Pedagogy in a New Tonality

Pedagogy in a New Tonality

Teacher Inquiries on Creative Tactics, Strategies, Graphics Organizers, and Visual Journals in the K-12 Classroom

Edited by

Peter Gouzouasis
The University of British Columbia, Vancouver, Canada

To Margaret,
One of the best in
every way – a great
colleague, researcher, artist
and teacher!
Peter
Nov 2011

SENSE PUBLISHERS
ROTTERDAM/BOSTON/TAIPEI

A C.I.P. record for this book is available from the Library of Congress.

ISBN: 978-94-6091-667-0 (paperback)
ISBN: 978-94-6091-668-7 (hardback)
ISBN: 978-94-6091-669-4 (e-book)

Published by: Sense Publishers,
P.O. Box 21858,
3001 AW Rotterdam,
The Netherlands
www.sensepublishers.com

Printed on acid-free paper

TABLE OF CONTENTS

BARRIE BENNETT

FOREWORD

Although most of us rarely think about it, we would agree that without 'students' we would not have ministries of education, teacher unions, faculties of education, and school districts. Given those stakeholders exist because of students, one would think those stakeholders would work collectively to make a difference in the life chances and learning chances of students. Unfortunately, collaboration between stakeholders is rarely the case, which begs the question, why wouldn't they work together? Anyone who has worked with a group of students for approximately six hours a day for 200 days, year after year, understands the complexities of the teaching and learning process. And tangentially, logic would tell us that all stakeholders should be working together to increase the life and learning opportunities of students.

Over the last 29 years I have been involved in working with districts on long-term systemic change in Canada, Australia, and Ireland. I've experienced the complexities, frustrations, and successes of attempting to create partnerships between stakeholders. This text represents one of those 'rare' success cases.

In the present foreword, I situate the efforts of Dr. Peter Gouzouasis in collaboration with school districts, specifically the North Vancouver School District, by sharing the stories of a few systemic change projects that I have been involved in over the last 29 years. These examples illustrate failures and successes.

In 1982, I was involved as a participant teacher, and later as a consultant, in a systemic change project that focused on instruction with Edmonton public schools. After six years, we had 154 schools (of 197) with teachers and administrators working in teams involved in the project. Even though the project was voluntary, no school ever left the project. As part of the project, we tried to connect with the Faculty of Education at the University of Alberta; however, they took no interest in our project.

In 1999, we started a project with the teachers' union in Western Australia. The union's leaders were clearly progressive in understanding the importance of assisting WA teachers to become effective practitioners. The union eventually formed a partnership with the ministry of education in Western Australia to create a statewide project to support teacher professional development. This is the most effective union/ministry project I have experienced. For whatever the reason, and 12 years later, we were only marginally successful in eventually connecting to the teacher education programs in the local universities in Western Australia. They were invited right at the start to be part of the project's initiation, but unfortunately they never committed themselves to being part of the project.

In contrast, the Ontario Institute of Education at the University of Toronto (OISE/UT) created a partnership with the York Region District School Board (YRDSB). YRDSB worked initially on an instructional intelligence project for two years—this project involved approximately 600 teachers working in teams with their principals. In the third year, YRDSB and OISE/UT created the Doncrest Option that involved 65 students doing their B.Ed. program at Doncrest Public School in YRDSB. The program was team taught by faculty from OISE/UT and YRDSB. That partnership is now in its ninth year. The B.Ed. students were placed with teachers who were involved in the project. The key benefit was the development of a common curriculum, contemporary assessment practices, and instructional language between the associate teachers and the B.Ed. students. Importantly, YRDSB has hired over 200 teachers from the Doncrest B.Ed. option. In addition, a number of teachers from YRDSB went on to do graduate studies on various aspects of the project. Moreover, they now co-ordinate this option.

This text embodies one of those rare occasions where university and school district stakeholders make the decision to work together, over time, for primary, middle school, and secondary students, as well as teacher-graduate students. In 2004, Dr. Peter Gouzouasis, from the Faculty of Education at the University of British Columbia, met with representatives from the North Vancouver District School Board. The meeting focused on enacting one of the conditions of North Vancouver School District's five-year project—to work with a local university to begin researching aspects of their project.

The focus of the five-year project was on instructional intelligence. Instructional intelligence implies exploring ways that curriculum, assessment, instruction, how students and teachers learn, change, and systemic change intersect and play out over time. In this text by Dr. Gouzouasis, you will read examples of research by teachers exploring the complexities of the teaching and learning process—how they enact aspects of being, and becoming, instructionally intelligent. You will learn what happens when universities and school districts work together to make a significant difference for students of all ages.

Barrie Bennett
Professor Emeritus
Ontario Institute of Education at the University of Toronto

PETER GOUZOUASIS

TOCCATA ON BECOMING ARTS BASED TEACHER RESEARCHERS

Trusting the Processes of Our Journey

> *Teaching matters. Above all else.* And we must not let ourselves off the hook in regards to continually improving our teaching. The research base is clear: the most important factor that affects and improves student learning is quality teaching. (Wilhelm, 2009, p. 36)

Teacher inquiry has become increasingly important since the latter part of the 20th century. As such, this book is for teachers and about teachers. It involves stories of practice and the journeys that dedicated, creative practitioners undertook in their quest to become reflective-reflexive practitioners. It is a collection of stories about their dedication to continued learning, and moving beyond the typical, everyday practices of K-12 teachers through their discoveries of how creative, arts-informed pedagogy may be applied in a variety of teaching and learning contexts. Creative pedagogy was the artistic force that breathed life into our research projects. We nourished ourselves and shared our knowledge with the students we taught. We breathed creativity and life into curricula and unit designs. With those perspectives in consideration, the roles that teachers play in learning about how creativity informs praxis dramatically changes both the curricula we teach and our pedagogy. As we changed and evolved into creative practitioners, we lived both our learning and our inquiries. We breathed new ideas both in and out. We moved outside of the "black box" of creativity in teaching and learning—we played in, around, over, under, and with the box of creative instructional tools until the boundaries of the traditional boxes of teaching and learning evaporated. I recalled and laughed at the song of Malvina Reynolds, "Little boxes on the hillside, little boxes made of ticky tacky…" and we left the ideas of those cynical lyrics in the circular file cabinet that sits under our desks, never to be recycled.

Robert Fulford (1999) believes storytelling is "how we explain, how we teach, how we entertain ourselves, and how we often do all three at once. They are the juncture where facts and feelings meet. And for those reasons, they are central to civilization" (p. 9). For the group of talented teachers who have contributed to this book, it is also how we learned and conducted our inquiries. Jeff Park (2005) believes, "Writing is both an individual act and a social construction …Writing in the expressive function is writing on the edge of self and the world" (p. 8). The stories we share in the present collection of research papers were collaborations, between me and the teachers, the teachers and their teacher peers, and the teachers and their students. Given that situational context, our research was more than what is typically considered as action research. Both traditional and "experimental" forms of research (Sparkes, 2001) informed our inquiries. In place of traditional action research, we used the lens of artography (Springgay, Irwin, Leggo, & Gouzouasis, 2008; Irwin & deCosson, 2003). To extend our understandings of traditional forms of narrative research, we explored poetic representations, autoethnography, and autobiographical work in social science research, especially in arts based educational research (ABER).

> … for teaching to assume the mantle of a profession a central tenet of that practice is the ability and willingness of its members to inquire into their own practice, into easy of improving and developing their practice consistent with the unique contexts in which they work and with an appreciation of current trends in education. (Clarke & Erickson, 2003, p. 3)

As a young teacher in the 1970s, I always wondered why so much of what teachers did in their classrooms was not valued as research by stolid academics that edited journals that now lie dormant and dusty in the bowels of university libraries. I believe we have arrived at a point in history where our professional understandings have matured to the extent that we can find overwhelming value in the systematic study teacher-learner experiences, and acknowledge that stories in the form of teacher inquiry is fecund, living research (Lewison, Seely Flint, & Van Sluys, 2002). We revel in the notion that our inquiries are embodied in a professional approach to practice (Sachs, 1997), and in the use of "self" as a legitimate way of writing research (Etherington, 2004). That said, I do not believe that "heaven knows, anything goes" (with apologies to Cole Porter), to the extent that arts-based educational researchers have been accused of "navel gazing" and other related activities. Instead, what we trust you will read is that our stories are more rooted in "mindful gazing" and "star gazing." We reached for the stars and made the seemingly impossible—dramatically changing our praxis by infusing it with research and creative instructional tactics, strategies and graphics organizers—possible.

With criticism from traditionalists in mind, when we begin to question why, how, how long, when, and what we do in the curriculum, as well as why, how, how long, when, and what we do (in)form pedagogical perspectives, we begin a regenerative journey for answers. That said, most meaningful research poses as many questions as answers, and most dedicated practitioners end their day with as many questions about how they taught and what the children learned as answers to what worked and did not work in their quest to improve teaching and learning. We look to theory and research to help guide our emerging perspectives. We take risks and live with tensions as we examine our teaching practice in a transparent, critical manner. Ideally, teacher inquiry is a dialectic—an endless cycle of reflection, inquiry, and action (i.e., reflexion). And reflexivity is not the final step in the teaching, learning, and research process. Rather it places the creative, teacher-learner in a position of trying and applying the inquiry process in both old and new contexts, then beginning the process of questioning one's practice, inquiry, and actions anew. Kim Etherington, in her quest to understand how practitioners become researchers, believes that

"Reflexivity is a skill that we develop … to notice our responses to the world around us, other people and events, and to use that knowledge to inform our actions, communications and understandings" (p. 19).

Becoming a reflective-reflexive practitioner involves an intense commitment to both teaching and learning—it is a lifelong endeavor and not one that merely ends because one believes that they *are* a "master teacher." Becoming (Allport, 1955) is a never-ending process, and to *become* a master teacher means that we never truly attain the ultimate endpoint or final goal (i.e., there is no *telos*) of *being* a master teacher. Thus, by its very nature, the cyclical process of learning to become a reflective-reflexive practitioner never ends. We strive to constantly become better at our craft. Moreover, our human need to ask questions is unending. We possess the potential to always learn, and through our commitment to lifelong learning—working with children, learning with peers, keenly observing, tinkering, honing our craft—we may begin to design our personal, unique, research infused, creative approaches to teaching and learning. Even though much of the creative pedagogy we explored and applied in these inquiries seems to lead us to specific, particular outcomes, the uniqueness of each story is inevitable. "Each person is an idiom unto himself, an apparent violation of the syntax of the species" (Allport, p. 19). Those perspectives have implications for the kinds of theories, research methods, and teaching approaches that are required to understand creative pedagogy and the individualistic nature of both learning and teaching.

> We are told that every stone in the field is unique, every old shoe in the closet, every bar of iron, but that this ubiquitous individuality does not affect the operations or the progress of science. The geologist, the physicist, the cobbler proceed to apply universal laws, and find the accident of uniqueness irrelevant to their work. The analogy is unconvincing. Stones, old shoes, bars of iron are purely reactive; they will not move unless they are manipulated. They are incapable of becoming. (Allport, p. 21)

When people ask if I play guitar (and I've been studying and performing music for 47 years) I always respond, "Yes, I'm a lifelong learner." I will never stop learning—that is my commitment to myself as a dedicated educator and to teaching and learning with my students. That notion also aligns with Allport in that, "It is the unfinished structure that has this dynamic power. A finished structure is static; but a growing structure, tending toward a given direction of closure, has the capacity to subsidiate and guide conduct in conformity with its movement" (p. 91). That perspective is enhanced with the acknowledgment of tension, between the individual and the collective, as well as between what is thought to be known and the unknown, as we imbue ourselves with the exploration and implementation of creative pedagogical approaches.

How, What, Why We Learned

> "Good teaching cannot be reduced to technique," wrote Palmer. "It comes from the identity and integrity of the teacher." (Thompson, 2009, p. 15)

That we learned in a professional community, made strong relationships with peers in our cohort and in our home schools, and learned our new craft in our schools working alongside our students (Hargreaves, 2000, p. 165) was a hallmark of this group of practitioners. Our classes usually met on Saturdays. We experimented and learned in the same ways that we planned to teach in our classrooms. Rather than rely on traditional, transmissive lecture and examination techniques, we discussed and unpacked our research and professional readings using all of the tactics, strategies, and graphics organizers that we used in our classrooms. We assessed our own learning using these same approaches. We made mistakes, we regrouped and reorganized, we redesigned our plans, and we practiced. We learned that the more teachers play with creative tactics, strategies, graphics organizers, visual journals, and variations of those constructs the more that learning (and teaching) transcends the commonplace and becomes a magical experience. Not only were we as teachers transformed, so were our classrooms and the students who walked alongside us.

All of the creative pedagogy we designed, explored, and applied led us to a place of rejuvenation and renewal. All of the teachers whose research is included in this book became leaders in curriculum and pedagogy and have been acknowledged as such by their peers and school administrators. Many have become administrators and curriculum leaders in their school districts. I believe that we went beyond becoming good technicians to *become pedagogical* in our practice and daily lives.

"Instructional Intelligence" as Creative, Arts-informed Pedagogy

> I say that you make a great, a very great mistake, if you think that psychology, being the science of the mind's laws, as something from which you can deduce definite programs and schemes and methods of instruction for immediate schoolroom use. Psychology is a science, and teaching an art, and sciences never generate arts directly out of themselves. An intermediary inventive mind must make the application, by using its originality. (James, 1899, p. 2)

Instructional intelligence (Bennett & Rolheiser, 2001) is a creative endeavor from the perspective that these tactics, strategies, graphics organizers, visual journals and collaborative learning concepts are strongly influenced by arts-based teaching and learning constructs. "Intelligent instruction" and "intelligently designed instruction" are intelligent, per se, because they are informed by numerous sources—brain research, the arts, social sciences research, psychology, and best practice. In that manner, it takes us "Beyond Monet."

Over the past 15 years, brain research has revolutionized the ways we understand human development and learning. In perhaps the most striking work, researchers have revealed that the study of music changes the neurobiology of the brain and enhances sensorimotor and cognitive capabilities in humans (Schlaug, Janke, Huang, Staiger, & Steinmetz, 1995; Hyde, Lerch, Norton, Forgeard, Winner Evans & Schlaug, 2009). It is but the tip of the iceberg of how social scientists will change the ways they think about outmoded, dualistic notions of nature and nurture in human development (LaMonde, 2011). On a related note, to an arts educator, the ways we design learning environments (i.e., both the space and the lessons, units) and teach music, dance, drama, and visual art can profoundly change and influence the ways that teachers (re)present mathematics, language, social studies, and science (Sarason, 1999). Moreover, for Grade 11 students' music achievement predicts academic achievement in Grade 12 (Gouzouasis, Guhn, Kishor, 2007). We also know that the arts are meaning makers in their own right and that visual, kinesthetic and musical representations are powerful forms of human expression—artists and the arts in general possess the power to change not only the ways that we think and learn, but also the physiological structures of the brain itself (Wan & Schlaug, 2010).

To extend that notion, basic pedagogical principles from the arts have strongly influenced the ways that teachers sequence their teaching. For example, since 2000, I have taught adults and children to play with computers the ways that I teach guitar—we learn to *play* guitar and *play* computer. When one approaches a computer as a form of music instrument, a learning tool, one can borrow much from music pedagogical principles. Metaphorically speaking, learning a simple chord progression is not unlike learning a simple progression of steps to record a voiceover for a movie clip. Rarely do two people learn to play an instrument the same way and with the same learning outcomes. Learning to create a digital movie is not a "click here, now move the mouse here, now drag this object and drop it here" step-by-step, group process. Learners frequently move at their own pace, discovering short cuts, making mistakes, and creating their own unique expressions. Discoveries are shared with learning partners or small groups and reapplied in either similar ways or in unique variations.

The ways that I teach everything are influenced by the ways that I teach and learn through music and movement. Play and imagination are the foundation of creativity (Singer & Singer, 1990). Since creativity may be considered as encompassing both divergent and convergent thinking, practitioners who play with and implement creative, arts informed tactics, strategies, graphics organizers, and visual journals enable all forms of creative thinking, across the curriculum, for both themselves and the learners.

> The arts are a matter of the heart. Science is thought to provide the most direct route to knowledge. Hence, "aesthetic modes of knowing" is a phrase that contradicts the conception of knowledge that is most widely accepted. (Eisner, 1982, pp. 23–24)

From yet another related perspective, teachers need to be as accomplished as performers as are successful artists. The more a teacher is aware of the inherent creativity of the arts and artistic pedagogy, the more they can harness and transform their practice. Through the ongoing development of an artographical (Gouzouasis, 2008) practice, the teachers who have contributed to this book were challenged to think like artists, and to embrace their artistic selves not only in ongoing coursework, but also in the ways that they approached their classroom inquiries. For some teachers, the challenges created tensions between what they initially believed constituted research and what they learned, as well as between their personal notions of self as science or mathematics teachers and ideas rooted in the science of teaching.

> While science is thought to provide the most accurate and direct route to knowledge, the arts are devalued and submerged as mostly a matter of the heart. Thus, "aesthetic modes of knowing," as well as artistic ways of seeking, knowing and doing contradict commonly accepted notions of knowledge acquisition (Eisner, 1982, pp. 23–24).

Some may consider that there is a scientific aspect of pedagogy, but for me, pedagogy is the *art* of teaching and learning, and as an extension of that notion, teaching may be considered a performing art (Sarason, 1999). I *perform* when I'm teaching. Whether it is music, research methods, the psychology of music, or instructional intelligence constructs, I consider it all under the umbrella of creative pedagogy. The ways that I teach everything are influenced by the ways that I teach and learn through music, movement and music and movement activities. As William James once said, "The art of teaching grew up in the schoolroom, out of inventiveness and sympathetic concrete observation" (p. 3). Metaphorically thinking, the art of teacher inquiry is rooted in the classroom and as such is embued with the inventiveness and creativity of teachers and students.

My junior high school classroom methods professor once asked our class what we believed to be the most important aspects of teaching. I blurted out, "Playing with the kids, having fun learning, performing!" and she thoughtfully paused before responding, "No." I was puzzled and silenced. The conversation went on to emphasize knowing the curriculum and other factors that I likely tuned out after my idea was rejected. While I placed my beliefs in the back of my mind, it haunted me throughout my teaching career. Sarason's brilliant book (1999) confirmed and reinvigorated my ideas, and influenced not only my leadership in and the creation of the Fine Arts and new Media in Education cohort (FAME; The University of British Columbia, 2000–2010) but also the Curriculum Leadership Instructional Intelligence masters program cohorts (2005–2010) from which this research is born.

> The state of mind which enables our actions to promote growth and generate awareness is so bound up with the flux of the moment that it is hard to analyze. The bond between the teacher and the taught, and the dancer and the dance, is at once intimate and tenuous, ever changing, ever bonding, and always new. (Morningstar, 1986)

Codetta

The title of this book refers to *pedagogy in a new tonality.* Tonality is defined by the organization of pitches in a scale. Traditionally speaking, most Western music is written in diatonic tonality, and a diatonic scale is made up of 7 pitches separated by half steps and whole steps. If one imagines a piano keyboard, when one plays from the note C, and ascends seven steps on the keyboard to C', the space between the pitches are whole-whole-half-whole-whole-whole-half. That relationship between pitches creates the sound of what we call major tonality. Regardless of the key signature, all major keys have the same arrangement of pitches. Major tonality is overwhelmingly used to compose popular music and folk songs in the West. Depending upon one's vocal range, one can sing any song in 12 different keys; a singer can change the key (i.e., starting pitch) of a song, but it still sounds like the same song. However, there are 6 other diatonic tonalities—dorian, phrygian, lydian, mixolydian, aeolian (natural minor), and locrian that can be played across 12 key areas (e.g., A natural minor, D natural minor, G natural minor, etc.). When the composer Gustav Mahler drew upon the French folksong "Frère Jacques" ("Bruder Martin" in German) as the theme of the third movement in his *Symphony #1 in D major*, he changed the tonality of the song from major to aeolian (i.e., D natural minor). Unless one listens very carefully, one would never notice that the theme is a transposition of a traditional folksong from major to minor tonality. That seemingly simple shift in tonality—also referred to as mode—changes the character, mood, and feeling of the theme, as Mahler's extra-musical, loosely based dramatic idea is that of a procession in a hunter's funeral.

In jazz, all tonalities—and the scales that emanate from those tonalities—have specific, interesting functions and complex applications. By the mid-1950s, jazz musicians were experimenting with the implementation of different tonalities in composition and improvisation (e.g., Lenny Tristano in New York City, Dennis Sandole in Philadelphia, and other early innovators that they influenced). By the early 1960s, "modal music" (i.e., music composed in dorian, phrygian, lydian, mixolydian, aeolian, and locrian tonality) dominated the music soundscape (see Miles Davis's Quintet and subsequent groups that were formed by members of Miles' band).

There are at least two reasons why this book is a tonal, and not merely a "keyal," shift from tradition (with all due respect to Suzanne Langer's notion of a "philosophy in a new key"). First, the research inquiries that are storied in this book exemplify a radical shift away from descriptions of traditional, transmissive approaches used to teach in the K-12 classroom. The authors embraced change and challenged themselves in their own learning, in their teaching, and in their student's learning. Metaphorically speaking, they did not simply sing the same songs in different keys. Secondly, because we used non-traditional, "experimental" modes of conducting research, I believe we have composed our inquiries using alternative—dorian, phryigian, lydian, mixolydian, aeolian, and locrian—tonalities.

This book is not finished, in the sense that I am now working and learning with my third group of dynamic, creative teachers in our pursuit of changing our praxis. Our journey is truly ongoing and defined by trusting the process (McNiff, 1998), imagining transformation, embracing change, designing creative teaching and learning, inventing new variations of instructional tactics, strategies and graphics organizers, designing new applications, and improving learning. We are already playing with creative classroom tactics, strategies, and graphics organizers in a variety of keys and tonalities. This book is for my colleagues in the classroom and many other teachers who will follow us in the quest to not only improve their practice, but radically transform it—to free themselves from the stifling boxes of traditionalism and emerge as teachers who revel in the ongoing quest of becoming creative, reflective, reflexive, artistresearcherteachers (Gouzouasis, 2008).

Peter Gouzouasis
The University of British Columbia
peter.gouzouasis@ubc.ca

PART 1

STORIES OF COLLABORATIVE LEARNING AND CLASSROOM CONFLICT

MARGARET PAXTON

THE HEART OF TEACHING

A pedagogy of community in the classroom

Prelude

The concise Oxford English dictionary offers this definition of the word, community, which come from Latin *communis*, or 'common': a group of interdependent plants or animals growing or living together or occupying a specified habitat. I like this biological perspective on community as a way of describing a classroom environment, for a classroom *is and should be* a place where a group of interdependent people are *growing* and *living* together. I wonder how teachers can enable students to be part of this kind of community, to become interdependent and place pure self-interest aside at times, for the greater good of the group. Is teaching just a form of manipulation? What motivates some children to want to learn more than others? Is teaching just means of indoctrination? Why do we seem to value compliance more than nonconformity and individualism? These are some of the big questions that I wrestle with as I near the end of my second decade of teaching. These are the questions that intrigued me the most when searching for an appropriate line of inquiry for my research project. I believe that it is possible to build a community within a classroom. I believe we can create learning environments in which students and teachers are truly interdependent, in which the motivation for the group to succeed is as strong as the interest in individual successes.

Setting the Story

SEPTEMBER 12TH

Today the students wrote letters to me to introduce themselves. I liked the last line of Luke's letter.

Dear Mrs. Paxton,

Hi my name is Luke. I like to play hockey and skate board. I have two dogs and three cats. My two dog's names are Jinger and Triesie. My three cats names are Mocha, Daisie and DJ. I have 2 sisters and 1 brother. My two sisters' names are Coral and Dirdre. My brother's name is Sean. This letter is almost about my life.

Your student, Luke

P. Gouzouasis (ed.), Pedagogy in a New Tonality: Teacher Inquiries on Creative Tactics, Strategies, Graphics Organizers, and Visual Journals in the K-12 Classroom, 3–18.

As a teacher of twelve and thirteen year olds, I am always looking for ways to work smarter, not harder. Early in my career, I would leave school at the end of the day exhausted, dragging my marking bag to the car, dreading a long night of ticking and x-ing papers and projects. As well, too much of my energy was being spent managing my students, trying to control their behaviour, so that I could "teach." On occasion, I caught glimpses of a different way of practicing teaching and learning. I saw that there were fragments of time in the school day when there was a hum of learning and active engagement in the room, when we were all working together on something that really mattered to everyone. It was what Csikszentmihalyi describes as a state of flow: "joy, creativity, the process of total involvement with life" (1990, xi). In recognizing the potential of flow in the classroom, I began to seek ways of creating more of it, but I also realized I would need to change my patterns of teaching. I would need to find ways to inspire students to work together with a common goal, and to learn to satisfy their own natural curiosities. My enthusiasm was buoyed in a summer institute with the North Vancouver School District. In their text, Bennett & Rohlheiser (2001) state, "Teachers are involved in one of the most complex, demanding and important professions in the world – a profession where changes emerge in the blink of an eye …To respond to the ever-increasing demands and complexity, teachers must be aware of and act on the science within the art of teaching – a challenging task" (p. 3).

Through the integration of an art and science of teaching, I believe one finds the essential, creative, *heart of teaching*. Bennett & Rolheiser (2001) describe the absolute necessity of creativity. "There is no guarantee," they argue, "that a teacher who is knowledgeable, has an extensive repertoire of instructional practices, and is kind and caring will necessarily be an effective teacher" (p. 5). It is the ability to be imaginative, to be spontaneous, and to teach intuitively, that characterizes an effective, creative teacher. Throughout my graduate courses, as I read and listened, and read and listened again, I realized that many educators shared my desire to teach with a sense of flow—with a sense of creativity.

From Sylvia Ashton-Warner (1972) I learned that with creative teaching, "the drive is no longer the teacher's but the children's own … the teacher is at last with the stream and not against it: the stream of children's inexorable creativeness" (p. 82). I liked everything about Ashton-Warner's description of teaching "organically." She wrote about "the preservation of the inner resources, the exercise of the inner eye, the protraction of the true personality" (p. 87). I, like Ashton-Warner, appreciate "unpredictability and variation; I like drama and I like gaiety; I like peace in the world and I like interesting people, and all this means that I like life in its organic shape and that's just what you get in an infant room where the creative vent widens" (p. 87).

I craved a more creative practice, but also a more cooperative one, in which students did not merely "work in groups," but worked collaboratively. From Johnson & Johnson (2004) I learned that since 1896, over six hundred studies have been conducted on cooperative, competitive, and individualistic learning, with the results indicating that achievement, quality of relationships, and psychological health all show gains when cooperative learning is taught and positive interdependence created. They believe that "humans are small group beings" and that "the social competencies necessary for interacting effectively with others are central to quality of family life, educational achievement, career success, psychological health, and creating a meaningful and fulfilling life" (p. 40). Johnson & Johnson argue that cooperative community, constructive conflict resolution, and civic values are three essential conditions for social and emotional learning (p. 41). My own experiences taught me that when these conditions are in place, at least to some degree, the practice of teaching is less of a Sisyphean struggle, for we are all engaged in pushing the rock up the mountain together.

Once community is established in a classroom, a remaining feat to accomplish is delivery of the curriculum. What time is left for learning about the Ancient Greeks, exponents, and quotation marks, when we are simply trying our best to get along? Wrigley (2003) proposes pedagogy of hope, in which, "curriculum is reshaped, remade, reborn, recoded in what we do with kids in classrooms" (p. 92). He speaks of the importance of meta-learning, or learning how to learn, as superceding the prescribed curriculum. That fits with my desire to empower students, to give them the confidence that they can learn what they need to learn, when they need to learn it, just as a castaway learns what he needs to learn to survive.

I taught my students that their survival depends on the satisfaction of basic human needs. Some of these are physical needs: food, water, protection form danger, and so on. But there are also psychological needs: freedom, fun, power, and most of all, belonging (Glasser, 1984; Bodine, Crawford & Schrumpf, 1994). Teaching students about these four needs enables them to think about their behaviour in a new way. They learn that they are always working toward satisfying these needs in either positive or negative ways. They learn that in order for us all to survive and thrive together, the needs of others must also be considered as well as their own.

The aforementioned authors inspired my new hope for a creating a classroom environment in which the members of the community (including me) worked together, learning how to learn. I decided to document the process of building community in a classroom. Having been assigned to a new school, with a fresh sea of faces, it was the perfect opportunity to put into practice the many strategies, tactics, rituals and belief structures that I had been practicing in a more piecemeal fashion over the past few years.

The Research Project

OCTOBER 3RD

Today we discussed the advantages of sitting in groups, or "pods," as opposed to sitting in rows. Students said it is quieter in rows, but not as much fun. I think back to what my Tribes trainer said, "If the amygdala is happy, kids will learn."

The present research project began on the first day of school and ended in the early Spring. My elementary school is in the northern end of Squamish, in a working-class neighborhood. Most families own homes or townhouses. The population is more stable than transient. Ten per cent of our population is Aboriginal. My class consisted of 28 students, evenly divided between Grade 6 and 7, with 17 boys and 11 girls. Four of my students had severe learning disabilities and behaviour difficulties. One student suffered with an undiagnosed metal illness, suspected to be bi-polar disorder. Eight of the students lived with one parent. Reading assessments indicated that 20 of the students were reading at grade level, while eight struggled with fluency and comprehension. No students received support for E.S.L., although two spoke another language at home. I was clear that this group was not without its challenges. However, my first impression was that this was a class with great potential, for they smiled at my attempts at humor and appeared to be interested in what I had to tell them.

In conducting my research, I collected evidence about my teaching practice and my student's learning through observations (recorded in a journal), informal discussions with students in large and small groups, and with reflective "exit slips" upon which students wrote their thoughts or feelings about a particular activity. Every two weeks, I took time to sit and write a reflection, focusing each time on one particular aspect of my practice. I also referred back to letters that my students wrote to me on the first day of class, in the first hour we met, in which they told me a bit about themselves and their hopes for the year. As I got to know the students better, I found it very interesting to return to these letters, as I could view them with a keener, more informed eye.

I spent a number of hours each week searching for and reading other authors' words on the topics of community building, cooperative learning, multiple intelligence theory, differentiated instruction, and autoethnography as a qualitative research method. For my everyday teaching, I relied heavily on two resources: *Tribes* (Gibbs, 1995) and *Beyond Monet* (Bennett & Rolheiser, 2001). I was also very interested in the use of storytelling as an educational tactic (Egan, 1986, 2005).

I returned again and again to the following three questions: (1) Which strategies, tactics, and activities help to build inclusion and improve students' feelings of safety in the classroom? (2) How can I effectively model compassion and cooperation in my teaching? (3) What are some of the stumbling blocks to building community I will encounter, and what can I do to overcome them? My hope was to complete a project which would help me to solidify the thinking/feeling, or intuitive parts of my practice with clarity of purpose and direction for myself as an ever-learning professional, but also an authentic research document which might be of interest to other teachers.

Using an autoethnographical approach, I recorded my observations of the students' participation in activities that encouraged them to practice cooperation, attentive listening, and mutual respect. I reflected upon my own participation in these activities, as well as how my praxis evolved throughout the year. I chose an autoethnographical approach for a number of reasons. I knew that I would struggle with the feelings of self-indulgence and fear of narcissism. Indeed, this is a criticism on the research methodology that Holt (2003) describes. He states that the two challenges researchers must overcome to justify the method are (1) representation and (2) legitimation. The researcher must be seen to be representing the social world accurately and truthfully—which is difficult for others to verify—and at the same time, interpret the data in a manner that ensures validity, reliability, and objectivity.

When we are conducting research on children in classrooms, it seems only fair to acknowledge that classrooms are very messy places indeed. How can one possibly measure a child's creativity, imagination, or resiliency? What is an accurate rating scale we could use for friendliness, tolerance, or trust? Surely, it is the practice of reflection that allows one to determine what words, actions, tactics, and strategies have had an impact upon students' learning. In *Professional Learning Communities at Work,* Dufour & Eaker (1998) quote the philosopher, Kierkegaard, "Life must be lived forward, but it can only be understood backward" (p. xv).

In using an autoethnographical approach to my inquiry, I hoped to document the process of community building in my classroom in a rigorous, honest, and authentic way. It is a way of taking full control and responsibility for what occurs in class, and to reclaim, as Tierney (1998) puts it, "through self-reflective practice, representational spaces that have marginalized those of us at the borders" (p. 66). Instead of placing myself as a researcher standing outside the classroom looking in, autoethnography allowed me to be a participant, in the midst of the sometimes chaotic, often messy place we call school, and allowed me to tell the story of the process from a participant's point of view.

Stories, however, are easiest to tell and understand when told within a framework. In school, we call it "story structure," and we have students map it, chart it, and describe it sequentially. In this project, I also sought a structure that would make the story more meaningful and accessible to readers. In *Discovering gifts in middle school: Learning in a caring culture called Tribes* (2001), Jeanne Gibbs cites the work of John McKnight (1992), who describes five indicators of community: Capacity, Collective Effort, Informality, Stories, and Celebration. These are the headings I employ to organize my narratives of teaching.

Capacity

NOVEMBER 4TH

> We began a new class tradition today – taking turns giving and receiving compliments. I thought the kids would hate it – think it cheesy. But they really rose to the occasion and gave each other sincere and thoughtful comments. I keep reminding myself – I need to provide frequent and authentic opportunities for the students to practice these interpersonal skills.

In my discussions with other administrators, we speak often about building capacity in our teachers. In planning professional development opportunities and staff development days, we attempt to assess the needs of teachers and provide in-service activities that will help to strengthen and enhance their skills and knowledge. In the classroom, how often do we take inventories of the variety of strengths, weaknesses, aptitudes, gifts of our students? One of the first activities I did with my class was, "This Is My Bag." I thought that if I encouraged students to think individually about their own capacity, that they might find some commonalities, the beginning of community.

"My name is Mrs. Paxton and this is my bag." Out of my bag I pulled, one by one, a number of treasures: a photo of my children and our dog, a running trophy, a seashell from Tofino, a stuffed rabbit, and a favourite book. As I removed each item from my bag, I explained its significance and how it represented a part of me. I asked the students to bring in bags of their own over the next few weeks and most were very excited about doing so. They liked the ritual of beginning with, "My name is … and this is my bag," and ending with, "My name is … and *that* was my bag." The audience politely and spontaneously applauded after each presentation. Presenters were very trusting in passing around their stuffed animals, video games, trinkets and treasures; every item was handled with respect. After every "This is my bag" presentation, I asked the class, "What did we learn about your classmate that we did not know before?" Two students, too shy to speak in front of the class, presented privately to me at lunchtime. The Korean children were adamant that they had brought nothing to Canada worth sharing. One girl just kept "forgetting" her bag. It was hard for me to imagine being so reluctant to reveal a bit of oneself to others, but I told them that I hoped they would reconsider, and bring in their bags sometime during the school year.

Another activity helpful to inventory the notion of capacity was the Life Map. On a large piece of paper, students "mapped" their own lives, recalling important events and many "firsts" such as "the first time I rode a bike," "my first day at school," and "my first ski trip." They added colour and photographs, and pictures cut from magazines. During the times that they spent creating their life maps, they were fully engaged and happy. They talked quietly to each other. They giggled and shared. They complained when I told them it was time to stop for lunch. In the sharing that came later, students were amazed at the similarities and differences they found between each other. It was as though some had never imagined that their peers had lives, families, and experiences similar and different from their own. Whenever we formed new groups, before any learning task or activity took place students got out their life maps and shared with their new learning partners. This seemed to be a necessary ritual to set a tone of mutual understanding for the new group.

In attempting to recognize the capacities of individuals and groups, I have also used the multiple intelligence inventory from the Tribes (TLC) middle school resource. Students completed the scoring of their own multiple intelligence checklists, and we discussed the eight different strengths that all people each possess in varying degrees. One student observed that musical intelligence was his "weakest strength." I like this oxymoronic phrase, "weakest strength," for it implies that there is still hope. After discussing our strengths, I gave each student an apple, farm fresh, some with a leaf on the stem. I told them that they were to study their apple intently and memorize its features so that, later, they might be able to pick it out of a pile of apples. They could not mark their apple in any way. After several minutes of intense study, they brought their apples to the window ledge and lined them up. I mixed them up like a magician with cups and balls. I then gave groups of four large pieces of paper and asked them to complete a Venn diagram explaining how apples and people are alike and different. Their ideas were very creative. They came up with many similarities and differences that I had not anticipated, beyond, "We both have skin and flesh, but apples grow on trees." They said things like, "We are both vulnerable to disease and predators," and "We both reproduce with seeds!" In collating their ideas, it struck me that this had been a great opportunity for all of us to practice creative thinking, and what fun it was for us all.

I thanked them for their participation and then took my own apple and cut it crossways through the middle. "Wow!" some exclaimed who had never seen the star shape inside. I said, "This star is like the brilliance in each of you, and the seeds you find within the star represent your potential." I thought a few eyes might roll with that statement, but they looked at me evenly. "And," I continued, "you might be able to count the number of apples that fall from a tree each year, but who can count the number of trees that come from a single apple seed?" With that, I gave them an exit slip to be completed before lunch. They were to write a one-sentence reflection on the morning's activities. Then they got to find their apple and eat it with their lunch. Some students wrote, "That was cool," and "I liked it," but the words that made me smile were Luke's, a very cool seventh grader. He wrote, "Mrs. Paxton uses very unusual teaching methods." I was pleased, because he had not dismissed me, or my teaching methods, but compared them to what he was used to, without judgment. Coming from him, it was a fine compliment.

Collective Effort

DECEMBER 22ND

> Today was our last performance of the play. I asked students to fill in a reflection sheet. Sammy wrote, "Before the play I thought I could never remember my lines. But now I think it's a piece of cake." Way to go, Sammy!

I found that my students are greatly motivated and enjoy learning activities in which we had a common goal. I have taught them some games that do not require much skill or fitness, but strategy and thinking, such as Group Rock, Paper, Scissors and Line Tag. The key to these games is that everyone must cooperate and communicate for the game to progress. They must work together, or it is not fun for anyone.

Another means by which to practice collective effort is with a whole class play. For years, my classes have been performing abbreviated versions of Shakespeare's plays. We invite other classes to come and watch the performances. I have been told that the plays are now something that younger students look forward to doing when they get to my grade seven class. This year, I decided to write a play based on C.S. Lewis' (1994) the *Lion, the Witch and the Wardrobe.* I was not sure if this particular class was ready for Shakespeare, and I wanted to give them practice working together on a story with which they were already familiar.

We cast the play as a group. Students were invited to "audition" for several parts and we quickly reached consensus as to who would play what role. Those who possessed stronger reading skills and more confidence in public speaking generally won the larger roles, such as Lucy, Peter, Edmund, and Lucy. Other strong readers, who did not wish to act, took the parts of the three narrators. Several students, with weaker reading skills, but more dramatic flair than others, were enthusiastic about their roles as Aslan, the White Witch, Father Christmas, and the Beavers. My quiet and shy boys decided to be the heroic mice that free Aslan from the ropes that bind him on the Stone Table. My most challenging student, Leslie, who struggles with bi-polar disorder, took on the role of Maugrim, the Wolf, as she loves to growl. Once the play was cast, the rehearsals began in earnest. During rehearsals, everyone read along. I insisted on this, because inevitably, someone cannot make a performance, and it is often a shy and quiet student who raises his hand to say, "I can play that part, Mrs. Paxton. I know it by heart."

The atmosphere in the classroom during rehearsals was intense. There was an urgency felt as students began to memorize their lines and movements. There was a spirit of teamwork as they coached and prompted each other. There was shared laughter at the funny mistakes and the "over acting" of some of the players. There was mutual joy when at last we were in our costumes and ready to perform. Student attendance was almost perfect during these weeks leading up to and including the performances, for they sensed the importance of everyone's presence and participation. We felt deep and collective pride when the performances were finished and the audience's applause rang in our ears.

I have many times experienced surprising outcomes of our dramatic productions: the revelation of a child's gift in acting, or in designing sets, that would otherwise lie undiscovered; the ability of one student to mentor another while keeping their dignity intact; the spontaneous gratitude children express for being allowed to learn this way. I do not feel I can adequately describe the importance of this collective effort in helping to build community in the classroom. The process of preparing a play for performance, allows students to work creatively and to use their kinesthetic, artistic, intrapersonal and interpersonal intelligences. I realize, now, that there are many more ways to allow students to "work" in this way, in a state of flow. It need not be a play—perhaps a fundraising campaign for charity, the creation of a mural or giant sculpture, or a "political" campaign to persuade some authority to action. What excellent rehearsal for real life.

Informality

FEBRUARY 28TH

The class loves it when we have discussions that take us in many different directions, and that, in their minds, distract me from the work that needs to be

> done! Today, the students got talking about wars, all kinds of wars. They don't know much about any of them, but are fascinated by the subject. After a lengthy discussion, Jazmin said, "Today I learned that people fight about the dumbest things." How true.

Gibbs describes the state of informality as existing when "transactions of value are based on consideration; care and affection take place spontaneously" (p. 82). Among teachers, I believe, there is often a fear that informality will lead to chaos. I also feel that fear, especially when I am attempting to relinquish some control that I have traditionally held to the students. I sometimes fear that if they're left to their own devices, my students' choices will not be appropriate, and their decisions may not be inclusive and kind. However, I have found that when given some structures, guidelines, and boundaries they inevitably solve problems in sound and creative ways.

There are several ways of creating these structures. The first is with the Four Agreements (Gibbs, 1995). When I meet my new students in September I always feel nervous. I hope to make a good first impression so that they will go home to tell their parents that they are glad to be in my class. I have learned that I can calm my own fears at the beginning of the school year by trusting myself. I trust myself to make this place safe for each one. I know that I do not have to rule through inciting fear. I do not have to control with threats and power struggles. I can be *myself*, and as I lead, they will follow. If they do not choose to follow, I can only be patient and hope that they find their way on the trail I have set. Still, I think that those first few hours together can make all the difference in the world. A teacher can either set herself up for success or for endless struggles in her initial choice of words and actions. The students want to know what the year has in store for them, what to anticipate, and what they might have to steel themselves to endure.

This year I told my new students something that amazed and delighted them. I said, "In our classroom, there are no rules and I give no detentions." There was a ripple of giggles and whispers. "But!" I continued, "I *do* invite you to agree with me, that we will treat each other, our selves, and our belongings with respect. Any "rules" that we could ever make will be covered by that agreement." There were nods of understanding. This is what I love about grade sixes and sevens: one does not have to explain every little thing. "Also," I continued, "we will learn about the other three agreements: Listening Attentively, The Right to Participate and Pass, and Appreciation/No Put Downs. All of these agreements fall into the bigger one of Respect, don't you agree?" More nods. "And as for detentions," I said, "if you need extra help with math or reading, I will be here after school to give you that help. If you need extra help with time management, because you do not get your homework done, I will be here after school to help you. And if you need extra help to learn to manage your behavior, I will also be here after school. So I may ask you sometimes, to stay after school, not as a punishment, but to get the extra help you need." I said all of this with a big, benevolent smile, and they love it, because they know exactly what I mean.

On our first day together, I was keen to begin building inclusion. I wanted to begin with the Name Wave, so I had the students to push some of the desks aside and stand in a circle. I explained that the Name Wave was a way for us to get to know each other's names. It began with me saying "Mrs. Paxton" and performing a gesture, a circling of clasped hands in front of me. I asked the student to think of a gesture to go with their names, and one by one, they were to say their names, perform the gesture, and the other students were to echo it, one by one, around the circle. Although everyone was cooperative, it did not go as well as I had hoped it would. The students were still too self-conscious, they got antsy waiting for their turn, there were so many of them, and it took too long. A few took me up on my offer to pass and so their names were not circulated. When we did this activity in Edmonton with twenty-five teachers, it felt like a big hug as others repeated my name and gesture around the circle. Here, it felt awkward and uncomfortable. I realized that many of the inclusion-builders I hoped to use would have to wait until there was more safety and trust in the room. The students were not all happy to be there and eager to learn. Many were fearful, anxious, embarrassed, and reluctant to be part of the group. I resolved to move more slowly and carefully in the days ahead.

A much more successful activity was the creation of personal shields. We brainstormed adjectives that described the people we admire. Words like brave, athletic, smart, determined, funny, friendly, trustworthy, and honest filled the chalkboard. I showed the students samples of family shields, with mottos and symbols that represented the family's values. I instructed the students to choose two or three of these positive adjectives to describe themselves and gave them an outline of a paper shield. I asked them to make their names and the words they had chosen big and bold, and to then add pictures or symbols of things they liked. Everyone was very keen to begin and fully engaged. It was only a day or two before they were all complete, cut out and ready for display.

I mounted the shields on the bulleting board in the classroom, including mine. When the parents came to "Meet the Teacher" they eagerly sought out their child's shield. Some laughed and some marveled. One mother sighed. Her son's shield was illustrated with little fighting guys with swords and robots and spacemen. She said, "He does that to cover up who he really is and the fact that he is all about bunnies and love. He thinks he has to draw these things to be cool and fit in. When he brought it home to work on I said, 'Oh dear, Daniel, they are going to send you to the counselor's office.'" I tried to reassure her that what he was doing was normal, developmentally speaking. She expressed her fears for him, but also her hopes. She said that he was very happy in my class and that he was, for a change, happy to come to school. She said, "Did you notice how he signed his name on those paper pencils in the foyer?" I had not. Our librarian had given each class a large paper "pencil" already labeled with the teacher's name, and asked us to have the students sign it. She then made a display of the pencils in the front hallway, with the words, "Brackendale Elementary School, Home of the Sharpest Students!" Later that evening, on my way out, I looked at our pencil. Daniel's name was printed as small as could be, tucked inside the capital M of Mrs. Paxton. It gave me goose bumps, both then and even now, as I reflect upon that moment.

Transactions of value are the risky exchanges of thoughts and ideas and feelings. We express ourselves with the hope that we will be heard, will be taken seriously, will be accepted and will be valued. Part of the art of creating Informality is in allowing students' voices to be heard and acknowledged frequently. I tried to establish some rituals that allow this to happen in a non-threatening way. Every day we took part in a "community circle" in which everyone was invited to speak in turn. Sometimes it was simply a word, sometimes it was a sentence, other times, an anecdote. Of course, students had the right to pass. It was hard, as a teacher, to resist the urge to say, "Come on, now! Everyone *has* to participate!" I had to give up that power, and be patient with those who chose to pass. Sometimes they simply needed more time, and after everyone else had had their say, they were composed and ready.

To further encourage learning conversations, I began the year with learning partners. Pairs of students sat with their desks touching, in two rows of five pairs and one row of four. During lessons, I frequently posed an open-ended question, then said, "Turn to your learning partner and tell him or her what you think." This allowed some rehearsal and preparation for answering the question. I found that more students were willing to raise their hands and provide an answer or idea when they had had time and opportunity to practice. Think/Pair/Share is one of the simplest, yet effective strategies to promote student engagement and learning (Bennett & Rolheiser, 2001). Still, some partners wore each other out. Boys were reluctant to sit with girls, and vice versa. No one wanted to sit with Lindsey, as her tantrums and hypersensitivity were tiresome.

On the first of November, I asked the students if they would like to continue sitting in pairs, and many replied that they would like to try groups of four—just what I was hoping. I wrote their names on popsicle sticks and we formed groups by drawing sticks. This strategy was their choice, arrived at after lengthy debate and discussion around the pros and cons of teacher-created versus student created, versus randomly formed groups. I was very proud of them for coming to that decision, but they may not have done so if I had not given them some structure. I said that whatever means they chose had to be fair and ensure that no one's feelings could be hurt by exclusion. Care for others' feelings was the deciding factor. After going through this process, I was amazed to see my adamant grade six boys, who said that they could never, ever work with grade seven girls, were now sitting in their groups—a mix of grade sixes and sevens and boys and girls, resigned to do their best because they owned the class's decision, having has a voice, a "say," in the process.

When observing students working in these groups, I noticed many examples of "care and affection" that I know would not have occurred had the students sat in rows. For example, Carys helped Lindsey with her multiplication, pre-empting the usual explosion of frustration. James, a grade six boy, helped Donna, a girl in grade seven, to find the circumference of a circle, allowing me to help other students in need. Meagan helped Henry, from Korea, with his spelling. She did this spontaneously, without any prompting from me. I was in awe of my students' common acts of generosity and kindness. Schaps, Battistich & Solomon (2004) reviewed many studies before concluding that students need "frequent opportunities to help and collaborate with others" (p. 190). This is one of the four key components they regard as essential in a caring community of learners, along with respectful, supportive relationships among students, teachers and parents; frequent opportunities for autonomy and influence; and emphasis on common purposes and ideals.

Stories

> *MARCH 5TH*
>
> I love reading stories to them more than anything. I love when they cry out, "Read us another one! Read us another one!" Reading and listening together makes the words seem animate and important. When we finished our whole class novel study, they mourned. They did not want the story to be over. The act of sharing literature aloud so that even the struggling readers are part of the experience is like sitting at a banquet together and feasting!

More than anything, my students loved stories, both from fiction and "real life." Shared stories seemed to satisfy some deep need, some raw hunger in their bellies. When we had a few minutes before recess or lunchtime, they begged for a story. Sometimes I read to them from my ancient, battered book of Grimm's *Fairy Tales*. They loved the gory ones best. They delighted in hearing how the one of Cinderella's wicked step sisters cut off her toes, and the other her heel, in order to try to win the prince, and how the witch in Hansel and Gretel was pushed into the oven and "burned to ashes and bone."

The students also loved picture books, and there are so many that are appropriate for intermediate students. They were moved to tears by *The Faithful Elephants* (1988), filled with moral outrage by *Rose Blanche* (2001), and *Teammates* (1990), delighted by the possibilities of *Westlandia* (1999), and provoked into thoughtfulness by *The Mysteries of Harris Burdick* (1984). Sharing stories aloud helped me to both activate my students' imaginations, provide topics for class discussions, and model what good readers do: visualize, predict, ask questions, draw inferences, and so on.

I have found that stories are the best means by which to gather and hold their collective attention, even if it a simple anecdote about me and my daughter getting ready for school. We shared stories constantly, throughout the day. During social studies, I told them how I once mummified a chicken and how it mysteriously disappeared, leading to legend of "The Curse of Tutanchicken." In science class, I told the story of Galileo, who was persecuted for his new scientific theories. Cries of "That would never happen today!" were countered by, "Or would it?"

In *An imaginative approach to teaching* (2005), Kieran Egan continues his discussion of teaching as story telling. He writes, "The great power of stories, then, is that they perform two tasks at the same time. They are, first, very effective at communicating information in memorable form, and, second, they can orient the hearers' feelings about the information being communicated" (p. 10). A statement Egan makes near the end of his book conveys even more distinctly the need for storytelling in a classroom community. In explaining how successful teachers hook their students into content through storytelling, he concludes, "Teachers who do find that emotional engagement typically find themselves energized rather than drained by the end of the day. And their classes have more children who are themselves imaginatively engaged, and that in turn energizes the teachers further" (p. 215).

Gibbs describes stories as "reflection upon individual and community experiences (that) provide knowledge about truth, relationships, and future direction" (p. 82). More than anything, the act of sharing of stories helps to build community because it requires all of the behaviours that enable people to function in a community: attentive listening, taking turns, practicing restraint, participating, respecting others ideas and opinions, and most importantly for school: making meaning.

Celebration

APRIL 12TH

> Aaron never gets more than ten or twelve words out of twenty-five correct on a spelling quiz. I always say, "Never mind." I tell him that being able to spell well is not a sign of intelligence. Something got into him this week. He must have studied like the dickens. He got twenty-three words correct. Even though it was not a perfect score, everyone recognized his accomplishment. Andy, my severely learning disabled student, was the first to stand and lead a spontaneous ovation. We all stood and applauded, until Aaron was red in the face, but so pleased with himself.

The fifth indicator of success is Celebration. In functional communities, people socialize, and in doing so, "the line between work and play is blurred and the human nature of everyday life becomes part of the way of work" (McKnight, p. 90). Celebration, I have learned, is not merely about parties. I think it is more about reflection, and can happen many times a day. It is a ritual acknowledgement of something important that has taken place. In the course of conducting my research, I have found a number of ways to celebrate student learning in the classroom.

This year, I began each morning in a new way. As I opened my classroom door, and the students filed in, I attempted to make eye contact with each one, say "Good morning" and their name. Most made eye contact with me and returned the greeting. I was afraid that my Korean students thought this making of eye contact is inappropriate, and so I did not insist on it with them. Some of my shy students tried to sneak past without participating in the greeting. Sometimes I let them go and sometimes I pulled them back. One day I was flustered and in a hurry, and forgot to greet the students one by one, as I hurried to unload my piles of books and marking on to my desk. "Hey!" someone exclaimed indignantly, "You didn't say good morning to us!" So I ushered them all outside again and began the day properly, celebrating the fact that each one was at school, ready to learn (or not).

In March, I thought that perhaps I should end the day in a similar fashion, and so I began standing at the door saying "goodbye." I have observed that primary teachers do this more frequently than by intermediate teachers, and it is rarely practiced by secondary teachers. The effect I noticed is a sense of closure. Even if a student and I had a disagreement during the day, saying goodbye to them somehow conveyed, "Everything is okay. I care about you. Tomorrow is another day."

Other ways in which we celebrated were through applause, awards, and public praise. As the school year progressed, I found that the students celebrated spontaneously when someone had experienced success. In previous years, I would "drag" classes into clapping for a fellow student. Now, they do it without any prompting: when Justin arrived on time for school for the first day in months, when Daniel scored high on his spelling test; when Lindsey publicly apologized for calling Rachel an idiot; when Sandy recited all of the twelve times tables in under three minutes.

I have tried to find ways of celebrating the behaviours that I want, and ignoring those that I don't. Recently, only a handful of my students completed a homework assignment, a character chart for our novel study. Rather than lecture the rest, I decided to give "Homework Completion Certificates" to those who had done their work on time, in a little ceremony at the end of the school day. I thought that perhaps this would be seen as silly by both the recipients and the rest of the class, but the next day, I retrieved a voice mail message from one recipient's mother, thanking me for recognizing her son in that way, and telling me how proud he was of his certificate. It made me realize that no matter how old and "mature" we become, we still enjoy recognition of our achievements.

What impact has Celebration had on the sense of community in the classroom? I cannot prove that it has lead to greater academic achievement or improved test scores. That is another research project. I do believe it has served to heighten the importance of social competency, for I have observed evidence of increased confidence and what Gibbs describes as social competence, "trust in others, perspective taking, sense of personal identity, awareness of interdependence" sense of direction and purpose" (1995, p. 49). Through daily, small acts of celebration we are reinforcing what Watkins (2005) calls the "hallmarks of community," namely, agency, belonging, cohesion and diversity. We are saying, "Everyone can be successful at something and we will acknowledge that success. People can improve and we will acknowledge that improvement. We all belong and despite our differences, we are equally important and deserving of respect."

Précis

MARCH 17TH

I have been teaching grade sixes and sevens since my practicum in 1991, in two different districts and six different schools. This class, by far, has been the most fun and the most professionally satisfying. The students make me feel like a good teacher. What has made the difference? Are these kids special or have I changed?

Much of the evidence I have gathered about the practice of community building has been anecdotal and based on my own observations. I would also like to recognize the voices of my students. I began to use exit slips as a means of encouraging reflection on a particular activity, and now use them frequently at the end of the day as closure. We called them, "I think, I feel, I learned slips" and the students are free to write whatever they wish and give them to me without putting their names on. The following are some of their words.

- *Today I learned more about that black bears eat acorns.*
- *This morning I learned about a pelecon and we discussed humoruse stuff.*
- *I learn English and I feel now I am not shy to talk with Canadian and foreign. I think Canada is good to improve my English.*
- *I think today was good because I just made good friends with Luke and Nicole. At first I didn't like them. Now I think their cool.*
- *I learned that are (sic) class is really funny sometimes.*
- *I think it is fun to be goofy in class. I feel that it is great to have plays in class. I learned it is ok to have a calm down time.*
- *I thought it was funny when we all started to say "are."*

The last comment was in reference to one of the funniest moments we have shared as a class. I was enthusiastically telling a story and at one point my brain was searching for a word. I stalled and stuttered in the middle of a sentence. "You see, sometimes people are, are, are…" David, my little mimic, repeated, "Are, are, are!" like a seal. Suddenly the room was full of little seals crying, "Are, are, are!" We laughed and laughed. They still tease me about it months later. It is one of my favourite examples of how we have grown together as a community: the fact that we have such shared, inside jokes, that no one from the outside would understand.

To conclude, I would like to return to the three questions that guided my inquiry. The first was: Which strategies, tactics and activities help to build inclusion and improve students' feelings of safety in the classroom? There is an endless array of strategies described in many excellent resources. No single strategy, however, is worth its implementation without the sensitive consideration of students' needs and strengths. I learned that the first step in building community is to help students get to know themselves, with activities such as This is my Bag, the Life Map, and the Personal Shield. Once they have reflected upon whom they are and what they value, they are primed to consider the qualities and interests of others. It takes a long time to build mutual trust and respect, but the time invested is paid back when the teacher can put her energies into teaching, not managing, and when students can help each other. Learning in the classroom becomes not one teacher helping thirty students, but thirty-one teachers helping each other, positively interdependent (Johnson & Johnson, 2004).

I also asked, "How can I effectively model compassion for others in my teaching?" My inquiry has reinforced for me the importance of modeling. In the past, I would lecture. I now model reading strategies. I model thinking skills. I model practical things like how to fold and cut and paste, rather than assuming that they come to me knowing how to do these things. I model good manners. When my most challenging student has temper tantrums and calls me names, I try to model patience, compassion, and most of all—forgiveness. I saw the effect this has had on my students. They know that there are bottom-line behaviours that cannot be tolerated, but they also know that everyone may be forgiven. This aspect of forgiveness plays a huge role in establishing the positive interdependence that is crucial for cooperative learning. I tell the students, “We are like a team. When one of us is successful, we are all winners.”

My teaching practice has changed dramatically as I have begun to contemplate these two questions. The use of the various strategies, tactics, and activities I have learned over the past few years has certainly made teaching more enjoyable. I cannot help but remember an occasion years ago, when I told my class to answer some questions on Ancient Egypt out of the text book. There was so much frustration in the room, so many hands waving in the air, so many who could not read the text, that in the end, I wrote out the answers on the board for them to copy. I am very grateful to have found much more effective methods of teaching, for my own sake as well as the students’ sake. I *feel* differently now, when I step into the classroom—more optimistic, calm and patient, less tense, less fearful and discouraged. In giving away some of the control and decision-making power to the students, I actually feel more in control, more balanced.

When I asked, “What are some of the stumbling blocks to building community?” I thought that one might be student attitude toward cooperative learning and community building. What if they hated it? What if bad experiences with group work in the past limited their ability to buy in? I also feared that one or more students might sabotage the process, making it impossible for others to feel safe. Another prediction was that parents might object to too much time being spent on the “soft” curriculum, and not enough on the prescribed one. It may be the particular make-up of this particular class and their families, but none of these scenarios, to my knowledge, have arisen. The greatest impediment to building community in the classroom has been time. It feels that there is too little time to accomplish everything that I wanted to, both in the overt and covert curricula. I console myself by rereading Terry Wrigley’s (2003) words in *Schools of Hope*:

> Curriculum is reshaped, remade, reborn, recoded in what we do with kids in classrooms. Pedagogy re-mediates, frames and rearticulates what will count as knowledge in classrooms. So no matter how we theorize or “fix” the curriculum – either centrally of locally – it won’t make much difference if our pedagogy isn’t up to scratch. (p. 92).

Like a pedagogy of hope, a pedagogy of community seems to me to be not only reasonable, but an essential part of school. My practice has changed dramatically since I began to teach with community in mind, to the point that I do feel I am working smarter, not harder, I am enjoying my students’ company, and I am finding my professional life more fulfilling. Through emotional engagement with my students, and in allowing them choice in and responsibility, I have witnessed the power of the creative, imaginative, and compassionate potential that exists in every student.

Margaret Paxton
Sea To Sky School District 48
mpaxton@sd48.bc.ca

LISA OTTENBREIT

LINKING STUDENT LITERACY

Building Community Through Cross-age Tutoring for Reading

> Any genuine teaching will result, if successful, in someone knowing how to bring about a better condition of things than existed earlier. (John Dewey)

Making Connections

I delight in the resultant power of people coming together. When people connect for the purpose of learning, there exists a luxurious, alchemic potential for greatness. One of my greatest fascinations as a teacher is to walk into the classroom on the first day to face a myriad of personalities, shapes, and sizes all assembled together for the purpose of change and growth. It is that initial moment of potential, in the spirit of dynamic possibility, that I derive my challenge: how am I going to bring these 35 unfamiliar, possibly reticent, individuals into one, cohesive, supportive, collaborative group? One of the most valuable things I have learned in my seventeen years of teaching is that a sense of belonging, that sense of valued participation, is a critical ingredient for creating connections from disparity. It is when we reach out to one another that we can enable and promote strength and grace. In the words of the inimitable bell hooks (2000), "When we drop fear, we can draw nearer to people, we can draw nearer to the earth, we can draw nearer to all the heavenly creatures that surround us" (p. 213).

It is with this goal of making "heavenly" connections that I initiated a cross-age reading program called *Reading Rounds*. I was aware of a group of Grade 9 students (all male) enrolled in a Literacy support class who felt marginalized and unsuccessful due to their inability to read effectively. I also knew of a teacher at a nearby elementary school who was finding her young readers struggling to make sense of the words on the pages. So I brought them all together in the spring of 2006, and Reading Rounds was born. The results of this "experiment" grew into an initiative that will hopefully continue long after I have retired from North Vancouver School District (NVSD44). What resulted from one school reaching out to another in the spirit of promoting reading to struggling learners was a connection that reaches far beyond the classroom. I believe it promoted community by linking students through literacy. This paper examines the insights gained from and learning outcomes of the second exploration of a Reading Rounds session in which I was involved.

P. Gouzouasis (ed.), Pedagogy in a New Tonality: Teacher Inquiries on Creative Tactics, Strategies, Graphics Organizers, and Visual Journals in the K-12 Classroom, 19–34.

Accessing Background Knowledge

The effects of cross-age tutoring for literacy learning have been extensively researched and documented (Cohen, Kulik, & Kulik, 1982; Labbo & Teale, 1990). There are important implications for students and teachers when it is clear that older students who struggle to read can benefit from being placed in the role of a reading mentor with younger, emergent readers. The positive outcomes of cross-age "buddy" reading programs are manifold: older students gain the opportunity to examine and strengthen their reading comprehension strategies, they build competence as a role model, and they develop confidence as a learner while the younger students benefit from small group explicit reading comprehension instruction and authentic, meaningful reading practice (Gensemer, 2000).

When a well planned, low-cost, cross-age tutoring program can be offered between two schools, there are not only increased opportunities for literacy learning for all students involved, but also benefits in the increased development of social skills and community. North Vancouver School District has excellent potential for establishing cross-age reading programs as "schools in North Vancouver are organized into 'families of schools' with each of seven secondary schools serving a geographical catchment, or attendance, area made up of a number of elementary schools" (Catchment Areas, 2005).

Where students from elementary "feeder" schools pair up with older students in the neighboring high school, this fosters a heightened awareness of a "family of schools" model and a greater knowledge of the schools included within that family. The younger students, in visiting the older buddy readers, become more familiar with their future high school and the older students delight in their roles of responsibility and leadership with their younger peers. Initiatives, focused on literacy, instructional intelligence practices (Bennett, 2001) or otherwise, that link the elementary schools to their "mother" school also help to promote richer connections between students, teachers, administrators, and the surrounding community.

A qualitative examination of the sense of community developed with Reading Rounds provides a valuable source of information about the relationships that can develop between students and teachers within a family of schools. *Reading Rounds*, which began in March 2006, involved a class of Grade 9 students who were identified as struggling students from a local NVSD secondary school and who were paired with a class of Grade 2 students from a nearby elementary school. As researchers have documented great gains for both tutees and tutors, even when the children being tutored or the tutors themselves are from special education backgrounds (Topping, 1987), there was less trepidation with the implementation of a buddy reading program with these two groups of students who represented a wide range of challenging needs.

With the present reading initiative, the older students acted as reading mentors to the younger students, but in some cases, ironically, the Grade 2 children were more proficient readers than the Grade 9 adolescents. In other words, the reciprocal teaching that occurred was not solely limited to the older students teaching the younger students. In a cross-age tutoring situation, older students often develop in areas beyond literacy and language development such as self-esteem, confidence, risk-taking, and initiation (Urzua, 1995). With Reading Rounds, both groups gained from this experience together as they built knowledge, and a sense of accomplishment. Further examination of the perceptions from the journal responses of the students and feedback from the teachers involved, with regards to their awareness of building community in this cross-age tutoring experience, reveals a sense of connection extends beyond the classroom setting.

One of the major goals of NVSD44 is to strengthen connections between elementary schools and the central high school in each family of schools, with a focus on creating "safe and caring" schools or "tribes" (Gibbs, 1999), and I would propose that Reading Rounds is an excellent means of supporting that district plan. From that perspective, the purpose of this inquiry is to elaborate the successes of Reading Rounds. Specifically, I explored the question of how *Reading Rounds* helps to create community between students, teachers, and the school community.

Reading Rounds

Prior to meeting their younger reading buddies, the Grade 9 students had three classes to learn about their roles and expectations as reading mentors. Equally important was the explicit instruction about reading strategies that they would be modeling for their younger counterparts. As District Literacy Facilitator, this opportunity to teach and review reading strategies with the older students allowed me to learn more about their personal reading strengths and weaknesses. This process with such at-risk middle year students revealed that there is a further need in NVSD44 to create and provide effective reading programs for struggling readers.

To facilitate successful reading with these two disparate age groups, I purchased highly interesting and visually engaging picture books that the older boys would equally enjoy reading with the younger students in their small groups. (NB: A list of the books, most of them fractured fairy tales, may be obtained from the author). I worked collaboratively with the Grade 9 and Grade 2 teachers to discuss the program and prepare the students for the rounds. It was decided that the Grade 2 children would walk from their elementary school (rain or shine!) to read with the Grade 9 students in the high school library for six sessions, once a week for six weeks, during which they would read a picture book aloud together and focus on one reading strategy which would be explicitly discussed and practiced. The initial information outlining the Reading Rounds that the older students received was in the form of a handout (NB: available from the author).

During our three "preparatory" classes, the Grade 9 students were taught the twelve reading strategies as outlined in *North Vancouver's Reading 44: A Reading Framework* document (NVSD, 2004) and offered the opportunity to practice those reading strategies. The Grade 9 students also had the chance to read and discuss a variety of the picture books with peer partners. They were also given a brief lesson on how to read expressively to others. All of this "front-end loading" and reading practice was necessary as each of these boys, for various reasons, struggles to read fluently. Practicing to read aloud with a partner helped to diffuse some of the anxiety they initially felt about their reading skills and the effect they would have with the younger students. It also provided us with a sense of which students were more nervous about the project. It should be noted that, in future, more than three lessons would be more effective in providing the guided instruction that many of these students need. The following journal entries, written prior to meeting their Grade 2 buddies, reflect an anticipated sense of failure for these Grade 9 students.

It is interesting to note that this young man, despite his trepidations, had one of the most successful experiences with Reading Rounds. Further entries from other students included the following comments (copied exactly as they were written).

> To improve in my reading skills, I could be louder, expressing myself a bit better and making voices to sound like the characters. Today when I was reading, I fell that I did a pretty good. I also feel that I could have improved a lot. And I soon will.

> I think I need to use different voices for every character. I also think that I should read louder and slower so the kids could understand. Making it more exciting so the person I am reading to don't get bored. I also should practice the words that is difficult to say. I think I need to make more eye contact to the person I read to.

> What I think I need to approve on is reading a bit slower and finishing the last words to a line instead of mumbling the last few and skipping to the next line. I also should thing about making my voise change for every character and each character will have its own voise so it will be like a movie but other then that I don't think I need to improve on anything els other then getting a few words mixed up so mabey I should practice those.

These particular entries reveal hesitation and insecurity about their performance with the younger peers. These adolescent boys were rarely successful in school and had assimilated their feelings of inadequacy. The wonderfully ironic element of reading with the Grade 2 children was that the younger children never noticed any shortcomings of the older students. Building relationships through connected experience allowed for the older students to transcend their learning difficulties and bond with these younger people of their community.

Observations

The following section provides an overview of each of the Reading Rounds sessions including the weekly reading strategy focus and instructional plans. My personal observations for each visit focused on (1) the interactions of the younger students as they walked to the high school and (2) the social connections and learning outcomes that resulted each week with the older boys. Grade 9 students wrote the journal responses after each session with the Grade 2 children. These responses offer powerful insights to the reading experiences for these adolescent boys. I have presented the comments of Jeff, Cole, Tyler, William,

Shane, and Hesam pertaining to connections that they made with the younger students, and their reading experiences in a sequential fashion in an effort to illuminate the growth and changes in their attitudes, their self-esteem and their growing fondness for their younger peers (NB: they are presented exactly as they were written, in the same order each time reflections are noted; names have been changed for the sake of anonymity). Clearly, connections were made that were obvious and meaningful.

WEEK ONE READING STRATEGY FOCUS: PREDICTING

Instructional Plan

The older students will ask what the younger students predict about the story based on the front cover visuals. As well, twice throughout the story, at an opportune place in the story, the older students will stop and ask each of the younger students to predict what is going to happen next. Post-reading discussion should include whether the students' predictions were correct or not. Student journal responses were as follow.

> Today the Grade 2s came to read. I had three boys we readed "The Three Silly Billies". I tried involving all of them during the reading. I also tried using the things that Mrs. O told us like predicting. One of my kids readed really well and one was not as good. One of my kid read slowly. But he did a good job. One kid cheated when we were predicting he kept going ahead. All the kids did a really good job. They were really friendly. I also met my old teacher Mrs. Bondar.

> Today the Grade 2s came to read and I really enjoyed myself. I feel that I had a lot of reading experience. I never really knew I could express myself in reading this much, but I finally tried and I feel I did pretty darn good for a newbie.

> Today the Grade 2 come to read before they came I felt ok about. I had three kid there names were William, Ethan, and Trisha. William was more talkative while Ethan was semi-talkative and the girl Trisha was shy.

> Today, the Grade 2s came to read. I felt really tired today to I let the kids read and when they made a mistake I corrected them. My partner, Tyler, wanted to read some sentences but this kid beside him kept wanting to read. I didn't care but Tyler probably wanted to read. We had four kids in our group. One wants to read the whole book, two is just noisy, three and four are shy and doesn't want to read. I was actually kind of surprise that they could read that well. If they keep reading like that, they won't need us to help them.

> Today the Grade 2s came to read but I didn't like reading all that much because when I was done I was starting to lose my voice and my throat was hurting. I hope next time I am reading shorter books so my throat doesn't hurt but otherwise it was good because the kids were really good and

> predicting lots and I think they were having a good time because they kept on wanting me to read more and more.
>
> Today the Grade 2s came to my school. I think they were really nice and funny and cute. One of them had troubles reading but I like that fact that he wanted to read even though it wasn't his turn. I think one of the kids I was reading with will be really good at reading in a couple of years and I think he will probably be the smartest. I think it's fun to do this every 'Tuesday. I like things that are different.

Personal Observations & Reflections

Today, I was with the older boys in the library prior to the younger students' arrival. The Grade 9s were nervous and apprehensive about the experience. This was quickly dispelled as in marched a long line of adorable children who were so enthusiastic and accepting. There was a wonderful energy in the library as we introduced the program, organized the small groups and conducted introductions. I observed the change with the older students as they immediately realized that Grade 2 students are, overall, quite charming. The students quickly settled down to reading and the other two teachers and I mingled around the room offering help if needed. The Grade 2 children were very focused in their reading and I think that this was encouraging for the older boys. When they finished their books, they had conversations that were allowed them to get to know one another. Some of the older boys had been students at the same elementary school and had siblings who attended the same school, so there were many discussions around these coincidences. I noted that the reading became secondary to the blossoming friendships.

WEEK TWO READING STRATEGY: VISUALIZING

Instructional Plan

Once during reading and after reading the whole story, the older students will ask the Grade 2s to draw a quick picture they have in their heads of their "movie version" of the story. Have each student present and speak about their "mind movie." Student journal responses were as follow.

> This week in buddy reading I had a new person in my group his name was Alexander. He was a really good drawer all of them were. It was hard keeping them in control but I did it. One of my buddies was coping the picture from the book and the other two were making their picture from there head. I think Alexander did a really good job making pictures in his head. All of them did a really good job of paying attention when I was reading the book. One of my buddies made a really good connection when I told them what the title was he told me if *Jim and the beanstalk* and *Jack and the beanstalk* were the same story. I wasn't really sure what to say to him

because I ever read Jim and the beanstalk before. Amir one of my buddies made a good prediction when Jim finish helping the Giant Amir said that the giant was going to eat Jim because he was happy again. I like my group a lot because they pay good attention.

Today I think my buddies drew pretty well. They did not draw nearly as well as I can draw (I don't mean to brag) but they did draw pretty doggone good. I also think that they listening skills was absolutely fantastic, and that really impressed me because most other kids I work with are not as good as my buddies were. Mine were probably the best listeners I could possibly have. They were not very talkative, but they were very interested in me I think, and also, I hope. I am like totally looking forward to next Tuesday, I absolutely cannot wait. Even talking about it makes me want to do it more.

I had three kids in the group. Ashlegh had good pictures and Jin was quiet but had good pictures too but one wasn't. Eugene had good pictures and he loved to read so he read two pages in the book. They called my name when I came to the table. I think they are getting to know me.

One of my buddies was actually doing a great job. He was focused on me when I was reading the story to them and did what I told him to do. Though, two of the buddies were though. They weren't really focused on me when I was reading the story to them but they all did drew lots of good pictures and I think they all did good job drawing.

My reading buddy's were super good drawers one of my buddy's named Ceci was a fantastic drawer probably even better then me and they were doing great they were listening and predicting and had no problem drawing or thinking of what to draw. I think they did a super job and they weren't copying the from the book and they were coming up with there own idea's and if I had to mark them out of 10 I would give both of the 10 out of 10 because they were excellent drawers and picturing what they were going to draw they weren't talkative and they were listening with eyes and ears and following along together with the spare books they had and what really impressed me was they both remembered my name without the name tag. And I am really happy I got those two girls for my reading buddy group because I wouldn't pick any other kids there because the ones I had were perfect.

I think there really good at reading and there really smart some of them!

Personal Observations & Reflections

Today as the Grade 2 children entered the library, they quickly checked out where their older reading buddies were sitting and RAN to them at their tables! It was so delightful to see the looks on their faces as they connected to these older boys. We took some time to sort out who was with whom, but once again, they settled down with their books to read and draw. Today was a little more frenetic as there were papers and crayons to manage, but I think the older boys were happy to see the children again and to have them so focused. Many of the older students are not familiar with being "leaders" and Reading Rounds places them in a position of responsibility that they seem to enjoy. The younger students regard them with awe and it is this "unconditional" admiration that is wonderful for the older boys' esteem. I witnessed several occasions when the older boys were referring to reading strategies to engage the children. I hope this reciprocal teaching will help to support their personal reading challenges and enforce the importance of explicit instruction. I also noticed that the other teachers really seemed surprised at how much the children were enjoying themselves. Both of these teachers have been very supportive and they like coming together Reading Rounds – it provides an excellent opportunity for collegial sharing.

WEEK THREE READING STRATEGY: CONNECTING

Instructional Plan

Using sticky notes, the younger students will be asked to find places in the story where they connect to either something in their own lives, another book they have read, or a "world" connection. Discussion after reading should include sharing their various connections. The older students are encouraged to share their ideas of their text-self, text-text, and text-world connections as well.

Personal Observations & Reflections

Today, we learned, after we arrived at the high school that there was a power outage due to the incredible wind storm the night before. It was so disappointing to make the effort to get to the high school, only to arrive in a library that was pitch dark. The Grade 2s had practically RUN all the way to the school in their excitement and I was sorry to have to tell them that Reading Rounds would have to be cancelled that day. The decision was made that we would convene in the classroom to await the principal's announcement about early release. It was eerie walking along the dark corridors, lit only by emergency lights, and I was worried that the younger children would be frightened by the expansive hallways and lack of light. They were rather hushed as we assembled into the classroom and they all sat in the "big kids'" desks while the older boys huddled at the front of the room. To distract the younger children, I asked if they had any questions for the older boys about "life in high school"...to our surprise they had MANY! They queried about the size of the desks, what the lockers were for, and what big kids carried in their backpacks, amongst other questions. Tyler came forward and "entertained" the kids by emptying the contents of this backpack and patiently explaining each of the items and what they were for. Tyler has written output issues and had a NEO keyboard in his backpack that was very fascinating for the younger children and he proudly explained its use and why he needed it. As teachers, we all observed an interesting phenomenon in that darkened room that day: the students were all becoming friends. The reading strategy we had planned to focus on was "connecting to text", but we connected in other ways. It was magical to witness! As it turned out, the principal did ask everyone to leave the school and Reading Rounds was not held, but all was not lost, because it was a visit that changed these students from reading partners to true reading buddies!

WEEK FOUR READING STRATEGY: FINDING THE MAIN IDEA

Instructional Plan

After reading, the younger students will be asked to discuss the main idea or lesson of the story. They will then be asked to write one or two sentences on a slip of paper about what they think was the main idea of the story to share with the group. The older students will be coaching. Younger students who cannot write well can verbally or visually represent their ideas. (NB: The original plan for this week was replaced by the previous week's lesson that had been cancelled due to the power outage).

> Today reading was very easy because I got to read a very short book. We got a lot of confusion during the beginning (around) who was in my group but we sorted that out. My buddies made a lot of good connection with the book. One of my buddies made a connection with other book called frog prince. Other connection was somebody liking motorcycles. I had to read one book twice because we finish to fast the second time I let the little kids read the book and I think they did a good job reading it. One of my buddies was very good reader I had no problem with him. Other one need more help than the other. During the end they kind of got bored and started to play around with my nametag also at the end Mrs. O ask Grade 2s which book they like the best. I think I need to stop more often and ask questions what that little part was about and ask what was going to happened next.

> Today my reading buddy and I did some rocking fantastic reading. We read "The Three Silly Billies" and "The Paper Bag Princess". They were pretty da*n good, especially the "Three Silly Billies". It was very funny and cool. Anyway, 4 the connections, with ze "golden stickiest", my reading buddy wats her face, um Sara I think or somsing like zat. Anyway, she inserted her "golden sticky" on this big page with a bear family who was just about to cross this bridge, because it reminded her of her own family, and I placed mine on the last page of the book where it said under construction, because I am going 2 build a toll booth when I grow up as well and um ya that about covers it. (P.S. read the book for more information).

> Today in buddy reading, it was annoying to me because my head hurts and reading to the buddies when my head hurts it's really hard to focus. But my buddies were paying attention to me and respected me so it was easy to read for them. I didn't really feel good today. If my head wasn't killing me, I would probably able to read lot better than how I read today.

> Today went really fast and was easy because one of my buddy's offered to read today and then the other one wanted to read so barely had to read and

> connection thing went really well and there was no problem with that and one of my buddy's was such a good reader she was just speeding threw at a good pace and not making any errors. I thought the connection thing was a good idea because it was making the Grade 2s thing hard about the book and then the thing that they connected with so I thought it made them focus a bit more and the color and shape of the stick helped because they were really attracted to the sticky and one of them wanted to keep it and take it home. And next time I could maybe do a bit more predicting because I didn't do much of that this time because I was doing the connection thing.
>
> I think it's good that they come to high school before they become a Grade 8.

Personal Observations & Reflections

Today's lesson was focused on making connections. The objectives facilitated discussions around the books and how they connected to their lives which in turn elicited stories about their own lives that they shared with the group. I think the older boys did a wonderful job managing the sometimes rambunctious children in their small groups. Now that there is a high comfort level with the Grade 2s, we saw more behavioral challenges than in the past few sessions. Having three teachers and two aids in the room helps to keep things under control, but I also saw the older boys stepping up to this challenge and doing a great job. We only intervene if there is difficulty. Often I see the older boys managing to keep the Grade 2s on task and focused on the activity. They are reading so much! Some small groups are getting through more than three books during the session. It is so exciting to see them read, read, read!

WEEK FIVE READING STRATEGY: SUMMARIZING

Instructional Plan

After reading, and using a story summary graphic organizer the students will discuss the story and make a summary in their own words. The older students will fill in the worksheet with the younger students' ideas.

> Today it was a very easy day for all the big kids because there wasn't a lot of little kids. So that meant we had to have smaller groups. I only had two little kids in my group and they were every good. We read "Who's Afraid of Grannie's Wolf." It was an every good book we took turns reading. At the end we had to say a summary in are own words. They did a very good job about that. I think both of them need to read louder. When Mrs. O came and read they got more excited about the book. I'm very excited about the Christmas party next week.
>
> Today I had some fun reading with my hey ya buddies. I read the stories "rumplestilskin" and "princess smarty pants". Both of these books are very good books and my buddies and myself really enjoyed them. Today, my

> buddies were paying very good attention and were focusing much better than last time and I really appreciated them giving me that type of behavior. That way thing went smooth and I could manage to read to them just fine.
>
> Today, in buddy reading, I didn't really feel well so I read the book fast and my buddies didn't even care. We read the same book again! This is our third time! My buddies listened well but they didn't answer any of my questions though it was okay. Even though I was tired my buddies paid attention.
>
> Today my reading was easy because I only had to read one book and my buddy did the rest. I don't think she could improve on any thing because she was so good and she had no problem reading. She didn't stumble on any words and she was speaking clearly. She even summarized at the end of both books. When we were done she memorized what we read and we predicted on one of the books because the other book we had already read. I think my buddy is getting better at reading ever time she comes. Today she was reading really big words and I was surprised she could read them.

Personal Observations and Reflections

This week I walked with the Grade 2s to the high school. They LOVE the walk! They almost run all the way. It is a challenge to keep the group together because half of the kids run while others want to stop and pick up every rock! The beauty of this walk is that it offers the kids exercise and fresh air and some of them need this very badly. It also teaches them about the surrounding area and the route to the high school. We chat with the kids as they walk along and today I learned all about their pets, their favorite video games, their friendships, and their daily lives. This time allows for building connections that are outside of the classroom and that shines a light on the things that are important to them. It is a wonderful chance to get to know the students on a personal level.

WEEK SIX

The last Reading Rounds session was turned into a Christmas celebration. I gathered a number of Christmas books and the children were free to choose their own text. By this time, they were having so much fun together that it almost seemed a shame to spend the time reading. They wanted to chat and spend time together. There were no journals after this class; the observations are mine only. Moreover, I have included the observations of the Grade 9 and Grade 2 teachers respectively.

Personal Observations and Reflections

Today was our last day of Reading Rounds. A grey drizzly day, I said a little prayer for sun, but unfortunately this request was not granted. Jewel had asked that I walk them to and fro and this was a first for me. After dropping off the Christmas books and materials required for the Christmas craft at Carson, I zoomed off to Queen Mary to join the Grade 2 children in their march up to the high school. It was interesting to see the children as they readied themselves for Reading Rounds. Usually I merely greet them at the school and then walk them back, but today I was provided a glimpse into their preparations for leaving the elementary school on their journey. There was lots of chaos as the students put away their chairs and tidied the classroom before they donned their jackets and lined up at the door. I was reminded of how much time in school is spent lining up and "getting ready." It took this Grade 2 class a solid 15 minutes to get themselves to the point where they could depart.

There were several students who did not have appropriate outerwear for the walk in the rain and cold, but seven year olds don't seem to mind the cold as much as I do …The walk was not uneventful. As I lead the pack and the classroom teacher brought up the rear, I walked along with a First Nations boy who told me about how he used to play football. Another boy was trailing too closely behind him and this was annoying enough for the first boy to extend his led back and kick the student who was bothering him. There was a great wail of despair and tears! Jewel came forth and reprimanded the First Nations child who was most indignant and stormed off. That was the end of the journey for him! The teacher took him and the other sobbing child and marched back to the school while I carried forth with the others. Sadly, I had not wanted them to have to end on this note, but I am aware that there is a history of behavior/conflict with both of these students and I respected their teacher's decision.

We finally arrived at the school, gathered in the library and were just sitting down to read with the buddy readers when the fire alarm sounded! What timing! There was a flurry of commotion as coats were grabbed and students – both Grade 2 and 9 – were corralled out of the school to the sidewalk out front. The younger students were quite concerned and there were lots of questions: "Is this real? Is this a fire?" One young girl was disappointed when we told her it was merely a prank! The kids were all very excited and it was quite the challenge keeping them all together, but then Tyler took over. Quite handily he began playing a game with the children to keep their minds off the situation and to keep them engaged. What a star! By far, this Grade 9 boy has shown that he has incredible talent with younger people. He is incredibly learning challenged and yet he demonstrated remarkable leadership and confidence with the younger students. We were fortunate to have his talents today! One thing I noticed when we were all rushing outside was that the older boys were watching out for the younger ones. They really stepped up as responsible leaders in that hectic situation. I was thankful for the extra help, as Jewel had not returned from her walk back to Queen Mary with her "trouble makers." Again, the sense of community was significant as the older students were curious as to why the "little kids" were at the school and several of them recognized neighbors or family friends. The students have now experienced a power outage *and* a fire drill. They have experienced the high school setting at its most frenetic.

Once back in the library, the children chose their Christmas story and they were able to read at least two stories with the big buddies. It was lovely to see them so engaged and so focused. One of the older boys was missing today and so I approached an older, senior student sitting on the back couches and asked him to read with the younger kids. He was most enthusiastic and he started right in reading with the two little girls in his group. His teacher walked over and told him that he would get extra credit for doing so – he beamed! I hated to interrupt the reading only after fifteen minutes as the students were really enjoying themselves (as seen in the photos) but we had lost so much time with the false fire alarm that we had to end promptly, disregard the Christmas craft due to not enough time, and move directly to the thank yous. Tyler and Jeff spoke for the older boys and thanked the younger students and myself. The younger students handed their thank you cards and treats to the older boys and there was a lot of praise and a feeling of warmth from all. Finally, little William, often an easily distracted, unfocused Grade 2 student asked to pass around the donuts to the older students. He seemed so proud to be able to provide the older boys with their snacks. I would have to say that I am sad to see this project end. Both teachers have stated that they will absolutely want to continue Reading Rounds next fall. I think they enjoyed it even more than the kids.

Making Inferences

The importance of the collegial capacity for this project cannot be underestimated. Working with both the Grade 9 and Grade 2 teachers to coordinate Reading Rounds was essential for the successful outcome of this project. Their reflections reveal a connection that was made on a collegial level that might not have been possible without an opportunity to collaborate on a cross-age reading program like Reading Rounds. Their comments show that building community comes from teacher leadership and a desire to work with others when improving education. Thomas Likona (1988) reminds us that "to build a sense of community is to create a group that extends to others the respect one has for oneself … to come to know one another as individuals, to respond and care about one another, to feel a sense of membership and accountability to the group" (p. 421). The observation from the Grade 9 teacher is below and the Grade 2 teacher's response follows.

SECONDARY TEACHER REFLECTION

"Reading Rounds has always been a fabulous, community building experience for everyone involved. Professionally, it is always a pleasure and an insightful learning experience to spend time peering into the daily life of a colleague. Furthermore, seeing my future students at such a young age and hearing about where they are in their literacy development is interesting and valuable. Collaboration and communication between colleagues within our family of schools (in particular because of the socio-economics) is paramount if we aim to provide a learning continuum and raise life long learners and responsible citizens in our diverse and needy community.

I believe Reading Rounds does just this-provides collaborative, communicative opportunities, encourages life long learning and literature appreciation, and certainly builds community and responsible citizenship. We know that when students enjoy their time at school, they go to school more often. Sharing in the Reading Rounds experience is an opportunity for the older students to remember where they've been and how far they've come, while it is a vision of the future for the younger ones. Personally, I love watching my older boys interact with the younger students. It is an opportunity for me to see them shine in such a way that they might not have the opportunity to in my classroom. At Reading Rounds, my boys are the experts and the successful feeling of being the authorities is written all over their faces. They always look forward to spending time with their buddies!"

PRIMARY TEACHER REFLECTION

"Reading Rounds allowed for the creation of a special and motivating environment in which the Grade 2 students felt excited and special to be apart of. Further, the Grade 2 students looked forward to pairing with their "big buddies" and increased their reading volume and time on task because they wanted to be able to "do a good job for their buddies." As a teacher, I felt this to be a wonderful connection between my former students and my present students. This opportunity afforded me the opportunity to get to know a high school colleague and to discuss many aspects of literacy regarding our students. It allowed both of us to give feedback to students and one another and to determine strengths and weaknesses. Reading Rounds allows for a meaningful and real life connection between elementary school and high school. Many of the Grade 2 students will be going on to Carson Graham Secondary. This experience affords them the opportunity to become familiar with the layout of the highs school and an introduction to behavioral expectations within the new setting."

Finding the Main Idea

It was evident from the data collected and the observations of those involved that what started out as a buddy reading initiative grew into a small reading community. When we attempted to bring two disparate groups of students together, there was a spark. When two teachers came together to wonder and learn there was accomplishment. Reading Rounds was merely a vehicle for connecting students in a school family that resulted in a rich appreciation for one another. The supportive environment provided by the administrators, teachers, and students of both schools played an important role as well.

This cost-effective, buddy-reading program can improve reading attitudes, increase motivation and self-efficacy, and provide authentic opportunities to perform strategically in a structured and safe environment for students—not unlike the adolescent Grade 9 boys in this study, who are often abandoned by the regular school system. It behooves district administrators to closely examine the benefits of programs like Reading Rounds if they wish to strengthen connections in their families of schools. In the future, it would be important to study the positive impact on the younger students in terms of their perceptions toward reading, high school, and the effects of linking students through literacy.

Summarizing

I return to the introductory words of John Dewey that would suggest that effective teaching, indeed, genuine teaching inherently requires a change. With Reading Rounds, Grade 9 students who typically struggled to read grew to embrace their individual strengths in leadership and responsibility for teaching reading strategies to younger children. As a result of their own teaching experiences, they were able to articulate some of their own reading issues and identify specific strategies to improve upon. They became more familiar with common language used to identify particular reading strategies as outlined in *Reading 44* such as "predicting" and "visualizing" (NVSD, 2005). Struggling readers are often denied opportunities within school settings to participate in authentic, affirming and non-threatening language interactions that can scaffold their learning (Cazden, 1983). Reading Rounds provided a situation when these boys could shine. This socially based reading experience may have helped both groups feel better about school, although this was not measured. The older boys' journal entries and comments from their teacher revealed an improved attitude about the significance of reading and academic growth.

There are many considerations for future reading initiatives, including allowing for more time in preparing the older students for their tutoring responsibility. Some recommendations for a well-designed tutoring program might require certain factors deemed necessary for high-quality implementation, according to researchers with the U.S. Department of Education's Planning and Services.

- Close coordination with the classroom or reading teacher
- Intensive and on-going training for tutors
- Well-structured tutoring sessions in which the content and delivery of instruction is carefully scripted
- Careful monitoring and reinforcement of progress
- Frequent and regular tutoring sessions
- Specially designed interventions for children with severe reading difficulties

It might also be important to include the parents of the students in an effort to increase the role of literacy support in the children's homes. Successful community building through literacy initiatives should ideally involve teachers, students, administration, district support staff, parents and neighboring public libraries.

The sense of familiarity and community that grew from the Reading Rounds experience resulted from the strengths and sensitivities that the older boys brought to their teaching roles. In her research on mentoring programs, Gensemer (2000) found that "cross-age tutoring is most successful since older students are seen as role models" (p. 3). In the present inquiry, the Grade 9 students were often reading with Grade 2 children who were equally delayed in their literacy development and the Grade 9 students' insight to this lack of fluency allowed for greater empathy and non-verbal communication. The tutors' sensitivity to the needs, abilities and struggles of the younger students, enabled them to take chances, modify tactics and implement reading strategies effectively which gave them a higher sense of purpose. The relationships between the peer tutors were deepened by a common understanding of what it means to have difficulty and from this understanding grew an unspoken bond of trust. It is this deeper connection that is possible when a cross-age reading program can exist between two schools that share common experiences.

Engaging in rich, collaborative and cooperative learning experiences can make a difference to a school, and on a broader level, an entire school district. North Vancouver School District embarked on a remarkable journey with its commitment to the Instructional Institute and the creative strategies, tactics, and skills inherent in this pedagogical approach. Through further commitment to engaging literacy initiatives, it is my hope that the enlightening responses that were collected in this qualitative study will inspire and encourage other families of schools in NVSD44 to adopt a similar cross-age reading program that can benefit middle year students and primary students who struggle with their literacy development. Elementary schools and neighboring high schools can support one another by linking students together through literacy initiatives such as Reading Rounds.

Lisa Ottenbreit
North Vancouver School District 44
lottenbreit@nvsd44.bc.ca

SEAN KELLY

AT THE CROSSROADS

A Teacher's Journey in Understanding Classroom Conflict

Signposts

I began the present inquiry with the intent of examining my role in the conflicts that occur between me and my students in our classroom. According to Long (2000), in many conflicts between teachers and students, the teacher is responsible for escalating the conflict. Although students may initiate the conflict, in most cases, the teacher's responses trigger further inappropriate behaviours. My goal was to examine my actions when dealing with students who exhibited some kind of inappropriate behaviours, and then look for patterns or habits that either improved the situation or made it worse. Instead, I discovered that the amount of inappropriate behaviour in my classroom has decreased considerably since I started my master's degree program. Instead of students either losing their tempers, swearing at teachers, or simply being noncompliant, the worst I now have to respond to is students talking in class or straying off-task at their desk. Something had changed in my classroom, something in my behaviour, and perhaps something in my understanding of what it means to be a teacher. That changed the focus of this inquiry.

The three-year pursuit of a master's degree was a combination of academic and emotional growth. Through a blend of personal reflections, exposure to pedagogical theories and practical applications, awakened memories, and observed behaviours, I came to other realizations of myself as a teacher and as a person. Articles and essays I read resonated with childhood experiences. New understandings of classroom tactics and strategies intersected with personal beliefs and ideologies. With those influences in mind, this paper emerged as a collage, or portrait, of these intersections—an autoethnographical examination of my interactions with my students, revealing not only what I learned, but also what I unlearned as new knowledge and increased awareness transformed previous values and beliefs. It is not merely a culmination of learning and research, but rather a new beginning in praxis.

CHILDHOOD REFLECTION

The boys were playing marbles in the dirt, out underneath the eucalyptus trees near the edge of the playing fields. The magpie nest was empty, so there was no threat from above on this day. Their shoes were long discarded in the classroom, and the shirts and shorts of their uniforms

P. Gouzouasis (ed.), Pedagogy in a New Tonality: Teacher Inquiries on Creative Tactics, Strategies, Graphics Organizers, and Visual Journals in the K-12 Classroom, 35–53.

were dusty with the red clay of a Queensland primary school recreation yard. For a half-hour, the boys were free of teachers' discipline, of sitting in silent rows, of copying their times tables neatly inside the lines of their notebooks. They didn't have to worry about saying "Sir" or "Miss" at the end of each sentence. They were free of the slapping of the ruler on Sir's pant leg. They weren't scared of not having the right answer, or making a smudge on their slateboards as they practiced their letters and numbers, again staying between the permanent lines on the same slateboards their parents must have used. The marbles were all that mattered at this moment.

He focused on the mib on the edge of the group inside the circle. The blue one was his favourite and he had it right where he wanted it. These games were keepsies and he had lost it yesterday. Now was his chance to win it back. The aggie in his hand was balanced on the end of his thumb. He went knuckle-down, ready to shoot. The boy across from him held his breath.

The aggie flew from his hand, but caught a pebble and skittered left of the blue mib, rolling futilely through the circle. "SHIT!" said the boy. From nowhere, a grown man's hand struck him across the side of the head and sent him rolling across the dirt, scattering marbles as well as other boys. The boy's ear rang from the impact.

"There'll be none of that kind of language, Mr. Kelly, or it'll be the headmaster's cane for you. Now pick these up and get back to your lunch area and wait there until the bell rings."

The boy cried all the way to his classroom area, expecting further punishment for his inappropriate language. Luckily, none came. He didn't tell his teacher what happened. He never even told his parents. Swearing was wrong and he knew it. He deserved what he got.

On-ramps and Merging Lanes

The topic of conflict in the classroom has received much attention over the years, and there are a variety of focal points in the literature. Colvin (1992, 1995, 1997) focuses on defusing confrontation in the classroom through a series of practiced steps. Riddle (2003) recounts her days as a student teacher and talks about the vital need for open communication between teachers and students in order to create a safe learning environment. Long (1986, 1995, 1996, 2000) developed the Conflict Cycle model to enable teachers to understand the evolution and escalation of classroom conflicts. Kottler (2002) describes the type of students whose behaviours trigger emotional responses in teachers. Yost & Mosca (2002) discuss the importance of reflection in the teacher's dealing with troubling events. A common element in all of these writings is the observation that when teachers react, either emotionally or reflexively, they usually exacerbate the situation.

Emotions often run extremely high at my school. My alternative secondary school is a school for students designated as having severe behaviour disorders. Anger management and dealing with frustration are common challenges for these students. Conflict, therefore, has been a common occurrence in my classroom, whether it's as minor as a discussion around the appropriate time to be programming an iPod, or as major as students losing their temper and destroying school property. Although my situation is not unique, in my teaching environment I have been exposed to a wide range of negative behaviours from students. When I started teaching at this school—my very first permanent assignment—conflict was a daily occurrence. In one month, I more than likely experienced more conflict than a teacher in a non-alternative school might experience in a year.

In my third year of teaching, I began working in a very small career preparation program called TASSC (Trades and Secondary School Completion), in which our Grade 11 and 12 students prepare for the working world after graduation. As in an elementary program, I teach these students multiple subjects and they are rarely out of my classroom. Although these students are older and more mature than the students I worked with in my first two years, conflict continued to be a part of the regular school day.

CHILDHOOD REFLECTION

The boy was a little unsure when the teacher called on him to pull down the map at the back of the room. He was unfamiliar with the spring-loaded roll-down maps mounted on the wall, and hesitated a little before rising to the task. He was pleased, however, when he was able to pull down the appropriate map from the large roll and point out various countries on the map of Europe. Since coming to this small Canadian town, he had discovered that his Australian education had prepared him well for the academic requirements of BC secondary school. Grade Eight Social Studies was one of his favourite classes, even if the teacher was a bit loud.

The other students followed his finger as he identified England, France and Germany on the map. The attention made him nervous, but he relaxed as soon as the teacher called everyone's focus back to the front of the room. Without being asked, the boy decided to return the map to its original position, but he couldn't figure out the spring mechanism. He had seen others perform the quick tug-and-roll manoeuvre and was sure that it shouldn't be this difficult. He tugged a few times, varying the length and speed of his motion, but the map would not roll up. He was about to sit down when a classmate reached over from his seat and yanked on the map. It flew up immediately, making the loud clattering noise so familiar to anyone who has been to high school, shooting up the wall and bringing the class to a standstill as it crashed to its rolled-up position.

The boy stood horrified, stunned by the noise and the suddenness of what had happened. Gone was his satisfaction at knowing the countries of

Europe. Gone was his small pride at being asked to help. His face burned in shame.

"All right, WORM!" The voice thundered in the room. The teacher's arm was outstretched, his finger pointing in judgment and isolation. The student who had pulled the map giggled a little at his desk.

"Now that you have disrupted my class, SIT DOWN AND BE QUIET." The teacher's face was as red as the boy's. His hand clenched in anger as he stared the boy back to his seat.

The boy somehow got to his seat without shrivelling and vowed to himself that he would be invisible for the rest of his years in school. Never again would he do more than he was asked. He should have known better. He should have left the map where it was. What the hell was he thinking? He didn't know how to work the damned thing, so he should have left it where it was. Never again.

Detour

I began the present inquiry with the hope of learning more about my keen awareness of students' needs for a safe learning environment, my knowledge of the teacher's role in teacher-student conflict, and my understanding of the benefits of personal reflection. I hoped that this newfound enlightenment would change the ways I responded to conflict between my students and myself. What happened was an inquiry into why conflict rarely happened in my classroom.

As I recorded the daily interactions that could be deemed conflict, I soon realized that I was documenting rather innocuous exchanges. Occasionally, I might have asked a student to watch his language in conversation with other students. Once in a while, I had to ask a student not to get involved in someone else's conversation. The most common situation, though, was simply asking students to stop talking about non-school related work and get back to their lessons. None of these could really be considered conflicts. It had been a long time since anyone slammed a door, kicked over a chair, or hurled a derogatory epithet. The most common reasons for asking students to leave class were (1) that they had either fallen asleep at their desk and needed to get some fresh air, or (2) that they had trouble staying on task and were being a bit disruptive to their peers. Those situations never led to angry exchanges, as they might have at one time, and they never harmed my relationships with the students.

My inquiry evolved into an exploration of how my experiences in the study of creative applications of tactics, strategies, and graphics organizers influenced my interactions with my students and led to a classroom in which conflict was a rare occurrence instead of a daily routine.

My Autoethnographic Journey

Ethnography enables a researcher to examine belief systems and values within an environment (Gay, Mills, & Airasian, 2003). Yost & Mosca (2002) argue that teachers' reactions to conflict are usually grounded in their prior beliefs and experiences. Long (1979), in creating his Conflict Cycle model, observes that stressful situations activate students' belief systems. In consideration of Yost and Long's perspectives, I used an autoethnographic approach to examine my own beliefs and values and how they affected my participation in the conflict cycle in my classroom.

The project was conducted daily, inside my own classroom in North Vancouver School District. At the end of each day, I documented, in the form of narrative field notes, any conflicts that I had with students during the day. The documents were as descriptive as possible and I tried to be as honest as I could in describing my emotions, actions, and intentions. Each evening, the field notes were converted to memos in which I reflected on the conflict and my role in it. Field notes and memos were filed chronologically. I also used a visual journal to reflect on the events in the field notes. At the end of the research period, which culminated toward the end of the school year, the notes and memos were analysed for patterns of behaviour and evidence of growth in my interactions with my students.

The end product of this inquiry is an a/r/tographical narrative (Irwin & de Cosson, 2004), combining descriptions of classroom incidents and the reflections that followed. Events from my childhood and from my first years in teaching are also included in this narrative, as I have attempted to draw comparisons between my life experiences, then and now. Linking the individual stories and reflections are discussions of the research literature that have contributed to my understanding of conflict. The narrative approach allows both a non-linear presentation of the research and the use of fractured narrative and textual cues to represent the findings of this study. Through my coursework in narrative and artographic inquiry, I have learned that research can be both an art and science. Linked to that perspective is the notion that pedagogy may be defined as the art and science of teaching and learning. Artographical autoethnography allows me to explain my development—my *becoming*—through the lens of an artist, researcher, and teacher.

A visual journal that I began during an artography influenced, action research course enabled me to reflect on the almost constant conflict with a particular student, Brooke. Brooke was always determined to do things her way. From her first days in TASSC, she struggled to meet the requirements of the program. For a long time, her toughest challenge was meeting the minimum attendance requirements. She came close to being withdrawn a couple of times. As she moved closer to graduation, though, she started to seriously question why she had to do certain work, or why she had participate in class activities. Whether it was out of a newly developed self-confidence or from a sense of rebellion, more and more she refused to cooperate with staff if she didn't want to do something.

After one particularly trying day, I turned to my visual journal and created two pages that focused on conflict and confrontation. From these images (see *Figure 1* below) came the realization that I am as much a part of any conflict or confrontation as the student. From that realization came the idea for how my inquiry would unfold.

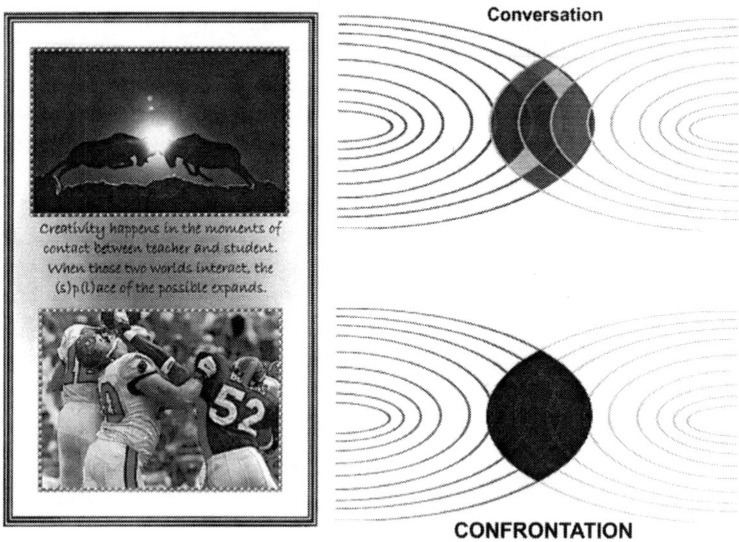

Figure 1. Visual journal images that illustrate conflict and confrontation.

Intersecting Pathways

The work that is most relevant to my inquiry has been conducted by Long (1986, 1995, 1996, 2000). According to Long (1996), the Conflict Cycle—which describes the circular and escalating nature of student/teacher conflict—involves five interactive steps.

1. *The Student's Self Concept* – in troubled students, this self concept is usually comprised of irrational beliefs developed over time and resulting from negative reinforcement from significant adults in their lives.
2. *A Stressful Incident* – this activates the student's irrational beliefs (i.e., "Nothing good ever happens to me!" "Adults are hostile," etc.)
3. *Student's Feelings* – the negative thoughts trigger negative feelings in the student.
4. *Student's Observable Behaviour* – the student acts out those feelings in an inappropriate manner, inciting staff.
5. *Adult/Peer Reactions* – staff react, often mirroring the student's behaviour. This reinforces the student's irrational beliefs, elevating the student's stress levels (Step 2), and triggering more negative feelings.

Long argues that teachers have their own emotional triggers and beliefs about themselves that influence how well they work with troubled students. He also says that troubled students can "greatly influence the behaviour of their teachers" (p. 243).

FIRST YEAR TEACHING REFLECTION

The teacher began the class by handing back some marked assignments. Two students came in late, interrupting his explanation of some of the marks. They barely looked at him and dragged chairs to a desk at the back of the room, talking all the while. He was three months into his first permanent teaching job and was finding a school full of "at-risk" students quite a challenge. One student was particularly determined to be dismissive in her comments and disruptive in her actions.

"Ariela, you're late. Stop talking and just sit down." He turned back to the class.

"Whatever. I'm just getting a chair. What do you want me to do, sit on the floor?"

Ariela stood facing him.

"Get the chair, and sit down," he said, his voice tinged with exasperation.

"Okay. Geez. I'm not even late. The bell just went."

She dropped her binder on the desk as she slumped into her chair. He turned to face her again.

"Ariela. You're three minutes late. You haven't been in class on time at all this week. And you always come in making a lot of noise. So could you please just be quiet and stop disrupting the class."

"Why? It's not like we're learning anything in here anyway. We don't do any of the stuff that I'll need to know when I get back to mainstream school, so why should I even listen to you. This isn't Grade 10 stuff we're doing. It's stuff you just made up. You don't even know what you're doing, do you?"

Ariela's voice rose in pitch and volume. The rest of the class turned to watch the teacher's reaction. Unfortunately, he took the bait.

"Of course I know what I'm doing. If you came to class more often, Ariela, you would actually be learning the stuff you'll need in Grade 11, but you don't show up half the time and when you're here you don't pay attention."

He could feel his face getting red with anger.

"I don't come because your class sucks. How did you even get this job? Kayla was a way better teacher than you are. They should fire you and get her back."

She laughed directly at him and smiled at her friend, triumph all over her face.

"All right, Ariela. You're outta here. Come back tomorrow when you've figured out how to behave in my class." He walked to the door with his hand motioning Ariela to the hall.

Ariela knocked her chair over as she jumped to her feet. She came right up to the teacher and said in a quiet voice, "You're just angry 'cause you know I'm right, ASSHOLE!" The final word was screamed into his face. He started backwards as she stomped out of the room. Ariela kicked a garbage can in the hallway and screamed down the hall, "LOSER!" The teacher turned to the support worker in the room, "Watch things for a minute, will you?" He went to the staff room for a drink of water, his hands shaking with emotion. He had never thought he would hate a student until that moment.

In his development of the Life Space Crisis Intervention program (2000), Long and his associates gathered and analysed more than 2000 hours of videotape recordings of interactions between teachers and students. In about 60% of the 140 crises that they witnessed, the situations were exacerbated by teachers' responses to the students' initial behaviours. Long describes three common problem areas for teachers who work with troubled students: "Avoidance Motivation," "Psychological Fit," and the "Conflict Cycle" (p. 96). From his research, Long concludes that teachers have a "good psychological fit" with about 60% of their students, a moderate fit with 25% of their students, and a marginal fit with about 10% of their students. He also believes that in every classroom there is one student with whom the teacher has a dysfunctional relationship.

CLASSROOM INCIDENT—MARCH 25TH, 10:30AM

Steven is clearly not intending to do any work in Art this morning. He has been talking to the student beside him for some time and has not even pulled his work out of his folder. Barb (the Special Education Aide) goes to him and asks him if he needs anything in order to start on his art project. Steven simply dismisses Barb. "Go away. I don't want to talk to you." He turns back to talk to the student beside him.

Barb tells him to leave class at this point and to go to the Longhouse (where students are supposed to go when they are asked to leave the classroom). She then comes to our classroom and tells me what has happened. She is stunned by his disrespect and his complete disregard for her authority.

I find Steven on the bench in the Longhouse and sit down next to him. I don't ask him what happened. I don't ask him to explain himself. I have decided not to be angry. I just want him to know that his attitude as well as his style of interacting with TASSC staff has to change.

I begin by saying that things are not working for him in our classroom, and that he is putting his continued enrolment in TASSC at risk. I tell him that the way he talks to staff and to Barb in particular is affecting her enjoyment of her job. I tell him that Barb is the "nice one" in TASSC, and that it doesn't make sense for anyone to be disrespectful to her. "Everyone knows that I'm the mean one," I tell him. He gives a bit of grin at this, though it might also be a smirk.

I tell Steven that we are all trying to be nice to him, to help him feel good about being in TASSC, but that we do have expectations that he work in class. We are not being mean when we ask him to work. We are not asking him to do something unfair. We are not limiting his personal freedoms or rights. We just want him to work during class time. When I say that it's really disheartening when he responds disrespectfully, he says it's just the way he communicates. I ask him if he can understand why it's not a productive communication style. He says "yeah." I ask him to think about how his interactions affect Barb's sense of well-being in the classroom. I finish by telling him that we will talk again, and I go back to the classroom.

For some time, I have been purposeful in my cheerful, casual interactions with Steven. I ignore his negative demeanour and give him positive, upbeat responses in all situations. I believe that students should never feel that we would prefer that they weren't here. Therefore, I have been very conscious in my exchanges with Steven to let him know that I want him in the classroom. The conversation in the Longhouse, though, was an attempt to be clear with Steven, without being confrontational, that his attitude and actions were not acceptable. Perhaps by talking to him honestly, and discussing the emotional impact he has on staff, I can increase his awareness of himself.

Long (1996) makes a number of recommendations for teachers who work with troubled students, and most of them centre on the need to put our students' needs and requirements ahead of our own. He also says that we need to use as many intervention techniques and skills as possible in order to cope with the diversity of behaviours and emotional issues that we encounter in the classroom. Most of all, we need to be honest with ourselves before we can be honest with our students.

CLASSROOM INCIDENT—MAY 14TH, 11:20 AM

Steven overhears me talking to Cathy about his Work Experience placement which will start on Wednesday. We have been working on this placement for a couple of weeks, arranging interviews, getting the schedule sorted out, and doing all the paperwork. Steven turns in his seat and nonchalantly tells me that he doesn't want to do it. His statement is a shock and seems to come out of nowhere. He had told me a couple of weeks ago that he didn't want to do a placement at this time of year, but I explained then that he has no real choice over the timing of the work placements. Students certainly get to choose where they do their work experience placements, but we have to send them out according to a schedule and it was Steven's turn. He seemed to accept that. As this particular placement came together, he said that he was looking forward to the placement because of the chance that it could lead to a new job. The interview with the employer went well, and Steven came back to class showing off the restaurant menu that he had to learn in time for the placement. So now, he tells me that he doesn't want to do it.

I ask him if he is serious, and Steven gives a little smirk and says "I told you I didn't want to do it." I begin to get angry at this point and ask him to come outside. Once on the landing, I tell him that he can't just decide at the last minute to cancel something that has been so long in the planning. I ask him why he doesn't want to do it, and he tells me that he doesn't like the idea that his Work Experience boss knows his restaurant job boss. He thinks that they will talk to each other about him. He says that if he quits or misses some days in the placement, he wouldn't want his real boss hearing about it. I get a little more angry at that. "So, you're planning to miss days on this

> *placement? You know, if you don't want to do the Work Experience placements, you need to find another program now, because you have to do them if you want to graduate from TASSC."*
>
> *He then says that he wants to do Work Experience but that Patricia (the other Work Experience facilitator) kind of pushed him into the placement. I ask him if he told her that he didn't want to do a restaurant, and he says that he didn't say that, but that he did say that he wanted maybe to try something else.*
>
> *At this point, I am frustrated and visibly agitated, but see no point in forcing him to do the placement. I tell him that I will call Patricia and get her to cancel the placement, but also that he needs to be clearer when talking to Patricia about future placements. Steven says that he doesn't really want to do a restaurant placement anymore, especially when he works at a restaurant. I tell him that we will go onto the database and have him come up with some ideas. I hold the door for him as we go back inside.*

Yost & Mosca (2002) anchor their article in Long's (1996) research, and argue that teachers' responses to students are more often a matter of routine, rather than thoughtful decision-making. They conclude that when conflict occurs in the classroom, teachers react based on "prior beliefs or experiences" (p. 265). Yost & Mosca have incorporated a reflective thought process into their teacher preparation program at LaSalle University in Philadelphia. Student teachers are taught to "name, reflect critically, and arrive at a plan of action" (p. 265) in dealing with classroom problems. Their article includes a case study to illustrate the process that a pre-service teacher would go through in coping with and solving a student's disruptive behaviours. Through critical reflection, the teacher would examine all aspects of the student's background and irrational belief system, arriving at a plan of action that best meets that student's needs.

CLASSROOM INCIDENT—MAY 16TH, 10:10AM

> *Janice and Emily are working together, but there are some giggles. Amy and Ryan are also sitting together and talking. Their volume rises above Janice and Emily. I catch Janice and Emily's attention and motion them to be quieter. They do. Amy and Ryan keep talking. I ask them to lower their volume.*
>
> *Amy responds "You didn't tell them to stop talking. They're being loud." I say casually, "No, no, I just asked you to bring the volume down. I didn't say that you had to stop talking." Amy and Ryan talk more quietly.*
>
> *Amy almost always responds to some kind of criticism as if we are attacking her. She frequently draws comparisons to others, as if to imply that she is being treated unfairly. I no longer rise to that bait, keeping the conversation focussed on expectations. I try to express things in terms of the behaviour we want instead of the behaviour we don't want. This reduces opportunities for Amy to defend herself. She always has reasons or excuses for what she is doing, so I ignore them and restate the expectations, keeping*

a reasonable tone and presenting the expectations as something that just makes sense.

Yost & Mosca (2002) expand on Long's ideas by proposing reflection as a way for teachers to work through conflict situations. They argue, "thinking through troubling events prevents teachers from relying solely on their instincts" (p.265). Their research is aimed at pre-service teachers enrolled in teacher education programs, but their recommendations apply to in-service teachers as well. Their goal is to empower teachers with management techniques that prevent "counter-aggressive reactions to troubling behaviour" (p.267).

CLASSROOM INCIDENT—MAY 28TH

It was a great day for a visit to the Vancouver Aquarium and a hike through Stanley Park. It had been planned for a couple of weeks, and we were lucky with the weather. Fifteen students and three staff made for a lively group, and we were all looking forward to the time in the park.

The morning had gone well, with a nice walk from the Seabus Terminal through Coal Harbour and to the Park. Once inside the Aquarium, the students were free to see the exhibits. We decided to let the students go off on their own, without direct supervision. Some of them were keen to see the Aquarium as they had never been there. Some remembered being here as a child and wanted to see the whales again. Some, however, just wanted to get away from the restrictions of the staff. Our primary goal had been the walk itself, so we weren't too concerned with students just sitting somewhere and having lunch.

Ryan, Andrew, and Sara found a table near the edge of the Beluga tank and were anticipating the scheduled show. Unfortunately, the Beluga show didn't start until after the time we had planned to leave. Although these three students arrived late to the restaurant, we gave them extra time to eat their lunch. When we decided to leave, however, they argued that they wanted to see the beluga show, and that they hadn't had the full thirty minutes for lunch that the other students had. We told them that they had arrived late for lunch and had used up all their time. We had other things to see in the park and it was time to leave.

We finally convinced them to leave the beluga area and head to the exit. However, they were clearly angry and were voicing their opinions. "This is stupid. Why did you bring us here if we can't even watch the whales?" said Andrew. Barb pointed out that they were able to see almost all of the Aquarium but that we didn't have enough time to stay for the whales. Sara spoke up, "But we didn't see everything. The others just ran around, but we were reading all the information and so we didn't get to see as much." "This is dumb," said Ryan.

We exited the Aquarium to find the rest of the students sitting outside near the Orca statue. "Are we heading back now?" asked Mike.

"No," I responded. "We're going to check out the damage in the park."

"Wait a minute," said Sara. "You pulled us out of there just so we could look at dead trees? But those were whales! We can see trees any time."

"This was the schedule," I said. "Let's go."

It was still sunny and warm, and we walked as a group up the hill. There was definitely some grumbling going on, however, and I knew that this could turn into a problem. As we neared the Miniature Railway, one or two students asked when we were going back to the Seabus. Ryan, Andrew and Sara had slowed down and were some way behind us. I could hear them talking as they came up the path.

*"This is f***ing stupid. We should just refuse to hike any more," said Ryan.*

"Let's just walk slowly, then they'll have to wait for us and we won't have to walk as far," suggested Sara. Ryan laughed out loud at that.

*"Yeah. That'll really f*** 'em over good," said Andrew. In these situations, Andrew always became somewhat aggressive in his comments and suggestions.*

When we reached the benches near the bus loop, I pulled everyone together, including the three stragglers. "Come on you three. Hurry up and join us over here." I had a big smile on my face as I called to them.

Rather than respond individually to students, I explained to the whole group what we would be doing for the next one and a half hours. "Okay. We are going to walk through the trails and look at the damage to the park. We'll be here for about an hour, and then we'll head back to the Seabus." The three plotters shared a bit of a laugh.

"And for anyone who might be planning to walk slowly just to screw us up, you can get on a bus right now and head back to North Van. But really folks, it's a nice day. We're walking with friends in a nice park, enjoying the fresh air and the sunshine. It's better than being in math class. We're not asking you to do anything really difficult or challenging. So let's just enjoy the afternoon and we'll be on Seabus before you know it."

After that, I made sure to be cheerful, outgoing and I try to engage everyone in experiencing the Park. Within a few minutes, the group was cheerfully walking the trails, and the rest of the day was as pleasant as it had started.

I had decided to address the three trouble students' actions directly, making it clear that their only options were to keep up with us or to leave. Their plan was more about posturing than any real dissention. They were really just egging each other on. But these three students sometimes have trouble staying within the boundaries of acceptable behaviour, so I thought I had better cut them off quickly. I didn't name them specifically, or physically address them directly, but rather made a blanket statement about disruptive behaviour. They knew, however, that I was talking about them.

As for the others, sometimes the students simply need a clear outline of what they are doing for the next while. If they know that everything is going according to a schedule, then they don't feel a need to voice their opinion on

> *what we should be doing. Also, if they are given a chance to think about what we are asking them to do, they realize that we are not being unreasonable and they settle right down. They are mature enough to see the purpose of the activity and so they almost always participate positively.*

Kottler's (2002) book encompasses many of the ideas raised by Yost & Mosca (2002), as well as Long (1996). He echoes Long when he says that every teacher has at least one student whose behaviour triggers counter-productive responses in that teacher. Like the aforementioned researchers, Kottler argues that teachers must examine their own actions in conflict situations if they are to succeed in changing their students' behaviours. He also agrees with Yost & Mosca about teachers falling into routine rather than thoughtfully choosing an appropriate response to students' actions. For most of his book, Kottler describes troublesome students and the myriad ways they frustrate teachers. He also suggests a number of strategies to use in changing their behaviours.

CLASSROOM INCIDENT—APRIL 5TH, 1:40PM

> *During a homeroom period when students are supposed to be reading quietly, the class is quite restless, and somewhat chatty. I have asked a few times for quiet, but three kids on the couch are still making funny noises. Andrew makes a goofy swallowing sound. Ryan is doing beeps and boops. Dave makes a duck sound. They have no interest in reading their novels, but they try to maintain the pretence. Their heads are down, as if reading, but their attempts to hide the grins and stifle their giggles are not working.*
>
> *I decide to raise my voice: "Stop it." I look at the students on the couch, using my best expression of disapproval. "You guys know that you're supposed to be reading silently. So please stop making noise." The three on the couch focus harder on their books. Other students in the class exchange a few grins and glances.*
>
> *There is silence for a moment and then Andrew makes one more funny noise. People giggle or grin. I can tell that they are barely holding back the laughs. I smile as well. Students are stealing looks at me to see what I will do. All of a sudden, I drop my head on the desk in mock surrender. Andrew sputters into laughter. A few others laugh out loud. The whole room is grinning as everyone simply settles down to read.*
>
> *I decided to raise my voice with the intent to shock them into quiet. I rarely get loud like that in the classroom, and so I thought they might realize that they had taken it too far. However, I wasn't really angry at all, and so when they giggled at Andrew's noise, I decided that it would be appropriate to show that I also found it funny.*
>
> *The kids' reaction to Andrew suggests that they knew they shouldn't be laughing, but they were keen to see my reaction. By reacting the way I did, I tried to show that I had a sense of humour. Once they started reading again, the tension in the room was gone and they knew that I wasn't mad.*

> *It's important to be reasonable. If something truly is funny, there's no sense in ignoring it. That just makes me look like an ogre. I've always connected to my students through humour, and try to be relaxed in all situations.*

Most valuable to the present inquiry is Kottler's (2002) discussion of the unresolved emotional issues that teachers bring to their classroom. He lists a number of insecurities, negative feelings, and irrational beliefs, and argues that when students "force us to look at our sore spots" (p. 44), we overreact and turn a minor situation into a larger conflict. Like Long (1996), Kottler argues that we must be honest with ourselves in evaluating conflicts with students. Like Yost & Mosca (2002), he recommends self-reflection as a means of dealing with our most challenging students.

Kottler (2002) prescribes some behaviours that teachers can develop to avoid the conflict cycle. His suggestions are concrete and almost obvious in their simplicity, yet they are presented in a way that acknowledges just how difficult it is for people to change ingrained behaviours. Kottler suggests, for example, that we must keep our sense of humour in the face of disruptive student behaviour. Yet he also recognizes that teachers often take those behaviours personally and leave no room for humour in their responses. He suggests that we remain flexible in dealing with difficult students, but also points out that while we think we are using a range of different tactics, those tactics are often just a variation on a single theme. Thus we do not know that we are not being flexible.

CLASSROOM INCIDENT—MAY 24TH, 1:20PM

> *Neil and Haley are talking to each other. Neil is supposed to be trying to get a lot of work done in order to stay in the program. He has been chatting to Haley for some time, even though she is trying not to talk.*
>
> *I go over to Haley and tell her, "You have to learn the 'stop talking to me' sign if you are going to sit next to Neil." I hold my hand up like a stop sign to demonstrate what I mean.*
>
> *Neil laughs. So does Haley. I smile at Neil, shaking my head a little.*
>
> *"Come on, Neil," I say. "You know how much work you have to do, and talking to Haley is slowing both of you down."*
>
> *Neil says, "Yeah, I know. I've been working, but I do talk too much."*
>
> *He turns from Haley and focuses on his work. I ask Haley how she is doing with the material and if she needs any help. Then I turn to Neil and ask if he understands the instructions on the thing he is working on.*
>
> *He says he does and I head back to my desk. Neil works well for the rest of the class.*
>
> *Neil is the chattiest student in our class. We have talked to him about this and we have moved him to different desks to try to minimize the chatting. He knows that his chatting is an issue but he says that he can't help it. We used to use a stern tone with him, to no avail. However, I have lately been playing up his status as the chattiest student, and he seems to enjoy the banter when I*

ask him in humorous ways to stop talking. It seems to be working. I now usually just have to give him a look and he stops, mostly while grinning.

Research by Colvin, Ainge, & Nelson (1997) and by Spitalli (2005) is also concerned with teachers' responses to difficult students, but it focuses mostly on the behaviours rather than on the reasons for those behaviours. Colvin, Ainge, & Nelson suggest a number of strategies that teachers can use in dealing with confrontation, and also describe the signs of agitation in students and how they turn into confrontational behaviour. They then provide a list of techniques for reducing agitation. Spitalli short lists what teachers should not do when disciplining misbehaving students. As with Kottler (2002), the list seems rather obvious, but it is somewhat unsettling to think that teachers need be told not to rant and rave in response to a minor, relatively insignificant infraction. Spitalli also cites research that demonstrates how bullying is becoming a more frequent teacher tactic in dealing with difficult students. Spitall's main argument is that many teachers do not realize how their reactions to student behaviour often guarantee failure and create a classroom environment of resentment and fear.

CHILDHOOD INCIDENT

It had been another fun chemistry class. The boy was enjoying working in the lab, especially with the Bunsen burners and the fascinating variety of chemicals. Mixing the various powders and crystals always produced interesting results and he liked working out the formulas and ratios.

As the class came to an end, the boy stood at the sink, washing the beakers and utensils that he had used in today's experiment. He lined them up according to size and function, turning them so that the spouts all faced the same way. He fiddled absentmindedly with the faucets, playing with the temperature of the water. He let the water run over his hands, through his fingers, as the noise in the classroom blurred in the background of his perception.

Other students were putting away equipment, talking to each as the class wound down. Books were closed, cupboard doors opened and shut. Some students finished their lab notes while others handed in assignments.

As the noise increased, the Grade 10 chemistry teacher called out to the room, "Settle down everyone. Settle down." The words registered on the boy's consciousness, but only as one more sound in the room. Still enjoying the running water, placing his clean equipment in a neat row on the table, he echoed the teacher's words, unaware that the room was a little quieter. "Settle down," he mumbled, almost singing. "Settle down."

A loud voice broke through his reverie. "Hey! If I wanted your opinion, I would have squeezed it out of you!" The boy looked up suddenly, to see his teacher glaring at him across the lab. He opened his mouth but the teacher cut him off. "Siddown wiseguy! And keep your comments to yourself."

The boy turned off the water and scurried to his seat, bewildered at what had happened. He thought the teacher liked him. He gathered his binder and textbook and waited for the bell to ring, keeping his head down and hoping no-one could see his watering eyes.

Rest Stop

The literature I selected relates to my research in its focus on teachers' responses to student behaviour, and the present inquiry reveals that I seem to have learned—at least for the present—how to put these theories and suggestions into practice. I have learned through my study of Bennett's (2001, 2004) work that a safe classroom is a necessary ingredient for student success. I've changed the way I frame questions during class discussion, allowing students a moment to consider their responses before I call on them. I give them a chance to discuss the question with a partner before they have to share with the class. Students feel less anxious in these situations when they know they won't be called on out of the blue to provide an instant answer. There is a more relaxed atmosphere in the classroom.

Through my research, I see that I have learned to reflect before I react, as Yost & Mosca (2002) recommend. I can see that my reactions to students no longer fuel Long's (1996) conflict cycle. Also, I have learned not only to use some of the strategies that Colvin, Ainge, & Nelson (1997) describe, but also to keep my sense of humour, as Kottler (2002) prescribes.

CLASSROOM INCIDENT—APRIL 2ND, 9:30AM

Mike is quite focussed on his Internet research project. He has been staring intently at the screen for some time. This is unusual for Mike because he rarely engages so seriously with his academic work. However, he has turned the monitor a little away from my view and this causes me to question his studious demeanour. I wander over towards his computer, but as I get close, Mike moves his mouse and quickly clicks on something on the screen.

I've seen this move many times with many students. I lean over his shoulder and examine his monitor screen. Sure enough, he has a valid website onscreen, but on his tool bar is the all the evidence I need. The YouTube icon is clearly visible. I lean over his shoulder and hit a few keys on his keyboard.

"You know, Mike," I say with a helpful tone. "If you really want to avoid suspicion, you should master the Alt-Tab combination. It's much more subtle than the mouse-click manoeuvre." I hit the Alt-Tab keys and up comes the hidden YouTube web page. Mike has been watching videos instead of doing his research project. I've seen this one before and it is actually quite funny.

"I love this one," I tell him, sitting down to watch for a moment. "But how about you watch it during the break, instead of during class." I close the website and ask him if he needs help on his project. He gives a bit of a groan, "No, I'm fine."

"Well, call me over if you need help. But stay off the YouTube." I go back to my desk.

In reflecting on my actions and responses to student behaviours, I have come to recognize the beliefs and values that govern those actions and responses. As Long (1996) and Kottler (2002) suggest, through an honest examination of myself, I have overcome the limitations I subconsciously placed on my efforts to provide for the needs of the troubled and at-risk students who sit in my classroom. I don't need to be either a taskmaster or disciplinarian who forces students into compliance. I ask instead of assume. I try to make students feel welcome, rather than force them to conform.

CLASSROOM INCIDENT—APRIL 4TH, 12:40PM

While the rest of the class is in the gym warming up on the exercise mats, I notice that Russell is outside sitting in the longhouse. I call him over and ask what is going on. He says that he doesn't want to do the kickboxing part of the afternoon and will join us when we play basketball. I explain that he doesn't have that option, and that if he doesn't join us at the beginning then he can simply take off for the afternoon.

Russell doesn't want to leave, but he says that he will feel foolish doing the stretches with everyone else. I tell him that everyone is doing them and no-one is laughing at anyone. We look into the gym to see what it looks like. Russell says, "See, they look dumb." He is getting agitated at not being able to just sit out this part.

I say, "Yeah, but everyone looks equally silly and it's not really that silly at all. It's just some stretches and then we'll be on to the kickboxing. Besides, you don't have to be good at it. You just have to give it a go, and have some fun trying it. It really is a lot of fun kicking the bag. Even Dave and Kent are into it." Russell kind of turns away, and then turns back and says, "Okay, I'll try it." In no time at all, he is laughing with the others and giving it a try.

Russell is fairly new to the program, but not to the school. He is a good athlete, and so I am at first surprised that he doesn't want to do this. I realize, though, that he is uncomfortable with how he will look while doing the exercises and so I try to minimize the optics and maximize the participation aspect. He can see that everyone else is doing it and no-one looks uncomfortable.

I don't berate him for trying to avoid the activity, nor do I saying anything about coming into it late. My goal is to help him see that he can simply blend in without looking foolish to anyone. Russell is a nice guy and is still a little unsure in this new class, so I wanted to help him feel part of the group. I knew that the other students would not make fun of him in any way, so if I could just get him into the gym then he would feel okay.

I have learned to bend when it comes to the requirements of the day. If a student is truly not comfortable for some reason, then there is no sense in forcing that student to participate. In order to make that judgement, however, I have to be sensitive to the student's emotions and moods. My focus has to be on the student's feelings of safety, belonging, and self-worth. If I am focused mainly on my own demands for my students, then I put my ego ahead of their well-being and I lose sight of my newly acquired pedagogy, my new found art and science of living with my students in a shared classroom, where relationships share an equal import with curriculum.

As Long's (1996) Conflict Cycle model highlights, most conflicts start with the student's self-image. Students who develop negative self-concepts usually behave in ways that reinforce that concept. My job, then, is to help my students develop positive self-images. The students in my program have been unsuccessful in regular schools, and many of them believe themselves to be either not as smart as others, or unable to cope in large groups, or unable to participate with complex activities. By focussing on their successes and on their positive qualities, I can slowly change some aspects of their self-image. By having specific academic expectations and helping them achieve those goals, I teach my students that they are just as smart as anyone else. By being sensitive to their emotions and moods, I teach them that they are worthy of consideration. By being pleased to see them and making them feel welcome in the classroom, I show them they are not social misfits. By expressing my classroom expectations as reasonable and rational, I want them to see and comprehend that they are being treated fairly and with respect. All of these things contribute to a message that my students are valuable and worthy of my efforts. When they learn that notion and accept it, they begin to respond in kind—not with suspicion, negativity, or confrontation, but with acceptance and a willingness to engage. If I respond to the needs rather than the actions of the student, it seems that I change the way students respond to me.

CLASSROOM INCIDENT—JUNE 7TH, 11:30AM

Ryan has been walking around too much in the classroom, talking to other students, and making random comments out loud to anyone who will respond.

He is in the middle of a random observation about something in the newspaper when I turn from helping a student and say to him,

"Ryan, it just isn't working for you in here today, is it?" I say it with a tone of mild exasperation and a bit of a smile on my face.

He stops and pauses, nods his head, and says, "Yeah, I guess I need to sit down."

He goes to his desk.

Ryan and I have talked a lot this year about his frequent lack of focus. He recognizes that there are times when he cannot stay at his desk. He is not disrespectful or confrontational in any way. He just cannot sit still for a full day. Unfortunately, though, Ryan reacts negatively to direct commands to sit down or to get back to work. He is very aware of the fact that he is 20 years old and still in high school. He chafes at the high school rules, and complains that he is being treated like a kid. We have talked about the reality of his situation, that he is in fact in high school and that the policies are meant for younger people.

When I do need Ryan him to change his behaviour, I try to say something that will get him to examine his actions at that moment. He usually always sees that they are inappropriate or a distraction to others. The amount of negative or angry responses from Ryan has dropped to almost none over this school year. He appreciates that he must conform to certain expectations, but he wants to be treated as an adult when we ask him to do it. Whenever I talk to Ryan, I try to keep this in mind, while still expressing our expectations about his behaviour.

The Road Ahead

The initial focus of my degree program was the work of Bennett (2004) and his Instructional Intelligence tactics, strategies, and graphics organizers. Through my reading of Bennett's work on framing questions and Think-Pair-Share strategies, among other tactics, I became much more aware of the need for emotional safety in the classroom than I was before I started this journey. Through an examination of my interactions with my students, I have begun to develop an understanding of which interactions contribute to a safe classroom environment, and which interactions simply escalate the conflict beyond my control. I began this journey of inquiry with the intent of learning some techniques for delivering curriculum to students. Instead, I have learned tactics and strategies for living the life of a teacher-learner-researcher.

My inquiry has become a journey of self-perception, learning, change, and growth. Now that I am more aware of myself and the ways I engage with my students, not only as a teacher, but as a human being, I am excited by the opportunity to put this new awareness into practice with each new student who enters my classroom. Knowing that I can make a difference makes me all the more eager to try more new ideas and grow as an artistresearcherteacher (Gouzouasis, 2008).

Sean Kelly
North Vancouver School District 44
skelly@nvsd44.bc.ca

PART 2

STORIES ON CLASSROOM APPLICATIONS OF TACTICS, STRATEGIES, AND GRAPHICS ORGANIZERS IN COLLABORATIVE LEARNING ENVIRONMENTS

ANDY WONG

IMPLEMENTING INSTRUCTIONAL INTELLIGENCE SKILLS, STRATEGIES, AND TACTICS INTO AN INTERNATIONAL BACCALAUREATE DIPLOMA PROGRAM MATHEMATICS CLASSROOM

Prelude

I was fortunate to have the opportunity for Barrie Bennett to observe my Math IB class at the secondary school in which I teach. His visit came shortly after I had read an article of his (Bennett, 2007) in which he asserts that the best predictor of student achievement is improving the instructional practice of teachers. That day, he was an active observer in the classroom, heavily involved in the discussions, and providing me constructive feedback. The class he watched was an introduction to logarithms. Since "logarithm" was such a foreign yet significant concept, he suggested that our class should do a Team Analysis the following class, re-defining the term and highlighting the key points of what makes a logarithm a logarithm by having a four-point follow-up on its definition.

During his observation I did a think-pair-share activity. He assured me that the students had a strong sense of safety in my class and that if I gave enough wait time I could call on individuals. His observations were encouraging and provoked an interest in me to further delve into the ideas of instructional intelligence in a senior math class.

Background

My school is in a period of transition, rebuilding its physical structure, and renovating its academic opportunities. There are two campuses with one full-time principal, with three vice-principals sharing their time across the two campuses. The Grade 11 and 12's study amidst the construction on Campus A, while all Grade 8 to 10's attend the other Campus B. While the physical transformation is dominant, academically, Campus A is also undergoing extensive changes; most notably it was awarded authorization for the International Baccalaureate Program – a Middle Years Program (MYP) and a Diploma Program (DP). The latter commenced in 2009-2010. It is a challenging two-year program that supports a globally recognized curriculum.

Even before IB, campus A readily accepted and embraced diversity, possessing a population that varies greatly in socio-economic and cultural differences. When the former IB coordinator surveyed Grade 10 students in 2008 about what defines the school, the top response was its acceptance of diversity. In fact, that year

P. Gouzouasis (ed.), Pedagogy in a New Tonality: Teacher Inquiries on Creative Tactics, Strategies, Graphics Organizers, and Visual Journals in the K-12 Classroom, 57–70.

enrolled students from 76 different cultures. The school displays its eclecticism through the numerous world flags at the entrance of the school to the collection of First Nations art works on display. The mission statement re-affirms this: "We strive for excellence in all endeavors, encourage personal and social responsibility, respect diversity, and work to develop a life long commitment to learning."

Defining the International Baccalaureate Program

The International Baccalaureate Diploma Program (DP) is a rigorous pre-university course of studies—leading to examinations—that meets the needs of highly motivated secondary school students (IBO, 2006a). It is comprised of a two-year comprehensive curriculum that is based on the pattern of no single country but intends to incorporate the best elements of many. It aims to develop inquiring, knowledgeable and caring young people who help to create a better and more peaceful world through intercultural understanding and respect (Skirrow & Barrett 2008). The program encourages students across the world to become active, compassionate, and lifelong learners who understand other people and their differences (Skirrow & Barrett 2008).

IB DP students come from throughout the district and, in several cases, from beyond the country. A successful student must be academically keen and possess a high level of intrinsic motivation to excel in this program. Ideally, classrooms are filled with inquiring minds, creating an ethos that is ideal for learning. Each DP student must complete a course from each of the six groups, as well as complete the Theory of Knowledge course, write a detailed Extended Essay, and complete the Creativity Action Service component.

Linking Instructional Intelligence and the IB Teaching Philosophy

The IB Learner Profile (IBO, 2006b) is a more specific document that highlights ten characteristics that are emphasized through learning. The characteristics embody students who are inquirers, knowledgeable thinkers, communicators, principled, open-minded, caring, risk-takers, balanced, and reflective. Their specific definition of curriculum fundamentally corresponds to the ideas behind instructional intelligence.

> The curriculum can be defined as what is to be learned (the written curriculum), how it is to be learned (the taught curriculum) and how it is to be assessed (the learned curriculum). This gives equal focus to content, teaching methodologies and assessment practices. The IBO prescribes, to varying degrees in each of its three programs, the written, taught and learned curriculum, but relies on schools for its implementation. The successful implementation of these three dimensions of the curriculum in each IB program depends on the culture and ethos of the school. The values and attitudes of the school community that underpin the culture and ethos of a school are significant in shaping the future of its young people. In a school that has a commitment to the values inherent in the IB learner profile, these

values will be readily apparent in classroom and assessment practices, the daily life, management and leadership of the school. (IBO, 2006b, p. 8)

Having a curriculum that emphasizes teaching methodologies and assessment practices as much as the content is ideal for infusing instructional intelligence activities.

The Learner Profile (2006b) specifically raises questions about the involvement of four classroom practices: 1) Is it possible to create more experiences and opportunities in the classroom that allow students to be genuine inquirers? 2) How much attention do we pay to how students interact with other students in group-work activities? Could we give more time to helping them work effectively as part of a team? 3) Could we create more opportunities to discuss the ethical issues that arise in the subject(s) we teach? 4) How well do we model empathy, compassion, and respect for others in our classrooms and around the school? The first two guiding questions are particularly in accordance to the principles of instructional intelligence. Bennett & Rolheiser (2001, p. 28) affirm that "instructional strategies increase the chances students are actively and meaningfully involved in complex forms of thinking and communicating. Learning improves. The strategies place the learning in the hands and minds of the learners."

Bennett (2007) lists five instructional areas—skills, tactics, strategies, concepts, and organizers. The present inquiry focused on the first three areas, as Bennett (2007) believes that skills drive tactics and skills and tactics drive strategies. It should be understood that there is much room for expanding these areas, and that there is considerable overlap within these areas. He mentions the complexities of instructional intelligence, and how it is actively changing, as evidenced in his statement, "Instructional intelligence, as a process, has evolved; it now merges curriculum, assessment, instruction, knowledge of how students learn, and theories of change and systemic change" (Bennett, 2007, p. 66). Bennett even differentiates the many levels of involvement of instructional intelligence. Thus when attempting to implement something for the first time, Bennett encourages teachers to be reflective for future applications.

Table 1. Teachers' level of use of an innovation (Bennett, 2007, p. 81)

Nonuser	Not using the innovation, but may have heard of it
Orienting	Interested and seeking more information
Preparing	Getting ready to apply the innovation for the first time
Mechanical	Applying the innovation in the classroom, but application is clunky
Routine	Has applied innovation often enough that it is working smoothly
Refined	Extending application of the innovation into new areas
Integrative	Connecting the innovation to other innovations
Refocusing	Searching for other innovations

Ever IB Diploma student must take a Group 5 mathematics or computer science course. IB offers three levels of mathematics, but given the on-going development of the program our students are mandated to take Mathematics Standard Level (SL). This course encourages students to be thinkers—exercising initiatives in applying thinking skills critically and creatively to recognize and approach complex problems, and make reasoned, ethical decisions (Skirrow & Barrett, 2008). It caters to students who already possess knowledge of basic mathematical concepts, and who are equipped with the skills needed to correctly apply simple mathematical techniques. The majority of these students will need a sound mathematical background as they prepare for future studies in subjects such as chemistry, economics, psychology, and business administration (Skirrow & Barrett, 2008).

The grading process is unique in IB. While students are formally assigned marks on report cards, their grade is the only predictor of their final mark. At the end of a two-year process, students take a calculator and non-calculator exam that accounts for 80% of their final grade, with the other 20% coming from two internal assessment projects. Consequently, the IB teacher has the autonomy to spend time over the two-year period exploring specific topics and assessing students in a variety of ways. The Mathematics SL course consists of approximately 150 hours of curriculum in which there are two years of course content to cover. Given the current timetable, there are over 200 hours of classroom time. This creates an advantageous situation, being able to gain a deeper understanding of the material through the application of various tactics and strategies without concern for time constraints one encounters with the implementation of creative instructional tactics, strategies, and graphics organizers. For example, although the students are given a 16 page formula sheet that they can have for all school tests and exams, we spend ample time understanding why the formulas exist and offer proofs to most of them. This differs from traditional classrooms in which Schoenfeld (1988) found that students were keen to accept formulas for what they were—they were not derived by the teacher, but rather, they were simply given as presumed knowledge to students.

Surprisingly, there is more of a disparity in math abilities and skills in an IB Math SL class than in any of my other classes. All IB students, whether they are Arts or Science students, were required to take the same math course. Several students came from different countries and knew certain units much better than others. Some students barely passed Math 10 Principles, while some have already finished Math 11 Honors Principles. The incredible diversity made the utilization of instructional intelligence in this setting even more applicable.

Most of the IB research is heavily concentrated on the Primary Years Program (PYP) and Middle Years Program (MYP). Relating instructional intelligence to the Diploma Program (DP) was a worthwhile endeavor. Similarly, most math education research literature seems to be based on elementary school studies. Overall, there is a paucity of research dealing with senior level studies in math. Thus, I believed it would be educationally valuable to merge these two areas of interest—Instructional Intelligence and Math IB DP, a topic that does not co-exist in current academic research. My hope was to create senior math class that has on-going active learning that is meaningful to the students. Schoenfeld (1988) summarizes what a good math class consists of—a good math class encourages students to think mathematically and to become proficiently numerate through learning the material, as well as become able to apply this mathematical knowledge to the appropriate situations.

Beginning the Journey

From April of 2010 to June of 2010, 20 students participated in the present study examining how the use of a variety of Instructional Intelligent (II) tactics, skills, and strategies promote a deeper mathematical understanding of the IB curricular outcomes. The research project took place during regularly scheduled block three class times and ran for approximately three months. Using II tactics and strategies, students learned the units on Trigonometry.

Data was collected in class time during the last few minutes of class throughout our study of trigonometry; a simple survey was handed out to complete at the end of class, approximately once a week. The survey took about five minutes and asked students to rate the effectiveness of the strategies/tactics/skills and to provide a brief comment on the process. The latter was intentionally open-ended in the hopes of generating honest and unbiased responses about the process. I did not use a Plus-Minus-Interesting (i.e., PMI assessment tactic) because I was concerned they might feel obligated to fill something in for each column and I wanted their most-honest feedback. Asking for a brief a response would hopefully best replicate their sentiments.

During the research component of this project, I consulted from time-to-time with three colleagues who were all members of the first Curriculum Leadership cohort (also advised by Peter Gouzouasis, 2004–2007) in NVSD44. They teach social studies and science. The fact that they were not mathematics teachers was beneficial because I wanted to hear their thoughts on teaching in general rather than in content and curriculum specific feedback.

INTRODUCING TRIGONOMETRY

The students were situated in tables of four with a left side and right side separated by an aisle. The seating changed from unit-to-unit. Typically, I taught a lesson for part of the class, standing at the front with my tablet and pre-typed notes, but in each class meeting I incorporated something that involved some aspect of instructional intelligence. For example, given that the students came from seven different schools, and the fact that they had not studied trigonometry in close to a year, I felt it was important to do an assessment for learning as an introduction to trigonometry. The students were randomly numbered into groups of four and asked to do a placemat graffiti listing anything they could remember from their previous years of trigonometry (e.g., formulas, diagrams, key words). After approximately five minutes, all the students went around to observe and comment on each other's work. Students were not allowed to add to their own responses at this time. To formalize this activity, the students then went to the library where they created a "Wordle" in their groups. In a "Wordle," which is described as a "word cloud," every time a word or phrase is used more than once it is featured and becomes larger than the previous words and phrases. Therefore, the most popular responses stand out more. Among the group members, one person was the recorder, one person read the responses, and two people were responsible to report back to the class. This exercise enabled me to properly gauge the classroom's understanding of the material as we began the unit. The class atmosphere was constantly active and time constraints were not an issue.

The first official lesson that was taught in trigonometry was the concept of radians. In the past, students had been exposed to the idea of measuring angles in degrees. Prior to learning about radians, students were asked to create their own unit of measure, and to be able to convert their measure into degrees. For example, students illustrated that there were 22 Moons in 360 degrees or 17 Hearts in 360 degrees. They were given ample time, and after they individually created a novel unit of measure, they were asked to share it with their partner and be able to report back to the class. That created a great discussion environment.

PARTICIPANT FEEDBACK

The formal part of the present study focused on a skill, a tactic, and a strategy that was used in class. For all three learning areas, I tried to use definitive concepts – things that were familiar to the students, things that were already being used consistently in class. In terms of testing a skill—implementing wait time, framing questions in certain ways, checking for understanding, and probing ideas are all skills that I implemented in class. I have a reputation for asking students to think about a question, but to not blurt the answer out loud to "ruin the surprise." Thus, they fully understood the definition of wait time and framing questions when explaining the present study. As an extension to this, I linked it to the tactic of a think-pair-share (i.e., TPS). They had been exposed to Venn diagrams and placemat tactics as well. This was great for informative assessment through learning. Certain tactics were very difficult to fit. For example, to get an opinion through four corners would be a challenging fit in the math class. However, I knew that this was commonly used in other settings such as the IB History of the Americas class. Finally, in terms of a strategy we did a jigsaw as a unit review in preparation for the formative assessment unit test. I had implemented concept attainment and mind mapping in the past, but was excited to see how interactive the jigsaw activity would be when students have the pressure of a unit test looming.

Data Collection and Results

From a class of 25 IB Math SL students, 20 of them returned both the parental consent and participant consent forms. During three separate classes, they used a pseudonym to fill out a short, five-minute survey clarifying the type of strategy/tactic/skill used and they rated it on a five-point scale (not at all helpful—a bit helpful—somewhat helpful—quite helpful—very helpful). As well, they were asked to briefly comment on the task. While the students had been exposed to a variety of tactics and skills over the course of the year, this was a way of officially formalizing the process. I was particularly excited to see the feedback from these students, as the majority of them are very good at expressing their ideas and are mature beyond their years.

WAIT TIME SKILL

As previously mentioned, the students possessed a broad range of mathematical skill levels; 25 students were brought together into one classroom that they would not have normally fit in a typical, non-IB setting. A challenge I had as a teacher was that the keenest and most confident students frequently had the urge to blurt out answers immediately and make comments about the simplicity of the content. Requesting that students hold on to their answers, and pausing between key learning outcomes, was imperative. Overall, this was a simple task to give as this skill was not driven by a predetermined process, but rather could work in combination with other areas.

Table 2. Wait time tabulation

Task Helpfulness	*Number of Responses = 19*
Not at all helpful	0
A bit helpful	3
Somewhat helpful	5.5
Quite helpful	7.5
Very helpful	3

Nineteen of the 20 students who agreed to participate in the study were present on this day. As can be seen in the table above, all but three of the students found wait time to be at least somewhat helpful. The students who felt otherwise were more concerned about the way it was implemented into the classroom. For example, Effy Strohem (NB: all student names have been changed to protect anonymity) found this to be "a bit helpful" citing that he didn't "like it, because the smart people always answer and it's not long enough to properly think." Others reported a strong preference to working independently. Dr. Oz asserted, "this isn't usually a big issue for me because I prefer to just work things out by myself." Students in favor of the wait time skill were very appreciative of not being hurried. Queen Elizabeth liked its proactive approach because for her, "hearing something rather than doing it is less helpful."

A question in contention was the amount of wait time that actually occurs. There was division among the class as to whether there was too much or too little time to think before answering. Valeria Guzman, a student who found it somewhat/very helpful, said she felt that "the wait time is sometimes too long, and my mind starts to wonder." Jamal asserted with a contrary opinion, "wait time is somewhat helpful. However, I take a long time to understand things and I find there is not enough time for me to think about the question before the answer is gone over. So I still remain confused." Similarly, a blank pseudonym reported: "YAY! Wait time is great! Maybe a little longer though…" Mathemagician wanted staggered wait time, suggesting that we "take 10 sec the first time you mention something, but the next time, reduce the waiting time so the class won't waste time." Other students thought the time was just right. Harry Potter stated, "I like the wait time. Mr. Wong gives us time because there are a lot of smart people in the class so it gives me the chance to try and find a problem out by myself without being told the answer." Sexauer asserted, "I really like the wait time. I find that I need time to 'digest' the ideas, before moving on so quickly." Finally, IBApro, who found it very helpful summed it up saying, "this technique is usually followed by a discussion and is therefore greatly beneficial to the student and environment of the classroom."

THINK-PAIR-SHARE

Traditionally, in this class the students did not have official partners, however, they were asked to change seats to start a new unit. Each time, they were assigned random new seating plans using basic tactics such as date of birth and alphabetized first names. This tactic ensures that students get to constructively work with new people all the time and have math conversations with them. They do not have an official partner, but in almost every class they are asked to take a few minutes to work on a problem on their own, consult with a person nearby after doing so, and then be ready to explain their solution to the class. I try to ensure a balance of safety and accountability for each of the students.

The tactic chosen was think-pair-share (TPS). In general, tactics are less complex than strategies and may not relate directly to one particular learning theory, although they often enhance or extend a particular strategy (Bennett & Rolheiser, 2001). As can be seen in the Table 3 on the following page, all but two of the students found TPS to be at least somewhat helpful. The two students who found think-pair-share to be only somewhat helpful believed that a weak partner could stunt learning. Effy Stonem stated, "it depends on who you sit with and discuss, because some people and their partners could slack off and let the other person do all the work." Freddy Mercury reported, "sometimes it works, but sometimes neither people understand the concepts, so nothing is learned. A lot of the time the conversation drifts off into non-math topics." Both negative responses revolved around a lack of work ethic. That was surprising considering that all of the students involved in the study were IB Diploma program students.

The majority of the class highlighted feelings of safety and comfort in the classroom, as well as an added confidence in discussing a problem before reporting to the class as a whole, regardless of skill level. Katie Fitch believed, "It was helpful because if you get called on and get the answer wrong, it's not just you by yourself that gets it wrong." Harry Potter thought, "I like how he let's everyone know what he's going to do, so if you get picked on for answering a question you knew it was coming." Nautical reported, "It helps people who do not understand what is being to get help from someone or to help workout the answer. Also, when called upon, to be more confident in answering." Sylvia Won said "I never feel unsafe, because math is easy for me, so it doesn't make much of a difference BUT it was fun and I enjoy tutoring." Tom Hanks added, "I think it will boost up confidence in terms of answering questions." Finally, Richie Carlos wrote, "I like that if you don't get a concept after the teacher explained, you can learn from a student." Several students stated that explaining questions to other students improves their own learning. For example, Alana Kinsman said, "if I know a question and I teach it to someone else I will be able to remember better."

Table 3. Think-pair-share tabulation

Task Helpfulness	*Number of Responses = 20*
Not at all helpful	0
A bit helpful	2
Somewhat helpful	4
Quite helpful	10
Very helpful	4

Ironically one of the students who reported think-pair-share as being "very helpful" didn't have the most positive things to say about the actual process of think-pair-share in the classroom. Pomegranatewalabe28 believed that "Mr. Wong keeps picking the same people, only hearing one opinion in the class. I believe the rest of the class is not involved, and should be to show better results."

JIGSAW STRATEGY

Our class was involved in a jigsaw activity to finish the trigonometry unit and to help prepare for the upcoming unit test. Specifically, the students were randomly numbered into five groups: Group A (Let's Get Tanned), Group B (Lawmakers), Group C (The Sinusoidals), Group D (The Plotters), Group E (The Wrappers). Each group had one or two questions from the IB Question Test Bank, and they were asked to collectively provide a worked solution. After several minutes, they were provided with an answer key to verify or modify their solution. The purpose was to create an expert from each group. The weaker students were partnered with a stronger students in groups of five based on my planned selections. Upon finishing their question, students were asked to not go on to the subsequent questions, but were encouraged to read them for understanding. I believed that approach would provide them with familiarity, as well as keep everyone on the same level. After twenty minutes of working amongst their peers, the students were each assigned a number (1, 2, 3, 4) and were asked to re-group in their numbered groups. One-by-one, the expert student worked and explained to the group how to complete their specific question. In my opinion, the task was extraordinarily successful. Each student felt like they had something to offer the group, regardless of their skill level in math. The negative aspect of the activity was the amount of time it took to complete. However, another teacher was generous to our class the first 35 minutes of her Theory of Knowledge block, which took place after lunch, to allow the students to finish their sharing. She commented on the high level of engagement that took place, and the fact that all students were on task. This was an excellent way to achieve an assessment as learning and to prepare them for assessment of learning.

Table 4. Jigsaw tabulation

Task Helpfulness	*Number of Responses = 19*
Not at all helpful	0
A bit helpful	1
Somewhat helpful	2
Quite helpful	7
Very helpful	9

In total, 16 of 19 students found this exercise to be at least quite helpful. The student who circled "a bit helpful" was Jamal, the same student who had earlier said, "I take a long time to understand things." This time he explained that he "did not find the task helpful at all and still did not learn anything better. I prefer standard style of teaching."

Most of the students who identified flaws in the jigsaw related it back to a lack of work ethic. For example, Sexauer said "I found that activity good to study the stuff. The only problem I found was we didn't have enough time to get through everyone." Effy Stohem said "some people didn't pull their weight, then you don't understand that question."

Most of the reviews were extremely positive, even adding a fun element to it. Dr. Oz exclaimed, "I like the game ☺." Harry Potter said, "When fellow students are teaching me, I think I can learn better because they can show me their strategies of learning, rather than the teacher just showing how to do it." It is interesting that students believe our traditional teacher-centered classroom includes a teacher saying how to do it with proper explanation. Similarly, Queen Elizabeth said, "It was very helpful to do the worksheet in small groups instead of just listening to Mr. Wong talk. It was a productive working class and I learnt a lot and was able to teach other people the answers." Passion Fruit shared, "honestly, out of all the strategies we've used in class before a test, I find these activities to affect me the most. As a group, trying to tackle questions can become quite fun, and a team-skill building experience. Not two, but three birds with one stone." Santa Claus enthusiastically agreed, stating, "I really liked this class! I learn better when I practice questions with friends. I like when we explain math to each other, and I also learn when I explain things again." Valeria Guzman wanted more activities like this, exhorting, "I REALLY like this because I learn a lot by trying to figure out questions with other people, because we get to explain it to each other, which is the best way of learning. DO THIS MORE PLZ." Finally, Marcela Lopez emphatically benefitted saying, "This strategy is the MOST helpful for me because working with a group gets me thinking more and allows me to listen to how others solve or thinks of a problem. Also, I learn when I teach so, when I go to my other group to teach what I solved, I understand it and remember better."

I believe that this activity really used the three specific aims of IB: 1) transfer skills to alternative solutions and to future developments; 2) communicate clearly and confidently in a variety of contexts; 3) develop patience and persistence in problem-solving (Skirrow & Barrett, 2008). Students were able to feel confident about questions they didn't normally have the time to work out on their own. They developed deep understandings of them and were able to share and teach with their peers.

PLUS

Overall the students gave fairly positive feedback all three times. The most positive feedback was based on participation in the jigsaw strategy. Compared to the other two areas, this took a considerable time to prepare, but the class ran itself. As well, the feedback that was not positive, mostly related to their dissatisfaction to "how" the instructional intelligence task was run, rather than the theory behind the task. As was anticipated, the feedback appeared to be honest and well thought out.

MINUS

In a class of more than 20 students who possess a wide range of capabilities, it is difficult to equally satisfy all learners. Thus, issues such as time will continue to be an issue with differentiated learning taking place. I was also particularly surprised by the number of responses that conceded to getting off-track when given time to think about questions. One may question if this was a lack of focus on their part, a reluctance to get involved, or a poor sense of planning on my part. Regardless, I was hoping for better efforts from an IB Diploma program.

INTERESTING: FUTURE RESEARCH IMPLICATIONS AND SUGGESTIONS

In terms of what is worthwhile and what is not, I conclude that the same skills, strategies and tactics that are used in a more traditional arts class can be effectively used in a higher-level math classroom. However, what does differ is the frequency of use among these strategies. For example, something like the tactic "Four

Corners" can be used in a math classroom, but rarely. During a Theory of Knowledge class we discussed how practical math is in our daily lives as well as how mathematics is a form of language. Debates arose from discussions like those, but they were not very frequent.

The present study was, for the most part, kept quite simple. Delving into the incorporation of other instructional intelligent areas such as concepts and organizers and the continued use of multiple areas simultaneously would be an undoubtedly interesting area of research. Bennett (2007) believes that concepts can be hard to objectively measure because concepts refer to authenticity, variety, relevance, and accountability. They guide rather than prescribe specific courses of action, but that they can be enacted through skills, tactics, and strategies. Thus it would be worthwhile to extend inquiries in that direction. Strategies would be difficult to implement because they are more complex processes that are (1) often driven by theory and (2) that usually provide theory-specified results (Bennett, 2007). Nevertheless, adapting current instructional intelligence strategies could provide something new for the mathematics education world. I believe that Bennett (2007) is attempting to make instruction more specific and focused so that we are more likely to demonstrate intelligent or expert behavior in the design and assessment of the learning environment. While many people see teaching as repetitive, I believe that teaching is constantly evolving. As Bennett (2007) explicitly states, "Teaching is one of the most complex, important, and demanding of all occupations; to be effective as an educator takes years of intense effort and constant reflection and dialogue" (p. 67).

As well, it would be valuable to find out what limitations exist in applying instructional intelligence to senior math classrooms. Moreover, it would be beneficial to compare a math classroom that uses the current BC Provincial Curriculum with an IB course to see what differences exist in instructional intelligent applications. Finally, a longitudinal study on the implementation of instructional intelligent ideas into a group of math students over the course of their high school career would be informative on the overall impact of instructional intelligence.

Beyond Trigonometry

Trigonometry is one of many units studied in IB Math SL. There are many applicable II tactics and strategies that can be used throughout the course that did not necessarily fit into this topic. For example, I have used concept attainment to define permutations versus combinations or what specifically defines a function, or even more specifically a quadratic function. In fact, concept attainment parallels the Math SL Guide (IBO, 2006a) objective of recognizing patterns and structures in a variety of situations, to make generalizations. As well, the international mindedness component incorporates historical perspectives, enabling students to appreciate the multiplicity of cultural and historical perspectives of mathematics. This can foster, in some instances, a classroom with a student-centered, historically contextualized atmosphere, enabling various opportunities to incorporate instructional intelligence strategies.

Changing Traditional Mathematics Classrooms: Positive Directions

There is a need to increase the amount of student-centered learning in a senior mathematics classroom, and to replace the daily complacency of repeating the process of a teacher-centered direct-instruction lesson followed by individual student class-work. There must be a stronger sense of ownership given to students, as ownership is strongly connected to motivation and engagement. One way that students demonstrate ownership is when they share and talk about their learning with their peers. An ongoing challenge to change in instructional practice is that no other type of classroom change causes more conflict than when administrators attempt to change the instructional practices of teachers (Bennett, 2007). There is an intransient attitude that stalls moving forward. Having an idea in place and actively pursuing it are two different things. In theory, the IB believes that the learner profile will provide a shared vision that will encourage dialogue and collaboration among teachers and administrators about how to create the best environment for learning (IBO, 2006b). Unfortunately many teachers and administrators are hesitant to embrace change.

Based on my experiences through this journey of inquiry, I would like to suggest four changes that can be initiated. First, teaching must proactively pursue instructional intelligence training. Epson & Junk (2004) found that in the implementation of a district-wide program, investigations foster a desire to continue learning because it helped the teachers formulate and address problems at the heart of their mathematical work. Secondly, colleagues should share instructional intelligence ideas that work in their own classrooms. For a period of time, we had moderate success with the Brown Bag Lunch group, a team of teachers who shared ideas at lunchtime. That activity needs to be extended and sustained. Thirdly, teachers in training should view instructional intelligence as “the way to teach” and bring much needed changes to the senior secondary school classroom. Fourthly, the proper steps must be in place at the elementary and junior math levels to enable higher levels of learning at the senior level.

Empson & Junk (2004) believe that the current teaching curriculum programs in elementary school settings require new kinds of mathematics knowledge, and that “teachers’ knowledge in these contexts remains largely unexplored” (p. 121). Finally, Stigler & Heibert (1999) look into the future and require the change be in methodology and practice when they report, “we believe that long-term improvement in teaching will depend more on the development of effective methods for teaching than on the identification and recruitment of talented individuals into the profession” (p. 133). Courses like IB Math SL are in harmonious accordance with this statement. In fact, IB requires training for new teachers introduced to the course, and recommends upgrades. For example, I went to Houston, TX in January of 2008 for Level II training in the Math SL course. As well, IB teachers get re-evaluated in our fifth year into the program. This is far different from traditional teacher education and professional development models, and helps eliminate some of the complacency that is possible once a teacher seems secure in their career.

In the IB program, teaching methodology and assessment practices are as important as the content itself. Moreover, the content of IB Exam questions in mathematics allows for student discussion on their own. For example, the jigsaw activity was based solely on IB Exam questions. They are multi-layered so that everyone can begin with a modicum of understanding, but they build up to something quite detailed. These questions are thought provoking, require time to think about, and benefit from peer-to-peer discussions. Schoenfeld (1988) writes "we have done a serious disservice to any student who emerges from a classroom thinking that mathematics only applies to situations that can be solved in just a few minutes" (p. 160). In other words, instead of being so focused on how to solve a problem that creates a fragmented understanding of the subject without a full understanding and an inability to relate it to other concepts, students are encouraged to seek out what process to do, and the reason why they are selecting that process before actually doing it. Steigler & Heibert (1999) exclaim that teaching, not teachers, is the critical factor, and that North America has focused too much on procedural skill, while schools in Japan are "distinguished not so much by the competence of the teachers as by the images it provides of what it can look like to teach mathematics in a deeper way, teaching for conceptual understanding. Students in Japanese classrooms spend as much time solving challenging problems and discussing mathematical concepts as they do practicing skills" (p. 11). The IB curriculum adheres to those principles and has implemented this approach into both IB Exam questions and internal assessments.

Finally, instructional intelligence promotes deep self-learning. Schoenfeld (1988) documented that good test scores don't necessarily translate into good results, as many students learn math without actually acquiring a depth of understanding. Schoenfeld adds that during this process, students develop bad habits at the expense of getting the right answer. Students learn that "understanding is not necessary when solving mathematics problems; one simply follows the procedure, whether it makes sense or not" (p.149).

Mathematics is a difficult subject to write about, as a teacher and student. It is one of the school subjects in North American society in which it is socially acceptable to say, "I'm not good at math." One could say that music falls into the same categorization. This gives the impression that math is neither innate nor learned, and seems to minimize perceptions of what can be accomplished in a mathematics classroom. In consideration, the IB DP Program has made tremendous strides to provide something that is academically worthwhile to a broad group of learners. Moreover, it is conducive to using teaching tactics, strategies and graphics organizers that will help all learners attain a deeper understanding of the various topics by providing a curriculum that focuses upon a rich, creative, artful pedagogy.

Andy Wong
North Vancouver School District 44
awong@nvsd44.bc.ca

SANJEET JOHAL

THE EFFICACY OF CREATIVE INSTRUCTIONAL TACTICS, STRATEGIES, AND GRAPHICS ORGANIZERS IN TEACHING AND LEARNING MATHEMATICS IN GRADES FOUR - SEVEN LEARNING PODS

So far, my life as an educator has provided me with a variety of challenges and skills. My professional journey has shaped me as an educator and has shaped my views on teaching, administration, and on education as a whole. In May of 2003, I began my career as a 23 year old teacher-on-call (TOC), freshly graduated from the two year Professional Development Program (PDP) degree program at the University of British Columbia. I recall my beginning substitute teaching days in North Vancouver School District as a smorgasbord of opportunities. I was a reliable TOC who worked any assignment for which I was called upon, from Kindergarten to Grade 12, at any school. However, my happiest and most fulfilling days were those when I had the chance to work at one particular community school. I was attracted by the school's ethos—its culture and environment—that is deeply connected to the Squamish Nation. I knew that, ideally, I wanted to be a part of this school as a full time teacher some day. Eventually, I was given the opportunity to come to the school as the Grade Seven teacher in September 2006. For the past three years, I have also had the privilege of serving as the Vice Principal.

The Setting

My school is the last "community" school left in the North Vancouver School District. It is situated in the southwestern region of North Vancouver near the Lions Gate Bridge. It is considered a lower socioeconomic area in North Vancouver and is surrounded by single-family dwellings, predominately rancher-style homes. An important part of the school is the First Nations heritage—the area surrounding the school includes the Squamish Nation Reservation located to the west of the school, an approximately 10 minute walk. There exist a combination of corporate business, as well as small private business, buildings to the north and east of the school. The south side of the school encompasses single-family homes.

I came to my community school in September 2006 as a Grade 7 classroom teacher, surplused from a previous elementary school position. The transition from a larger school to a smaller one was quite refreshing, as the smaller staff and

P. Gouzouasis (ed.), Pedagogy in a New Tonality: Teacher Inquiries on Creative Tactics, Strategies, Graphics Organizers, and Visual Journals in the K-12 Classroom, 71–83.

student population allowed for a deeper connection and a greater opportunity to get to really know and understand the culture of the school, the students, and their families, as well as all staff members. The school has eight divisions and approximately 160 students from Kindergarten to Grade Seven. There are two administrators, three office assistants, 14 support staff, eight teaching staff, and one community events organizer who brings in community speakers, coordinates after school programs, and organizes the two lunch programs. Although a smaller school, it has a vibrant culture and deep links to the community.

Rationale for the Inquiry

The idea of implementing this topic for study began in June of 2009 after reexamining the School Plan. The School Planning Council (SPC) is an important partner in maintaining the School Plan, a legal and binding document outlining two to three major areas of improvement required for the students of a school and the goal is to increase success in these areas. The School Plan for a community school is created by the SPC, which consists of the administrative team of a school and three parents chosen by the Parent Advisory Council (PAC). For our school, mathematics was identified as a weak area in which improvement was much needed, and, as such, improvement in mathematics was an important and integral objective outlined within the School Plan.

Once these goals for the school were distributed and discussed with staff, it was decided by the Intermediate teaching team (composed of the Grade Four to Seven teachers) and the Learning Assistance Centre teacher (me), that mathematics podded groups were going to be established and put into effect beginning in September 2009 and ending in June 2010. For the present paper, *podding* is defined as the grouping of intermediate students from Grades Four through Seven according to the mathematical achievement levels of the students. Based on formal and informal assessments and observations by teachers from both the present year and the past year, these groups were created in September 2009. One stipulation was that the groups would have fluidity; students could move back and forth between mathematics pods depending on teacher observations, student achievement levels, and intermediate team discussions and recommendations.

As the school's Intermediate LAC teacher, I could see first hand that there was an overall weakness in mathematics achievement for Grade Four through Seven children. Those that were most vulnerable in mathematics were not having their needs met. These students were struggling with the pacing of the curriculum, despite the best efforts of the teachers. Furthermore, there was not enough differentiated instruction to meet the diverse learning needs of all students. This was reflected in lower and failing grades in mathematics. Moreover, achievement levels had not been increasing, and the morale of mathematically "weak" students was low according to the intermediate teachers' observations. Many teachers and administrators thought that they just "couldn't get" mathematics and that this was an irreversible state. To compound pressures on teachers and students, the school was mandated to participate in province wide mathematics testing, the FSA, or Foundation Skills Assessment. The FSA's are mandatory tests for Grade Four and Seven students provided by the British Columbia Ministry of Education. Province-wide results in reading, writing, and arithmetic are published for each school. Results for our school were significantly lower than the district average. From that perspective, the implementation of mathematics podding was seen as a necessary step for improvement in this subject area.

My role in this school was as a Vice Principal, Librarian, and Learning Assistance Centre (LAC) teacher. In the latter role, I taught and offered support to a variety of grade levels, including mathematics to students from Grade Four through Seven. Therefore, I was able to use my LAC time to study the implementation of Instructional Intelligence (II) tactics and their efficacy on student learning in mathematics. My mathematics pod consisted of 19 students, 8 girls and 11 boys—one student from Grade Four, two from Grade Five, five from Grade Six, and 11 from Grade Seven. There were also two students in my class who were designated as "gifted" students by the Ministry of Education, and who do not generate any hours of Special Education Aide (SEA) support. The students in the class are from a variety of multicultural backgrounds and possess a narrow range of academic skills in mathematics. For instance, within any given intermediate classroom at my school, we found that the range of academic skills from the lowest test score to the highest test score, according to the mathematics portion of the Canadian Test of Basic Skills (CTBS), was a fairly large range; on average, the scores had a difference of 70%. In one class there was a range of 83%. However, podding these students according to academic skill levels minimized the academic skill range to 30% from the lowest test score to highest test score in my class. This minimal range, and the need to expand and improve the grades in the class, provided the impetus for the current study.

Purpose of the Study

Maintaining traditional teaching methods had not succeeded in improving mathematical achievement for the school. I saw this as an opportunity to experiment with instructional intelligence (II) techniques—tactics, strategies, and graphics organizers—to see whether II practices could improve mathematical achievement for my students. II is another way of looking at the art of creative teaching and student centered learning, of pedagogy. I saw my LAC mathematics class as the perfect opportunity to implement II in a controlled manner and as the ideal setting to monitor the efficacy of creative pedagogical ideas closely. Upon further thought, I decided to use numerous II tactics—singularly and in combination—in my daily teaching to assess (1) whether these tactics would aid students in the development of understandings of mathematics and (2) whether this implementation would translate into improved mathematics achievement in the form of higher grades in the classroom. I decided to use mind mapping (Buzan, 1993) as the cornerstone of my teaching practice, as well as other II techniques, and to assess their impact on student learning and academic achievement.

Why II?

The benefits of mind mapping and other II techniques may be considered fourfold. First, they could be important tools to increase understanding of mathematical concepts, thus resulting in the improvement of academic achievement in mathematics. Second, another benefit of implementing II tactics and mind mapping could be a trickledown effect on teachers, as more staff could begin using II tactics within their own classrooms more effectively and efficiently. Third, the podded mathematics students could learn to understand the benefits of mind mapping and independently apply this II tactic in other subject areas to enhance their own learning. This could include the Grade Seven students using mind mapping as an important note taking skill as they moved on to high school. Fourth, mind mapping uses a "graphic approach to unlock the full potential of the brain by engaging both the right and left sides to work as a whole" (Lane, p. 24)—this could only benefit the students in all areas of their schooling as well as in daily life outside of school. Therefore, I decided to focus on using the II techniques, specifically mind mapping, as the primary method of improving mathematics achievement for students in my mathematics pod.

Overall Design of the Inquiry

To teach students mind mapping and II techniques, I chose to use a few different resources. The techniques used in this action research project was based on components from Barry Bennett's (2002) teaching resource, North Vancouver School District's curriculum resource, *Math 44: Teaching for proficiency*, and *Mind maps for kids* by Tony Buzan (2003). Those resources have been distributed to most schools within NVSD and most teachers are familiar with them and/or have used them as teaching resources. The books contain comprehensive notes, lesson plans, and curriculum information for teachers. As well, NVSD has put in considerable resources to train the district's teachers in these techniques, providing professional development opportunities, both within the individual schools as well as within the district as a whole. These resources provided the theoretical and practical basis for teaching students mind mapping skills within a mathematical context.

After ensuring that I had a strong grasp of concepts presented in those resources, I clarified the objectives of my study—to determine if the use of II techniques could improve mathematical understanding and increase academic achievement levels. The use of pods seemed helpful to clearly determine improvements as well as to differentiate whether the techniques, especially mind mapping, was more effective in certain pods over others. The teachers in the Intermediate teaching team discussed placing students in mathematic learning pods. We studied previous assessments, such as the last year's report cards, as well as current teacher observations, school based assessments, and a formal mathematical test from the CTBS. All of this information was used to group the intermediate students into pods of similar academic skill levels. Four pods were created—a Grade Four and lower skill level, a Grade Five skill level, a Grade Six skill level, and a Grade Seven skill level. Teachers were then brought together to discuss the organizational results and to provide both feedback and objections to any of the podding. We were then involved in a discussion as to the distribution of the pods among staff and after a consensus was reached, each intermediate grade teacher became responsible for a pod. Through this process, I was assigned the highest achieving group of mathematics students, the Grade 7 skill level pod.

I used a journal to collect my personal reflections and observations on the efficacy of the II techniques and student learning processes. These reflections and observations on the implementation of mind mapping activities included the students' responses to and use of mind mapping. I also recorded the efficacy of results of in-class quizzes and tests. Holistically speaking, student progress was monitored and assessed through classroom work, academic achievement results, and my own personal reflections and thoughts on how mind mapping affected the students' overall mathematical understanding.

The Processes of Learning Mathematics in My Pod

Many of the students in my pod were familiar with II techniques, and before the study began (from September 2009 through February 2010), some mathematical concepts were introduced through the use of mind mapping. Front loading of mind mapping skills occurred from September 2009 to February 2010. For example, the following questions were discussed with students: What is a mind map? Why do mind maps work? How do you make a mind map? Furthermore, students were able to practice their newly learned mind mapping skills by creating a class-wide mind map of divisibility rules, and students further honed their skills when they worked with partners to create a mind map on the rules for concepts of area, perimeter, and volume. Finally, students individually created mind maps of numerical patterns, and other mathematical concepts to allow for further individual practice. I used that work as an assessment tool to give me insights on which students had learned the basics of mind mapping and which students needed more teaching and further practice with mind mapping. I then spent additional time with those students who were not as proficient with mind mapping, until I was satisfied with their level of understanding.

The next step was to begin using mind mapping and other II techniques for the focus of my inquiry. Creative instructional tactics and strategies centered on the use of mind mapping. Math units taught throughout the 2009-2010 mathematics podded groupings included patterns and relations, numbers, shape and space, and statistics and probability. I mapped out each unit into lesson plans and decided when and where I could use II techniques to teach various concepts. Once my unit and lesson plans were complete, I had a clear organizational picture of the curriculum that I would teach and how I would teach it through II.

I began to implement my lesson plans in April 2010. I specifically examined the general effectiveness of II tactics during the period beginning on April 1, 2010 and ending on May 31, 2010. I introduced various mathematical concepts using both traditional teacher-directed approaches such as lectures, note taking, and handouts, as well as contemporary student-centered approaches such as the II tactics of concept attainment, concept formation, and mind mapping. I tried to create a healthy balance between the two styles of delivering curriculum. After the teaching of each mathematical concept, an examination was given. In addition, prior to a regularly scheduled examination, which was part of their ongoing school assessment, students were required to create a mind map. Students had the option of using their personally constructed mind map during the test. The subsequent test and assignment scores formed the basis of my data to determine if there was improvement in mathematics achievement. In my daily journal, I reflected on the daily lessons as well as interactions with students and between students.

Lessons and Teacher Actions

My teaching had to be flexible as I played with II techniques to teach the curriculum. I decided to begin with concept formation. A concept formation activity is the process of comparing a group of objects or events that share similar properties to groups of objects that do not contain concept-relevant features (Bennett & Rolheiser, 2001). Students were required to simultaneously compare and contrast groups or categories into concept-relevant features that they conceive as relevant. Therefore, multiple concepts may arise and this concept "invites the brain to find patterns" (Bennett & Rolheiser, 2001, p. 190), thus resulting in more complex thinking and intellectual growth amongst students.

I wanted the students to feel ownership of their learning rather than to see me as the imparter of curriculum. I beleieved their own awareness and understanding of the material could only improve if the learning came from them rather than from me telling them what needed to be learned. As an introductory lesson, I enjoyed using concept formation, as it enabled the students to take ownership of their learning and promoted a student-centered approach. As well, this II tactic allowed for a range of concepts to unfold, as well as discussion and dialogue to occur among the students. I saw this strategy support as a shift in power from the teacher to the students. I allowed the students to place themselves into four groups—two groups of five and two groups of four—and handed out a foolscap sheet of paper to each group that had a T-table with "yes" and "no" headings. As well, each group received a total of ten pictures that they were to placed onto the T-table under the "yes" or "no" columns, depending on what they considered to be the concept. Whereas the "yes" column represented the concept, the "no" column did not represent the concept. Students were very eager to begin, and after explaining the activity and answering a few questions on process, they had ten minutes to work as a group and come up with their own concept.

As I walked around, I noticed each individual participating within their group; all groups were thoroughly engaged in the activity. I noticed one group that spoke about a few concepts, and students argued as to which one made the most sense.

On the other hand, the other three groups came to a consensus quite quickly and had a summary of their concept ready to share with the rest of the groups. This part of the activity also helped improve both debating and listening skills among the students, and allowed students to come to a decision via a democratic process. After the initial ten minutes, group members had five minutes to take part in a gallery walk where one student from each group stayed behind to explain their concept while the rest of the students walked around to look at the other groups' work to listen to the variety of concepts. Next, all students returned to their original group to share aloud their concepts with the rest of the class in a group setting, one at a time. As a result, three groups came to a conclusion of the concept of patterns, whereas the last group had a concept of pictures that encompassed written text. The mathematics lesson for the day was planned around the concept of patterns, and the fact that the majority of students had revealed that discovery themselves seemed to create more interest in learning.

To foster differentiated learning, the next step involved bringing technology into the classroom through the use of laptops. Students played games that involved concepts of patterns. They visited the website http://resources.kaboose.com/games/math2.html, which contained an array of games for them to play and hopefully develop a deeper understanding of pattern concepts. I observed the students enjoying themselves throughout this part of the lesson while learning more about the concept of patterns. The use of laptops within the classroom was greeted with eager learners and was a successful transition into deeper mathematical understanding. Moreover, all students were engaged in their learning and I became a participant as well—I had the chance to challenge some of the students in a few of the computer-based games, something that we all really enjoyed.

Following the technology portion of the lesson, students were given photocopied notes that I had prepared. This allowed for further information, development, and understanding of patterns. Furthermore, the prepared notes allowed me to make sure the Prescribed Learning Outcomes (PLOs) outlined by the British Columbia Ministry of Education could be discussed and the integral concepts covered. Practice questions as well as homework were also part of this section, and this also helped students gain a better understanding of the concept of patterns. Moreover, the practice and homework allowed me to assess which students gained knowledge of patterns and which students needed more tutoring. The following day the class peer-marked their homework. In my classroom, peer marking is defined as groupings of two or three students that go over their homework together and discus any differences that may arise in the final answers. It is a great way to empower students, as this tactic enables students to become peer tutors. Furthermore, students stay on task because each student is involved in a discussion on the concept at hand. We then marked the homework aloud and reviewed questions and concerns any individual had on the homework on the whiteboard.

My role in developing the mind map was that of a facilitator. As a facilitator, I provided the opportunity for the students to construct the mind map. Therefore, the final part to this project was to create a mind map on the concept of patterns. I felt that this allowed "students to express their own personal understanding and generate their own description" (Howitt, 2009, p. 42) on the concept of patterns. Students could use any size of paper or material; however, basic mind mapping rules were imposed. According to the mind mapping rules outlined with the classroom, a mind map needed to have the main concept, in this case patterns, in upper case letters in the middle of the page, centered. Each subheading was connected to the main concept via lines similar to limbs of a tree that represented subheadings, and was connected to its trunk (i.e., the main concept). Moreover, the subheading had to begin with an uppercase letter followed by all lowercase letters. The next step involved lines extending from each subheading to its own specific ideas similar to branches (i.e., ideas) connecting to each limb. Those ideas all began with lowercase letters. The second last step was that the students were to use a variety of colours—each subheading required a different color from the next to show different ideas. Moreover, the difference in the variety of printed text from one level of the mind map to the next also helped indicate the distinction of each step in the process of creating a mind map. Finally, images that were printed, drawn, or cut out were used to help explain the concept of patterns. As well, a rubric was handed out for two reasons, (1) to outline necessary components of a mind map and (2) for student clarification and guidance on the task.

At the end of the unit on patterns, students had the option to use their own mind map during the examination. Approximately half of the students used their mind map regularly during the test, whereas a few of the students used it minimally or as a reference point. A few did not use their mind map at all. Moreover, out of the few who did not use the mind map during the test, a couple did not have a completed mind map or had forgotten it at home. Overall, after my observations, test results, and discussions with students about the use of mind mapping in mathematics, an overwhelming majority of students felt that they gained a deeper understanding of patterns due to the use of this II tactic. They also disclosed that they were eager to use this tactic in future mathematics lessons, and a few were optimistic about using mind mapping in a variety of other subject areas such as science, social studies, and language arts.

For another lesson, I introduced integers using an application of the II tactic concept attainment. Concept attainment is defined as "an inductive strategy [that] pushes the analysis level of thinking [and] invites the brain to find patterns" (Bennett & Rolheiser, 2001, p. 190). Additionally, it is believed that students "remember information longer and understand the design of concepts more quickly and more deeply when asked to think at more complex levels and to discuss their ideas with one another" (p. 190).

Prior to the lesson, I had written 16 words and symbols, in no particular order, on the whiteboard in a web-like pattern using a black erasable pen: negative, positive, mountain, %, student, number line, zero, –4, +11, Canada, (+), (–), water, 0, cake, and fire. Once the lesson began, I explained to the students that we were going to play a silent game, and I outlined the rules of the game to the students. I used two erasable pens to illustrate words that were part of my concept and words that were not related to my concept. For example, use of the green erasable marker represented "go," or words that were part of my concept; the red erasable marker was used to represent "stop," that is, words that were not related to my concept and had no relation to it. All students had equal opportunity to share their thoughts, however, it had to be done silently and by using their thumbs only. For example, if the student thought she knew the concept, she would signal and put her thumb up. If the student was somewhat sure, but not entirely, she would put her thumb sideways. Finally, if the student felt that she did not know the concept, she would place her thumb upside down. After answering a few questions, we began the learning with this II tactic.

I first stated, "the following word was part of my concept," and used the green marker to circle the word "positive." In turn, I then stated, "the following word is not part of my concept" and used the red marker to circle the word "mountain." I continued with two more rounds and circled two more words with the green marker, and marked two more words with the red marker. After six words had been circled with either the green marker or the red marker, I turned to the class and asked if anyone knew my concept. Students showed me by using their thumbs, and most students had their thumbs pointed sideways. A few students had their thumbs facing down, and a couple of students had their thumbs facing up. I continued with the concept attainment lesson with one more round and then asked to see thumbs again. At that point, more students had their thumbs pointing up. I chose one of those students and asked him to give me an example of a word or a symbol from the whiteboard that represented the concept. He chose the symbol (-), which was correct. I then asked another student who had their thumb up for an example of a word or symbol from the whiteboard that did not represent the concept, and she chose the number 0, which was correct. After choosing a few more students for either "yes" or "no" examples, I noticed that more and more students pointed their thumbs up. After eight total rounds, students had one minute to discuss what they felt the concept may be. Following the brief discussion, one student explained the concept and thought the concept was about positive and negative numbers—that was the correct concept.

I then continued on with a Think/Pair/Share (TPS) activity where students filled out a Know/Wonder/Learn (KWL) chart to enable students to think critically about their understanding of positive and negative integers. The first five minutes were allocated to independent work and completing the first two columns, the K column and W column. The next five minutes facilitated paired work, and allowed students to pair up with one another to discuss their first two columns. In this manner, ideas were shared in a small group setting and students were able to exchange and add ideas to their own first two columns of the KWL chart. After five minutes of paired work, students then shared aloud as I completed a master KWL chart on the overhead. Students experienced both oral and visual representations of their peers' thinking and allowed for further connections with other students who possessed similar thoughts and understandings about positive and negative numbers. At that stage, students had the option to add onto their own individual KWL charts.

To facilitate deeper understanding on both positive and negative integers and support a differentiated learning style within my classroom, I brought in laptops for each student to play games at a great website, http://www.onlinemathlearning.com/ integer-games.html, where they had the chance to play various topic-related games, both individually and with peers. I observed all students really enjoying this part of the lesson, and all were keen participants while staying on task. This part of the lesson allowed me to observe student understanding on the concept of positive and negative integers, have informal conversations on the main points of the lesson, and work one-on-one with students who needed further understandings and support.

The next part of the lesson involved handing out notes to reinforce the necessary subtopics of negative and positive integers such as adding and subtracting integers, using the number line, and absolute zero. Also, students had a chance to practice their newly learned skills in a group setting with practice questions, and each student further honed their skills by completing their homework assignment that was handed out prior to the end of class. The following day we discussed the homework as a class, and I reviewed the difficult questions on the whiteboard.

The final part of the positive and negative integer lesson was that each student created their own mind map, outlining each subtopic that was discussed within the class. I noticed that some students lost their motivation for mind mapping and that a few disliked the II tactic because we had completed this type of assignment so many times in previous lessons. Therefore, I modified the mind map and told the students to use their imagination to allow the "individual developing the mind map to make it more interesting, thereby making ideas easier to remember" (Howitt, 2009, p. 42). For example, I allowed for more choices in presentation. For example, students had the choice of using any size of paper they liked (8 × 11, 11 × 17, or larger). As well, students were allowed to use a variety of forms of expression such as paint, pastel, and fabric. I noticed with this modification in presentation, the majority of students worked eagerly toward completing the assignment. There were still a few students who did not enjoy mind mapping, yet they completed the assignment. At the end of the unit study, a test was given and students were allowed to use their mind map during the test. In a culminating activity, I handed back the KWL charts and we completed a TPS activity that fostered individual thinking about their learning in this unit. They then filled out the L part of the chart, paired up and discussed their findings with a partner, and shared aloud with the rest of the peers.

In another lesson, I used the II tactic of Jigsaw. Jigsaw "exploits both cooperation and interdependence in its attempt to maximize intergroup harmony and educational gain" (Walker & Crogan, 1998, p. 382). In my Jigsaw lesson, students were grouped according to both grade level and academic ability level. In theory,

> "each student in each Jigsaw group must learn a unique segment of information, which he/she then teaches to the other members of the Jigsaw group. The Jigsaw group members therefore depend on one another to

> acquire the composite parts, which, as they are combined, constitute the entire lesson" (Walker & Crogan, 1998, p. 382).

The subtopics were mean, median, mode, and range. I photocopied each subtopic on different coloured paper to allow students to be able to distinguish between each area of study. I explained how a Jigsaw activity worked and I emphasized that the power of teaching was leaving me and empowering them, as each student was responsible to teach their own subtopic and include a hands-on demonstration and a few practice questions for their group members. After answering some questions on process, I placed students into their jigsaw groups of four. I then lettered students off from A to D, whereas each letter represented a subtopic, and each student was responsible to learn their subtopic and teach it to their jigsaw group. The letter A represented the subtopic mean, B represented the subtopic median, C represented the subtopic mode, and the letter D represented the subtopic range. Students then placed themselves into their letter groupings and worked on their own subtopic. For example, the group of letter A students sat together with the mean subtopic; they read, studied, and created a lesson on how to teach their individual jigsaw group their topic. This enabled students to work together, gain more insights on their specific subtopic, and take on a leadership role (especially the quieter students). Overall, I believe that this lesson empowered my students.

After a few classes of working in their own letter groupings and honing their skills in their specific content area, students returned to their Jigsaw group and orally and visually presented and taught their subtopic. I was witness to amazing presentations by all students. Furthermore, my class was asked to teach the concepts of mean, median, mode, and range to the lowest academically achieving math pod—Grade Four and lower—and my students were eager to take on that responsibility. I received much positive feedback from my students and they all felt excited and empowered by the overall experience.

A follow-up activity resulted in students creating a mind map on what they had learned in conjunction to mean, median, mode, and range. Furthermore, I administered a test at the end of the unit and as in previous exams, and students had the option of using their own mind map during the examination. It seemed evident that students gained a deeper understanding on mean, median, mode and range after the mind mapping assignment.

Findings

In consideration, reviewing my personal reflections and observations in my journal responses and reading over the key conversations I had with students or overheard in student discussions, I found four key outcomes that were persistent throughout the two month study. First, mind mapping facilitated the study process for examinations. Second, mind mapping helped many students, especially those who I considered as visual and kinaesthetic learners, gain a deeper understanding of the mathematics topics. Third, mind mapping made learning more enjoyable and fun for both me, the teacher, and the students. Finally, mind mapping improved mathematics achievement.

In relation to the first outcome, "[n]ote taking is generally the initial step in a study process" (Nada, Kholief, Tawfik, & Metwally, 2009, p. 257) and many of students felt that mind mapping helped them in the study process as it allowed students to move away from traditional text-ridden notes toward a new-age, spiced up, graphic organizer such as mind mapping that is a "highly effective tool" (Howitt, 2009, p. 42). A mind map is illustrated with the primary concept at the center, with subordinate ideas, or branches, radiating from it. Its design "encourages the use of colour and imagery" (Gripman, 2009, p. 26). The idea of mind mapping is to "make the note-taking process more natural, more like the way the human brain operates" (p. 26). Furthermore, mind mapping assignments were completed at the end of each unit of study, which helped summarize key concepts and reinforce main points. This notion is considered in the following quote, in that a "[m]ind map reinforces teaching strategies that encourages learning through multiple intelligences" (Nada et al., 2009, p. 256) and supports higher order thinking skills.

Third, the use of II tactics, specifically mind mapping, made teaching and learning more fun and enjoyable for the teacher and the students as it brought a creative, artistic element to the academics. I enjoyed teaching mind mapping as a note taking skill. It was "more spontaneous, creative and enjoyable, both for the educator and the students" (Nada et el, 2009, p. 260). Mind mapping moves away from traditional teacher-centered approaches to teaching mathematics with a student-centered approach. Students became empowered as they created a graphic organizer to encompass the important details of a unit of mathematical study and they were able to use it during their tests. Mind mapping inspired "students through a brain-friendly, interactive approach to learning" (Nada et el, 2009, p. 260).

Finally, I feel that the students benefited, academically speaking, through the use of II in the classroom. Through my observations, personal reflections, communication with students, test scores, and class assignments, the students in my mathematics podded group have achieved deeper understanding about mathematical topics covered within the classroom. This is evident in the overall academic achievement attained by the class as a whole. For example, the students in the class collectively achieved an average mark of 81 percent during the study beginning on April 1, 2010 and ending on May 31, 2010. This was an improvement of approximately 15 percentage points when compared to test results prior to the study. I believe this increase to be an excellent indicator of how II tactics and mind mapping have helped increase academic achievement levels within mathematics. Moreover, on a variety of occasions, many students disclosed that mind mapping helped them gain a deeper understanding on the variety of mathematical topics learned in class, and that the II tactic better prepared them toward writing the final examination after each unit of mathematical study. This directly resulted in higher achievement levels within mathematics.

In Reflection

Throughout my inquiry, I believe students gained a deeper understanding of various topics based on various II tactics, specifically mind mapping. "Brain research informs us that the brain is a pattern seeker and that talk is important for intellectual growth" (Bennett & Rolheiser, 2001, p. 190). From that perspective, it is critical that educators give students many opportunities that tap into both the left and right sides of the brain, the whole brain. In addition, "[m]arrying the strengths of the right- and left-brained clears the path to real open-mindedness. The results can be thinking that has no barriers" (Lane, 2009, p. 25). This newly acquired skill enabled students to bring in an element of visual art and heightened creativity to their academics. "Imagination and association are the keys to high-level memory and creative thinking and mapping supports this" (Nada et el, 2009, p. 255). They gained deeper understandings about mathematics through unorthodox note taking methods that support and break the "top-to-bottom, left-to-right, text-only bonds of traditional notation" (Gripman, 2009, p. 26).

I am not saying that traditional note taking methods are inadequate; on the contrary. However, I support and nurture an environment where students are allowed to use any form of note taking they wish. As an educator, I taught my students that web diagrams, concept maps, mind maps, and other forms of graphic organizers are as sufficient and acceptable as traditional note taking methods. Moreover, I provided opportunities for both traditional and non-traditional note taking techniques. The "nature of mind mapping is skill based rather than content driven … [and] in this manner, learning becomes more dynamic and enriching" (Nada et el, 2009, p. 256). Furthermore, I believe that not only does teaching students a variety of note taking tactics increase student engagement, it also enables students to expand their note taking skills and use whichever note taking tool they so choose across the curriculum.

Finally, only when we, as educators, support opportunities for choice and marry traditional teacher-centered teaching methods to non-traditional, student-centered teaching techniques such as II tactics, strategies, and graphics organizers within our classrooms, the result will be that more students become engaged with their learning. In my mathematics podded groups, there were times that I provided teacher-centered instruction, however, I fostered a classroom environment that helped promote self-efficacy among and between the students. My goal in teaching II tactics in my mathematics podded group, specifically mind mapping skills, was to reach a larger audience of students and enable them to gain a deeper understanding of mathematics. I achieved that goal, and as a result my students learned more, not only about mathematics, but about their own learning.

Sanjeet Johal
North Vancouver School District 44
sjohal@nvsd44.bc.ca

KEVIN WARD

MENTORING MYSELF

The process of becoming an instructionally intelligent intermediate educator and mentor of pre service teachers

> In praxis, there is always an element of action; that is, some kind of application to the lived in world, although it is not about mere practice, the routine repetition of an act. There is always a reflective component wherein one describes, contemplates, and considers what is being thought or felt or is happening. There is always a critical component involving analysis and questioning of motives, purposes and ideology. There is always an evaluative component, though not always explicit, as one takes heed of the worth of the thought and action. There is always an interpretative component, as the question "What does it all mean?" is inevitably posed. (Pearse, 2004).

Overview

I investigated the role of instructional intelligence in shaping myself, my practice, and my philosophy or pedagogy. I wished to study myself, to discover the spaces where my theory and practice collide, deconstruct my praxis, and rise from the ashes of the internal discourse to do battle with my reflective consciousness. How does this complex process shape me as a teacher of young minds? I was overwhelmed by the enormity and complexity of studying myself, as well as the "dynamic dialectical relationship between theory and practice" (Pearse, 2004). I realized that I needed to focus my lens a little more or be swept away by a tsunami of research and professional literature. I hypothesized that if I narrowed my area of study to investigate a specific area of my theory and practice I would be more likely to scale my Everest and reach some findings that informed my praxis. To do so I focused on the implementation of instructional concepts, strategies, and tactics. I hypothesized that if I could experiment in my own practice with certain Instructional concepts and reflect upon, critique, and evaluate their use and learning outcomes in my classroom, then I would be more likely to be cognizant of their implementation and, therefore, better suited to informing my praxis one small step at a time. I decided that I needed to find 15 tactics and strategies that were suited to the Kindergarten through Grade 7 learning environment so that I could manage the enormity of becoming a more reflective practitioner.

In doing so, I also wondered how my reflective process could be useful in mentoring pre service teachers. This thought occurred to me at a time when I was mentoring a pre service teacher from the University of British Columbia's (UBC)

P. Gouzouasis (ed.), Pedagogy in a New Tonality: Teacher Inquiries on Creative Tactics, Strategies, Graphics Organizers, and Visual Journals in the K-12 Classroom, 85–101.

Fine Arts and new Media in Education (FAME) cohort. At the time, I was struggling with how to effectively model the implementation of Instructional intelligence (II) strategies and tactics for my pre service teacher. I questioned how could I do a bang up job of mentoring implementation when I was unsure of my own practice. I hypothesized that if I were to determine what constituted best practice for me, that I would be more confident in modeling the experimentation that is required to become a reflective-reflexive practitioner and thus, become an effective teacher. I believed that just being more aware of one's own teaching and learning processes would be enough to help an emerging teacher question their own practice and engage in reflection of their own praxis. I hoped that through inquiry I would be able to target II tactics and strategies that would be beneficial to a pre service teacher. I then hypothesized that if pre service teachers went through a process of guided self-observation they may be more likely to experiment with II.

The Journey of Discovery and Verification: Scaling My Everest

I may be barking up the wrong mountain when I suggest that Sir Edmund Hillary, the famed explorer and conqueror of Mt. Everest, had no idea he would attempt to climb Everest 14 years after completing his first summit climb of Mt. Ollivier in 1939. With that first summit climb began a process that changed Hillary forever. A process that began before Hillary himself was even aware of what his end product might look like, what it would entail, and who would be along for the ride as confident, colleagues, mentors, or climbing partners. It may be quite a stretch to compare scaling the tallest peak on earth to scaling my own Masters of Education degree, but it is an analogy that I am sticking with. Like Hillary, I did not even consider the possibility of scaling something that seemed insurmountable. I also, like Hillary, never knew what my support crew would look like before beginning the journey. How could we? Hillary never even met his Sherpa, Tenzing Norgay, until his famous 1953 ascent was in the planning stages.

I started my own journey in my first year employed as a full time teacher. I was unaware of it at the time, but in hindsight that was the first time I encountered the notion of the Instructional Institute. Fast-forward from 2003 until the present school year (2010/2011) when I have finished my thesis and placed an exclamation mark on my learning process. I have reached the summit in my own development as a teacher, at least until tomorrow when the ascent continues. I possess a great fear that one day I will become unreflective of my person, theory, and practice. Will I stop thinking and evolving just because I have planted a flag at the top of my Everest? I take great faith that this will not occur because my ascent, the process of attaining my masters, has helped me come to terms with my praxis as well as my view of the evolution of humanity. It took a long time to get to this point and to the realization that there is no finish line, just a series of summits. When I moved from unofficially studying for my master's degree to actually joining a graduate cohort of peers, I was very anxious about the process of research, data analysis, and attempting to quantify the complex role of teaching. I questioned how my data would be beneficial to others and to what purpose would this process serve. It turns out that the goal was not about writing a final research paper but about the journey to a new summit, of finding myself, and becoming a better educator. As a result of working with other dedicated teachers and my fellow graduate students, I have come to embrace this awareness. My peers have enabled me to think, to reflect, and to be creative in my research and my teaching.

During my exploratory process, I took many courses under the guidance of my graduate advisor. He was to become my Sherpa and was as instrumental to my successful navigation of my masters as Tenzing Norgay was to Sir Edmund Hillary's ascent of Everest's summit. The guidance, teachings, courses, and experiences designed for my program were invaluable in helping me come to terms with my own learning. My graduate advisor provided learning environments that engaged my peers and me in ways that allowed us to question, explore, and value a broad range of qualitative research. No longer did I worry about the value of my data, in light of the notion that there was no such thing as 'pure data' (Pepper, 1942; Gouzouasis, 2008). As part of our qualitative journey, our graduate advisor encouraged us to explore the value of different forms of research representations. These notions were planted so that they could germinate until each of us was ready to harvest the growth.

"The growth of new writing practices in sport and physical activity signals a growing awareness in this community that there is no single way, much less one "right" way, to stage a text or to know about a phenomenon (Sparkes, 2002). How liberating to be freed of the expectations of having to do something the "right" way. In essence, we were encouraged to engage in the creative process, accessing Mihaly Csikzmentmihalyi's notion (1990) of creative flow where the right mixture of challenge, interest, and ability clashed, and that by doing so we would be able to consider creative forms of inquiry and representation of our own research. Being told to "trust the process" (McNiff, 1998) and to try and achieve "flow" (Csikzmentmihalyi, 1990) was both terrifying and liberating, and yet it allowed me to move forward and see value in studying my own creative use of instructional strategies and tactics. The following journey ensued.

Over the course of the past eight years from 2002 to 2010, the North Vancouver School District (NVSD) has been undergoing a transformation designed to target the effective use of instructional tactics and strategies. This process of shift can be labeled in many different ways, such as creative instructional tactics, instructional intelligence and tactics, or simply as a reflective and reflexive analysis of what constitutes 'best practice' teaching strategies, tactics, or techniques. As teaching professionals can attest, this is a necessary process to any teachers' career and when ongoing can be the most powerful tool at our fingertips. In other words, it can be said that what the NVSD is trying to accomplish is by no means new and revolutionary. Successful teachers have long been known for being reflective of their teaching practice and applying their self-reflection through the evolution of their teaching tactics. However, the NVSD's long-term plan in partnership with Barrie Bennett, to implement Instructional Intelligence through the Instructional Institute in a systemic fashion, was both a worthy and ambitious goal.

This project has put me, by pure coincidence, in a very interesting situation to develop some insights and questions surrounding the implementation of the

Instructional Intelligence Institute. In 2002, the first year of the Instructional Institute implementation, I entered my Professional Development Program at Simon Fraser University, finishing the program in April of 2003 after completing my practica at Lynnmour Elementary School, located within the North Vancouver School District. I was hired in May of 2003 having never heard of Barrie Bennett, Carol Rolheiser, or Instructional Intelligence. It can be said that I entered the system at the beginning at what was hoped to be a systemic instructional change. In the 2002-2003 school year, I received my first teaching assignment in a Grade 7 classroom. Under the mentorship of the acting principal, I was introduced to "instructionally intelligent" tactics, strategies, and the *Beyond Monet* resource.

I was duly impressed when I was asked if I would attend an Instructional Institute workshop under the instruction of Barrie Bennett himself. I jumped at the chance. I could not believe how fortunate I was to be working and learning in a district that was willing to invest the time and money in a beginning teacher. This, I thought, was how grassroots change happened. Unfortunately, like most change, it happened very slowly. Three years later, I was finally given the release time to attend a Barrie Bennett Instructional Institute workshop. Three years! In each of those three years as I chalked up teaching experience in a Grade Four class sandwiched by Grade 6/7 combined classes at three different elementary schools, I was asked by each administrator if I would like to attend an Instructional Intelligence workshop. Each time I stated my desire to attend and each time I was denied release time due to a lack of educational leadership release time. I began to wonder, is this really how we support beginning teachers? I am now in my eighth year of teaching, just like the district is in it's eight year of implementing the Instructional Institute, and I still wonder if our profession provides enough support for both beginning teachers and pre service teachers in implementing best practice tactics like those found within the Instructional Intelligence umbrella? Given my experiences, I decided that if I was ever to be an effective mentor I needed to study my own practice.

Taking what I had learned from my cohort's engagement with II, I began the process of studying my own use of instructionally intelligent strategies and tactics. In the *Beyond Monet* resource that I had become reliant upon, I found a vast array of Instructional concepts, strategies, skills and tactics at hand. In fact their where too many ideas within the resource to simplify my area of study. Around this time a colleague introduced me to a document that was created by the Otterville Public School Teachers, *Instructional Strategies for K to 12: Strategies for Teaching,* that summarized the strategies and tactics found in *Beyond Monet*. The authors (Ellis, Keeling-Walter, Evans & Reissner, 2006) condensed the 33 strategies and tactics into a reference booklet for teachers. The booklet provided a description of each strategy as well as procedures to follow. It also provided classroom management considerations and any prior knowledge that would be required to make the implementation successful and a three-column chart that listed the Key Benefits, Effective Uses and Extensions, and

Modifications. With the aid of this invaluable document, I began the process of experimenting with my practice in a systematic way, one strategy at a time. Over the course of two school years, I used the Otterville document to try each strategy several times. What I discovered is that I had my favorites and narrowed those down to 15–20 that became a fluid part of my practice. The use of these strategies became an extension of my lessons and my self. I was well on my way toward creating a list of 15 tactics and strategies that I felt might guide a pre service teacher through their practicum experience. In the 2009–2010 school year, I began recording reflections on the use of 10 tactics and 5 strategies employed in my Grade 7 classroom, that I felt would be beneficial to my study of pre service teachers and their experimentation with II tactics and strategies.

Self-study: The Implementation of Instructional Tactics and Graphics Organizers

As I went about the task of teaching my Grade 7 class that school year, I recorded many journal or reflections on the strategies and tactics I used. The following ten tactics and five strategies were the most prominent in my practice. I firmly believe that their prominence and frequency speaks directly to how seamless and effortless they became part of my instructional repertoire. I also believe that their prominence is directly related to an evolution of my instruction and concern with student engagement. I shall summarize their importance to my instruction beginning with the following ten tactics.

NUMBERED HEADS

Numbered Heads is one of the simplest tactics to implement in a teachers classroom management and it can be used effectively in any cooperative learning activity (Bennett & Rolheiser, 2001). It allows teachers to assign a number or letter to a small group so that each student has a pre determined order or responsibility to the group. Numbered Heads is a very effective tactic to increase the concept of accountability because each student is aware of their responsibilities to the group and is given the opportunity to share within their group, and thus practice, before having to publicly share ideas and information with the greater classroom community. My own reflections on my use of this tactic suggest that it does increase accountability and I would suggest that this occurs because each student feels safe in their respective roles. The opportunity to share with a small peer group reduces stress and anxiety and allows the group to scaffold or correct any wayward thinking that confuses the concept being considered. In essence, the students get a dry run in digesting and processing the concept and a system of checks in balance are in place to ensure individual and group success. Over the course of my ten-month self-study, I noticed that the frequency in which I used this tactic increased from a few times per week until it became almost a daily tactic. In addition to the benefits previously mentioned, I found that the numbered heads tactic was very effective in aiding transitions between activities or subjects or in collecting group work.

INSIDE/OUTSIDE CIRCLES

This tactic is very effective at providing each student with the opportunity to share ideas and thoughts with their peers while classroom building and fostering oral communication skills (Bennett & Rolheiser, 2001). Inside/Outside Circles employ an inner ring and outer ring amongst a group of six or more students. The outside circle faces the inside circle with each student facing a student in the other circle. Starting with one of the circles the students are expected to dialogue for a period of time. The students could be discussing a concept, solving a problem, sharing a story, poem or piece of art or at the beginning of the school year, sharing information about each other as a community building activity. After the first circle is finished sharing, the other circle has a turn to share or extend the thinking of the first person. After one round, the circles rotate one person in opposite directions and the process begins again.

When I reflected on my own use of Inside/Outside Circles, I noticed that I preferred to use this tactic to have students share their work such as a poem or short story. The tactic allowed the students to hear their own creations being read aloud, thus acting as a editing and revision tool and allowing for feedback from the other peer circle. It also enabled students to practice delivering their poem or story several times, which helped to prepare them for a public presentation to the entire classroom. During my poetry unit, this tactic was used twice weekly and students shared their work in small, intimate settings before having to select which poems they would later present at a classroom poetry coffeehouse.

GALLERY TOUR

Gallery Tour is another simple tactic that can be incorporated quite easily into one's repertoire of teaching and classroom management. It involves students "touring" the classroom to observe peer work that has been completed (Bennett & Rolheiser, 2001). I noticed that a Gallery Tour allows students a safe environment to share their work and see other interpretations of work. It also allows students the opportunity to observe and collect ideas to store in their own toolbox that they may be able to incorporate into their own creative process, while showcasing the collective efforts of the classroom community. Allowing students to see multiple representations of a similar task or assignment encourages (1) diversity of thinking and creating by (2) nurturing and valuing the diversity found within the classroom. I found myself using this tactic for those students that were having difficulty getting started on an activity. In my own practice, I specifically employed a modified version of the tactic when beginning a visual journal activity. While the majority of my students dove right into visual journaling, others had a hard time getting started because they could not figure out what was the "right way" to visual journal. Providing the opportunity for these students to see that each person in the class had a different way of representing their ideas and experiences freed them from the expectation of doing a visual journal the "correct way." The short stories that were eventually produced from the visual journals were stunningly diverse and valued in our classroom community.

VALUE LINES

This II tactic is a thinking or emotional organizer that is designed to have students demonstrate their opinion or feeling on a topic by standing on a Value Line that ranged from strongly disagree to strongly agree (Bennett & Rolheiser, 2001). This tactic is particularly effective with any topic that involves discussions about opinions or feelings. The more informed the group is on the topic of debate, the more valuable the tactic becomes. However, it can also be used to shed light on a topic on which the students may be naïve. In my ten-month self-study, it came to light that the majority of students in my Grade 7 class believed that the Internet was a very safe place to post information about oneself. During a current events session, a student introduced social networking as a dangerous place for pre teens to meet other pre teens. I requested that he only share certain parts of the news article so that we could form a Value Line along the principle that Social networking sites like Facebook were safe havens on the Internet. The student that introduced the topic, having been informed by the article, was the only student to place himself on the strongly disagree end of the Value Line. This tactic and topic led to a very serious discussion about the perils of sharing personal information and social media online. The tactic lends itself very well to academic controversy and debate on a topic. It also challenges the students' thinking, which in many instances results in a complete reversal of opinion (Bennett & Rolheiser, 2001).

THINK PAIR SHARE

Think Pair Share (TPS) is a cooperative activity in which individual students are given either a topic, idea, or question to think about. After an appropriate amount of wait time, determined by the level of *thinking* expected relative to Bloom's Taxonomy, the students are expected to *pair* with another student and *share* their ideas about the topic of discussion (Bennett & Rolheiser, 2001). Each student in the pair is allotted an opportunity to share with each other. Then all the pairs If students may report to the larger class community allowing for the possibility that some pairs may not feel safe sharing and thus employ their right to pass. This tactic ensures accountability as any pair may be called upon to share their collective thoughts, agreements, or disagreements. Students are provided with an opportunity to practice their oral language skills, attentive listening, taking conversational turns and suspending judgment or respecting alternative perspectives. In my own practice, Think Pair Share became a tactic that had the potential to be used several times a day as it was so easily implemented and effectively used by my students to practice their thoughts before being invited to share their thoughts or pass to another group.

GRAFFITI

Bennett & Rolheiser (2001) suggest that this II tactic is effective as a brainstorming process for recording the collective wisdom of the group. Graffiti involves placing students in small groups of three to five and providing a large piece of paper or poster to allow them to Graffiti words and or images. In the centre of each piece of paper, students are provided with a topic. Students are allowed thirty seconds to think about the topic and then sixty to ninety seconds to individually and simultaneously Graffiti their ideas on the paper. Each group then moves to a different piece of paper where the process is repeated until each group has visited each piece of paper. In my own practice, I noticed that I used this tactic often at the beginning of a unit to access background knowledge about a particular topic. The collective background knowledge then provided a visual display for all the students to benefit from. In one instance, I used this tactic to create ideas for a short story that fit the criteria of twisting plot and character of popular culture to create an alternative fairy tale. The students utilized the graffiti walls so well that there was very little room left on the majority of the sheets. The graffiti walls were posted around the room and used as part of an ongoing Gallery Tour throughout the story writing process.

FOUR CORNERS

Four Corners is an ideal structure for getting students to operate at higher conceptual levels of Blooms Taxonomy by employing more creative and evaluative ways of thinking (Bennett & Rolheiser, 2001). Four Corners involves a statement, issue, or debatable question that allows for several different perspectives. Each perspective is represented by one of the four corners (i.e., of the classroom; more "corners" may be created if required), where students are expected to place themselves in accordance with their thoughts and beliefs on a particular issue. At each corner they meet like-minded students at which time they Think Pair Share their thoughts on the topic as well as discuss aspects of the corner they find themselves in. The tactic lends itself to debate because the potential to have four different perspectives is present. Each corner should expect to be asked to share their response to the original question. In my own practice, I found that employing four corners was an excellent tactic to draw the student's passion into a debate. I mainly used this tactic in conjunction with current events and social studies. I found that class discussions were more meaningful when the topic was explored in this way. In one instance at the end of the school year, I asked the students to place themselves in one of the four corners after making the statement that the Ancient Chinese invention of gunpowder has had the most profound impact on today's society. The statement was given after exploring the innovations of Ancient Egypt, Greece, Rome, and China. A gender split ensued with the majority of the girls placing themselves in the "disagree" or "strongly disagree" corners. The boys were the polar opposites with the exception of two who also strongly disagreed. The girls were passionate about the subject because they believed that either writing (i.e., using hieroglyphs and papyrus) or organized farming were the greatest innovations of the ancient civilizations. The boys were equally passionate about the effects and devastation caused by gunpowder and the genesis of weapons and explosives. Both groups were persuasive and we ended the activity with the notion that sometimes we must agree to disagree.

FISHBONE

This II tactic is a graphic organizer that is often used in problem solving or to identify, organize, and classify factors (Bennett & Rolheiser, 2001). It provides students the opportunity to display ideas and concepts at the analysis and evaluation levels of Bloom's Taxonomy. The fishbone tactic can be used as a whole group, small group, or independent brainstorm. I utilized the fishbone organizer frequently throughout the year in all core subjects. It could be applied to explore a character's development in a novel, as a way to classify different species of animals, early humans, or ecosystems, as well as in math to consider multi step problems.

Two instances of note came to light during my ten-month, self-study. The first was when reading the novel "The Sea of Trolls" by Nancy Farmer. The main character develops from a powerless farm boy to a powerful bard while questing to save his younger sister and himself from their abduction by North men raiders. Along the way he encounters different classes of creatures including Anglo Saxon humans, North men humans, trolls, mythical animals, half-humans, and unclassifiable creatures. Each of these classifications contributed to his development as a bard in some way. The fishbone organizer acted as a wonderful tool for the students to evaluate how the main character developed. They also acted as powerful visual displays of the students' learning and made for a very dynamic Gallery Tour. The second notable instance was when we classified the different species of early humans. What struck me about the fishbones in this case was how my students were inspired to create their own Fishbone skeleton from the tools, bones, and skulls of Australopithecus, Neanderthal, and Homo erectus. They may not have been anatomically accurate, but they sure looked great.

PLACEMAT

Placemat is a cooperative tactic that enables students to simultaneously work and think independently from each other before they share their thinking in a group (Bennett & Rolheiser, 2001). It keeps students accountable to the group allowing the teacher and group to see each member's independent contribution. The activity involves a large piece of paper being divided into quadrants with a central square in the middle. Each student responds to the question posed, story read, or poem analyzed in his or her own quadrant. The use of a different color marker is an excellent method of tracking individual student contributions. After each person has contributed, the Placemat may be rotated 90 degrees so that each student can read and respond to the first entry. This allows alternative perspectives or ideas to be considered to scaffold other students or to simply allow students to see how their peers feel or think about a particular topic. This process can be continued, either until a consensus is reached or until the topic has been exhausted. In my own practice I loved to use this activity to explore poetry and other uses of figurative or sensory language. Lyrics or a poem would be the focus of the placemat and the students could write their interpretation of the text, or explore different uses of simile, metaphor or other instances of figurative language. My students were particularly engaged when they were encouraged to bring in lyrics from popular music as a focus of a Placemat activity.

THUMBS UP, THUMBS DOWN

Thumbs Up, Thumbs Down invites students to actively participate in a discussion or decision by putting their thumbs up if they agree or understand a concept or thumbs down if they disagree or are unsure of a concept (Bennett & Rolheiser, 2001). Students that are unsure can place their thumbs sideways to demonstrate that they are unsure. Thumbs Up, Thumbs down keeps students accountable to a discussion because they are expected to elaborate if called upon. It is a non-threatening way for each student to participate and it provides the teacher with a very quick visual snapshot of where the students are at in relation to the concept being discussed. This tactic can be used in conjunction with almost any other II tactic or strategy to ensure that active participation is present when exploring any issue. In my own practice Thumbs Up, Thumbs Down was rarely used as a stand-alone tactic as it would be incorporated into most tactics, strategies, activities or discussions.

Self-study: The Implementation of Instructional Strategies and Graphics Organizers

The strategies chosen for my self-study, which included Jigsaw, Concept Attainment, Concept Formation, Mind Maps, and Concept Maps, were all very powerful to engage my students and even more so when the strategies were combined with one or more of the tactics explored above.

JIGSAW

This II strategy is a cooperative strategy in which students are part of a cooperative group that is called the Home Team (Ellis et al., 2006). Each member of the home team meets with a different expert group to learn about a different aspect of one topic of study (Ellis et al., 2006). Employing Numbered Heads is essential to the success of this activity. Each student is numbered or lettered within their home team. For example, each student could be labeled A, B, C or D. All the A's from each home group would meet to form an expert group that is expected to learn material that they will become experts on. The experts then disperse back to their Home Team armed with their new expertise or 'jigsaw piece.' In their home team each expert shares their expertise with members of their Home Team thus ensuring that the group covers all areas of study. Each expert provides one piece of a jigsaw puzzle that is assembled by the home team. This strategy is very effective at covering large amounts of information quickly and is also effective in keeping students accountable to their group. During my ten- month self-study, I used this strategy to cover large amounts of information in an efficient manner. One such time was when we were studying the effects and consequences of drug and alcohol use. Each expert group was assigned a topic, such as alcohol, crystal methamphetamines, marijuana and tobacco, that they needed to explore through which they would become experts. Once the material was covered they were sent back to their home groups to educate their peers in their area of expertise. At the end of the activity the students were able to identify the effects and consequence of using these substances.

CONCEPT ATTAINMENT

Perhaps one of the most powerful instructional strategies is the inductive thinking strategy of Concept Attainment developed by Jerome Bruner (Bennett & Rolheiser, 2001). Bruner's work on how humans construct meaning and how instruction affects learning has been critical in increasing our understanding of how the brain seeks patterns and how the brain develops with consistent thinking at the analysis level. The Concept Attainment process helps students engage with concepts by creating a game like environment to explore examples of a concept, thus helping students to remember information longer and increasing their understanding and design of a concept. The strategy provides opportunities for students to think for themselves at the analysis level of understanding, thus ensuring the development of critical thinking skills. The strategy itself is game-like and novel for students because they are asked to analyze, compare, and contrast *like* and *unlike* examples of a concept.

In this data set of yes and no examples, the students are expected to analyze the different attributes, purposes, and models of the like and unlike examples and attempt to crack the code to figure out what the concept may be. Several examples of a yes and no example of the concept being explored are given in turn to allow students to look for connections and patterns to help them confirm, deny, or readjust their thinking. At the end of several rounds the students are provided with testers that remain unlabeled as like or unlike examples. The students then check their understanding by identifying the testers based on their knowledge of the data set. In my own practice, I employed the Concept Attainment strategy across all subject areas. I found that my students were engaged and excited to be learning in a way that they perceived to be game-like. In one instance I combined the strategy of Concept Attainment with a Jigsaw strategy to explore the concept of a protagonist. After completing a literature circle, which included six different reading groups having read five different novels, I placed an expert from each novel group to form five groups of six book experts (i.e., each group for the concept attainment portion of the lesson had at least one person that had read one of the five books). This ensured that each member of the group would need to be actively participating to help compare and contrast attributes of each character. I made a data set that demonstrated yes and no examples of protagonists from each novel. I then used the placemat activity to have the groups keep a running record of their thinking as each round of yes and no examples were revealed. Each group worked toward identifying the concept I had been modeling. In the end, each group was able to demonstrate their understanding of the concept of a protagonist while having a great deal of fun doing so.

CONCEPT FORMATION

This strategy is almost the inverse operation of Concept Attainment as a small group of students are given a data set or are asked to generate their own data set (Bennett & Rolheiser, 2001). The data set, which can be words, pictures, formulas, or processes, is sorted into classifications based on common attributes. This inductive thinking method encourages students to identify critical attributes of a concept allowing them to make generalizations and discriminations, create connections by comparing, contrasting and evaluating the design of the concept. Once students have created their concept formation data set they can share with other groups to facilitate discussion and engage each other in Concept Attainment games. At this stage of the activity, each group of students engages other groups in the process of interpretation of the Concept Formation they created. Concept Formation lends itself well to any subject area and therefore makes it very versatile for classroom use. I found that I employed Concept Formation at the culmination of a unit in conjunction with a Concept Attainment lesson. I would give a lesson in Concept Attainment then ask the students to make a data set with a related concept. For example, after the concept lesson on the attributes of a protagonist, I asked the students to generate a data set from some other aspect of the novel they had read during their literature circle. The students then presented their Concept Formation to other groups to see if their peers could interpret their thinking and classifications.

MIND MAP

Mind Mapping is a strategy that involves creating a graphic organizer by integrating a combination of concepts, words, colors and visuals that are all linked to a central theme (Bennett & Rolheiser, 2001). Mind maps increase the brain's capacity to store and recall information because the brain is actively engaged in the construction and design of the mind map. Students use the central theme to create main branches that radiate out from the general to specific. The use of images, symbols, words and colors to capture the essence and complex relationships of a concept is essential to a powerful mind map. I used mind maps quite often over the course of my self-study in each of the core subjects. In science we explored the Earth's crust and the forces that shape our planet, which included excellent opportunities for key visuals such as volcanoes, plate tectonics, and erosion.

CONCEPT MAP

Concept Maps are another way to visually represent a person's thinking in the form of a graphic organizer. Concept Maps are different from Mind Maps in several key ways. Concept Maps generally begin with a major term or idea that is the top of a hierarchy (Bennett & Rolheiser, 2001). The term radiates downwards, shifting from a major idea to a minor idea, terminating that "branch" of thinking with an example. Along the branch and between concepts, joining or linking words, usually in the form of a verb, are used to state relationships between the concepts. Cross-links from one independent branch to another are also employed to represent connections between concept hierarchies. Unlike Mind Maps, Concept Maps usually do not involve pictures, images, or other visuals. They are simply connections between concepts in the form of words. In my own practice I found that Concept Maps could be done quite quickly at the end of a unit to demonstrate the big understanding of the unit. For instance, in social studies we evaluated the importance of the Nile River to ancient Egyptians. Concept branches that were formed to demonstrate the importance of the Nile included the river's ability to provide, food, water, transportation, shelter, papyrus, defense, and communication. Students then cross-linked their branches when appropriate.

At the conclusion of my ten-month study of my own practice, I was able to look back and reflect on the II strategies that I utilized over the school year. The fifteen strategies and tactics that I selected for the pre service teacher study were the most prominent in frequency and efficacy for my praxis. I felt as I used these tactics and strategies that they became a part of my pedagogy because after practicing them and focusing on them for over a year they became a fluent part of my instruction. I began to feel that if this were an indicator of best practice then perhaps I would become a better mentor of pre service teachers. These fifteen tactics and strategies were used to form a checklist that could be used to collect data (NB: A copy may be obtained from the author).

The Pre Service Teacher Study

The purpose of the following phase of my inquiry was to explore whether pre service teachers are likely to use Instructional Intelligence tactics and strategies as part of their practicum experience. Successful, innovative, and creative pre service teachers are future employees of our school district and can be extremely effective in a grassroots effort to achieve the systemic change we would like to see in implementing the Instructional Institute district wide.

The rationale for pursuing the line of investigation lies in my own experience as a beginning teacher and most recently as a fifth year teacher when I had the opportunity to mentor a UBC teacher candidate from the Fine Arts and new Media in Education cohort (FAME). When compared to my own experiences as a pre service teacher I noticed a great deal more Instructional Institute opportunities for FAME teacher candidates and began to wonder how effective those opportunities were for pre service teachers. This was partly because my experience as a School Associate (i.e., classroom mentor of pre service teachers) seemed quite different from other colleagues I witnessed mentoring other pre service teachers.

In informal conversations with my colleagues it was reported to me that some Teacher Candidates were attempting Instructional Institute tactics while others were not, despite all six teacher candidates having attended the Instructional Institute workshop presented by Barrie Bennet and having equitable access through the FAME cohort to the *Beyond Monet* resource and instructional methods courses. Browne & Hoover (1990) reported similar findings in their study of 79 pre services teachers—they found that student teachers "only variably employed instructional strategies emphasized in university instructional methods courses" (p. 21). Those findings, along with my own informal observations, made me ponder why some pre service teachers choose to omit instructional strategies that engage the learners and appeal to multiple intelligences. I also wondered that if pre service teachers were provided with a simple checklist, would they feel comfortable experimenting with their instruction?

Research Questions

I begin with the most obvious questions. How are we educators—whether we are a professor representing a university methods course, a district or school administrator, or a school associate—currently supporting pre service teachers in employing creative instructional strategies as described in *Beyond Monet?* Which instructional tactics and strategies are being emphasized in methods courses? Are these same strategies being modeled and supported by school associates and supported by district administrators? If so, are pre service teachers experimenting with the implementation of creative instructional strategies and at what frequency?

Daane & Latham (1998) suggest that a problem or criticism of teacher education programs "is how to encourage a stronger correlation between the effective instructional strategies modeled and taught in methods courses and those valued and modeled by supervising teachers" (p. 141). If district administrators are involved in school associate selection, are they selecting the school associates that are most likely to model the strategies recommended by the Instructional Institute model? Sudzina, Giebelhaus & Coolican (1997) found that student teachers perceived the mentor-mentee relationship as a process where a supportive, honest and positive role model helped to facilitate their learning and allowed for exploration of new teaching ideas. It is reasonable to suggest that it is critical to the success of pre service teachers and the district's implementation of II that school associates who support this type of exploration are being selected to foster II amongst pre service teachers.

Design, Procedures and Data Collection

To attempt to find some insight into the above questions, I followed the practicum placements of three FAME Teacher Candidates (TCs) within two of the 26 elementary schools found in the NVSD. Placements of the TCs were both the primary and intermediate levels and will be at the discretion of university and district administrators. Over the course of their thirteen-week practicum experience they were asked to provide the data needed by self reporting their experiences in implementing creative instructional tactics and strategies in their classroom placement. My method of data collection and inquiry into the above questions were centered on a series of three self-reports and three observational records. Both TCs and School Associates (SAs) were provided with a short description and checklist of 15 creative instructional tactics and strategies that are to be tracked. The fifteen strategies were selected based on my own self study and therefore are consistent with tactics and strategies found in *Beyond Monet*.

Teacher Candidates were asked to self-report, using the checklist, their attempts to employ these creative instructional tactics and strategies. School associates were also asked to record their observations of teacher candidates employing these creative instructional tactics and strategies. The two reports were then cross-referenced to see if there was agreement or a discrepancy between the Teacher Candidates' self-reports and the School Associates' observations. Ideally, I hoped to get a sense of whether these reports can be used to measure the frequency of II tactics and strategies during the developmental stages of a teacher's development. I also hoped to be able to determine whether the checklist was a valuable tool for Teacher Candidates and School Associates to open dialogue and reflection of their praxis.

The Findings – What Did I Learn from Climbing My Everest?

Throughout this paper and my process I posed questions that I thought have guided me well and focused my quest to inform my praxis and thus help me to grow as a mentor of Instructionally Intelligent instruction. Specifically, how could I do a bang up job of mentoring the implementation of II when I was unsure of my own practice? Borko & Mayfield (1995) noted that school associates sense of efficacy as a teacher educator plays a substantial role in their ability to play an active role in developing their student teacher. I wondered if my reflective process could be useful in mentoring pre service teachers. I hypothesized that if I were to determine what constitutes best practice for me, then I would be more confident in modeling the experimentation that I believe is required to become a more reflective and effective teacher and therefore have a greater sense of efficacy as a teacher educator. I may not have all the answers but I believe I have informed my praxis through the process of studying my own practice, with the purpose of growing as an educator of my school age students and as a mentor of future pre service teachers. This process helped me to realize which II tactics and strategies I prefer in my own instruction and allowed me to proceed with a checklist that I believe will inform others. I hypothesized that simply having a checklist present would help to guide discussions between the SA and TC about the TC's praxis and would increase the TC's awareness of the II tactics and strategies and therefore the likely hood that they would experiment with these methods.

This was corroborated in my pre service teacher study in two of the three TC-SA relationships tracked by the data collection reports. SA Participant #227 reported in the comments section of the report that,

> Having the list of strategies and tactics has given us a tool to use as a reminder to think about these methods and discuss which ones could be used … We have had many conversations about which strategies she could try during her lesson planning and have made many activities more

> meaningful and enjoyable for the class. I think that future groups of student teachers should use your study during their practicum as a graphic organizer or checklist to make sure they incorporate II strategies in their lesson. It is also a good reminder to sponsor teachers to discuss these tactics with their student teachers.

In the second instance, SA participant #7 reported in their comments section of one of their reports that: "The student teacher is a great role model for me and is reminding me of the value of doing these (II Tactics and Strategies) … some of which I have never tried and I am discovering are very suitable for even the youngest students." It seems that the student teachers' willingness to experiment with II tactics can have a positive effect on the School Associate as well as it does on the student teacher. This is one pattern I did not expect to glean from the pre service teacher study. In hindsight and reflection, this seems to be a very profound way of enabling experienced teachers to refocus their own practice.

I also posed the general questions about the role of educators in supporting pre service teachers in employing creative instructional strategies in a school district that has committed itself to the concept of the Instructional Institute. In creating my study, I had informal discussions with district teachers that had been seconded to teach the UBC FAME cohort in their professional program. I was pleasantly surprised to learn that the cohort was very familiar with II as they used the *Instructional Strategies for K to 12: Strategies for Teaching* document that I used for studying my own practice and for designing my checklist. So it seems that the FAME cohort was teaching the appropriate methods to place teacher candidates in NVSD. I also learned that two of the three School Associates had professional development training in the Instructional Institute which also confirms that, in this case, it seems that the district administrators are selecting appropriate mentors for the training of future teachers in our school district.

Postlude

I started this process or topic of research because of my own experiences as a beginning teacher and later as a mentor teacher. I was dissatisfied with my own experiences and therefore wanted to explore the topic in more detail to see if my experience was an anomaly or just a product of time and place. I believe now that having been on the ground floor of the Instructional Institutes launch that it was a case of grassroots growing pains. It seems that the district has come a long way in nurturing and supporting the school districts own initiative of Instructionally Intelligent teachers.

This could not be made more evident than by studying the frequency in which the pre service teachers experimented in their use of II over the course of my seven-week study. When all the SA reports were tallied it was revealed that all fifteen tactics and strategies were utilized at least once during their practicum. The TC reports revealed that all the tactics and strategies were employed once with the exception of the Four Corner tactic, which went unreported. The SA reports noted that these fifteen tactics and strategies were observed being implemented a total of

46 occurrences over the six-week observation period. The TC self reports indicated that these tactics and strategies were used in 52 occurrences. The reports were divided into three periods with the first SA report, which included ten teaching days from May 3, 2010 – May 14, 2010; it exhibited a frequency of 17 occurrences and the TC reports suggesting a usage of 16 occurrences. In the second report period, from May 17, 2010 – May 28, 2010, the SA observed 12 occurrences and the TC self reported 18 occurrences. From May 31, 2010 – June 11, 2010, the third and final report period, the SA observed the targeted II tactics and strategies being implemented on 17 occurrences. The TC reports for the same period suggested a usage of 18 teaching occurrences. The patterns that emerge from the SA and TC reports indicate that there is a willingness amongst TC to experiment with II tactics and strategies over the course of their practicum experience. This may also indicate that the SAs are being supportive of II in their classrooms. This was indicated by TC participant # 227 in the comments section of their report where they wrote, "I was encouraged to use instructional intelligence during this practicum by my SA."

I recognize that my pre service teacher study is by no means conclusive but it was a worthy endeavor for the simple fact that it informed my praxis and helped me come to terms with what Pearse (2004) suggested is inevitably posed, "What does it all mean?" My praxis has indeed an element of all the components that Pearse suggested is required of reflective praxis. There was an element of action throughout my Masters of Education journey that could be applied to my real world, the classroom. With those forces in play there was most notably a reflective instinct and process that was a perpetual thorn in my brain, accessing the analysis and evaluative levels of metacognition. The analysis of motives, purpose and relevance were constantly looping throughout my cognitive functions. Lastly, the interpretative component is subjective but to me it was a simple conclusion. Once a path is chosen, walked, and toiled upon there will inevitably be learning occurring as long as I remain reflective and cognizant of my own praxis. I can be an effective teacher of II tactics and strategies and I can employ this knowledge to mentor future pre service teachers in methods I believe to be both relevant and profound for my classroom and the young minds that I have the complex responsibility of shaping.

Kevin Ward
North Vancouver School District
KWard@nvsd44.bc.ca

SPENCER KELLY

CREATIVE INSTRUCTIONAL TACTICS AND STRATEGIES IN TEACHING SUMMARY WRITING TO INTERMEDIATE GRADE STUDENTS

Background

I have found that change is good. Just as I was to commence conducting this inquiry, I experienced a move to a new elementary school, in which I could explore my teaching practice. My move to a new school has been professionally and intellectually invigorating.

My new school has eight divisions of approximately 180 students, with two administrators, seven full time equivalent teachers, and ten special education aids (i.e., SEAs). The morning bell goes at 8:40 am, yet the first students start arriving at 7:30 am as the school is a safe place for all the members of the school community. The bell at day's end sounds at 2:35 pm, and the bulk of the students file into the Boys' & Girls' Club that offers after school care and additional programs that enrich students' lives.

My class is an intermediate class with 28 students from a variety of cultural and linguistic backgrounds. Within this group, six are designated learning disabled and there is one child with autism who garners full time SEA support for the class.

With my degree focused upon curriculum development, specifically the use of Instructional Intelligence (II) tactics and strategies, I wanted to explore the use of II outside of where I have utilized it, Science and Social Studies. I define Instructional Intelligence as tactics and strategies that allow students to develop their own understanding of a concept. This constructionist approach allows me to facilitate the lessons, as students engage in learning, often in small groups. I value this method of teaching because it empowers the pupils as they create their own meanings of the concept. I find II to be much more effective in students' retention of the concepts than direct teaching. II offers students non-threatening activities that enable all students to participate within the safety of a pair or small group. I use II across the curriculum; I was introduced to the tactics as a student teacher about ten years ago and have infused my teaching with II tactics and strategies ever since. It has also been beneficial that the North Vancouver School District (NVSD44) has supported II by holding a Summer Institute yearly for the last six years to train staff on the application and use of II in a classroom setting.

My original ideas for this project had to do with using II in staff meetings and then using II to prepare Grade 7s, the grade I have taught for the past seven years, for the province-wide Foundation Skills Assessment (FSA) testing. My school colleagues deemed the first idea as an awkward topic to research because I would

P. Gouzouasis (ed.), Pedagogy in a New Tonality: Teacher Inquiries on Creative Tactics, Strategies, Graphics Organizers, and Visual Journals in the K-12 Classroom, 103–119.

no longer be an active participant in the meetings, just an observer. The latter idea was changed out of necessity; I was teaching grades that did not participate in the testing (only Grades 4 and 7 complete the FSA). With wide ranging abilities and needs within the class, I wanted to be able to challenge all my students. No students were left out of the study due to a learning disability. After the first term in my new school, in a new classroom and a new grade level (leaving Grade 7 for 5/6), I began to see an academic weakness that I thought II might serve as a useful tool in teaching: summary writing.

Having completed *The Westing Game* (Raskin, 1978) as a guided novel in which summary writing was an aspect covered, the need to focus solely on summary writing became apparent. Some students had difficulty extracting crucial information to create summaries from texts. Often students would paraphrase the opening paragraph of the chapter as their summary attempt. After a few lessons of directly teaching summary writing the summaries improved, but important information was not being included in the students' work. I questioned whether the students understood the text, but the Reader's Responses they produced indicated they understood the storyline and the story's concepts; they were able to personally connect to the novel on many levels. Yet their summaries were insufficient, missing key events or including too many details that were not vital to the retelling of the text. Direct teaching summary skills were not effective in boosting student writing to the grade level standards, and the learning disabled students demonstrated next to no improvement.

The challenge was three fold: improving student comprehension while they read both fiction and non-fiction texts; identifying the main events/facts and some important supporting details from the text; and constructing a concise paragraph that effectively summarizes the original text.

With the reading component already being addressed through Guided Reading activities that were done twice a week, I needed to focus my attention to the second of two challenges. I would rely heavily upon the II documents, *Beyond Monet* (Bennett and Rolheiser, 2001), *Writing 44* (NVSD#44, 2007), and *The Developing Writer* (Abbotsford School District #34, n.d.) curriculum documents to help improve and refine student writing. These three documents would provide the basis of the activities that I, as the facilitator, would use to engage the students. My biggest challenge was the order and pacing of the activities for the greatest understanding, and hence improvement, of the basic concepts of summary writing. I considered identifying the main events (reading) activities first, followed by paragraph writing lessons. I also considered the opposite, with intensive writing lessons preceding the reading. After due consideration, I decided on a mixture of reading and writing as it would teach the students that the two are analogous skills that would compliment my teaching outcome. Summarization is a life-skill in both effective written and oral communication; it is needed for future academic success, a skill that successful pupils have acquired but for other pupils needs to be taught.

Methodology

The goal of the combined lessons was to enable the students to achieve greater summarization skills. This was monitored through student work, through student reflections on how they perceived their increased proficiency and understanding of the applicable strategies, but especially on my own reflections and thoughts on how the process of teaching the concept was being ascertained by my students. My reflections and analysis of each lesson are embedded within each II lesson to illustrate my thinking as the class progressed through the unit.

My role in conducting this inquiry with the class is one of being a reflective, reflexive practitioner. By being reflective and reflexive, I was able to adapt the learning process in the class to meet students' academic needs in understanding new concepts and the effective application of their summary writing skills. In context of an action research narrative, I will communicate my evolving understanding of the teaching process through my classroom experience; students will teach me what are successful methods.

Data is presented in the form of student reflections on the learning process and the work produced by the activities. The student products will be compared to their earlier work to see if improvement is occurring at both the individual student and class wide level.

For each section herein, I will briefly explain the tactic used and the concept I wanted students to learn from the lesson. I will then move on to describe what occurred in the class and how students responded to the activity, concluding each section with my reflections and analysis of the activity.

Lessons and Teacher Actions

It should be noted that the class had previous exposure to all II tactics and strategies used in this unit with me earlier in the school year. I did not want students struggling with a new activity in addition to trying to understand the concepts being taught; I wanted them to focus on learning one item at a time. With this in mind, I introduced II into the classroom's culture early in the school year through a review of last year's content; new tactics with familiar concepts allowed students to become aquatinted with II. This empowered the students to know the activities and the associated topic-specific language when the new concepts were introduced.

The II writing activities were specific to summary writing and paragraph construction, and were new to the students. However, throughout the year writing lessons were done on a weekly basis with the class in the form of guided writing lessons. In these lessons everything from basic grammar to sentence structure was addressed.

Setting the Environment: Class Meetings

I held weekly class meetings at the commencement of the year to set expectations for students when participating in group work, and held another at the beginning of the study to remind students of what behavior I expected. I needed to reinforce a positive and cooperative tone in class before commencing the study. As a class we agreed that we would all need to be respectful when working with classmates, this included giving people the chance to talk and listen to what others had to contribute to the discussion. I also stated that it was "okay" to disagree with others, but that these moments were opportunities for students to be open to new ideas and debate the issue in order to clarify their meaning.

Assessing the Data: Rubric Development

I wanted to know if the work the students and I were doing had a positive effect on their ability to communicate written main ideas from a text. With this in mind, I set out to have each student set a baseline in summary writing. My students were familiar with using rubrics and so I looked for a rubric that covered both writing ability and inclusion of the main events of a text. I started with the "Quick Reference" rubrics developed by the British Columbia Ministry of Education (http://www.bced.gov.bc.ca/perf_stands/writing.htm) for reading and writing, but found them to be too broad in purpose for the specific skill I was investigating. I turned to *Rubistar*, a web based rubric generating site for assistance (www.ribistar.4teachers.org), and found it helpful and so utilized some wording from its recommendations. I needed to further refine the rubric for the present inquiry so I incorporated some of the language from the Ministry's examples into my rubric. With the summary writing rubric completed (see Table 1 below), I selected reading material for the exercises.

Selecting the Readings

Choosing appropriate reading material was challenging given the Grade 5/6 class. Do I aim for a reading selection in the middle of the two grades (end of five, beginning of 6)? Additionally, I needed to address the huge range of reading ability within the class, ranging from Grade 2 to high school. How do I cater to these needs? I decided to select Grade 5 and 6 curricular materials. I came to the realization that the students will be facing grade level texts, regardless of their individual abilities, but that I as the teacher, in conjunction with my SEAs, could assist those students that had difficulty reading and writing. For many reading assignments, I usually have a tape or MP3 audio file to which a student can listen. Additionally, a peer or myself might read the text to an individual or a small group as they follow along. To adapt the writing portion of the assignments, I would have the SEA scribe for one student, while three others would use their NEOs (NB: NEOs are word processing units that resemble a laptop that can be used by individuals at their desks. It is used to assist students with written output difficulties).

The Study in Action: Learning to Summarize

The starting point was to have students produce a baseline representative of where the students are in their summary writing abilities. Summary writing is a skill (i.e., learned), not an ability (i.e., innate). I chose a one page, non-fictional text on Michael Jordan (Christopher, 2002). My class had recently completed a Physical Education basketball unit, and they were eager players. I believed that the topic would interest the children and the writing style was aimed at an easy intermediate reading level. I also thought the chronological retelling of Michael Jordan's life would allow students to find important facts about the athlete; each era of his life had a separate paragraph to help guide fact-finding.

After explaining to the group the purpose of the writing exercise, that this would set a baseline to which a final summary would be compared, I asked the students to try to summarize the page in a paragraph from five to ten sentences long. As students did their page set-up, I handed out the passage. What followed was not expected.

While some students quietly started to read, a lot of them highlighting and underlining segments of the biography, a few rebelled, refusing to read and participate in the activity. One child simply quietly wrote a story about her father, and yet another simply stated to me that this activity was "... not how this cow moos!" After calming this small, yet vocal group, they did try to complete the assignment. The results of the exercise reaffirmed that the class needed to improve summary writing. When assessing their work on the summary writing rubric, nine students were "Approaching Expectations," another nine "Minimally Meeting Expectations," six "Meeting Expectations," and four "Fully Meeting Expectations."

Table 1. Our summary writing rubric

Aspect	*Approaching expectations 1*	*Minimally meets expectations 2*	*Meets expectations 3*	*Fully meets expectations 4*
Topic sentence	There is no clear introduction of the main topic or structure of the paper.	Introduction states the main topic, does not adequately preview the structure of the paper; not particularly inviting to reader.	Introduction clearly states the main topic and previews the structure of the paper, but not particularly inviting to the reader.	Introduction is inviting, states the main topic and previews the structure of the paper.
Meaning	Some info may be inaccurate or copied. Few details; may be irrelevant or repetitive.	Generally accurate, but may omit key points. Includes details and examples; some may be irrelevant/ inaccurate.	Generally accurate, complete, and in own words. Some relevant details and examples.	Information is well chosen, thorough, in own words. Specific details or examples.

Table 1. (continued)

Form	Some of the paragraph information connects to the topic sentence. Conclusion is missing. Connections are awkward.	Most of the paragraph information connects to the topic sentence. Conclusion is abrupt. Connections are awkward.	Paragraph information connects to the topic sentence. Conclusion sums up the topic. Sentences linked.	All paragraph information connects to topic sentence. Conclusion sums up the topic, has impact. Flows smoothly.
Grammar	Frequent errors interfere with meaning.	Some noticeable errors; these may cause the reader to hesitate or reread parts to confirm meaning.	Few errors; these do not interfere with meaning.	Sense of control; few errors, usually the result of taking risks to use complex language or structure.

Those students, who were working at the approaching and minimally meeting levels, relied heavily on paraphrasing, and did not include important details that were critical to understanding the article. These students also had difficulty organizing the information, and although the article was presented chronologically, these pupils did not present the information systematically, instead adding details, some extraneous, to their summary paragraph.

THINK/PAIR/SHARE: WHAT IS A SUMMARY?

In a Think/Pair/Share (T/P/S) activity, students will first independently form an opinion or answer to a statement or question. Then, with a partner, they will explore and politely challenge each other's thoughts, allowing them to clarify, add to, or even change their reaction. After a brief discussion with a partner, the whole group comes together to explore the differing ideas present in the class. I find the benefit of T/P/S is that students realize that others often have similar reactions to the statement or question, and my current class is more than willing to share their feelings or what they think about a topic with the group.

As an introductory activity, I also appreciate T/P/S because it gives me a chance to learn students' level of understanding when a new concept is initially unveiled; the amount of background knowledge the group has may lead me to adjust the activities that follow.

I asked the class to consider two questions on the first day of the unit to gauge what should follow: "What is a summary?" and "What is the job of a summary?"

The students were given 30 seconds to consider the questions in turn, 45 seconds to share with a partner, and then I asked for volunteers to present their ideas to be recorded. After the difficulty some students had with the summary writing, I was happy that most students wanted to participate in this section.

The first question, "What is a summary?" garnered these responses from the class: *telling what happened without reading the book, preview of something you read, tell somebody about the book, only important stuff, main points of what you read, something that explains something that happens, know what a book's about, what happens in book without the detail, on the back of books.* I found it interesting that although I did not specifically relate summaries to literature, most of the ideas relate to fiction. Only "something that explains something that happens" seems comparatively unrelated to books. With this in mind, I felt confident that the class knew the characteristics of a summary. I moved onto the next question.

The class was equally eager to inform me "What is the job of a summary?" Before the T/P/S, I encouraged students to focus upon the job of the summary: what is the advantage of the summary over the full text or story? As a result, their opinions were completely different from the first set of responses: *tells main points, summarizes book, quick version of book, simpler/short version, understand "missed" sections, introduces characters, introduces story, shares main ideas of what happens in a story.* I find it compelling that all these answers, and the conversations between students that I heard, all indicate that students were speaking of summaries in terms of fictional texts. It might be because the class has, up until this point, only done minor work of summarizing non-fiction texts; their predominate experience within my class has been summarizing and analyzing fictional books. Having completed this activity, I had a strong indication from the class that they knew what a summary does, but I sought to expand their repertoire to include fact-based texts as well. This response also indicated that I needed to incorporate summary writing in a variety of subject areas, not just Language Arts. I need students to do more work with non-fiction. Since this activity, I have been using Science and Social Studies texts more frequently, especially to build students' background knowledge on a subject.

CRAZY CREATIONS

Following the summary activity, I wanted to have the students writing in order to strengthen their skills. I started with "Crazy Creations" from *The Developing Writer* (Abbotsford School District #34, n.d.). In the past I have found that students enjoy this activity, although they can sometimes become frustrated due to unintentional outcomes. In this activity, students "write a descriptive paragraph(s) that will be clear and detailed enough that another students, upon reading the description, can draw image(s) easily."

I started the session by providing each individual with a blank, letter size piece of paper and instructed the students to create a large, line drawing of an object. At this point I provided no other instruction, wanting students to be free to draw whatever they felt like without restricting them with further information. After three minutes, and before anyone was finished their image, I had students put down their pencils and observe my example of the activity. On the overhead I drew an oversimplified drawing of a door, and in point form we listed information someone would need to draw the door, using neutral language that would not give away the object (e.g., doorknob). With this in mind, some students either redrew or altogether changed their drawings so that they could adequately write instructions on how to draw their object. As I circulated throughout the class, students remarked to me that the level of detail needed to communicate how to replicate their image was difficult, with the majority of children bringing out rulers to precisely measure the length of lines and debating on how to describe curves in their art. After a few minutes of writing drafts, we again stopped and reflected that, like many step-by-step drawing books that the kids use, it was a good idea to break down their figures into basic shapes that could be assembled in order to create the desired picture. Their assignment was to complete their drawing and instructional paragraphs for the following day.

The first drafts were collected and randomly distributed among the children; the goal was to try to replicate the original drawing from the instructions, but few students were able to successfully draw anything that resembled an object, let alone the intended outcome. After hearing their frustration under their breaths, I inquired if anyone was having difficulty deciphering the instructions. An overwhelming "YES" was my answer, and the drawing attempts and the instructions were returned to the author. Laughter quickly spread as kids saw that the descriptions that they thought were clear resulted in misshapen diagrams that bore no resemblance to the original illustration.

As a group we then brainstormed a vocabulary list that might aid them in adjusting the paragraphs for effective communication. We turned to Math texts to assist us, pulling words such as *parallel*, *horizontal*, *vertical*, *perpendicular*, and *diagonal* to add to the paragraphs. It was also noted by several students that simply adding *left* or *right* would greatly clarify the instructions. With that in mind, adjustments were made.

One student in particular made huge gains in the clarity of her writing. Unhappy with her first attempt to render her drawing into comprehendible writing, she decided to start afresh with a new image as her focus. She simplified her picture and, as she drew, focused on the steps she used to create the illustration. Here is her example; I urge you to try following the directions.

DRAWING WRITING

> "First start with your paper horizontal. Now put two small brackets that meet together. Under the two small brackets sketch a medium circle. Now we are going to make adjustments in the circle and erase some of the circle. On the left side draw a small semicircle from the top to the bottom then erase the circle par on it. On the bottom part of the circle put a small semicircle going up then erase the circle part on this too. On the top put a "V." Now erase the circle on it, too."

The student also did some reverse engineering; she tried to have the instructions be based on a few simple shapes that were then adjusted to depict the image she wanted. Although not the only one to utilize this process, I believe that this is a good example of what the children accomplished when confronted with the problem of representing an illustration, however simple, as a set of written instructions.

The final product was typed, and on the back, hidden from the audience, the students drew their "answer" images so the participants could check their creations with what the writer had wanted. These were sent to the other Grade 5/6 class to be completed by an audience that had not had exposure to the writing process. The outcomes were still not as the students expected.

I had my students, who were laughing at what the other class had drawn, write a quick reflection in response to what had become of their instructions. The class was evenly divided into four groups in their remarks. One group, although noting that the picture was not identical to their original, commented that they really were happy with their set of directions and would not change anything. Another group had wanted to have the reader put more effort into the drawing, questioning whether the reader comprehended the directions. The last two groupings looked solely at the writing, with one group realizing that their comments were too complicated to complete, while the last group reflected that the level of detail in their paragraph was not at the level needed to replicate the image.

Crazy Creations assisted the summary writing process because it forced students to be selective in the language they used to communicate their ideas. Their writing needed to be concise and accurate, with no extra details beyond the direct information on how to replicate the image. It was also useful because students thought about the importance of sequencing within a paragraph. Like a summary, the order of the instructions had an impact on how the reader perceives the outcome.

My student's example? An apple, a logo the student felt would be known to most people, yet difficult to explain how to replicate without using key language (i.e., *apple*, *stem*) that would ruin the surprise of the creation.

THINK/PAIR/SHARE: PARAGRAPHING IS IMPORTANT

I incorporated a brief lesson on why we paragraph and basic paragraphing rules from *The Developing Writer* (Abbotsford School District #34, n.d.) and added the T/P/S tactic. I had them initially make a list of why and when a writer starts a new paragraph, encouraging them to look at the books they are currently reading. They all got books out and started to scan, jotting down ideas as they came across them. Once in pairs, the activity continued as the pupils compared notes and started comparing examples of what they were finding in the novels.

As a class they identified six reasons of why a new paragraph is needed: *new speaker, change of setting, new idea introduced (change of topic or describing different people), offset beginning, change of time, offset conclusion.* I was very impressed with the class; in a span of ten minutes they had found the reasons I had wanted them to find. Next, I had them share/read some of the examples they had found. I did not have to do the direct teaching I thought I would be needed.

THINK/PAIR/SHARE SUMMARY: FLY AWAY HOME

With all the previous activities being concentrated on paragraphing, I then started combining summarization with writing. Identical to the T/P/S activity already mentioned, the students will first independently, then in pairs, complete a summary of the picture book *Fly Away Home* (Bunting, 1991) that was read to the class. Afterwards, the class constructed a communal summary based upon the summaries that they prepared in pairs. This was followed by discussion as to why events were, or were not, included.

To begin the lesson I reminded the students of the format of T/P/S and that their partner in this activity would be the person adjacent to them and that they would be accountable for participating in the lesson.

I read the book and asked the students to make predictions about the book based upon the cover illustration. All the guesses offered publicly inferred that the cover depicted a father and son going on a trip given the packed bags and airport locale. A few students hinted at the somber facial expressions and predicted that the trip may have a sad purpose, or that they were leaving a sad place. These student responses reminded me of the power of illustrations in books, and I shared that the students might want to pay close attention to the pictures because the illustrations often add detail and emotion to the plot of the story.

I read the story, and often stopped to answer clarifying questions the students had concerning the plight of the main characters. The story revolves around a father and son who are homeless and have taken refuge in a massive airport. The story is told from the young boy's perspective, and my older students could infer from the family's experience to how difficult and sad their existence is in the airport's corridors; hiding from security and constantly moving between gates.

A student inquired if notes would be needed and I said it was an option and a good habit to keep track of the plot. As a result, approximately three-quarters of the children opted to keep some form of written record.

Once I completed reading, I gave the students a minute to organize their information, asking them to narrow the events they had to between eight and ten items. I then asked them to turn to the person next to them and for another minute compare thoughts about what was needed to communicate the story as efficiently as possible. Conversation was loud and animated as students, for the most part, agreed what should be included in the summary. Finally we came together to make a summary as a group.

We ended up making a web on the board because although the plot was presented in a linear fashion, the students were making connections between events that were not in the book chronologically. For example, the detail that the mother had died became massive in my students' minds: what ramifications of the death led the father and son seeking shelter in the airport? The seemingly minor detail that the pair always wore plain clothing becomes increasingly important when we learn of other homeless individuals being escorted out of the airport for not adequately blending in with the travelers. The summary that was formed also relied on symbolism, with the stranded bird standing for the hope of freedom and acquiring a home the boy had at the conclusion of the story.

At the end of the activity we agreed that although the major events need to be included to form an effective summary, it is sometimes necessary to retain some minor details to maintain the integrity of the plot.

PARAGRAPH PUZZLE

In this exercise from *Writing 44* (NVSD#44, p. 148), students took existing texts that were cut up, mixed up, and they pieced them together. The emphasis was on the clues that give away the sequence of the sentences within a paragraph. This was followed by class discussion concerning what patterns and clues they used from the texts.

I selected paragraphs from three novels that are for late intermediate students and would be challenging and promote discussion in the groups: *The House of the Scorpion* (Farmer, 2002), *The Thief* (Whalen Turner, 1996), and *The City of Ember* (DuPrau, 2003). All the passages were from the books' first chapter, and included language that gave clues to the sequencing of the information. At the time of this activity I had completed *The City of Ember* as a read aloud book for the class, knowing all students could relate and contribute to the discussion. A few students had read Nancy Farmer's book, and no one had read *The Thief* as I had withheld the book from students because it was to be a Literature Circles novel later in the term.

I formed seven predetermined groups of four, with all the groups having a Grade 6 boy and girl and a Grade 5 boy and girl; each group of students represented a mixture of student strengths. Before the puzzles were distributed, we went over the rules for this activity. As a group their job was to reconstruct the paragraph in the order the author intended, without outside help (some wanted to use the books or the internet to find the correct results). They were limited to the clues within the text for the order the sentences would be placed. I encouraged them to discuss the sentences and what clues they may or may not contain, and to do one paragraph at a time. To keep the groups focused, I timed the activity allowing for four minutes per paragraph for a total of twelve minutes to debate the sentence sequencing. Every four minutes I advised the students to move onto the next paragraph, but the groups were very fluid in their actions, finishing one then moving to the next, then double checking the previous work as new thoughts sprang up while working with new material. With time up, and a final check, the groups seemed happy with their decisions and were eager to hear the "answers."

But before finding the sentence order, I had the groups go back with this question in mind: "What clues in the paragraph gave away the order?" After a few minutes of discussion, the children offered these thoughts: *whether or not it makes sense, grouped sentences that are about the same thing, helps if you know the story, by how it was cut, what makes sense, a good feeling about it, some words are in the same sentence.* With these ideas as a point of reference, I read the paragraphs as the author had intended.

For *The House of the Scorpion*, most groups' responses were fairly close, with the only line "All that was hidden in the droplet" proving difficult. The groups agreed that this line, in particular, could be placed in a variety of positions within the paragraph meaning an exact placement would be guesswork; the language did not suggest a position.

The Thief proved even more difficult, with only a single group out of the seven groups matching the original paragraph. Groups felt that there was a lack of clues to signal where specific sentences would be placed. I disagreed, stating that some of the pronouns could be used to mark a sequence (e.g., "he" would have to refer to a proper noun that preceded it) and that similar material would be grouped together (i.e. everything about the chains and how they felt), a detail a group had pointed out during the discussion.

Four of the seven groups sequenced *The City of Ember* to match the novel. I think students had the most success with this passage for a few reasons. Having been a read aloud book, many students had a vague notion of the novel's events and could use this knowledge to assist them in reconstructing the paragraph. Also, the students felt the language in this set of clues provided the most information for them.

I believe this lesson was highly successful in having the children utilize language in a way they had not previously done. In hindsight, I think I misplaced this activity in my design; I should have placed this right before the drawing instructions activity. However, having placed it before the writing lesson, it would have provided students with ideas on using language to provide readers with clues.

CONVERSATION LINES

Conversation Lines (also known as Consultation Lines) is an II tactic I was introduced to on the first day of class for my Master's program. My students read an article about the fishing industry in British Columbia (Francis, 2000) that was tied to Social Studies and Science units. We also had an aquarium with salmon eggs in the classroom. I learned from selecting a text for the baseline and chose something from the easier side of the reading scale; my hope was all students would participate at a greater intensity than before and get involved in the activity, and therefore learn and understand the concepts surrounding summaries.

Before they began the activity, as a class we reviewed note taking and the purpose of summaries, then they read the three-page article and took point form notes. Students used the notes to construct a point form summary that they would share, albeit safely, with only one other student at a time. Students formed two parallel rows with their chairs and told a partner sitting across from them their summary. After a minute, the partners switched roles, and the summarizing student listened to their partner's version of the article. Next, one line shifted over by one chair and the process was repeated. Depending upon the length of the article, each student needs to talk, and listen, for about a minute each before moving onto the next partner. The entire activity is conducted with the summary and pen in hand, so notes may be made if needed to improve or alter their work.

What I like about this activity is the safety it allows the students; children can make adjustments between their retellings. Listening students will also review the effectiveness of their summary compared to that of the telling student. I have also modified the lines so that one line of stronger students will retell their summary to weaker students several times before the weaker student takes over and shares their summary. This allows the weaker student to hear several effective summaries before retelling, allowing more time to listen and incorporate facts and details they may have missed in their original summary attempt.

With the students set, I had them talk and listen for five times each; most children had more than enough information to talk for a minute and I encouraged those students to go back and try to eliminate some details. Exactly what did the other person need to know? What were the article's big ideas?

A few students were finished speaking with lots of time left. I asked these children to listen closely to their partner's summary, add more to their notes, and include more information the next time they spoke. These students became frustrated with the process, but I kept listening in on their conversations and they did talk for longer durations about the given topic.

THINK/PAIR/SHARE SUMMARY: ANGEL GIRL

With many T/P/S activities already successfully completed, I thought that this one would be done easily by the class—just another bit of practice of pulling out the big ideas from a text. I was wrong.

Since I was going to be reading the article to the class, I planned on reading *Mandela* (Schiller, 1999) to them: a short, biographical article about the man and his rise to power. The text was targeted for Grade 7 students, but since I was reading the text and the text was connected to an earlier conversation on racism and apartheid, I believed that the students would be able to connect to the article. The language of the article was not difficult, but the information was not presented in a chronological order and presented some abstract political concepts. That led to the class being confused.

I stopped the activity and the next day started anew with the picture book *Angel Girl* (Friedman, 2008), a true story about childhood in Nazi Germany. The students could connect to this story as it dealt with the difficulties of growing up amid war and the class really made a connection to the hardships the characters faced. With T/P/S lessons similar to this one previously conducted, the students knew what to expect and all took notes to enhance their ability to share their thoughts afterward.

They moved into pairs, and after a brief comparison of notes I grouped two pairs together forming seven groups. Their task was to come up with a "Master List" of the main events of the fact based story, aiming for just eight to ten events and big ideas from the plot. With these refined summaries, I inquired whether or not it was more difficult with a larger group to share information and opinions. The overwhelming answer was yes; the pupils summated that they had very different ways of doing things and put emphasis on different aspects of the story as well. This resulted in some people being detail oriented while others really wanted to get to the bare essentials of the story.

From this discussion I realized that, although the class was gaining proficiency at drawing information out of texts, I needed to do more on eliminating superfluous details from the summaries the pupils were creating. I briefly reminded them that details would have to be eliminated to keep summaries concise.

PUNCHY PARAGRAPH

In this paragraphing assignment from *The Developing Writer* (Abbotsford School District #34, n.d.), students were focused on proper paragraph form, specifically the topic sentence followed by approximately five supporting sentences. They could select their own topic, allowing students to write about a topic with which they are comfortable, have experience and, as a result, write from a position of power; they *are* the expert.

We reviewed the purpose of topic sentences and agreed that its job was to capture the reader's interest. I had students examine a sample paragraph, and had pairings discuss whether or not all the information was connected to the first sentence. They all concurred that all the details had a direct relationship to the topic sentence.

After a brief research period using both texts and the Internet, students wrote their drafts. I noticed an improvement in the use of effective topic sentences when introducing the topic and the ability to stay on topic without including extraneous information. As a result the focused paragraphs were easier to read than the baseline paragraphs the students wrote.

SUMMARIZING NON-FICTION TEXTS

The Developing Writer (Abbotsford School District #34, n.d.) supplies the lesson Summarizing Non-Fiction Texts, through which students are focused upon what constitutes a strong summary. Students had written short summaries that I had not evaluated, and in this lesson they were paired and exchanged their summaries. Pupils silently read each other's papers with the following questions in mind.

If you hadn't read the text, would you understand it from the summary? Why?
Is there anything important that should be added to the summary? What is it?
Is there anything unimportant that could be left out of the summary? What is it?

After reading, the pairs gave each other a review of each other's summaries with these questions leading their discussions. I noticed that if the summary was well written, the pupil discussions were brief; they did not have much to share beyond the first discussion point.

When I opened the discussion to the entire class, students recounted their private discussions. In response to the first question, students remarked that some summaries were difficult to read because they offered little information or had left in too much to be considered an effective summary. One student commented that their partner had in fact written a reader's response, and although started writing a summary had included their emotional response to the information as well.

The second question garnered very few comments from students, which I interpreted positively because it meant that the class' summaries were growing stronger. One frustrated student stated that her partner did not communicate the big idea; she was unsure what she was supposed to gain from the summary. Another remarked that although the summary included all the necessary information, he felt the sequencing of the information could have been better presented for the reader.

The final discussion point produced the greatest number of responses, and mirrors the first question in what students noticed in each other's writing. Again, too much detail, not focused on the big idea, and emotional responses were problems pupils found in the writing. But another aspect was also commented upon, the context of the writing. A student mentioned the importance of the topic sentence to establish the paragraph's content, and that in the summary she read the topic sentence did not completely match the paragraph's information. This led me to remind the class of the importance of topic sentences, and how it can easily mislead the reader.

An interesting element arose in connection to the second and third questions; should the author's name be included in the summary? I stated that it would help the reader by providing context if you included the title and the author's name in the summary. I related it to my own schoolwork for my Master's, and that other people might be interested in reading the original article or story. If you supply the information for the reader, it is easier for them to locate and enjoy the text you summarized.

I included this activity for two reasons, both I believe were achieved. This lesson allows students to practice their summary writing skills without the pressure of knowing that I will be evaluating their writing. I encouraged them to experiment with their writing. Additionally, it permitted students to read summaries written by their classmates, so they could discuss what they were doing in their writing.

Summative Evaluation

At the end of the project, the students read a grade level article on culture and how different cultures use their environment to meet their needs (Powrie & Sterling, 2001). The article also signified the completion of a Social Studies unit on endangered cultures and how cultures sustain themselves. The article was considerably longer than the single page article upon which the baseline summary was written. This was done to really test my students' abilities to obtain the major points from the article while eliminating details that would clutter the summary.

Before I distributed the article, I had the class brainstorm the role of a summary: a *brief summary of what happened, take out unneeded stuff, shorter version of original, easy way to describe it.* I used this as a reminder to the class of what their task was with the article. I continued the brainstorming process when it came to writing paragraphs. When asked what their paragraph needed, the class replied as follows: *a topic sentence, a description - some big details, indent, stay on topic, a concluding sentence.* At this point one pupil remarked that they would have to follow the paragraph hamburger model that was hanging in the class. I then distributed the student sheet, with the rubric on one side and the reverse side had space for the written summary. We went over the rubric, reminding the students that the key to success was an effective topic sentence, with supporting details within a paragraph form. I scheduled the time allotted for the work to be open ended, with students submitting their work and continuing on with other activities.

The work my class completed in writing summaries was effective. When compared to the baseline summary, the summative summary illustrated that pupils did improve their work. The level that were ‘approaching expectations’ fell from nine to four, ‘minimally meets expectations’ declined from nine to three, while those that were meeting or fully meeting expectations rose from ten to twenty-one. Overall, the summaries were much easier to read; correct paragraph formation and including only the big ideas of a single topic meant the paragraphs were focused.

The biggest improvements I observed in student writing was the ability to remain focused upon a single topic within the paragraph. The connections between sentences were also well linked, resulting in a better *flow* of their writing. One aspect that I believe could still be improved are concluding sentences; most were too abrupt to adequately capture the meaning of the paragraph.

Supplementary Activities

I had supplementary activities that I did not implement during the inquiry. The first activity to be deleted was a Place Mat summary: students would first independently, then in groups of four, complete a summary of a non-fiction article that is read to the class. Afterwards, the class would construct a communal summary based upon the summaries prepared in pairs. Discussion was to follow regarding why events were or were not included. I believed that this overlapped with the T/P/S and Conversation Lines strategies and that based upon the success of those activities further practice was unneeded; students had already completed multiple summaries with a variety of texts.

Sequential Transitions from *Writing 44* (NVSD#44, 2007, p.131) was another writing assignment that could have been utilized had I felt it necessary. A paragraph would be written with the emphasis on effective communication of events in a specific order. In this second exercise, students will write a paragraph of simple instructions on how to prepare a sandwich. Based on the directions, another student will follow them in an attempt to build the sandwich (or other simple task). This was omitted due to the strong similarities to “Crazy Creations;” I do not think the students needed more practice in the careful wording of a sequence. Also, the class took considerable time and care creating the drawing instructions, so I felt completing this would be redundant; the students had already demonstrated a sufficient understanding of the concept.

Additionally, with the year end looming time became a major consideration, and I did not want to rush the process. If I felt it was warranted, I was prepared to include these, as well as additional T/P/S and Conversation Lines for students to practice and reinforce their summary skills. However, students were prepared for the summative assessment on the unit.

Analysis

At the outset of this study, I intended these lessons to be a short-term unit to provide a “boost” to student skill. Given the amount of curriculum needed to be covered, I learned that a focused four to six week unit was often more effective in terms of student performance in skill development than longer units. I also considered that two segments would be useful for teaching partners to divide the work or, my preference, for a Learning Assistance Centre (LAC) teacher to team teach the activities. LAC becomes socially awkward in upper grades, so bringing the LAC teacher into the classroom provides the opportunity for students to learn from two experts. Occasionally the LAC teacher was able to co-teach a lesson with me. She was able to insert her knowledge as well as spend time with those students who possessed written output difficulties to frame their thoughts.

With these considerations in mind, I feel, and the student improvement suggests, that the focused unit was the correct approach. The intense pacing and the variety of activities enabled students to constantly practice their skills; if the program had been drawn out the repetition could result in student disinterest. Better they apply their new skill set in Literature Circles, Science, and Social Studies classes.

One thing that I would do in the future is to introduce this unit at the beginning of the school year, empowering the students to use and continue developing the skill throughout the year. Also, this unit would provide a good basis for intermediate students in paragraphing. Although I would do it at the beginning of the year, there are drawbacks to the application of the unit so early in the year. I spent considerable time introducing and having my students practice the II tactics I used in this unit (e.g., T/P/S/ and Conversation Lines). Doing so enabled the students to focus on the concepts, not the process of the activity. I am hesitant to introduce both II and a new concept on the same occasion; the students may be so process oriented that the understanding of the concept would be lost. Two new concepts might be too confusing.

The nature of the unit also leant itself well to reporting. The baseline compared to the summative assessment also empowered me to accurately comment on student performance in relation to the government's performance standards. I was able to comment on paragraph writing, summarization skill, as well as the ability to draw main facts from a grade level text when writing Language Arts report card remarks.

Completing this study also enlightened me to my classroom practice. I will use more non-fiction texts in the future. I have been too reliant upon fiction to teach the writing component, but with the selection of curricular readings available, I can provide my students with greater background knowledge, a variety of reading materials, and a better understanding of the concepts. This is especially true for Science and Social Studies, where I often use readings to supplement the activities that are occurring in the class. The implementation of these particular II activities will be a springboard for incorporating II strategies into other areas of my teaching given the positive results in summary writing achieved by the class.

Spencer Kelly
North Vancouver School District 44
SpencerKelly@nvsd44.bc.ca

KATHERINE ROSS

THE IMPLEMENTATION OF CREATIVE INSTRUCTIONAL STRATEGIES AND TACTICS IN A LATE FRENCH IMMERSION CLASSROOM

You Want Me to Do What?

For most teachers I know the idea of a Professional Development Day is exciting, a day without our students, a day to converse with other teachers in similar classrooms around the district or province, collecting valuable resources and strategies to incorporate into our classrooms. I always start looking at the workshops in advance, hoping that someday it will say something, anything, with "Late French Immersion" in the title, but to date, I have been sorely disappointed. I am one of a handful of Late French Immersion teachers in the province of British Columbia, and until recently was the only Grade 7 LFI teacher in North Vancouver School District (NVSD).

When I was interviewed for the position of LFI Grade 7 teacher, I had very little understanding of the program itself. A product of the Early French Immersion (EFI) program, I had a general understanding of what goes on in a traditional EFI classroom, but the Late French Immersion classroom was a complete mystery to me. I was a high school French as a Second Language (FSL) teacher, and was ill equipped for my new job. I immediately set about researching how to teach an entire language in two years, while still keeping up with an intensive Grade 7 curriculum. I found very little to assist me with my new job, that is, nothing that really inspired faith that I could meet this task. I observed numerous EFI classes, looking for anything to help me out, but quickly realized that a traditional teacher-centered learning environment would probably not work with my students.

On the first day of my new teaching assignment, I quickly realized that I was in over my head. The students were eager to learn French, but struggled to understand what I was saying even at a slow pace, the textbooks were something that most Francophone Grade 7 students would struggle with using, and we had a lot of ground to cover in a few months. I had my work cut out for me. After spending a few days in the classroom, it was obvious that the majority of my students were "talkers," so I knew that's where I had to start. They loved to talk, so I just had to figure out how to get them talking about various subject matter in French. I started with some basic cooperative learning teaching and learning ideas, which quickly morphed my whole idea of how to 'teach' a class in French.

P. Gouzouasis (ed.), Pedagogy in a New Tonality: Teacher Inquiries on Creative Tactics, Strategies, Graphics Organizers, and Visual Journals in the K-12 Classroom, 121–132.

So What's the Problem?

The Late French Immersion (LFI) program is a challenging program, with students beginning their French studies in Grade 6. The goal is to have students from LFI integrated with the Early French Immersion students for Grade 8, allowing only two school years for LFI students to become fluent in the French language. In 2001, my elementary school was the first school in NVSD to implement this program. The program entails intensive language instruction while following the BC school curriculum, an already daunting feat. All subjects are to be taught in French, although resources that incorporate mature content with simple French vocabulary are scant.

Since 2003, the NVSD has been engaged in a district-wide initiative to implement Instructional Intelligence (II) tactics and strategies in all classrooms and across curricular areas at all levels. Instructional Intelligence focuses on how teachers use a broad range of instructional strategies to positively affect student learning, weaving together strategies, tactics, skills and organizers with an understanding of the student, and incorporating the knowledge of curricular content and assessment and evaluation techniques. Over the past 4 years, through a series of professional development workshops, I have increasingly added these strategies and tactics into my teaching repertoire with a focus on using graphic organizers to demonstrate key knowledge. Graphic organizers—such as a Venn diagrams, fishbone diagrams, concept maps, and mind maps—are ways to visually depict knowledge. For students who possess limited vocabularies, such as LFI students, graphic organizers are a way to organize the information with limited vocabulary to demonstrate an understanding of a topic. Graphic organizers, such as concept maps, "assist in making meaning; they help the learner connect existing knowledge with new knowledge – to make knowledge dynamic rather than passive" (Bennett & Rolheiser, 2001, p. 276).

With those factors in mind, the purpose of this inquiry was to explore how instructional intelligence strategies could be used to increase language skills in Grade 7 Late French Immersion students as part of a Science curriculum. The specific research questions that were explored in this study are as follow.

1. What language benefits can students gain from using Cooperative Learning strategies in an LFI class?
2. Do concept formation and concept attainment lessons provide students with limited French vocabulary the ability to explain challenging concepts as part of the BC Grade 7 Science curriculum?
3. Are visual representations of knowledge (i.e., mind mapping, concept mapping) an effective way to build French language skills?

As there are so few LFI classes in British Columbia, there is a very broad understanding of what is to be taught and how curriculum should be delivered. However, students from one classroom to the next may possess very different skills, depending on the focus of the teacher. For the LFI program to be truly successful, LFI teachers need an understanding of the best practices for language learning at such an intensive level of learning.

Welcome to F01L

The participants of this study were the Grade 7 Late French Immersion class, known as FO1L, at an elementary school in North Vancouver, BC. My classroom last year consisted of 25 students, 20 girls and 5 boys, all ages 12 and 13. The students came from diverse backgrounds and possessed varied educational experiences. They were enrolled in English elementary schools through the NVSD from kindergarten to Grade 5. Late French Immersion is a choice program, offered to students of all academic levels, abilities, and skills. As such, there are no entrance exams or formal requirements. There was a typical range of abilities, including one student who had an Individual Education Plan (IEP), and three who were designated as gifted students. The majority of students chose the LFI program themselves, specifically looking for a more challenging educational experience. Many of the students were highly motivated to learn the French language. The majority of students spoke English at home, with only five students coming from a multilingual home.

Throughout my six years of teaching Late French Immersion (LFI) Grade 7, each class has had a different make-up and vibe. LFI students are traditionally highly motivated, social, and extremely verbal, in both English and French. Every TOC (i.e., a Teacher On Call is also known as a "substitute teacher") I have had over my career has mentioned that my class was "chatty," more so than most. Last year, the biggest challenge facing the class was speaking French, in class, with their peers. Relative to other years, the overall oral language development was slow, as students did not seem to possess either the ability or patience to discover and pull out new vocabulary. For me, this took awhile to figure out. My initial reaction to the slow development of oral language skills was to assume the students were at fault, either possessing no desire to speak French or simply being too lazy. My strategies of instruction had worked for all my previous years, so I questioned, why not this one? In discussions with the students, it became obvious that they were motivated, but the nature and processes of the instruction was not working for them. They felt disconnected from the material being taught and did not understand how it all fit together. As one student put it, "I like learning about something that matters and figuring that out on my own, not because you tell me it's important. I'll remember something if it matters to me." As soon as he said this, I knew I had to re-evaluate my teaching approaches.

The nature of the LFI program is to rush to the finish line, racing through units at breakneck speed to get it all done. Unfortunately, for these particular students, the rush to complete the subject matter in French took away from their actual learning of the French language. They were able to regurgitate all of the vocabulary I'd written out on the board for them over the year, but few were able to use any of these words in sentences. I needed the students to be 'front and center' of their learning, getting more involved in the lessons and communicating their knowledge to each other in French.

I decided to design the present inquiry around components from *Beyond Monet* (Bennett & Rolheiser, 2001) and *Cooperative Learning: Where Heart Meets Mind* (Bennett, Rolheiser, & Stevahn, 1991). Those resources provided a foundation that enabled me to further develop my students' French language skills through increased student engagement and cooperative learning.

So Let's Figure this All Out

The focus of the unit was Ecology, as part of the BC Grade 7 Science curriculum, specifically the outcomes related to interconnections and interactions amongst organisms and the environment. My class typically does not enjoy science class, so this seemed like a perfect opportunity to mix things up a bit. Moreover, the nature of the subject matter lent itself well to cooperative learning, considering it was all about the relationships amongst living things. That was something that was pointed out to me by my most intuitive student who said, "Mme, you did that on purpose! We had to work together to understand how things work together. Sneaky!" Twelve instructional intelligence (II) activities comprised the learning approach of the six-week unit plan. These included Placemat and brainstorming activities, Numbered Heads, a Concept Attainment lesson, Four Corners activities, a Three-Person Interview, Mind Maps, Team Games Tournament, and other games. The majority of the work was completed orally and in groups, both in small groups and as a whole class.

In the Beginning...

My first step was to assess their prior knowledge with regard to the subject matter. I wanted them to anticipate some of the vocabulary they would be learning in French by brainstorming all of their previous knowledge on Ecology in English. Most of the French words were similar to those in English, which generally decreases student anxiety in learning a new language or subject. Students were put in groups of five, with a large piece of paper in the middle. One student was asked to write "Écologie" in the middle of the page. Students were given five minutes to brainstorm everything they knew about ecology, in either French or English. Once finished, the group was asked to look over all of the words, looking for key themes and concepts. From a student centered perspective, I asked each student to write a key question down on the paper, one thing they would like answered through learning in the unit. Groups worked to refine these questions and presented them to the entire class. Those questions formed the basis of our unit.

When I started the lesson, it was clear that the students felt they had little information to offer in the brainstorming. In the initial responses in their journals, they stated that they knew absolutely nothing about ecology. As one student stated, "When the teacher first told me to write about ecology, I had no idea what that was, but by the middle of the class, I realized I knew more than I thought I did. It felt good to be able to show what I knew to other people in my group." Through that initial lesson, their confidence grew as they saw all of the words on the page, both in French and in English. Since French was so new for my students, it was very important to increase their confidence so that they could finally start to draw out the vocabulary on their own, a skill that is crucial for them to continue in the French Immersion program. In student surveys, it became clear that the students in my class have felt a large disconnect from their learning. They were shocked to find out that I was actually willing to incorporate their ideas into my unit plan. They also felt confident about the lesson, because they realized they knew more than they had thought about ecology. I really needed the students to "buy-in" to the unit, as my goal was to have everyone participate to the best of their abilities and skills.

The Big Picture

The second aspect of the unit was focusing on group work, seeing whether the students could work together, speaking in French, to solve a problem. I had a few very strong leaders who possessed a tendency to take over group discussions, but on the whole, most of the class liked to sit back and have someone else take the risks. One of the II tactics used was Numbered Heads, "one of the most effective ways of *increasing the concept of accountability*" (p. 106), while decreasing stress through group discussion. In my class, Numbered Heads was also the best way to separate the strong leaders into different groups, while limiting their role, and encouraging all members of the group to equally participate in French. Students were numbered off into six groups of four to five students each and they arranged their desks accordingly. Each student was given a role: director, secretary, editor, or presenter. I explained the lesson, stating that they were given a piece of a poem and they had to figure out what it meant and how it might fit with poems of other groups. They were not to show the poem section to anyone outside of their own group. The students were unsure how a poem could have anything to do with Ecology, so it took a little bit of trust on their part.

The students set about their task, speaking in French, throwing out ideas and generally working together to make sense out of single line from a poem that had no apparent connection to ecology. They spent 10 minutes discussing their ideas, and the majority of the discussion took place in French. This was the most French many of them had ever spoken in my class, and this was January, definitely not the beginning of the school year. I was shocked. In student responses, the majority of them stated that they felt safe to banter ideas about because they felt that no one person was the group expert. As one stated, "we all had no idea what was going on, so it was easier to be wrong! I didn't feel stupid giving out my answers, because we were all over the place." The students all had the same starting point, so there was no fear of not getting it right. The differences in strengths and weaknesses in my class made the majority of the students feel inept, and had handcuffed their ability to participate fully in the lessons. By leveling the playing field, so to speak, I had managed to open up the dialogue amongst the students.

Once the discussion was over, I asked the class which group they thought had the first line of the poem. One-by-one, a presenter from each group came up and added their line to the poem, explaining why it should go in that position and what the general message might be. After arranging the pieces on the board, I asked the students to come up with their own definition of a cycle, both in words and in a drawing. Within minutes, I had a solid, French definition of the word "cycle" and a handful of great illustrations on the board. Many of the students remembered the rock cycle we had quickly covered first term, but others drew the water cycle, oxygen to carbon dioxide, the school system, and other examples of cycles.

It was truly astonishing to see the students figure out the big picture, without using any English vocabulary. They were so engaged in the lesson that they were able to trust each other enough to try—to try new vocabulary, to possibly fail—but they wanted to share what they knew with their peers. They all quickly understood the interconnectedness of our Earth and were eager to put this knowledge to work in other areas.

Living Versus Dead

The next lesson was focused on Concept Attainment, an instructional strategy that incorporates information processing with cooperative learning. This strategy basically allows the students to play detective, working together to figure out a pattern. My students were bombarded with new vocabulary and text every day, so I decided to change it up a bit by using images. As a class, we had played this "game" before, with me writing words on the board and circling words that fit my concept in green and circling words that did not fit the concept in red. This was my first attempt at incorporating images and group problem solving into the activity.

Students were divided in to four groups, again using Numbered Heads. They organized their desks into pods, which enabled them to have a large work surface and encouraging "face-time." Each group was provided a plastic bag full of laminated cards with pictures on them. I had purposefully given them a large selection of cards, so the students would have to work at naming them as well as organizing them. The instructions were to divide the cards in to two groups. "Based on what, Mme? Color? Size? What?," asked one of my more anxious students. I reminded them to work as a group and as long as everything fit into two categories and they could justify their choices, then it would be correct. Many of my students were traditionally very anxious with broad activities, so I needed to reassure them that all answers were acceptable. I was a little worried this might backfire on me, as obviously I was hoping they would arrive at a particular, single concept.

In my previous attempts at Concept Attainment lessons, I had used colored paper backing to denote the two groups of concepts, yes and no, with black paper for the testers. However, I found that students spent more time focusing on the colors, rather than the concept itself. They would simply look at the colors, fling the cards into two piles, and then spend a few minutes discussing the testers. For this attempt, I put all of the images on black paper, using small green stickers to denote the cards that fit my concept and red ones for those that did not. I found that students spent more time discussing the possible concepts, manipulating the cards and communicating their ideas when the responses were not color coded. They were encouraged to pull out their new French vocabulary, throwing out possible concepts, until they had made a decision. The images themselves were quite straightforward, so I had faith that they would discover the concept.

While the students were organizing their cards, I wrote a set of new vocabulary on the wall. All the words related to ecology—biotique, abiotique, organisme, biosphère, communauté, écosystème, and habitat. Once the students finished grouping the cards, I asked them to pick two of the words from the board as titles for their cards. I chose the words with care, as I wanted some words with which they were already familiar that might lead them to infer the correct new words, biotic and abiotic.

All four groups were able to come to an agreement that the concept was living and non-living things. Many of the groups started our thinking about habitats of the animals on the cards, but quickly realized that, with only two groups, it had to be more general. The majority of the discussion took place in French, although some of the weaker French-speaking students had a tendency to slip into English when they got too excited to share their ideas.

Once the discussion moved to the labeling, the discussion became very interesting. All groups started out by translating the words they knew or recognized into English. As many of the words were similar in sound and look, they were then able to narrow it down to four or five unknown words. At least one student in each group knew the term biosphere, mostly from having visited the Biodome in Montreal. They knew it to be a place for living things, so many of them clicked in that "bio" must have something to do with living. This led to the inference that biotic must mean living and abiotic must mean non-living. It was truly exciting to see many of the lights go on, as they worked through the lexicology of the words. This is exactly what I had been hoping for, as it showed me that they possessed the skills to decode new words, something I had been concerned about. As a general rule, most students seemed to prefer looking a word up in a dictionary, rather than using their own knowledge to figure things out. The students proved to themselves and to me that they were capable of coping with uncertainty and use logic to solve a problem, without relying on a dictionary.

Students were asked to complete a survey after the lesson. Out of the 25 students surveyed, all 25 said that they felt the vocabulary was easier to remember based on the way it was taught. Ninety-five percent of the students surveyed felt confident in their ability to define the terms biotic and abiotic. "I feel I learn more when things are in images, instead of writing things down. I can also remember them more easily," wrote Mary Jane (all student names have been changed for this inquiry). "When you figure things out for yourself, you remember them better than you would from a textbook" wrote Jack. For me, it was exciting to see the students write down how much fun they had figuring it all out and that they felt they truly learned the concept of biotic and abiotic.

In a quiz the following day, all students were able to recall the new vocabulary and give clear definitions in French, something many had struggled with in the past. Two students in particular had struggled all year with definitions of new terms, but both managed to give clear, focused answers on the quiz. After the quiz, I asked these two girls specifically why they felt they were able to do better with these new terms. One girl, Katie, stated that she felt she remembered it better because she was actively involved in the lesson; she was able to concentrate more on the vocabulary because she had something to do with her hands. "I focus more when my body is involved, so moving the cards around really helped, plus I got to ask my friends for help when I didn't understand right away," she said. Becky said that her only way to learn new vocabulary is to use it over and over again in context, something we did in class. "I got to figure out the right word to use myself, and then we talked about it as a group, and then we talked about it as a class, so it just stuck in my mind more," Becky wrote. These two students had very different needs and learning styles, but were both able to achieve success on the quiz. Katie also stated, "I had fun in the lesson, so I felt confident I knew this stuff. The quiz was super easy after that."

Let the Sunshine In

More about different organisms was covered in our next lesson. I used a version of the instructional tactics Walk About and Four Corners as described in *Beyond Monet.* I needed the students to speak more French and put their new vocabulary to work, so I created cards with basic information about organisms from four Canadian biomes, specifically the Boreal Forest, Temperate Forest, Tundra, and Prairies. Cards were placed on a student's back with either a picture of an organism or information, including basic habitat, food, size, and other basics. Students were asked to move about the classroom, asking questions of their peers to find their match. I also participated, to make even numbers, and to model asking questions in French. The students spent 10 minutes finding their partners, with the majority of the time speaking in French. A few got frustrated trying to ask their questions in French, so I had to remind them to try as best as they could before switching to English.

Once in their partner groupings, I asked them to think about where these organisms lived. In the four corners of the classroom, I had put up signs, indicating the four Canadian biomes, with some very basic information. Students were asked to confer with their partners, and then move to one of the appropriate corners of the classroom. They then had to use the information from their cards to create a poster showing the key aspects of their biome. Next they presented their poster to the class, outlining key facts.

For the most part, this lesson went extremely well. By giving each student different information, they were more accountable when working in their groups. They had something specific to offer the group, so they were confident in communicating this information to others. They also had all of the vocabulary at their fingertips, which helped with the conversations. "I had something specific to say, so it took the stress off of me. Normally, I hate group work because I'm not sure what to say or exactly how to say it in French. I liked that I had my card to show everyone, so they listened to me. No one usually understands me when I give ideas in a group," wrote Sally.

For one particular student in my class, group work was traditionally very frustrating, as students rely on her for all of the answers. Lauren said, "I enjoyed working in a group for once, since everyone contributed and cooperated. Everyone *had* to help out, or we wouldn't have anything to write. I liked that the pressure was off me." For me, this journal entry was very telling. Lauren was not a girl to complain, so I had never really noticed how frustrated she became in our usual group work. In further discussion, she told me how much she hated it, because everyone just sat back, expecting her to know the answers and do all the work for them. She really enjoyed having just one piece of the jigsaw puzzle and being able to learn from her classmates, something that had been sorely lacking in the past two years. I realized that I had constantly been relying on her to help out the weaker speaking students, which made group work a lot less fun for her. I made a commitment to her to continue with this style of Jigsaw group work, encouraging more accountability and participation from my other students.

Can't it be Bigger? There is So Much to Say, Mme

At the beginning of the unit, I had outlined that the summative assessment would be a Mind Map (Buzan, 1993). One of the prime objectives of the present study was to see whether visual representations of knowledge are an effective way to build French language skills. I wanted the final assessment to show whether the students truly understood the concepts and vocabulary learned in the unit, without being bogged down by grammar, something that had tripped them up on previous assessments. "*Mind Mapping* is an analytical process that involves creatively integrating a combination of visuals, color, codes and connectors" (Bennett & Rolheiser, 2001, p. 289). Mind Maps involve key vocabulary and visuals, while encouraging students to demonstrate their understanding of a subject in writing. When deciding whether to do a mind map or a concept map, I considered how the wordiness of a concept map might take away from the general demonstration of understanding. I felt that the linking words might be a bit too challenging for my students at this stage of the learning game.

When introducing the cumulative assignment, many of the students panicked, as they were much more used to traditional tests or poster projects for science. There was a lot of anxiety that their final mark was going to be based on a "crappy artsy creative" project, as one boy described the Mind Map. We had tried a few small-scale Mind Maps and Concept Maps, but nothing this big. To make sure this assessment activity was successful, I had to figure out a way to decrease their anxiety about the whole thing.

I decided to create a word web on the back wall of our classroom, getting the students to think about the connections between ideas. Every time we learned a new word, I wrote it on a laminated piece of paper. A student was then asked to place it on the word wall. I asked them to think about the placement of the word, but did not put too much emphasis on the connections between words. At the beginning, students were very unsure of where to place the new vocabulary. On the fourth day, with only 15 words already on the wall, Martin was asked to add the word *'population'* to our wall. He simply grabbed the thumbtack and stuck it blindly to the wall. An immediate outcry went up from a group of girls in the front. "You can't put it there," said Lisa. "It has to go between 'communauté' and 'individu' because that's the order. Individu, population, communauté, écosystème. That's how it works," she stated. She went up to the board and helped Martin reorganize the words. Once that was done, a few other students took over, grouping the words in clusters based on what we had already learned. This was a great teachable moment, as I explained to them that this was a precursor to mind mapping and they had already gotten the basic premise. "But that's easy, Mme, and school is *not* supposed to be easy," Derek cried out.

Halfway through the unit, I officially assigned the mind mapping assignment. We had a rudimentary Mind Map on the back wall of the classroom as a reference for the students, which decreased anxiety. The majority of the students created their own framework, but a few chose to begin with our word wall and create additional details. I was fine with that approach, as this was their first major assignment using a mind map. Students were given a list of vocabulary to include and we created a basic rubric together. Emphasis was placed on the understanding and use of key vocabulary, while demonstrating knowledge of two specific Prescribed Learning Outcomes (PLOs) from the BC Grade 7 Science curriculum. These were as follow: (1) Analyze the roles of organisms as part of interconnected food webs, populations, communities, and ecosystems; (2) Assess survival needs and interactions between organisms and the environment. Over the next three weeks, students worked diligently on their maps during class time and at home. Students met in peer groups once a week to discuss their maps and get feedback. All assignments were handed in on time, a first for F01L.

The day the assignments were due, I had two parents at my classroom door. They were concerned that their children had misinterpreted the assignment, as they had spent a lot of time coloring and didn't seem to be working on a final project. The students in question were so focused on creating the Mind Map that they couldn't believe it was a 'real' assignment. They could not fathom that I would design a cumulative assignment based on art, so they immediately felt their child had got it wrong. Sadly, many parents were so dismissive of their child's language skills, to the point that they felt the child could not even read and interpret the assignment sheet (but neither could they). It was quite upsetting to both myself and the children involved that their parents had so quickly dismissed the value of our visually based assignment. I spent 10 minutes explaining the educational theories behind graphic organizers, even lending one parent a copy of my book *The mind map book: Radiant thinking* (Buzan, 1993), the man who coined the term "mind map."

Just seconds after I escaped this minefield, another parent walked in, this time critical of her son's effort at the presentation. He had *refused* to color-code his lines, even though he had finished a week ago. Oh my! I had just about had enough with the whole assignment until I really looked at the work she was flinging about with disregard. Travis was a student who had struggled all year to get anything finished on time. He was struggling at a Grade 3 reading level in French and most of class instruction was over his head. He had suffered from intense headaches and insomnia due to stress, and had already said he was going to return to English for Grade 8. As I pored over his assignment, he was looking at me with a look of complete dejection, expecting the worst from me as well. On the contrary, it was incredible, and he completely got it. His lines weren't always straight, and the color-coding didn't quite make sense, but he showed a thorough understanding of the subject. When I told him this, he absolutely beamed. In my original survey, he wrote that he didn't like science class at all because "Science makes me confused with the words." In his final survey, he rated the efficacy of mind maps a 5 out of 5, writing, "they explain things in a better way. I like them because it gives me freedom to do it how I learn best."

According to the student surveys, the majority of students saw great value in doing mind maps, even though they were not particularly comfortable with them. A number of students commented that they were unsure where to make connections, feeling that everything should be interconnected. In that manner, they ended up making the assignment more difficult than necessary. Two students who were very successful in a traditional learning style felt that the mind maps took too long, feeling that a test would have been more straightforward. On the other hand, students who struggled in school, even the boys, felt that this was a good way to review what they knew, as there was a lot less pressure to succeed. As one student said, "I get very stressed out by tests, and this was stress-free. I liked drawing the pictures, and it was nice to be able to look up things if I forgot." On the whole, the comments were very positive on the learning process itself.

For me, the proof was very much in the projects. I was absolutely stunned by the quality of assignments my students produced. They took a lot of care and effort to produce beautiful pieces of art, and enjoyed the creative process. They took their understanding of a concept and presented it beautifully. According to a rubric that we co-created, 19 students received a level 4 (an A), with four students receiving a 3 (B) and two students receiving a 2.5 (C+). Initially I was a little leery, worried that the rubric was too easy. The rubric focused on their knowledge of the material, not the attractiveness of the map, so I was hoping they were accurate. I had already planned on having the students complete a traditional test, one that I had given to my classes in previous years. The test results were comparable, with one subtle difference; the students struggled on more complex questions with answers that required complete sentences. Despite their knowledge of all the key vocabulary, it became obvious that it was their understanding of grammatical structures that was holding them back, not their understanding of ecology. Plus, they looked incredibly stressed throughout the test. It was no fun at all.

So What Does it Seem to Mean?

When the unit began, I must admit that I was very skeptical of the possible successes that could emerge from the present inquiry. I had hated teaching science in French for years, even arguing my case with district personnel about the feasibility of teaching such an important and challenging subject in French to new language learners. Results had always been poor and the kids hated it. Many of them struggled in high school, falling behind in basic scientific vocabulary. It was quite an eye-opener for me that my teaching approach was one of the primary reasons for these challenges, not merely their language skills. In the past, my lack of enthusiasm for the subject definitely influenced the amount of time and energy I had spent preparing to teach science. Science was always the last thing for me to prep, so it was pretty dry, very textbook in orientation, and worksheet based. I now realize that the students were quite intuitive, easily knowing which subjects I liked to teach and which ones I didn't enjoy.

One of the biggest challenges for me, going in to this classroom-based inquiry, was finding the enthusiasm to do of the extra preparatory work. When designing the study, I had to really consider the amount of time it takes to prep many of these lessons. I wanted to make sure I could reuse all of the materials, so it took a lot of time and forward planning to get everything laminated. Whenever I give a manipulative to the students, it has to be laminated or it comes back all ripped up, or not at all. All of the preparation made the actual teaching of the unit so much easier, as I was able to be fully engaged in the lessons, rather than running around finishing up photocopies and other last minute chores. Advanced planning has never been my forte, so the study was a great opportunity for me to think things out well in advance. My attitude toward teaching the unit was much calmer and even keener. I was incredibly surprised, and so were the kids. In one student's pre-study survey, she wrote "Mme. Ross looks excited to teach us ecology, so I think it will be fun!"

A primary goal of this study was to determine the language benefits students could gain from using cooperative learning and instructional intelligence strategies in a Late French Immersion (LFI) classroom. I feel that aspect of my inquiry was a resounding success with students reporting feeling more confident, with both speaking French and using new vocabulary. Confidence is probably the biggest challenge to learning a new language, especially considering how much participation is needed in the lessons. By asking their opinions on the direction of their learning, students felt more connected and therefore more accountable, both to themselves and me. They wanted the lessons to be successful, because they had had a say in the direction of the unit, something they had never been given in the past. I needed them to "buy-in" to using the tactics and graphics organizer, which they did, wholeheartedly.

Student participation in French was at the highest I had ever had in previous classrooms. More French was spoken in my classroom over those six-weeks than the entire remainder of the year. Although they still occasionally chattered in English, the students were committed to using French. They were given the resources they needed to participate, right at their fingertips, so it was a little easier to continue speaking in French. Only when they struggled with their second language would they switch back to English. Students themselves were shocked by how much French they actually knew, realizing that they had learned more than they had realized, but again, confidence was key. In small group work, they were all on equal footing, so there was less of a fear of looking foolish. They all had something to offer, so they felt a part of the group.

This inquiry enlightened my classroom practice—my praxis. In the future, I will incorporate more instructional intelligence strategies, tactics, and graphics organizers on a regular basis. In the past, I used preparation time as an excuse to neglect one of the most successful teaching tools I have—planning and creating valuable learning tools. Watching the students beam when they got their final marks of the unit definitely proved to me how valuable II tactics, strategies, and graphics organizers can be. In consideration, I can't wait to get started in my new classroom next year.

Katherine Ross
North Vancouver School District 44
kross@nvsd44.bc.ca

PART 3

STORIES ON THE CLASSROOM USES OF VISUAL JOURNALS, GRAPHICS ORGANIZERS, STORYBOARDS, AND NOTEBOOKS

CHRISTINE BIEG

VISUAL JOURNALS AND PRIMARY CHILDREN

When learners speak, write, or draw their ideas, they deepen their cognition.
Ritchart & Perkins (2008)

Introduction

Although this masters program started three years ago, I believe the kindling that started me on this path began smoldering about 11 years ago. That was when I first met a UBC faculty advisor for a new student teacher program entitled FAME (Fine Arts and Media in Education). This change to the pre-service teaching education program appealed to me because of it strong commitment to the arts. Since I had just completed a Visual Arts diploma through another university, it is where my interests as a teacher had evolved. During those years of mentoring and visiting my classroom, Peter often mentioned various programs that the university was starting but I never gave it much thought; after all, I had a full life juggling teaching, family, coaching my daughters' soccer team, and playing the sport myself. When would I find the time and when would I consider myself capable of doing such a challenging thing. However, as the years went by, my family became more independent, my coaching commitments decreased and the plan of returning to work full time loomed in the future. I had spent so many years with a teaching partner and doing things a certain way that it was time for a change. Working with creative student teachers on a regular basis had given me glimpses of some of the changes that had been occurring in the teaching field but this was not enough. I needed a change, a chance to step out of my comfort zone, to grow as a person and a teacher. A new masters cohort was the perfect catalyst for this to happen.

When the program started I really had no idea what I was getting myself into or what would be expected of me. Was some major thesis involving data collection and analysis required? I hoped not, since I have never been terribly comfortable with writing; what type of study would I do as a primary teacher looking for ways to improve my teaching and myself? We started by investigating applications of Barrie Bennett's (2001) collection of instructional intelligence tactics, strategies, and graphics organizers. Many of these pedagogical ideas were completely new to me, so the learning curve was significant from the start. However, right from the beginning, my husband noticed a change in my attitude about school and my job. He said I seemed more excited about each day and that I came home in a much better frame of mind, brimming with stories about my day and the students I taught. *Beyond Monet* (Bennett, 2001) became my bible as I stumbled through attempts to implement II strategies in my classroom.

P. Gouzouasis (ed.), Pedagogy in a New Tonality: Teacher Inquiries on Creative Tactics, Strategies, Graphics Organizers, and Visual Journals in the K-12 Classroom, 135–147.

In addition to learning about these strategies, I had some heavy-duty readings to tackle. The titles of these books became the theme of our masters' cohort, Mihaly Csikszentmihalyis' (1990) *Flow* and *Trust the Process* by Shaun McNiff (1998) were phrases I heard and used throughout the two and a half years of class meetings. These became especially true during times of doubt or uncertainty as to why I had started this journey and what I was expected to do. As I progressed through my program I learned, "flow is important because it makes the present instant more enjoyable, and because it builds the self-confidence that allows us to develop skills and make significant contributions to humankind" (Csikszentmihalyi, p. 42). Ultimately, this was what I wanted for my students and myself. As I learned to "trust the process," I learned to trust myself. I learned that "in order to create freely we need to get beyond our self-consciousness and especially beyond the attitude that we have limited gifts of expression" (McNiff, p. 87).

In the summer of 2008, I enrolled in the first of two elective courses required to graduate. Both courses were based at the Vancouver Art Gallery and The Museum of Anthropology at UBC. They were intense two-week programs with the first week spent visiting the gallery and museum and the second week completing a final project. It was during the first week of each of these classes that visual journals were a requirement. "The journal is not new, but moving it into the teacher education context as a reflective tool in teaching and as part of coursework has helped change the nature of journaling" (Kalin, Grauer, Baird, & Meszaros, 2007, p. 202). It certainly changed the way I looked at journals since I had always thought of them as a place to write, something I did not really enjoy doing. I had never created a visual journal before, let alone heard of them, but found them the most fulfilling part of the course. Looking back, I see my first attempt as being somewhat simplistic and crude but by the time I completed the second course I had developed a better understanding of how to use a journal effectively. Given the choice, I would have spent the entire two weeks working on my visual journal.

In between courses at the Art Gallery were two other classes that had a lasting impression on me and probably had the strongest influence on my choice to use visual journals for my research study. The first was a course in narrative inquiry. In the class I was asked to write about family, to drag up old memories, and share them with my peers—something I was not comfortable doing. However, with our professor's support and the encouragement from my cohort peers, I found I could do it and that people might actually listen to what I had to say. Once I got past my fear and lack of confidence, I saw that writing was not something to fear but something to celebrate and share. The second course introduced me to the world of artography, Miksang photography, hermeneutics, and metonymic metaphor. Our professor gave us each a journal to be used as a visual diary to document our experiences during his class. Once again, I found this an ideal way to represent my thoughts and ideas because of the choices it allowed me in expressing myself. Therefore, when it came time to make a decision on what type of research inquiry I would implement with my students, my thoughts kept going back to visual journals and how much I had benefitted from there use so why not try it my students.

Review of the Literature

During these courses, a number of readings were introduced that had a profound influence on my decision to include visual journals in my classroom. In fact, they affected me in a way that changed my pedagogical thinking and my outlook on life. In *Walking in wonder* (de Cosson, Irwin, Kind, & Springgay, 2007) the authors discuss walking as a method of visual living inquiry and state, "pedagogy attends to how one teaches and is profoundly affected by learning itself" (p. 138). Over the last few years, walking played a large part in my masters' journey. It was during these walks that I did a lot of thinking. "Recursively, I circled back, in my mind and in my walking, to rethink what I had never questioned" (p. 143). This time allowed me to slow down and get away from everyday interruptions and return to the ideas and concepts that were new to me. It was a time to think about how I looked at teaching and my world, and what I could do to improve them. It gave me a chance to reflect, rethink, respond and revive, and as such I come to understand the notion that "it is through living inquiry, brought alive in walking, that we re-envision our teaching and research praxis"(p. 148). When I returned home from these walks, my visual journal became the tool to record these recollections.

Weber (2008) discusses the importance of visual images in research. As a visual learner myself, I found this informative into how the use of visual images can promote academic development. She includes several reasons why visual images are useful to research. I argue these reasons also relate to the use of visual journals by primary students. The first reason, and the one that relates to young children, is that images can be used to show something that words cannot always capture. "Some things just need to be shown, not merely stated. Artistic images can help us access those elusive, hard-to-put-into-words aspects of knowledge that might otherwise remain hidden or are ignored" (p. 44). When I think about this statement, it reminds me of those students I have taught who may understand a concept, but when asked to write about it were unable to do so. Given an opportunity to show their understandings through images allowed them an alternative method to be successful. "Images are likely to be more memorable" (p. 45). Grade Two students enter school possessing a wide range of abilities, yet some may not possess well-developed reading skills. Given this situation, they are more likely to remember an image before a word. As is, in many cases when we introduce written words to young children, we include an image with it to help foster recall. On the other hand, a child who cannot write a word or thought may be able to draw it and thus use an image to represent their knowledge. Another argument for using visual images is "the possibilities for using the visual to make effective and economical theoretical statements" (p. 45) through metaphorical symbols. In today's culture, many images represent ideas that even young children understand and can use to demonstrate their ideas. As well, "images can be more accessible than most forms of academic discourse" (p. 46). In my experience, most children are more likely to engage in a picture than text and are better able to understand what the image represents as opposed to engaging with and understanding a passage of words. "To sum up, this ability of images to evoke visceral and emotional responses in ways that are memorable, coupled with their capacity to help us empathize or see another's point of view and to provoke new ways of looking critically, makes them powerful tools for researchers [and students] to use in different ways"(p. 47).

While the work of Ritchhart & Perkins (2008) does not relate directly to the use of visual journals, they discuss the value of teaching students thinking routines that "jump-start thinking and make it visible" (p. 57). There are six key components of Visible Thinking, including "fostering thinking requires making thinking visible"(p. 58). They state, "effective thinkers make their thinking visible, meaning they externalize their thoughts through speaking, writing, drawing, or some other method" (p. 58). In relation to the present inquiry, a visual journal is the perfect vehicle to show this kind of thinking as a reflective tool. Ritchhart & Perkins describe another thinking routine, "See-Think-Wonder," which is useful for young children using visual journals. Students are asked to observe an image or object and answer three questions: "What do you see? What do you think about it? What does it make you wonder?" (p. 59). Since this activity allows students of all skill levels and abilities to participate, it is a useful tactic to show their thinking and visual journals the perfect tool to record them in.

Kalin, Grauer, Baird, & Meszaros (2007) portray personal journals as "a source of inspiration" and can be "used for documenting, reflecting, critiquing, and collecting ideas and inspiration"(p. 202). Although the article focused on teachers as the learners and the value of visual journals in representing their learning, I felt that these same arguments supported my plan to introduce journals to primary children. The visual journal enabled teachers to "select, according to their preferences, what and how to highlight, understand, re-represent, extend, and challenge the information presented" (p. 205). I argue that this statement could apply to children as well, since the use of visual journals allows students to choose what is important to them and how they would like to represent a particular idea.

Sanders-Bustle (2008) writes, "visual artifacts such as this photograph serve as valuable springboards for meaning making in visual artifact journals" (p. 8). As well, she describes "the magic of the sketchbook as a space for ideas to take shape [and] imaginations to wander" (p. 9) while discussing the value of using visual artifact journals with her students. She follows these statements up with the views of Blecher & Jaffee (1998) that "suggest that sketchbooks can become liberatory tools for "widening the learning circle" to include often marginalized learners" (p. 9). When I think of the differences in each of the students I teach, this idea makes me believe that I am on the right track in using visual journals as a means to engage all my students. I feel strongly that by allowing the children choices as to what they would like to put in their books it provides them "with a creative and critical space to explore and represent the contents [...] of their daily lives" (p. 9).

Acknowledging the children's lives is an important aspect in teaching according to Ted Aoki (1993), because this is the world of my classroom and the varied lives of my students. The lived curriculum dominates my day as I deal with one issue to the next, therefore, using visual journals as a place for children to represent their lives, providing them the opportunity to respond and reflect on their lived curriculum acknowledges this as being an important aspect of school life. Allowing the students to use visual journals as a personal reflective device "ultimately provid[es] a more democratic space for students and teachers to share ideas, reveal lived experiences, and make their worldviews public" (Sanders-Bustle, p. 14). This idea of choice was an overriding theme throughout my inquiry, as the students repeatedly commented on the fact that they were allowed to choose what to do when working on their journals.

The Setting

Bordered by the Upper Levels to the south, mountains to the north, Lonsdale Avenue to the west and Princess Park to the east is the catchment area of my elementary school in North Vancouver School District. The neighborhood is a collection of beautifully cared for character homes, 1960 post and beams as well as remodeled and brand new monster homes, many of which have basement suites. On the southern edge are some older apartment and condominium complexes. This is where the majority of students live. However, we do have a number of children from other areas that come to our school for various reasons. High results from the Fraser Institute, support for special needs students, and a full day Kindergarten class have all added to our school population.

This past year, I taught Grade Two and my class consisted of 22 children, unevenly split with 14 boys and 8 girls, from a wide variety of backgrounds. Upon completing a cultural crest with the class, I discovered that we had children from all parts of the world—including Iran, Hong Kong, Jamaica, and South Africa. In a class that had such diverse backgrounds, it was not surprising to find that four of the students were Level Five English as Second Language (ESL) students. Their verbal skills were quite good, but they needed some support from our ESL teacher. Three other children from the group received additional help for reading and writing through our Learning Assistant Center (LAC) four to five times a week. One of these students was designated learning disabled and the other two were up for further testing to determine their linguistic strengths and weaknesses. The remaining students demonstrated a wide range of abilities from minimally meeting to exceeding the expected learning outcomes for grade two. They were a very lively, talkative class always full of energy and life, especially considering the large number of boys that enjoyed being the center of attention. All parents consented to allow their children to participate in the study.

Methodology

This inquiry was conducted in my Grade Two classroom from April 9 to June 25. Before starting the inquiry, I needed to get parental permission for students to participate. My teaching partner, Deb Anderson, explained what the research project was about to the class and collected and kept all permission forms until the study was complete. The project took place during regularly scheduled class times and all students participated in the activities. At the end of the data collection, I was not surprised that all parents had given their children permission, considering the excitement the students exhibited when we started the visual journals. All references made to individual students are anonymous. The journals were an integral part of study as they enabled the children to represent their learning. These were collected at the end of the study, and reference points and pictures of their work supplied examples of the different ways in which the students represented their ideas (photographs of student work are available upon request). Nothing that identified individual children was included in these pictures. As the students worked in their visual journals, any anecdotal comments made by them were recorded. These comments were part of the data collected to assess individual learning on an ongoing basis. Mini-interviews of approximately five minutes were conducted with the students—that enabled them to explain orally how the images they used represented their learning. Furthermore, observations of students working were used to analyze students' engagement and work habits during the time spent working in the visual journals.

Implementation of the Research

After all the parental permission forms had been signed and returned to my teaching partner, it was finally time to get started. I had purchased coil bound scrapbooks for each of the students; they were 22 by 30 centimeters in size and contained 30 sheets. I preferred the coil bound book because it gave the children easier flexibility to maneuver the books into different directions or page sides. They were so excited to get these journals and begin using them, especially when I explained there were no real rules as to how to use them. If they wanted to write, they could. If they wanted to draw, they could, and if they wanted to do both that was okay too.

By the time I was ready to begin the formal aspect of the study, I had decided upon a number of teacher directed activities as well as setting aside time for the students to work in their journals independently. The first activity was for each child to do a name page. I felt this was an important starting point for the children to give them real ownership of the books. I asked them to flip the book open to any page they wanted, it did not have to be the first page but anywhere in the scrap book, and create a page with their name on it. Looking back at the journals, it is interesting that only seven of the students chose pages other then the first to use for this activity, and only two of those students were boys. That is of special note because throughout the study the boys kept mentioning how they liked the freedom to do what they wanted in the visual diaries, yet when I gave the name page location choice at the very beginning they all went to the first page as they would with all other new notebooks.

In addition to their name, I asked the class to add some words to describe themselves or their personal interests to the page. Most of the children found it easier to explain what they were fans of, such as sports and computer games, then describe themselves. That said, I did get a couple of kids who included words that described their characteristics and personal strengths. Two children used being a good friend while several included words like creative, artistic, kind, pretty, nice, and awesome. As the students worked on the pages they were very engaged with the activity and eager to share with each other what they had done. One of the students could write his name in Farsi and was keen to show his friends, the next thing I new the other children were getting him to write their name as well. This same student begged me at the end of the day to take his journal home with him to work on. I was a little leery because things that go home rarely make it back to school but he was so eager and promised to return the journal that I decided to let him; I did not want to discourage his enthusiasm. When he returned to school the next day he had the book with him and had added several pictures with captions about some of the trips he had gone on when he was younger. The name pages are unique and represent the different personalities in my classroom but I did not photograph any of these pages as examples due to the fact that they clearly show the children's identities.

After the first session working in the visual journals, I told the students that if they wanted, they could start bringing pictures from home to add to their journals. They had seen examples of my journals that displayed a variety of photographs and were very keen to add pictures to their own books. The next day several children arrived at school with envelopes full of photographs depicting family, friend's, pets, and vacations ready to be included in their books. The first thing they asked me when they got to school was when do we get to work on our visual journals again.

Over the next week, the students were given the opportunity to glue these pictures in and add comments about the photos. Alternatively, some students did not bring family pictures but cut out magazine pictures of things they liked or had me photocopy their favorite book covers and hockey cards to include in their journals. One boy created a storyboard by gluing pictures of Lego building pieces together.

Figure 1. Part of the Lego storyboard.

It was at this time that I met with the students individually to discuss their progress in their journals. The consensus was that they were very excited about the project and were keen to share them with me. Most of the children picked their name pages as the favorite page and explained they liked creating a page about themselves, especially seeing their name in different languages and styles of print. One child stated that she had done her name in rainbow colors because she really liked rainbows, while another said that it was cool because they had to be creative. I also saw examples of problem solving as one student explained they had started drawing a heart but it did not work so they changed it into a butterfly. Another child showed me how he had changed the size of the letters in a quote I had given them to show how the tone and character of the quote changed.

Figure 2. Visual journal entry after walking the dog.

For the next directed activity, I found a beautiful story *Flowers for Mom* (Marton, 1991), which was full of descriptive passages. The plan was that as I read the story the students would respond in their visual journals. This response could be done through words, pictures, or both. I felt that by giving them the choice, all children would be able to respond in some form or another, and that is what happened. Some students retold the story in their own words using brightly colored felts, while others simply wrote words that they heard. Other children drew colorful pictures to go along with the events of the story in a timeline, while one boy drew a large heart with some flowers and the caption "I love you Mom" under it. I asked him about his picture and he stated that the story made him think about his own mom so he wrote that in his book. In addition, some students used both pictures and words to respond to the story.

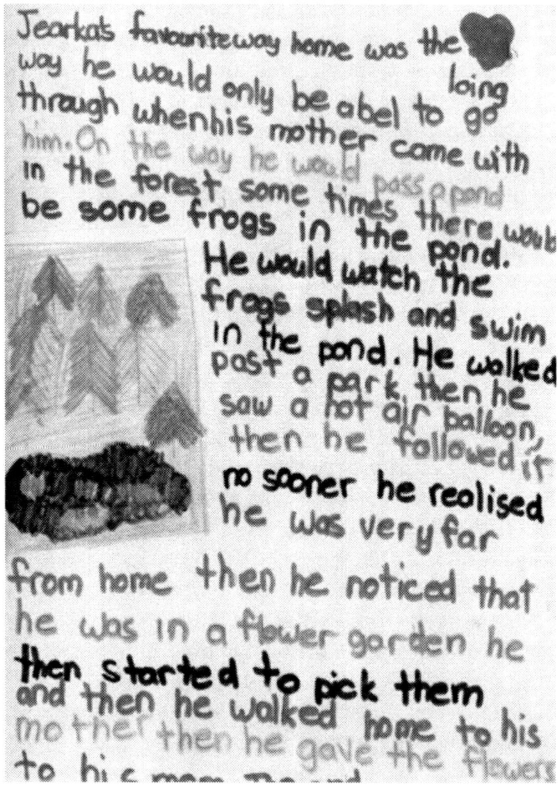

Figure 3. Use of images and words.

After rereading the story a couple of times, I finally showed the children the pictures and then gave them some free time to finish up what they had started or do their own thing in the journals. Looking back at the students' work, I found it rewarding that even my students who struggled the most were able to independently participate in this assignment by responding in a way that they felt successful.

The next time we used the visual journal was to respond to a field trip the children went on, as well as respond to a couple of assemblies they attended. Our field trip was to the Seymour Salmon Hatchery and we returned to the school about thirty minutes before it was time to go home. I asked the students to show me something they had seen or learned at the hatchery, and once again got a variety of responses. Some children drew pictures that showed the salmon life cycle or the large ponds that the fry were kept in, while others wrote about catching bugs in the water or the lonely spawner they saw in the holding tanks. Three children kept the stream survey that each group had done while at the hatchery and included these as visual artifacts to go with their responses. As well, most of the students glued their nametag into their books as reminders of their time at the hatchery.

The two assemblies the class watched involved water conservation and fire safety. After the water conservation program, I asked the children to choose something from the assembly that they either learned about or enjoyed. The presentation was a series of short skits demonstrating what the children could do to help care for our water systems. Geared for a primary audience it used a lot of humor to get its message across which appeared to be effective since all the students were able to recall something from the play. While some children drew pictures of their favorite characters from the presentation, others wrote statements such "don't take an hour to shower" or "turn off the tap while you are brushing your teeth." One student used picture symbols to get his message across; although they were very simple, it was clear what he was trying to say. This reminded me of Weber's (2008) thoughts on the value of visual images, "Through metaphor and symbol, artistic images can carry theory elegantly and eloquently" (p. 45). After the fire safety assembly, I asked the students to respond with two different ideas from the presentation. The first was to show something they had learned about fire safety, and the second was to come up with a plan on how they could get out of their room in case of a fire. The class was learning about mapping in socials studies, so drawing an escape plan seemed like a good extension activity. Although this was a more challenging activity, the students were able to draw a picture of their home and then explain their escape route to me. In addition to drawing or writing about what they knew, several students used pictures relating to safety that they had found in some kids magazines donated to the class.

Following these activities, I wanted to do something a little different in their visual journals. I had a wonderfully detailed print by Toller Cranston called *The Ship of Fools* that I chose for a "picture word induction" brainstorm. A picture word induction brainstorm is a strategy that uses a picture to generate vocabulary from the students. The print showed a ship, which looked like a dragon, full of fantasy characters that were colorfully dressed in ornate costumes. With the children sitting on the carpet, we examined the picture and then students called out things they saw or shared ideas about the print and what it made them think. I wrote these ideas on the board as a reference for students to use later when they went to their desks to work in their books. Half of the children chose to use words and pictures in their journals while the remaining students were split between just words or drawings. One student stated during the brainstorming session that it looked like the characters were going to a celebration and this became the predominant theme for most of the pupils. According to Sanders-Bustle (2008), "by self-selecting and writing about objects of importance, learners make personal connections between art and their lives" (p. 14), which is what one boy did when he went a completely different direction and claimed that the horn in the print reminded him of going to a Canucks game—thus, his book described this idea. I was not as happy about the outcome of this activity because I felt the children could have done more with it, however, since it was the first time I realized that more exposure to this type of activity would help. As McNiff states, when attempting something new, "give them plenty of time and sustained practice. Nothing will sink in and become an ally unless you stay with it …" (p. 87).

Our annual school sports day was quickly approaching and the class was getting very excited about it, so I decided to use that energy for the next activity. With the help of the class I planned a learning station for the primary kids to do the day of the big event. It focused on a Hawaiian theme and I asked the children to come up with their own idea for a sports day station. We discussed a few potential ideas and I sent them on their way to design a plan. They needed to have a name for their activity, develop the rules, and include any equipment they would need. They were so excited they could not wait to get to their desks to get started. This ended up being several of the students' favorite activity, as depicted in their visual journals. The results were extremely varied—from a sushi-eating contest (only with cucumber rolls) to a lava surfing race; every child had something unique from their neighboring station. In fact, only a few students used the same equipment, such as field hockey sticks or soccer balls, but had different rules for their station. Almost every student included illustrations with their design to enhance their station and ensure that one could understand what they wanted to say. This activity really showed how much the students enjoyed having the freedom to make up their own event with only a few guidelines to help get them started.

The final assignment was an activity that normally is done at the end of the year. It was written out on an open-ended worksheet, describing some of the students' favorite parts of the year. I wrote the sentence starters randomly on the board in different colors and asked the children to use these as a guideline to tell me about their year. One journal that really stood out to me was completed by one of my students who really struggled academically this past year. Besides writing about his favorite activities in each subject area, he included detailed pictures for each. For many of the other children this was the norm, but for him it was not an easy task to get his ideas down on paper—to have managed both visual and written expression was a real accomplishment. As well, one of my English Second Language students put all the ideas together in a well-constructed paragraph instead of using point form (see Figure 4 on the following page). After gathering all the children's visual journals it was easy for me to tell, what their favorite activities are at school i.e., centers still rule.

During the last week of the study, I again interviewed each of the students. I asked them four questions: (1) What was their favorite page and why did they like it? (2) What did they like about doing the journals? (3) Was there any thing they disliked about the journals? (4) Would they want to use visual journals again and if so was there something they would want to do that they did not do this time?

The responses were all quite different from which page they liked the best to what they would like to do next time, but the overwhelming view was that they really enjoyed working with visual journals. I saw evidence of this every time the children worked in their journals either during teacher-directed activities or during their free time. The level of engagement was usually high and the children were very enthusiastic workers, eager to share their ideas. When asked what they liked about visual journals many stated they liked being able to do what they wanted, but that they did not like being told what to do. However, what I found interesting with some of the students who stated they liked the freedom, without any guidance, was that they sometimes struggled getting anything down in their books. I need to take this under consideration in the future when I implement visual journals in my classroom.

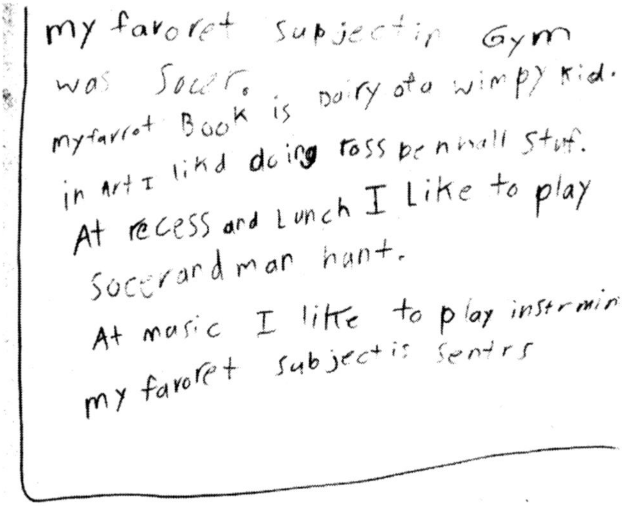

my farorет subject in Gym
was Socer. is Dairy ofa wimpy Kid.
myfarrot Book is
in Art I likd doing ross penwall stuf.
At recess and Lunch I Like to play
Soccerardman hunt.
At music I like to play instrmin
my farore t subject is Sentrs

Figure 4. A paragraph from an ESL student.

By giving them a starting point, the students were able to focus on a particular activity but they also voiced that they must also have the choice to determine how they want to share their ideas. As far as the last question, they all said they would definitely want to do visual journals again, and they had some very interesting suggestions for future activities. I found a couple of the boys' answers interesting, because during many of the journaling sessions they always seemed to be in a hurry to finish. Although I could not fault them for what they produced, I secretly wished they would spend a little more time and take a little more care in how they presented their ideas. That noted, when asked what they would like to do in the future, they both stated they wished they had colored more in their books and had not scribbled on some of the pages. Those students usually chose writing over drawing, so it was good to see them expressing an interest in trying a different tactic to share their ideas. All the students stated they would like to do visual journals again with one stating he would like more pages; another student said she would like to start it earlier in the year.

Closing Thoughts

In consideration of my experiences this past year, I believe that visual journals can be a useful tool in a primary classroom. As I became more comfortable with using a visual journal to explain my own learning, I now know that young children can too. After all, I had the opportunity to do a journal for three university courses, so I think the more exposure children have to using visual journals the more skilled they could become. As with any activity, some children took to it faster than others. However, even students whose first language was not English or possessed a writing challenge were able to express themselves in some way. Moreover, they were excited about doing it. One boy stated he did not like writing but loved showing his ideas through comic strips while another student enjoyed it because it felt like doing art.

To sum the experience up, "visual journaling within the (classroom) invites (students) to personalize their meaning making in more non-literal ways than just taking notes" (Kalin et al., p. 202). Learning is a continuous journey and finding a way to explore and facilitate that journey is the role of a teacher. I began my masters program at a time when a challenge was necessary to further my growth as a professional. I found that challenge as I attempted to understand a broad variety of new approaches to teaching and at first felt confused. Searching for new answers I have passed through a state of aporia—απορία, the unknown, the things that cause us to wonder and to question (Gouzouasis, in press)—and have transformed my praxis. Yet, I realize there is much more to learn about visual journaling and the benefits to students, young and old, so I plan to keep expanding the use of journals in my classroom. The students in this project taught me a lot about myself as a teacher as did the research involved in writing this study. I look forward to pushing myself and continuing my journey. Naths (2004) summed up my thoughts beautifully, "as I continue to define myself as inquiring and reflective, I simultaneously refine and define my philosophy and pedagogy" (p. 118).

Christine Bieg
North Vancouver School District 44
christinebieg@shaw.ca

JI AI CHO

IMPROVING SCIENCE LEARNING THROUGH THE USE OF AN INTERACTIVE SCIENCE NOTEBOOK (ISN)

It is the visions of our students,
their courage, determination, and triumphs,
that awaken our most cherished memories.
It is the visions of youth at its most impressionable,
when teachers and students gather nectar,
that causes flowers to bloom,
weaving garlands of their most wondrous lives.
Mary Catherine Swanson
(from Freedman, 2000, p. 1)

Prelude

The purpose of this study was to discern whether the Interactive Science Notebook (ISN) was useful in enhancing student learning in a Science 10 class. Science 10, being a required course for graduation in British Columbia, is a major hurdle for many students. Not only is there a huge curriculum with many Prescribed Learning Outcomes, the students are required to write a comprehensive Provincial Exam at the end of the course. I wanted to find out whether using the ISN would be beneficial to the students in helping them learn science in Grade 10. The specific research questions that guided this study were as follow:

1. How does the Interactive Science Notebook help students learn science in Grade 10?
2. Does the use of an Interactive Science Notebook (ISN) increase student achievement in Grade 10 science?
3. How do Instructional Intelligence strategies such as "Left-Hand Side assignments' help teachers monitor student learning as a formative assessment strategy?

The Setting

Students from my two Science 10 classes at a large secondary school in Squamish, BC participated in the study. There were 650 Grades 8 to 12 students with about 100 Grade 10 students this past year. The school has students from

P. Gouzouasis (ed.), Pedagogy in a New Tonality: Teacher Inquiries on Creative Tactics, Strategies, Graphics Organizers, and Visual Journals in the K-12 Classroom, 149–165.

mixed socio-economic classes and ethnicities. The town is going through a transitional period from a history of blue-collar, paper-mill industry to tourism, outdoor sports, and service focus. As part of the transformation, the school possesses inner city elements.

There were 25 students who first volunteered to be part of the study. One student withdrew early on, one student withdrew from the class later, and two students did not return their parent consent forms. In the end, 21 students were involved in the study. Out of the 21 students, 10 had used the ISN last year with me in Science 9. The other 11 students were new to the ISN. There were fourteen female and seven male students. About half of all my Science 10 students this past year participated in the study. All students were 15 or 16 years old. About one third of my students are second or third generation Indo-Canadians. Two students were of ESL and two others are second generation Filipino students. Half of the students were of European descent. Each student was given the same identification number for the both surveys for comparison of responses at the beginning and at the end of the study. Their identities were kept confidential throughout the research period.

I was first introduced to the ISN during an AVID (Advancement Via Individual Determination) conference in San Diego, USA about ten years ago. The AVID program uses inquiry based learning techniques, collaboration, rigor and intensive writing to help students challenge themselves academically to get ready for college. AVID is a program that helps students to reach high academic goals by rigor, self-determination and hard work. One tool that the AVID program utilizes is the Interactive Notebook.

The design of the present inquiry involves components from the work of Bennett & Rolheiser (2006) and Gardner (2006). Those resources provided the pedagogical and conceptual foundation for the lessons, in the aim to further develop the science understanding of my students. Instructional Intelligence (II) focuses on how teachers use a broad range of instructional strategies to positively affect student learning, weaving together strategies, tactics, skills and graphic organizers with an understanding of the student, and incorporating the knowledge of curriculum content and assessment, as well as evaluation techniques. Over the past 22 years, I have increasingly added these tactics into my teaching repertoire, with a focus on using the graphic organizers, art work and poetry to reach and enrich learners who possess different learning styles typically found in any class.

A Review of the Literature

A search on the UBC library ERIC database, Google Scholar and Google search engines, using the descriptors "interactive notebook," "multiple intelligence," "learning styles," and "brain and learning" located several articles. The books I used were from my own collection. The age of the literature used ranges from 1974 to 2008. As well, various articles from National Science Teachers Association (NSTA) publications such as *The Science Teacher*, *Science and Children*, and *Science Scope* were used.

DIFFERENT MODELS OF INTERACTIVE SCIENCE NOTEBOOKS IN THE CLASSROOM

There are different models of interactive notebooks used in classrooms. Hartley & Marshall (1974) and Baker & Lombardi (1985) demonstrate that college freshman were taking an inadequate amount of notes during lectures due to their inability to judge what parts of the lecture were important or not. Complete lecture notes were provided to the students and the students participate by "interacting" with the notes through: adding drawings, color-coding, marking important concepts with colours, and working on problems. They believed that having the students spend more time reviewing their notes, they generally do better on tests. Structuring a complete set of notes with spaces for personal additions to the notes were found to be beneficial. This model of interactive notebook is different from the notebooks traditionally used in the AVID (Advancement Via Individual Determination) program.

Interactive notebooks used in the AVID program are set up with much more rigid requirements. The spiral notebook is set up so that the notes are written on the right hand side pages. This is referred to as the "input." Next, the students participate by making up questions and summaries for their notes. On the left hand side page facing the notes, students interact with the notes through creative assignments known as "output." The LHS assignments are supposed to show the processing of notes. According to Young (2003), this type of interactive notebook set up is based on brain research of the 1990s; the left hemisphere of the brain is supposedly more "logical" and the right hemisphere more "creative." The different hemispheres control the opposite sides of the body. The right and the left sides of the notebook represent the opposite sides. Hence, the logical left brain controls the right side of the notebook where the notes are taken in orderly, sequential manner and the creative right brain controls the left side of the notebook where creative assignments are created based on the notes. That perspective noted, there seems to be no evidence of the brain regions working in isolation for either type of those tasks.

In the present study, the ISN used in the research loosely followed the AVID model. The RHS included the Cornell notes, questions, summary and reflection. The LHS was used for students to process and internalize the science concepts through doing a variety of II tactics.

INTERACTIVE SCIENCE NOTEBOOKS AND MULTIPLE INTELLIGENCES

Frames of Mind (Gardner, 1983) and *Multiple Intelligences* (Gardner, 2006) were written based on research from physiology, anthropology, and personal and cultural history. According to Gardner (2006), there are multiple ways that one can be considered intelligent.

> It is a pluralistic view of mind, recognizing many different and discrete facets of cognition, acknowledging that people have different cognitive strengths and contrasting cognitive styles. I introduce the concept of individual-centered school that takes this multifaceted view of intelligence seriously (p. 5).

The Multiple Intelligence (MI) theory tries to explain the content of learning and its relationship to the disciplines. Gardner identifies eight intelligences: *musical, bodily-kinesthetic, logical-mathematical, linguistic, spatial, interpersonal, intrapersonal,* and *naturalistic*. In the present study, before the use of the ISN, my students were introduced to the theory of MI. A survey was administered to the students and the students subsequently identified their own MI strengths. I believe that using the ISN, there are many opportunities to take advantage of a student's strengths and to nurture weaknesses.

For example, note-taking in the ISN may enable students to practice strengthening *linguistic* intelligences. Use of specific scientific language for recording information, summarizing and reflecting on one's own understanding of the information requires the development of specific skills. Vocabulary cards, by using definitions, usage sentences, and link words may help students learn a deep understanding of words and their usage. Riddles use humour to reinforce the definition of words as well as showing the literal and figurative meanings of words. Poems such as haiku and, acrostic may make students sensitive to the musical qualities and rhythms of words. Concept and mind maps may link visually the linguistic connections.

I intended that the LHS assignments help to develop *interpersonal, intrapersonal* and *naturalistic* intelligences. When sharing their work with others, the students had to be sensitive of what they said about one another's work. Informal sharing during gallery walks allowed students to reflect on his/her work in comparison to others. When writing the reflective paragraph after each set of ISN notes, the students were asked to gage their own understanding and, feelings about the topic that was discussed. *Naturalistic intelligence* was explored and reinforced through drawings made on the vocabulary, riddle and cartoon cards. All left hand side (LHS) assignments were accompanied by illustrations that distinguished the diverse organisms and other naturalistic phenomena such as plate tectonics and weather patterns.

While these were considerations in the set up of the present study, there are some weaknesses to multiple intelligence theory according to Silver, Strong & Perini (1997). They believe that multiple intelligence theory categorizes intelligences too broadly and does not consider individualized process of learning nor consider variations within a particular intelligence. Regardless, Gardner's theory has had a broad influence on educational research and practice, thus my decision to consider these dimensions of human learning in my inquiry.

INTERACTIVE SCIENCE NOTEBOOK AND LEARNING STYLE THEORY

Learning style theory focuses on the process of learning based on personality. It takes into account different ways that people process information. According to Silver, Strong & Perini (1997), there are four styles of learning: *mastery, understanding, self-expressive,* and *interpersonal.* I believe that the use of interactive notebook exposes students to all four types of learning styles. The *mastery style learner* best learns information through concrete, sequential, step-by-step notes such as those that are used in the Cornell style notes. The *understanding learner* benefits from questioning and reasoning. In the ISN, the student is required to make up questions and summaries of their notes. On the other hand, the left hand side "creative" assignments provide opportunities for the *self-expressive style learner* to use different styles of poetry, graphic organizers, riddles, 'foldables,' and others creative means of expression on the paper to learn the content of the notes. Lastly, the *interpersonal learner* has an opportunity to share the learning through regular sharing time in class. Limitations to the learning style theory have been made clear in the article. As the authors explain, learning style theory does not take into account how the styles may vary depending on different content areas. As well, there is no emphasis on the importance of *context* in learning.

According to another learning style expert, Lamarche-Bisson (2004), learning styles can be explained through multi-sensory ways. The *auditory learner* learns best through listening and speaking; the *visual learner* includes the learners using print and pictures; the *kinesthetic learner* best learning from tactile ways. From my perspective, the ISN was best suited the needs of the *auditory* and *visual learners*. The notes are read and explained to the students as they write the notes and the students are required to do creative assignments afterward. The verbal learner does not have the opportunity to speak during the note-taking time. Therefore, I believe that in the present study it was beneficial to give students time to express what is learned verbally through follow up activities such as "think-pair-share," "inside-outside circle," or "conference lines" after the notes were taken.

It was surprising to learn that using colours and pictures would help the *visual picture learners,* but for the *print visual learner*, illustrations and diagrams may actually interfere with learning. Graphic organizers such as Venn diagrams, T-charts, and fishbone diagrams may help the *print visual learner* organize their thoughts more efficiently. Kewra & Robinson (1995) describe the use of graphic organizers superior to the use of outlines in improving learning from text. Graphic organizers use spatial arrangements to relate concepts. They require students to interact with the text more deeply, resulting in durable encoding that will show longevity in students remembering the concept. When these dimensions are taken into consideration, for the *kinesthetic learner*, there are obvious limitations to the interactive notebook.

Using the ISN exposes students to all types of intelligences and learning styles. Some researchers have demonstrated that when students received instruction specifically tailored to their preferred learning styles, they perform poorly on tests of the material (Salomon, 1984). When students received instruction in their preferred learning styles, they put less effort in learning resulting in lower levels of learning. Olson (2006), thinks that this is due to the students being overconfident in their ability to learn the information. Instead of trying to tailor the lessons to the students' learning styles, she thinks the following should be considered first : (1) What representations are best suited to a concept?, (2) How is the instruction scaffolded from concrete to more abstract?, and (3) How abstract is the concept and how well can the students understand? By exposing the students to different learning tactics in using the ISN, I thought that the student would be prepared better to deal with various types of learning.

Further to those perspectives, Lamarche-Bisson (2004) categorizes children's personality into *types A, B, D, I, S* and *C*. *Type A* child is competitive, goal-oriented to the point of being irritable if anything interferes with his learning. *Type B* child is more balanced, with a tolerance for being imperfect and is therefore more relaxed. *Type D* child likes challenges, control and is active and task-oriented similar to type A. Active but more people-oriented, *Type I* thrives on having recognition and approval. *Type S* child is passive and people-oriented who works best in groups and routines. Lastly, the *Type C* child is more passive and focuses on correctness and quality of work. The personality profile explains why a child behaves in a particular way and how the behaviour may affect his learning. ISN empowers all types of personality traits because it (a) requires active engagement with course concepts, (b) incorporates self-reflection, (c) allows students to express their personal values; experiences and feelings, (d) teaches organizational skills, (e) creates pride in and ownership of class work, and (f) helps students visualize and demonstrate understanding as evidence of self-regulation (Waldman & Crippen, 2009, p. 52).

INTERACTIVE SCIENCE NOTEBOOK AND BRAIN RESEARCH

According to Jensen (1998), key steps in memory storage process includes a piece of information with stimulus registering through our sensors both consciously and unconsciously. There may be millions of bits of information. Short-term memory lasts 5-20 seconds with only a small amount of stimulus stored temporarily. It is theorized that to push the information into long-term memory, the information has to be actively processed through discussion, thinking, debates or mapping. Long-term memory includes explicit memories that have been processed through implicit learning. Retrieval of information is dependent upon state, time, and context of learning. Wolfe (2001) states that biologically, a memory is made when a group of neurons are involved in the learning experience and fire together in a particular neural circuit. Using laboratory animals and exposing them to "enriched" and "deprived" environments, scientists were able to show, through various imaging techniques, that one can grow dendrites and synapses between neurons.

Historically, as far as the functions and the roles of the two hemispheres of the brain are considered, there have been different ideas. During the 1970's and 1980's, some scientists believed that there was a dominant "leading" hemisphere commonly referred to as right-brained or left-brained. The interactive notebook tries to justify the organization of the notebook with its right and left sides with the same idea. For me, this seems too simplistic. Later researchers demonstrated that the brain is much more complex. The two hemispheres of the brain are joined by a connector bundle of nerve fibres known as the corpus callosum. Although each hemisphere is specialized in what they do, both hemispheres inform each other to coordinate incoming information and the processing of information. Therefore, it is more important to teach to both sides of the brain. To learn content with text, the left hemisphere is able to process well, the right brain has to be involved to decipher the context.

According to Kewra & Robinson (1995), using graphic organizers such as in ISN are effective in increasing students understanding and information retention. The non-linear structure of the graphic organizers, resemble the structure used by the brain to organize information.

Rhythm and rhyme used in poetry may also be in effective in long-term retention in information. Students are required to make their own haikus, limericks and acrostic poems based on the notes. Learning by embedding rhythm and rhyme in the ISN and then sharing the poems with their peers seem to help learning.

Emotions also play a big role in learning. Wolfe (2001) and Jensen (1998) have demonstrated that learning is more powerful and long term if there are strong emotions, positive or negative, involved. From that perspective, one may surmise that if students have more fun creating their own left hand side assignments, then the hope is that they will remember their notes better in the long run.

INTERACTIVE SCIENCE NOTEBOOK AS FORMATIVE ASSESSMENT TOOL

> Every day, science teachers are asking questions, listening carefully to students as they explain their ideas, observing students as they work in groups, examining student writing and drawing and orchestrating classroom discourse that promotes the public sharing of ideas. The purposeful, planned and often spontaneous teacher-to-student, student-to-teacher, and student-to-student verbal and written interactions involve a variety of assessment techniques. These techniques are used to engage students in thinking deeply about their ideas in science, uncover the pre-existing ideas students bring to their learning that can be used as starting point to build upon during instruction, and help teachers and students determine how well individuals and the class are progressing toward developing scientific understanding" (Keeley, 2008, p. 3).

LHS assignments are useful not only for student learning but for teachers to monitor student learning. A quick check on the LHS assignment easily informs the teacher of any common misconception about the topic at hand. Dependent on the extension of the topic shown by the student, it can truly show understanding and deeper learning by the student. By changing my next instruction to adjust these findings, I am better at meeting the needs of the students.

The Research Project

At the beginning of second semester in the first week of February 2010, my school principal came into my classes to explain the study and to distribute the student assent forms. The basic premise for the project was explained to the students. My principal explained that I was conducting the study to explore whether ISN can be used to improve science learning and student achievement, and to help students monitor their own learning. She explained to them that various Instructional Intelligence (II) strategies were to be used, as well as the Cornell note-taking tactic and reflective learning logs.

As well, the procedures for the two surveys were explained to them. Importantly, it was made clear that the participation in this study would have no effect on their Science 10 grade, since the Interactive Science Notebook would be used as a regular learning tool for all students whether they decided to participate or not in the study. Parent consent forms were distributed. If their parent or guardian chose not to give consent, they would not be part of the study. The student assent forms and the parent consent forms were distributed by the Principal.

All of my students were introduced to the Interactive Science Notebooks (ISN) as part of typical instruction in their Science 10 class. Each student was asked to bring a spiral bound notebook. One block of class was spent on setting up the notebook. It was explained to the students that all the notes would be taken in Cornell style on the Right Hand Side (RHS) page of the notebook. ISN is a technique used for students to "interact" with the learning in classroom. It uses a coiled notebook to keep all the notes and completed work, subsequent to taking the notes, together. According to Waldman & Crippen (2009), "At its best, an interactive notebook provides a varied set of strategies to create a personal, organized, and documented learning record " (p. 51).

On the Right Hand Side (RHS) of the notebook, the page is further divided into one- third and two- third sections. After taking the notes on the two thirds section, on the one- third section, the students were urged to write questions for themselves on the notes they took. The questions can vary from simple to more complex. It follows the Bloom's Taxonomy model of questioning. At the bottom of the RHS, the students are then encouraged to summarize the notes in a paragraph. Then, they were asked to write a reflective learning log that monitored self learning (NB: please contact the author for logs, rubrics, and surveys mentioned in the narrative). A sample page was photocopied for the students and the students had it pasted into their notebook for reference.

At the beginning of each ISN use, the students were given the notes from the overhead projector. During this time, each Left Hand Assignment was introduced with an explanation, sample work and guided practice. All students, including the students who were not part of the study were required as part of the course to keep the ISN. The ISN were checked after each lesson and were collected for marking twice during the study. The marking rubric was explained and pasted into the notebook at the initial set up.

On the Left Hand Side (LHS) facing the notes, the Instructional Intelligence (II) strategies were used to help students learn the science concepts as well as help monitor their own learning. Essentially, the school work generated from these activities formed the data for analysis in the present study. The only change in the Left Hand Side assignment from the originally planned activity was to substitute using cinquain, a five line poem that has one topic that describes the topic's action or feelings, for the Venn diagram. With the grade level and the type of subjects explored in Science 10, I felt that the Venn diagram was more useful in helping students learn.

After completing the Cornell notes, questions, summary and reflective learning log, the students were asked to do a LHS assignment chosen from one of the ten, Instructional Intelligence strategies through which they learned. This was usually completed at home in order to make sure students were learning and internalizing the new science concept. In the reflections, the students were asked to assess their learning the vocabulary and the scientific concepts. They gave feedback as to their feelings on the lesson itself, and were urged to think about how the lesson relates to everyday life or some other topic. Students had the opportunity to share their work with others in the class orally or by doing a gallery walk. This process verified the student's understanding of a concept as well as helping them to learn from one another.

After the initial introduction to using the ISN, during regularly scheduled science class time, I gave the participating students the first survey to complete. The survey took approximately thirty minutes and it included twenty yes/no questions and two open-ended questions. The questions were about science note taking, use of the notes for learning, instructional strategies that work the best or worst for the students, and self assessment for learning.

The project ran for approximately ten weeks with a two week Spring break included. On average, the students used the ISN two to three times a week. When not using the ISN, the students were involved with variety of classroom activities and experiences such as labs, different types of group work, videos, peer presentations, discussions, peer tutoring, tests, guest speakers and fieldtrips.

At the end of the project in mid-May, I administered the second survey with 18 multiple choice questions, and open-ended questions that helped students to reflect on the aspects of their learning that related to my main research questions (see the opening *Prelude*).

Results of the Two Surveys

The first survey was administered to obtain a sense of how much the students knew about the ISN and its various components. The results were tallied. It was a pleasant surprise to see that the majority of the students found taking notes as a useful activity and that at least half of the students took notes three times or more in typical academic classes. Approximately 50% of the students reviewed their notes once or twice after taking them, 10% never looked at them again and about 30 % of the students claimed that they reviewed them three times or more. Nearly half of the students in my study group had used the ISN with me from last year; the other half were new to the ISN. Over 71% of the students had used Cornell style notes previous to taking my class. Sixty seven percent (67%) of the students had made up questions to ask themselves after taking notes and 62% of the students had made a summary of their notes to review. Only 29 % of the students had ever written a reflection to monitor their learning. Reflection is a critical part of learning. According to Keeley (2008, p. 25), "Encouraging reflection and self-assessment helps students develop important metacognitive skills that help them monitor their own thinking and learning." As well, "A metacognitive approach to instruction can help students learn to take control of their own learning by defining learning goals and monitoring their progress in achieving them" (Brandsford et al., 1999, p. 18).

For the Left Hand Side (LHS) assignments, questions were posed to the students regarding their familiarity with using the various Instructional Intelligence (II) tactics. Analysis revealed that 72% of the students had made vocabulary cards but only 38% had made riddle cards to help them learn. About half of the students had made cartoons to help them review.

Some of the students were surprised that poetry would be used to learn science—81% of the students had composed Haikus, 86% cinquains, and 76% used acrostic poems. Concrete and graphic poems were also familiar with 81% of the students.

It was great to see that substantial number of students were used to using graphic organizers as an aid to learning. Seventy-six percent (76%) of the students had made Fishbone diagrams and, 62% had made concept maps but only 43% had made mind maps.

Overall, when the students were asked if they thought the LHS assignments would be helpful to their learning, 57% thought that they would benefit, 24% were unsure and 19% did not think that they would be helpful.

I also surveyed the students regarding their "learning styles" based on Gardner's Multiple Intelligence (MI) theory. Interestingly, 38% chose their strongest learning style as Musical, 24% each for Logical-mathematic and Interpersonal. Fourteen (14%) of the students identified being strong in Bodily-Kinesthetic, Linguistic and Intrapersonal traits. Only 10% were Naturalistic and 5% Spatial characteristics. Approximately 29% of the students identified more than one learning style.

For the long answer section of the survey, when asked if the students thought the ISN would be helpful in students learning, 81% thought that they would benefit. The majority of the students thought that the ISN would be a good resource for reviewing. Some of their comments were "all notes in one place," "if I have a question, I can refer to it before my tests and exams," and "better than just taking a lot of notes, making up questions help me remember."

Some students thought that the ISN would be a fun way of keeping notes, making comments such as "makes it more interesting, variety," and "… can always look back on what you wrote not only in the form of notes but also in poems and pictures; it makes everything different and interesting." One student alluded to changing memory patterns "instead of confusing your muscles, making them stronger – you are doing that to the brain." To do the Cornell notes, summary, reflections, questions and the LHS assignment, the students would be looking over the notes at least three times. This requires active engagement by the student with the material at hand.

One student thought that using the ISN would probably be helpful but did not give reasons why he or she thought so. Three students did not answer the question. I assume that they were also unsure of the note taking efficacy.

When asked what II tactics for the LHS assignment the students preferred, there was a huge variety in the answers. About half of the students thought that the vocabulary cards would be useful. Some comments were "help me remember words that are difficult but important" and "helps to test myself." The popularity of the vocabulary cards were followed by strategies and organizers such as fishbone diagram, Haiku, cartoon, concrete poem, acrostic poem, mind map, concept map in that order. Students mentioned "fun," "creative," "remembers artistically," "helps to stick in your head," "set the image of the definition" when associating the LHS assignments to learning. One student thought that all of the II tactics would be helpful and two students did not know.

After using the ISN for a 10 week period, the second survey (see Table 1) was given to the students. The first survey had 18 Yes/No questions. For the second survey, I thought that the Yes/No answers were too limited to give a full, rich voice to the students' perspectives. Therefore, I had the students rank their answers in a Likert-based rating scale: (1) Strongly agree, (2) Somewhat agree, (3) Unsure, (4) Somewhat disagree, and (5) Strongly disagree. There were also three open-ended questions where the students could elaborate on their thoughts.

HOW DOES THE INTERACTIVE SCIENCE NOTEBOOK HELP STUDENTS LEARN SCIENCE IN GRADE 10?

Twenty-nine percent (29%) strongly agreed and 57% somewhat agreed that Cornell notes were useful in learning science. Ten percent (10%) were unsure, and only one student somewhat disagreed. No student thought that Cornell notes were useless. Fifty-eight (58%) of the students reviewed their Cornell notes more than other forms of notes from their other academic courses. Taking Cornell notes requires organization. Many students struggle with school in general due their lack of organizational skills. I observed numerous instances where the students referred back to the notebook when they needed a quick reference.

After the Cornell notes were taken, the students were asked to condense their notes into a four to five sentence summary. This process makes students focus on the lesson and discover the main ideas. Many students had trouble summarizing. By having them share their summaries orally, having gallery walks where the students were able to see a variety of samples and discussing what criteria made a good summary, the students were able to improve upon their own work.

The last step in taking the Cornell notes was to write a reflective summary. The students were asked to think about the day's learning, what they found easy or difficult. If they did not understand the material, the students were asked to think of steps to learn it. Some comments such as " I love physics so this stuff is easy," "I get it completely," "I learned some new vocab though," "Starting to understand it—Still need to work on it to master it," and "I really like to learn about the earth. I find it very interesting to learn about the land we live in and how it works." By reading their reflections, I was able to monitor the students' level of understanding.

Having to make up questions to ask themselves after taking the notes was useful to 72% of the students. Sixty six percent (66%) of the students found summarizing the notes in their own words helped them learn science. Only 38% of the students thought that reflecting on their learning helped them monitor their own learning. Thirty-three percent (33%) were unsure and 29% somewhat disagreed. The questions that the student asked about the notes were classified according to Bloom's taxonomy and Costa's system of classification. The students could ask simple Level 1 recall questions such as "What," "Where," "Describe," and "List." For Level 2 questions, there had to be some information processing that the students had to do to answer them. The students had to "Compare and Contrast," "Explain," "Make analogies." For Level 3, the students were involved with higher thinking skills. They asked questions that involved going beyond the notes. They "Hypothesized," "Predicted," and "Speculated." I believe strongly that being able to ask questions of oneself is a critical part of the metacognition process.

Table 1. Interactive science notebook survey # 2

Questions	*Strongly agree 1*	*Somewhat agree 2*	*Unsure 3*	*Somewhat disagree 4*	*Strongly disagree 5*
1. Generally, I find taking Cornell notes useful in learning science.	6(29%)	12(57%)	2(10%)	1(5%)	0
2. I review the Cornell notes more often than notes taken in other forms in other academic classes.	6(29%)	6(29%)	7(33%)	2(10%)	0
3. Having to make up Questions to ask myself after taking notes is helpful in learning science.	5(24%)	10(48%)	4(19%)	2(10%)	0
4. Having to write a Summary to review my notes is helping me learn science (1 provided no response)	7(33%)	6(29%)	4(19%)	3(14%)	1(5%)
5. Having to write a Reflection to think about my learning helps me monitor my own learning.	3(14%)	5(24%)	7(33%)	6(29%)	0
6. Vocabulary cards help me learn science concepts.	6(29%)	7(33%)	3(14%)	5(24%)	0
7. Riddle cards help me learn science concepts.	0	9(38%)	8(38%)	3(14%)	1(5%)
8. Cartoons help me learn science concepts.	2(10%)	9(38%)	5(24%)	4(19%)	1(5%)
9. Haikus help me learn science concepts.	1(5%)	12(57%)	5(24%)	3(14%)	0
10. Acrostic poems help me learn science concepts.	4(19%)	10(48%)	4(19%)	3(14%)	0

Table 1. (continued)

11. Concrete/Graphic poems help me learn science concepts.	2(10%)	13(62%)	2(10%)	3(14%)	1(5%)
12. Graphic organizers such as Venn diagrams help me learn science concepts.	9(38%)	7(33%)	1(5%)	3(14%)	1(5%)
13. Graphic organizers such as Fishbone diagrams help me learn science concepts. (1 response blank)	8(40%)	7(35%)	3(15%)	1(5%)	1(5%)
14. Concept maps help me learn science concepts.	5(24%)	8(38%)	4(19%)	3(14%)	1(5%)
15. Mind maps help me learn science concepts.	3(14%)	11(52%)	4(19%)	2(10%)	1(5%)
16. Left-hand side assignments are helpful in my learning science.	7(33%)	7(33%)	4(19%)	2(10%)	2(10%)
17. Doing different Left Hand Side assignments exposed me to different Learning Styles.	5(24%)	9(38%)	4(19%)	1(5%)	1(5%)
18. Doing different Left Hand Side assignments helped strengthen my own Learning Styles.	3(14%)	11(52%)	5(24%)	0	2(10%)

For the LHS II tactics, 62% found the vocabulary cards useful. The vocabulary cards not only had the word definition but included a link word to help students remember, a picture and two usage sentences. Only 38% of the students found riddle cards somewhat useful. Many student had difficulties creating riddles. The riddles did not have to be funny. Some of riddles involved puns. Thirty-eight percent (38%) were unsure about it's usefulness and 19% found the riddle cards not useful.

Forty-eight percent (48%) of the students stated that the cartoons helped them with learning science. Not surprising, the students who enjoyed doodling and drawing usually were enthusiastic about cartoons.

Using poetry in science was a novel concept to many of my students. However, 61% found haikus useful, 67% Acrostic poems and 73% concrete poems. While making haikus, I observed the students struggling to come up with descriptive words that also met the syllable criteria. Both the haikus and the acrostic poems required the students to find the vocabulary beyond their notes to describe a concept. Many students enjoyed visually representing the concepts that they were learning. I used *Poke in the I, a Collection of Concrete Poems* (Janeczko & Raschka, 2005) to introduce the concept.

Graphic organizers were popular. Seventy-one percent (71%) found Venn diagrams helpful, 75% fishbone diagrams, 61% concept maps, followed by 66% mind maps. Having the students make different types of graphic organizers forced the students to re-organize the information in their notes.

Overall, 66% of the students reported that the LHS II tactics were helpful, 19% were unsure and 20% found them useless.

Sixty-two percent (62%) reported that doing different LHS assignments exposed them to different learning styles and 67% reported that the different assignments helped to strengthen their own learning styles.

It was to my surprise that all 21 students reported that the ISN was useful in learning science concepts. They found the notebook "easy," "organized," "helpful," and "convenient." A student remarked that the ISN "makes me think about what we are learning." Another added that ISN added to the "variety" and the LHS assignments helped them "expand knowledge." Another student noted that "It would help me if I actually did it – add to work load" as another student observed, "more effort but better notebook."

DOES THE USE OF AN INTERACTIVE SCIENCE NOTEBOOK (ISN) INCREASE STUDENT ACHIEVEMENT IN GRADE 10 SCIENCE?

In terms of ISN helping to increase student achievement in Science 10, eighteen students out of twenty one (86%) agreed. Five students alluded to "understanding lessons better" and "deeper learning." Many students reported the effectiveness of the ISN in reviewing and preparing for tests—"LHS and notes helpful in remembering things," "helps you learn in different ways," "variety," "helping you get good grade," and "did well in exams." Two students thought that the ISN probably helped to increase achievement in Science 10. One student didn't think that the ISN was helpful but did not comment on the reasons.

After completing the ISN assignment, the students were quickly checked for completing the assignment. I checked and signed each notebook that was completed. If there was no signature, that meant that the student had incomplete work and it needed to be done for next day. The ISN were collected twice during the semester for marking. ISN had two parts for assessment. For the Cornell notes, Summary and Reflection, the three (3) point rubric was used. For the LHS assignment, a five point rubric was used. The students were able to earn bonus marks by teaching a parent or a guardian what they learned. The parents then had to sign the parent signature sheet explaining what they learned from their child. This opportunity not only gave students better understanding by teaching someone else but it also kept the parents informed about what the students were learning and how well they understood the subject. To compare the students grades in the course and their grades received for the ISN, I took their marks and drew a correlation scatter plot graph (see Table 2 above). The reader may observe that there is a strong, positive relationship between the course and ISN grades.

Table 2. The correlation between Science 10 grades and ISN grades

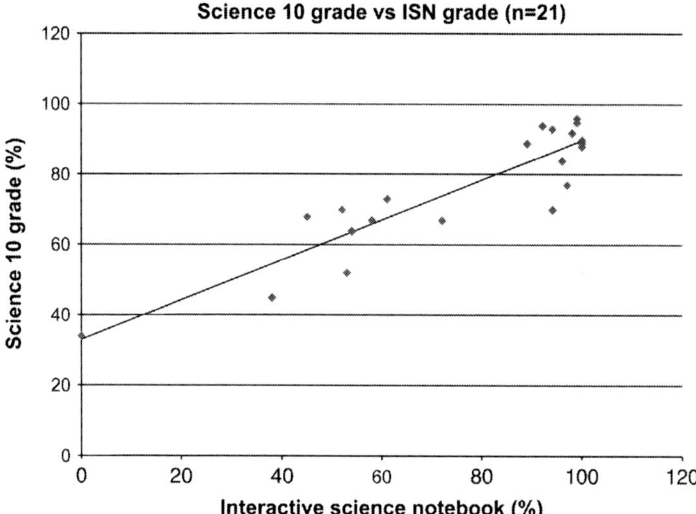

HOW DO INSTRUCTIONAL INTELLIGENCE STRATEGIES SUCH AS "LEFT-HAND SIDE ASSIGNMENTS" HELP TEACHERS MONITOR STUDENT LEARNING AS A FORMATIVE ASSESSMENT STRATEGY?

When asked to choose two most useful LHS II tactics, the ranking was as follows: Vocabulary cards, Venn Diagram, Fishbone diagram, Haiku, Cartoon, Mind map, Acrostic poem, Concept map, Concrete poem. One student listed none and no explanation was given.

Lastly, the students were asked about the role of LHS assignments in helping the teacher monitor student learning. Six students thought that it was a way for a teacher to see "how well the students understand, learn." Four students thought that it showed "how much effort the students are putting in." Other comments included "see what the students are thinking," "creative deeper learning," "monitor what methods each student learnt the best," "see how the student understand the notes," and "different learning styles seen." Whether the LHS assignments were done or not gave me an opportunity to have a conversation with a student about the reason for it not being done. I wanted to find out if the student had no time to do the work, did not know how to use the II strategy that was assigned, did not understand the notes or did not know how to transfer the content into the II strategy. This quick check was a formative assessment strategy that helped me gage where the students were at and how I can proceed with my next lesson.

Summary

When I started my investigation, I had three questions in mind—(1) Does the use of ISN help students learn science? (2) Does ISN help improve student achievement? (3) Do the II strategies used in the LHS assignments help with teacher monitor student learning? As a result of my inquiry, I believe that the ISN can be a useful tool in student learning. In concert with multiple intelligence theory, learning style theory, and brain research, it seems that learning can become more powerful with the use of Interactive Science Notebook. Using the ISN seems beneficial in student learning and the acquisition of new science concepts. It also seems to have positive relationship with student achievement. As important, the LHS assignments help the teacher monitor individual student learning. When using the ISN, it seems that the students take ownership in organizing, processing and reflecting on their learning. As student engagement is vital to student learning, ISN has the potential to be used not only in a science class but can be a strong learning tool in all classes. In retrospect, I believe that while learning new science concepts, the ISN helps to personalize and document the student's own learning.

Implications and Suggestions for Further Research

Teachers are always searching for ways to enhance student learning. In teaching science, I found that it was difficult to engage all students at all times. The reasons for this may be varied. Some students are eager to learn anything. Others only want to learn things that interest them. Some come to class not ready to learn anything. By providing a variety of instructional strategies, differentiated and adapted instruction, I hoped to engage as many learners in my classes. I believe that all educators must explore best practices to enhance learning in all students, and using the ISN was a valuable tool.

Because of the BC Provincial Examination at the end of the semester, I felt rushed to "cover" the Science 10 curriculum. In doing so, sometimes I was able to do a quick check on the ISN. Usually the Summary, Reflection and the LHS assignments were due the day after the notes were taken. If the students were not able to finish the assignments, they were given a chance to finish for the next day. A final chance for completing their work was given to the students upon ISN collection for marking. Having the expectation that the work is due but also giving the students some flexibility provided students some room not only to finish their work but to pay attention to quality. Many of my students lead busy lives with extra-curricular work, family life and jobs as well as full time school. The students appreciated the flexibility. Some students complained that it was a lot of work to keep the ISN. But at the end, 100% of the students agreed that ISN was a valuable learning tool. Using ISN was an attempt to organize the student learning in a cohesive and personalized manner. Many students with established good work habits had no trouble. Some students struggled at first with many issues: forgetting to bring the notebook to class, not doing the homework, having "written output issues," resisting a different way of taking notes, challenging the idea of learning through various II strategies, not liking certain II strategies an others. Few students who did not do the notebook homework, did not do any homework in general. Exposure to different II strategies was important in providing students with different tools for learning. By providing choices on the II strategies, students were able to do work that they preferred or had fun doing. Fun and novelty are two elements of student learning that educators are always in search of to enhance both their practice and student learning.

One student could not take legible notes. This issue was resolved by having the student word-process on a computer, printing out the notes at home, and pasting it onto his notebook. If the ISN could be set up for a computer-friendly model, it may be helpful for students who possess written output problems.

In comparing the ISN grade and the final Science 10 grade, there is a strong positive correlation. The class mark is based on a compilation of marks through ISN, tests, group work, presentations and others. Thus, if students kept a good ISN, they also seemed to do well in the course. According to the graph in Table 2, the reader may interpret that the students who scored 90% or higher on the ISN, scored 80% or higher in the course grade. One exception was an ESL student who put in a lot of work on the ISN but scored low on exams and quizzes. Her mark was pulled down by the test scores. It is questionable that there is a causal relationship between the ISN and grades. i.e., the ISN 'caused' learning that directly led to good grades. Rather, I think that it is accurate to say that the more effort the student put into their notebook, more time was spent reading their notes and processing the content while summarizing, reflecting, and creating the LHS assignment. In turn, the students were more likely to learn. In general, the students who did not keep good ISN, did poorly in the course. Because participating in my research was voluntary, my study may have been biased. The students who felt that they were not organized to keep a good ISN may not have volunteered. Also, these same students were more likely to not remember to bring back the student assent form and the parent consent form. Therefore, the less organized students were more likely not to be part of the research group.

I found the Summary, Reflection and II strategies used on the LHS useful in monitoring student understanding. In turn, it guided my instruction to an extent. However, due to time constraints, it was very difficult to be flexible in my pacing even though I knew that some of the students were struggling with certain concepts. In teaching a course with less time constraints such as Science 8 or 9, it would be interesting to see if this formative assessment strategy is more useful to the teacher.

I am encouraged by the results of my study. The survey student responses confirmed the usefulness of ISN learning science and relationship with student science achievement. As a teacher, I found the ISN a valuable tool for differentiated learning and assessment. I would like to expand the use of ISN by introducing it to my colleagues at my school not only in the Science department but in other departments. Furthermore, it would be interesting to see if the ISN is useful in disciplines such as Mathematics and English.

Ji Ai Cho
Squamish School District 48
JCho@sd48.bc.ca

CAREN J. HALL

THE EFFICACY OF VISUAL JOURNALS FOR AT-RISK FIRST NATIONS STUDENTS

A Sense of Belonging

Working at an Alternate Secondary School poses unique challenges and opportunities. The students in the grade 11 and 12 program are at high-risk not to graduate. All students have an Individual Education Program (IEP) tailored to their specific circumstances. These youth at risk students are complex and have many emotional, social, physical, and mental blocks to learning (Bennett & Rolheiser, 2001). Many students have learning disabilities, moderate to severe mental health problems, or social problems. Accordingly, our alternate program is structured so the same teachers teach students in both Grades 11 and 12, a journey taking two to three years. This enables relationships to develop between students and teachers and deepens the teachers' understanding of the complex student needs. I have a great opportunity to slowly build a strong relationship with each student and develop a classroom community that many in mainstream schools may not experience.

Throughout my teaching career I have actively sought teaching positions and professional development involving First Nations Students. Many seminars outline the history of problems, an explanation of factors that lead to labeling First Nations students as youth at risk, but few documents offer concrete tools for classroom teachers to use to encourage academic and social success in the classroom. My experiences in the alternate education classroom and with First Nations students often parallel the experiences of teachers in remote communities and cities alike. The writings of Cohen (2006) and Brokenleg (2002), whose research and stories touched me deeply as an educator, and echo the stories of First Nations educators across British Columbia. The British Columbia Ministry of Education reported a province-wide high school graduation rate of 89.5% (including First Nations students) in 2008. The First Nations graduation rate in 2008 was merely 49% (BC Ministry of Education, 2008).

Based on an awareness of those statistics and their practical implications for the classroom, it seems there is a need for educators to understand the broad notion of "belonging" and its critical importance in the classroom. The purpose of this study is to research the efficacy of visual journals for First Nations students in an Alternate School setting. Visual journals allow students to represent their understanding of the curriculum in the form of drawing, collage, poetry, or a mix of different mediums. The efficacy, in an alternate setting, is strongly tied to the sense of belonging the student has to the school community and the importance of

P. Gouzouasis (ed.), Pedagogy in a New Tonality: Teacher Inquiries on Creative Tactics, Strategies, Graphics Organizers, and Visual Journals in the K-12 Classroom, 167–183.

this to academic success for youth at risk to dropout. Therefore, my primary component is to study the efficacy of visual journals to determine if they contribute to First Nations students' sense of belonging in the school community.

What is Belonging?

Belonging is the basic psychological need for human bonds, present in every human being (Brendtro, Ness & Mitchell, 2005; Brendtro, Brokenleg & VanBockern, 2002; Osterman, 2000; Sax, 2005). Creating an environment that fosters feelings of belonging in the classroom is essential for teachers, especially educators who work with First Nations youth at risk. Adolescents may feel alienated at a school for numerous reasons. Without the basic need of belonging addressed and considered with its many implications, it is often difficult for these students to experience academic success.

Students are happier when they are connected to their work and community. Brighthouse (2008), Osterman (2000), and Brendtro et al., (2002) speak at length on the importance and characteristics of belonging in a classroom environment. A first component of reclaiming learning environments, especially for First Nations students, is to ensure students "experience belonging in a supportive community, rather than being lost in a...bureaucracy" (p. 4). Brendtro et al., (2002) quotes Desmond Tutu who urges educators to "surmount the 'us and them' syndrome" and learn to treat each person as a part of our family" (p. x). My literature review does not include the importance of belonging in peer relationships, groups, or families where there is ample literature. Instead, I focus on teacher-student relationships, the teacher's role of creating belonging in their learning environment, and teaching strategies and tactics intended to foster a sense of belonging.

Belonging and Academic Success

Every person has a deep need to belong (Brendtro et al., 2002; Brendtro et al., 2005; Johnson & Johnson, 2004; Osterman, 2000) especially in adolescence (Anderman, 2003; Osterman, 2000). For centuries, humans lived in small hunting and gathering groups and farming communities. We interact daily with our families, friends, and people who share common interests. Essentially, we belong to these groups. For students to flourish, Brighthouse (2008) believes that students need to be connected with their classroom community and the work they are doing. He found students with the greatest unmet needs for relationships are the most alienated from adults and peers.

Brendtro et al., (2002) are concerned that society is creating an increasing number of youth at risk due to impaired relationships. Historically, the nuclear family is less important than tribes in building healthy and growing civilizations. Education occurred in the home, with extended family, and through apprenticeships (Brendtro, et al., 2002). Today, teachers in many high schools rarely communicate with students as whole beings, as teachers are often seen in a narrowly defined role.

Osterman's (2000) extensive and compelling literature review studies how schools address the need for students belonging to their school community. Her review is valuable to educators as she goes beyond explaining why creating a sense of belonging is important to how to create such an environment. Osterman adds that the satisfaction of emotional needs leads to an overall experience of wellbeing and health. She reports the findings of Leithwood & Aitken (1995) who found that when needs are not satisfied at school many studies predict lower motivation, participation, development, performance, engagement, dropout rates and alienation. In discussing the research of Baumeister & Leary (1995), Osterman found that the "lack of belongingness is a primary cause of a wide range of psychological and behavioral problems" (p. 327). She summarizes that the school environment has a more direct influence on academic motivation and behavior than family does. Therefore, she argues, educators cannot afford to overlook this variable in their classroom environment.

Osterman (2000) challenges the assumption that belonging is not a precondition for engagement, achievement, and compliance, and that the student's emotional needs are met at home or in other social relationships. She refutes a quantitative study where Anderman (2003) researches the academic and social perceptions as predictors of change in students' sense of belonging at school. Anderman drew her data from a larger, longitudinal research project examining instructional practices and student motivation. There were 618 participants (253 boys, 365 girls) in grades 6 to 8 from seven middle schools in southeastern United States of America. Students completed surveys consisting of 130 items and focused on student perceptions of the classroom climate in their teacher relationships and academic motivation. The items were presented in a 5-point Likert-type format. The purpose of Anderman's study was to examine change in a sample of middle school students' self-reported sense of school belonging through three semesters. She specifically asked questions relating to sense of school belonging, perceived classroom task and goal orientation, expectancy for academic success, perceived teacher support for mutual respect, and academic achievement.

Anderman hypothesized that "one should expect both academic and social variables to predict the sense of belonging…academic achievement is likely to influence students' sense of belonging" (p. 6), it seems "likely that students with a high grade point average may feel reinforced in their sense of school belonging, while students with a record of poorer performance find it difficult to maintain a feeling of legitimacy and place in their school" (p. 7). She concludes that a sense of school belonging and teacher promotion of mutual respect used in the study is not as well established in the research literature, as are academic motivation measures. She reports that students who possess high Grade Point Average (GPA) scores also are more confident about school success and more positive associations between perceptions of their teachers' support for mutual respect.

Notwithstanding, Anderman seems to make oversights in examining the fundamental issues for belonging. First, she does not separate gender. Second, she does not differentiate between ethnic minorities. Finally, despite evidence in other comprehensive studies such as Osterman (2000), Anderman does not mention the possibility that a sense of belonging precedes and is predictor of academic success. This distinction is important because there is little evidence demonstrating that belonging is directly caused by achievement; however, there is substantial literature that suggests a sense of belonging influences achievement through increased engagement (Osterman, 2000).

The Importance of a Positive Teacher-student Relationship

A practical question educators must ask themselves concerns their role in supporting students. For students to experience a sense belonging, relatedness, and community in the classroom they must feel worthy of respect by their teacher. Research shows teachers' perceptions of students' engagement and ability influence the level of support students receive (Osterman, 2000). As Canadian educators, we must be aware of such biases, especially with First Nations students, to ensure we are not shortchanging those who need words or actions of encouragement, empathy, or assistance.

In their book, *No Disposable Kids,* Brendtro et al., (2002) describe 'Synergistic Relationships' as positive individual relationships between educators and students. These relationships are the foundation of successful classrooms. Teachers can enhance their legitimacy by showing respect for their students and themselves. Brendtro et al., (2005) describe techniques to use in the classroom that focus on the student's self-worth and dignity, and offer specific ways to create successful problem solving alliances with students. This appears very practical for Alternate Education. The authors appear to adhere to the common principle that positive experiences can occur in a classroom climate characterized by mutual respect.

Brendtro et al., (2002) profile that many of today's classrooms are unfriendly, and are a place of discouragement. When negative expectations, punitive outcomes, boredom, lack of adventure, irresponsibility, or the lack of assigning demanding tasks creates environments of disengagement, students do not feel they belong. Cultures of disrespect spark aggression, and a breakdown of relationships (Brendtro et al., 2005). That said, Osterman theorizes that teachers should be encouraged to facilitate dialogue and supportive interaction with their students in and out of the classroom. She states her findings are "strong and consistent" to support the theory that "students who experience acceptance are more highly motivated and engaged in learning and more committed to school. These concepts of commitment and engagement are closely linked to student performance and . . . to the quality of students learning" (p. 359).

Brendtro et al., (2002) support Osterman's claims that teachers need to create an environment of belonging in the classroom. Traits of such a classroom include a student feeling attached, loved, befriended, and trusting both of the teacher and the classroom environment. If First Nations students' needs for belonging are not met at home or in the classroom, youths may feel rejected and find artificial, distorted belongings through behavior such as attention seeking, risky behavior, or joining a gang (Anderman, 2003; Brendtro et al., 2002; Brendtro et al., 2005; Sax 2005). This can be changed by corrective relationships, trust, and intimacy (Strand & Peacock, 2002; Brendtro et al., 2002). A survey of over 90,000 adolescents of multiple ethnicities showed that there were specific school related factors in the avoidance of harmful behaviors including teachers treating their students fairly, feeling close with others at school, and experiencing positive interactions with teachers and other students.

McNeely & Falci (2004) explore the association between teacher support and social belonging to the participation in six adolescent health-risk behaviors. This study directly relates the relationship the student has with their teacher as a method of reducing at risk behavior. Their sample was drawn from the National Longitudinal study of Adolescent Health of 80 high schools and 20,745 adolescents in Grades 7 to 12. The survey contained six questions that tap into aspects of connection to school, social belonging, and perceptions of their teachers. Their models included five sociodemographic characteristics: ethnicity, age, gender, family structure, and household income. Those critical distinctions are not differentiated in the Anderman study.

Their findings have major implications for teachers of adolescent youth at risk. School connectedness is associated with mental health and decreased rates of involvement in risky behaviors including drug and alcohol use, sex, violence, suicide, and delinquency (McNeely & Falci, 2004; Brendtro et al., 2002). McNeely & Falci state that social support generates a strong sense of "belonging, which, in turn, leads to increased engagement and academic motivation" (p. 284). They demonstrate that when students believe their teachers care about them personally, they are more likely to be engaged in school and perform better academically, and participate in fewer health-risk behaviors. McNeely & Falci conclude that teacher support is protective against the initiation of risky behaviors, but not on the reduction or cessation of behavior once initiated, with the exception of violence. McNeely & Falci end with a compelling question that that warrants further inquiry: can support from teachers compensate for the lack of an intimate, positive, parent-child relationship?

Belonging and First Nations Students

My research did not unearth any studies that specifically addressed belonging and Canadian First Nations students. *Reclaiming Youth at Risk* (Brendtro et al., 2002), based on the experiences of American First Nations youth at risk, seems to be the primary resource for First Nations educators in North America. This book is referenced in the British Columbia Teachers Federations (BCTF) guide for educating Aboriginal students and in the North Vancouver School District's Aboriginal Educational Agreement (2006). Other than this book, there seems to be a significant gap in both research and literature regarding Canadian First Nations students and belonging and academic success.

Reclaiming Youth at Risk is similar in principle to *No Disposable Kids* (Brendtro et al., 2005), yet focuses on more of the spiritual and emotional development of youth at risk from the spiritual healing practices of First Nations peoples. It offers solutions to the dislocation that often happens between adolescent First Nations students and their teachers and schools. It argues that youth at risk can be reclaimed through encouragement, responsibility, and gaining life purpose. I was pleased to see a chapter focusing on brain research and scientific data that support the need for emotional and spiritual healing of students. This research reinforces the innate, physiological need for belonging in schools, and scientifically reinforces the importance of emotional and spiritual health.

Brendtro et al., (2002) weave First Nations knowledge of child rearing into their philosophy of education First Nations adolescents. Although Aboriginal societies were conquered by advanced military and technology beginning in the 1700's, they argue that many aspects of their civilization were highly developed and much to offer modern society. Brendtro et al., discuss how First Nations tribes in North America possessed profound child psychology wisdom. While Western education systems put First Nations children in residential schools to "Kill the Indian to save the Child," the First Nations philosophy of the central purpose in life was to educate and empower children. They adhered to a holistic approach fostering self-esteem, teaching the child that they were significant, competent, powerful, wise, and that they belonged to both family and tribe. The authors argue that this philosophy should not be unique for First Nations children, but for all children. Research shows that belonging to one's community continues to be a significant factor in First Nations communities (Brendtro et al., 2002; Strand & Peacock, 2002).

Strand & Peacock's (2002) literature review focuses on school success in American Indian students. The authors used a nationally representative sample of more than 90,000 young people of all ethnicities, then, a sample involving in-depth interviews with 120 Native students from across the United States and Canada. Strand & Peacock identify connections to both teachers and schools as major contributors to the success of First Nations students. They found that a key factor to staying in school was being well grounded and connected to their tribal culture. They found that students who were bi-cultural and felt they belonged in both worlds experienced the most academic success compared to students who felt alienated in one community.

Strand & Peacock's literature review includes a study of 117 American Indian adults who classify themselves as 'bicultural' were least likely to suffer from depression. The authors state that there is too little research done on the subject of First Nations people in North America and the collection of data at this point is more suggestive than definitive. This is a necessary and worthwhile thread of inquiry to increase the academic success of our First Nations students.

The Students in the Present Inquiry

> I have no absolute answers, I only share experiences: do they have meaning to you? Represent something to you? (Sparkes, 2002, p. 73)

Susan is a seventeen-year old girl enrolled in my class since May 2009 (NB: all students names have been changed). She is of mixed ethnic heritage—First Nations, Chinese, and German. It took me over six months to learn of her First Nations heritage as she never spoke of it. Susan lives with her mother and has no siblings. She struggled with school attendance problems, and her attitudes toward school and authority figures were aggressive and detached. In her first month at school, she was withdrawn; her attendance was at 48% and she was officially documented as "disrespectful and argumentative." We did not get to know Susan very well, but she returned in September 2009 with a new set of issues including migraines, depression, and sleep problems limiting her success at school. We would often wake her up while she was asleep at her desk during class. We soon discovered her love for art and offered for her to take Art Therapy first block in the morning as an incentive to get to school on time. Susan began Social Justice 12 in October, and began using painting and collage as methods of expression in the course. By November her attendance was at 86% and she seemed more at ease in the classroom and with teachers.

Ben joined us from the Kamloops Reservation where he lived with his mother. He moved to Vancouver to live with his aunt after several drug-related problems at his Kamloops Band school. He is nineteen years old and started grade 11 in October, 2009. We knew of his drug dealing before he arrived and he was suspended in November, 2009 and April, 2010 for possession of drugs. Ben had moderately good attendance, averaging 78% in the first few months of school. By Christmas of his first year his attendance dropped to 57%. He is very quiet and has little connection with the school or his peers. He has not chosen to attend First Nations studies or see First Nations counselors that work within our school. He began Social Justice 12 in February 2010.

Elias is a member of the Squamish Band and is well connected in his First Nations community. He is a talented carver and works with his extended family learning traditional art. He is involved in the First Nations studies program at the school. Elias has attended our Alternate School sporadically since the fall of 2005. In elementary school his teachers described him as "cheerful, enthusiastic, polite, conscientious, and pleasant." However, they reported attendance problems: one year Elias missed 38 days of school. He was suspended four times during his grade seven year for drug offences and teachers suspected a substance abuse problem. During his first year in the Alternate program, Elias' attendance averaged about 60% likely an outcome of his drug use. He struggled with his academic courses and was below his grade for reading and mathematics. He was also described as "helpful in the classroom" and "athletic." Elias dropped out of school in 2007 to work. He re-enrolled in 2008 but rarely attended. After 18 months away from school, and 19 years of age, Elias enrolled in our program to complete the Adult Graduation Program. His attendance is good, and he seems motivated to finish high school.

Anna is a member of the Burrard Nation where she lives with both her parents. She was expelled from her previous school for poor attendance, marijuana use at school, and physical altercations with other girls. Anna has attended learning assistance programs since grade one and has had trouble reading since primary school. While attending the Alternate School, teachers noted that she was an "independent worker who needs high structure" and is "smart, friendly, and very capable." Anna volunteers at a local elementary school once a week with the primary students, and has earned "Student of the Report" (i.e., high academic grades and good attendance) twice. Upon finishing grade 10 at the Alternate School, Anna tried to continue her studies in her Reservation's Band school but dropped out after four months. She took some time off to work and then returned to our Alternate School in January 2010 to begin grade 11.

Interviews

> We too often fail to realize we exist professionally because of students … how often we fail to stop and ask students what they think about the instructional methods we enact. (Bennett, 2009, p. 84)

Interviewing First Nations students is a difficult task. The cadence of conversation with First Nations students is different than with non-native students. I have found, over the years, speaking with First Nations people has taught me to be a more contemplative listener. The presence of the tape recorder on their desk appears to be unnerving. However, as students talk through their visual journals they are eager to share their stories, opinions, and insights into the visual journals process. I saved Ben for last as his entries are so personal and meaningful I am almost afraid of delving into his innermost thoughts. I was deeply moved during Ben's interview, as he appeared to get emotional when he described one of his journal pages. He said the Social Justice course lent itself to opening discussion of difficult issues and subjects, but the visual journals enabled him to make the curriculum personal and make connections through art that writing alone could never achieve. The visual journals enabled me to get to know my students on a deeper level and open dialogue with them that was never possible without the journal as a bridge.

Visual Journals Foster Engagement and Challenge

It is important the learner is actively involved in the learning process. Von Glaserfeld (1989) states that sustaining motivation to learn is dependent on the student's confidence in their potential for learning. Bennett & Rolheiser (2001) note that brain research has shown that classroom activities and instructional tactics need to be stimulating, challenging, and engaging. This links with Vygotsky's (1978) "zone of proximal development" where learners are challenged, yet close to their current level of development (Santrock, 2004). Delving into art enables and allows students to make connections, seek relationships, and analyze new knowledge in a new, more challenging way.

For example, Elias is more introspective when he physically and artistically organizes his academic ideas and appeared to portray a deeper evaluation of course material. At times Ben found it difficult to understand what he perceived to be foreign concepts in the course. He acknowledged that the use of images helped him understand these concepts on a deeper, more concrete level. Moreover, he indicated it was difficult to think up artistic representations of complex concepts, however, the challenge kept him engaged and on-task.

Ben said that the most important part of his academic success was the need to be challenged by his assignments. Feeling bored or feeling like assignments are a chore sometimes led to him leaving school before the school day was over. Also, Ben expressed that learning new things and feeling a connection that what he was learning was relevant and personal to his life helped him stay engaged.

I felt the visual assignments were beneficial because the students appeared challenged and enjoying what they were doing. Consequently, they directed more time and effort completing assignments. Anna adds, "time flowed by and I never was bored." Ben shared that using visual journals was better than "just getting through the work and waiting for the day to end … I enjoyed every second of it." Previously, Susan was often reprimanded for doodling and painting during class time, and now she is given encouragement to do what brings her happiness as an assignment. She spends more time on task in other subjects because she has the chance to have an artistic outlet in journal assignments that seem relaxing and enjoyable.

Students enjoy their work when meeting both the curricular expectation and have "gone beyond what they have been programmed to do… (and) achieved something unexpected" (Csikszentmihalyi, 1990, p. 46). The emotion the students pour into art is powerfully connected to their thinking. Art makes the curriculum come to life. Visual journals provide opportunities to express internal tension, creativity, personal discovery, and, unexpectedly, happiness. Pearse (2001) argues that there should always be an element of action in students' work that applies what they are doing to the real world. Visual journals cover his three criteria of a critical component where (1) students analyze the content, (2) evaluate through action and application, and (3) employ an interpretative component to connect meaning to the curriculum.

Ben found by intertwining his story with the curriculum he could place himself in the assignments. He felt safe putting personal things in the visual journal because he believes his art may help other people when viewing his stories. Ben liked how he could "see the images that represented how you felt at the time." Anna felt the most challenging thing was putting 'herself' into the answers because she had to reflect on her beliefs before she could respond to the curriculum. She did put herself there, in her entries, alongside the people and cultures she was studying, building connections with the outside world.

Elias found a challenging aspect of creating visual journal pages was the freedom to let himself 'trust the process' (McNiff, 1998). Elias is an artist, and I watched him in the flow of working on his art and poetry. Despite the fact it took the students more time to complete an assignment visually, this did not necessarily mean it took more class time. During the process, they were on task and were not wasting time and procrastinating. Elias wants to try visual journals in every subject to get him more engaged as he appears to think from the perspective of an artist most the time.

VISUAL JOURNALS AND BELONGING

Brendtro et al., (2005), Brendtro et al., (2002); and Strand & Peacock (2002) describe four steps to create an ideal learning environment for First Nations youth at risk. First, all youths need to feel they belong–in a classroom and with their teacher. The next step is to master their world–mentally, emotionally, and spiritually. Only then will they gain responsible independence (third) and, finally, be of value to others.

Bringing First Nations stories into a course based on contemporary global issues is beneficial because of the importance of students' identity. Their history travels with them through every visual journal entry as they look at the world and curriculum through the lens of being First Nations. They feel that they cannot separate their personal story from the learning process and, therefore, the ability to express how they connect with both the curriculum and society is important.

As Naths (2004) discovered, using artistic strategies help the students testify to their being and solidifies their existence in the world. In essence, through the visual journal students create an autoethnographic study of themselves and how they belong in their communities, classrooms, and the world (Suominen, 2006). This is critical for self-acceptance and self-understanding. The process is very personal. Ben revealed that, "it will be hard for me to find my place in the world…for some people it will be easier…for me, I look at things in a deep way and finding my place in the global community will be difficult." He feels dislocated and this is evident in his journal responses. He compares the struggle of the First Nations people to that of other people groups (see Figure 1 below) who seem lost in the modern world. He documents this struggle in some of his pages. "How do you represent that? How do you feel you belong in a world when you feel lost all the time?" was Ben's response when asked if he felt like he belonged in this society.

Elias felt he belonged at our Alternate School, "accepting him" through the relationships of teachers who "really knew him." While Ben and Susan still seem to be struggling with belonging, Elias and Anna truly feel they belong in this program, and school, because of the relationships they have built. Anna felt the relationships she developed with staff were the biggest pull for her to return to our Alternate school with plans to graduate.

VISUAL JOURNALS FOSTER COMMUNICATION AND RELATIONSHIPS

Brendtro et al., (2002) believe that building relationships is the key to academic success in adolescent First Nations students. Their research shows that the quality of healthy relationships between teacher and student may be more influential than specific techniques used in the classroom or interventions run by the school.

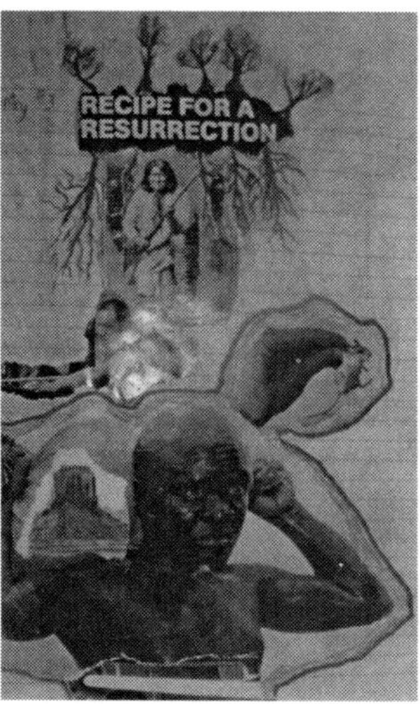

Figure 1. An example from Ben's visual journal.

Teachers need to be warm hearted, consistent, and stable in order to have a relationship where youth are more responsive to receiving encouragement or correction that comes from an adult whose opinion is valued. A critical factor in socializing children is to replace disruption with engagement by creating an alliance with the student (Brendtro et al., 2002) and students who are securely attached to significant adults become more curious, self-directed learners, and more empathetic.

Relationships in the classroom are made through dedicated actions, some of which are curricular. Pinar (1999) states that curriculum is "historical, political, racial, gendered, phenomenological, postmodern, autobiographical, aesthetic, theological, and international" (p. 366). The visual journals, as an instructional tactic, can be a meeting place of new knowledge and relationship. It allows curriculum to be more of a conversation that is a two-way, sincere interaction between the student and teacher.

Aoki's notion of an educated person is to, "ever be open to the call of what it is to be deeply human, and heeding the call to walk with others in life's ventures" (1987, p. 365). It is particularly interesting to see how the First Nations students interlace their culture and cultural worldview into the curriculum. Images help the student convey their points of view and provoke critical questions from multiple perspectives. Aoki (1993) advocates a lived curriculum, where the delivery of curriculum acknowledges each student's uniqueness and enables students to tell their own story through interplay, dialogue, and written work.

I learned more about my students from their journal entries than I ever thought possible. The depth of responses sometimes seemed like a cry for help, like Ben's entry in response to an assignment involving colonization.

> I can only speak from my experience; we're invisible. Ghosts. Shadows. Nothing beautiful, nor honorable, we've been shunned from our own Mother Earth. Sk'lep couldn't trick me into false fantasies of "hope", because I know my culture is dead, the language, beliefs, practices, songs, all of it is dust now. The knowledge will die with our elders, and we'll fade into something else. I'm not saying I don't believe in the old ways, I just know that the beliefs cannot survive like it used to. Which is just as good as being dead, because these things don't pertain to us anymore. We cannot live by the ways as fully as they were meant to be.

I believe the words and images Ben chose to describe colonization are more powerful than any textbook could describe. To have a teacher-student relationship based on truthfulness and integrity, I need to create opportunities to listen to my students through speech, words, and images.

As the teacher-researcher, I am actively 'researching' my students as I assess their artwork to see how critically they have analyzed the topic. I also use it as a checkpoint to assess where my students may be emotionally. Images have the ability to evoke emotional responses. All students started to develop their "inside eyes," a term Ben used to describe his lens through which he views the world. The colors they use, the heaviness or lightness of the lines, the patterns and images they choose, and the words they share all are clues to the inner workings of their personal histories and present emotional state.

In the present study, students often sit at a group table while working on journal assignments and had the opportunity to share and compare their work with their peers. I observed they did not put down or laugh at their peers work, they were proud and their own self-respect grew. Others commented and learned from their work and often sparked new ideas. Porter (2004) describes visual journals as "no longer a school space but their space" (p. 110). These interactions of sharing and learning together demonstrated a shift in power from teacher to student, a clear indication that student-centered learning was taking place.

As I assessed their journals, I invited all the students to engage in dialogue describing their work. I noticed that as students began to develop a sense of empowerment over the processes of creating their own learning, they also began to pursue issues and topics more deeply and take more risks with their presentation format. For example, Anna said she was proud of herself for being a self-reliant learner because she did not have to ask for help as much and she felt she had the time to think through and understand the issues on her own.

Discussion

> Education must be transformed by moving toward a reclaiming of the fullness of body and soul. (Aoki, 1990, p. 359)

Bennett & Rolheiser (2001) strongly advocate that teachers make instructional decisions based on the unique needs of their learners. The lens I look through in the Alternate School focuses mainly on the development of emotional intelligence: self-awareness, self-control, motivation, the development of empathy, and the creation of better social skills. The biggest hurdle we have to overcome for student success is to create a learning environment that is safe (Bennett, 2009). Visual journals offer a safe place to express innermost feelings and experiences in students' lives and enables them to make links to their educational experiences. I recognize my learners need to develop self-confidence, a sense of connection and belonging to the school community, and motivation to stay at school, using visual journals can help achieve these essential goals.

Visual journals facilitate active, engaged learning. Through my personal journey of learning and inquiry, I see how effectively teachers can become the facilitators of a course. The interpretation of a lived curriculum lies in the creation of art. Von Glasersfeld (1989) argues that the responsibility of learning should reside with the learner. Therefore, Instructional Intelligence strategies such as the mind and concept maps and Instructional tactics such as *Seeing Both Sides*, *Plus/Minus/Interesting, Concept Formation,* and *Think/Pair/Share* are incorporated into the journal to enrich and strengthen the learning experience. Some activities are structured to meet a specific learning outcome, while some are more reflective and contemplative in nature to nurture the social and emotional learning of the student.

As a facilitator, I have chosen an assessment rubric that reflects the depth of understanding and interpretation of themes rather than a factual recall (see Table 1 on the following page).

Students are free to create a method of knowing that acknowledges their personal life and pays attention to her feelings and thoughts (Sparkes, 2005) in this rubric. Sparkes notes that our social construction of events comes from the inside and we interpret academic work through our own stories. This allowed them to express contradictions within their identity as related to the curriculum. Art is a method where there are no absolute answers, but offers deep analysis and evaluation of topics (Bennett & Rolheiser, 2001).

The novelty of using visual art instead of a traditional textbook approach appealed to my learners. The students found they researched topics more than when merely searching for a single, written answer. Extended research skills developed through the process of gathering information, researching appropriate images, and putting the page together. This process was much more involved than reading a passage and responding in text. They felt more freedom and safety because they knew there was no concrete answer, and could explore issues more deeply through their own lenses. These notions are supported by Weber's work (2008), where visual images are considered as unique; they can convey multiple messages and pose questions with one glance. This also enables a teacher to pay attention to her students in new ways, as art is a more holistic and memorable way of conveying meaning and meaning making.

Table 1. Assessment for visual journals

Each entry will be assigned four marks.

4 Powerful
Journal entries are complete, personal and thoughtful. The student combines previous experience and learning with frequent references to classroom and video activities. The thinking goes beyond the surface level and indicates a deeper understanding of learning.
3 Competent
Journal entries are complete, consistent and logical. The student shows some ability to combine precious learning and experience and makes some reference to the documentary and activities. The entry deals with ideas on a surface level.
2 Developing
Some of the entries are incomplete or inconsistent and the student shows little integration of learning and experiences. There is an incomplete understanding of the lesson.
1 Beginning
Journal entry is incomplete, inconsistent and illogical. The student does not provide examples of the connections to learning or experiences. There appears to be little or no understanding of the lesson.

Our real lives are elsewhere. Art finds them. (Pearse, 1996, p. 194)

The visual journals, as a meeting place, can be placed in Aoki's curricular theme of bridges. Aoki (1996) discusses (curricular) bridges as places where students and teachers "intercept and come together" (p. 311). The journal becomes a dwelling place for reflection and conversation, a (s)p(l)ace (deCosson, 2004) across, amongst, and between cultures where all participating parties belong equally. A large thread of inquiry is the role of how the arts facilitate a sense of belonging to a group, in this case, school. My students experience flow (Csikszentmihalyi, 1990) while participating in visual journals activities. This may have positive impacts on other academic work. Moreover, the flow experience can bring self-confidence and help students experience academic successes where they haven't experienced it before.

We may be able to understand why many of our students have major mental, emotional, and social barriers to graduation and becoming responsible citizens. The question is what teachers can do in their instruction to create a classroom environment that fosters positive and lasting change in their students. Bennett (2009) argues that instructional methods have the power to affect learning, and integrating different methods such as visual journals is an effort to respond to the diverse needs of our students.

Chalmers (2004) adds specifically that since "historical research depends on images" (p. 173), thus, the use of images should be a prominent part of a teacher's repertoire. Students who work through courses in the social sciences such as Social Justice 12 are looking to the past for patterns and clues on why the world is the way it is. Representing these historical experiences—past and present—in images enables the students' own stories to be woven into the images with narrative texts or poetry to resonate with the reader and invite the viewer to participate in the assessment and evaluation process of the assigned curriculum.

Summary and Considerations

> I did not expect anyone to adopt my own position; however, I think it is possible that readers may recognize their own personal stories in parallel with mine. (Suominen, 2006 p. 148)

Since belonging is a deep physiological need in adolescents, schools must plan and be deliberate in providing nourishing relationships in a culture of belonging (Brendtro et al., 2002; Johnson & Johnson, 2004; McNeely & Falci, 2004; Osterman, 2000; Sax, 2004; Strahm, 2007, Bennett, 2001). Informing educators of the importance of building relationships with First Nations youth at risk and creating a culture of belonging both in the classroom and at school to enable students to be lifelong learners, cultivate their purpose, and strengthen their resolve to finish school. My inquiry enabled me to share the powerful social and academic importance of fostering a sense of belonging and community in the classroom as it has implications on graduation rates and academic performance for First Nations students.

Senior level secondary school courses challenge students to delve into complex issues and Social Justice 12 is no exception. I was worried that students would not feel connected ideas and realities of other people who do not live in suburban North America. I was wrong. First Nations students seem to have a deep connection with their own past and with other human groups who struggle to maintain their communities and identities as they battle with poverty and social inequalities. The visual journals helped make complex issues clearer to students and more accessible for me to develop deeper sensitivities and sensibilities. Naths (2004) describes her journaling process from the perspective of how "the images testify to my being, my doing, my existence" (p. 120), so did I see the same process unfold for my students.

During my interviews, I was intrigued by the students' sense of self and how it was often repeated. Their core values and sense of being were always put into their artwork, woven within the curriculum and complex issues. It was as if the students were planting themselves in their work, placing them on the same continuum of time and social context that they were studying. Talking to the students about their work and delving into their minds and pages created a deeper ethic of caring in my classroom. Their journals were a bridge where we could meet and discuss topics on a safe, middle ground.

I was touched by Ben's statement of his pursuit to find where he belongs. His journal entries were very strong messages of dislocation, suffering, and although he found connections with other cultures and their struggles, his sense of place seemed groundless. His knowledge about himself is a struggle. The visual journal was a more authentic experience than I thought it could be. The students felt safe creating personally meaningful touches on/in/through it, and while assessing their pages, I could see patterns in their analysis of the curriculum that enabled me to reflect on their growth. Partway through his interview Ben was having difficulty answering questions and then said "I'm sorry, today I didn't eat, and I have so many things in my head right now I can't concentrate." It was 2pm. I was reminded that my students have bigger things on their minds than getting through school, and in order for at-risk students to 'buy into' their educational program, there are a lot of variables that need to be addressed before academic success is achieved.

I am a firm believer in the holistic nature of teaching and learning. The process of creating journal assignments that both cover the required curriculum and deepen the sense of belonging and community in my classroom seemed like a daunting task, but it wasn't until I placed the students in the center of our classroom universe that could I see the process take care of itself. Smits (1997) reminds us through hermeneutics that the "space of human understanding is within the lived world of practice and human relationships ... that space cannot be presumed to exist without the active intervention of human thought and activity" (p. 293). Since teacher caring and concern requires me to discuss values and beliefs that are not comfortable for teachers or students, the journals opens up the space for conversation and one-on-one time with each student. This created a fresh look at the relationships between what I teach and the students' experiences of the assignments I create for them.

Naths (2004) argues that "students need to be active participants in the construction of their knowledge" (p. 123) and I have never felt this to be true in such a powerful, meaningful way before I began to use visual journals in my teaching repertoire. I believe the students' personal journey to connect and belong in the classroom, their immediate community, and the world by creating teaching strategies that challenge them and increase their engagement while at school is central to life and learning. Using a visual narrative allowed my students to learn in a way that is relational, social, and interactive as it built on self-understanding at the same time they constructed understandings of the assigned curriculum.

The process of adding visual journals to my curriculum allows me to re-define my purpose as a teacher of at-risk students, and the unique needs of First Nations students. My students are neither static nor predictable. With this knowledge I recognize my teaching strategies and assignments must also not be static or predictable. I am deeply interested in my research both personally and professionally, and I have come to the realization that teachers are indeed phenomenologists and need to be intimately aware on a daily basis of the processes that guide the classroom atmosphere and the progress of individual students.

Since teaching is a living practice (deCosson, Irwin, Kind & Springgay, 2007), the interconnectedness of a teacher-student-classroom model provides (s)p(l)aces (deCosson, 2004) for learning and understanding that can be filled through valuable tactics like the visual journals. The journal facilitates a space of (re)searching and (re)questioning that is an ongoing, active space for inquiry. It is engaged with real life. My inquiry is intended as a call to action among teachers to create powerful learning environments based on relationships, dialogue, and well-researched teaching strategies and tactics such as visual journals to ensure students are ready and able—mentally, physically, emotionally, and spiritually—to live successfully in school and society.

Caren J. Hall
North Vancouver School District 44
chall@nvsd44.bc.ca

GERRI KARR

WRITING IS MORE THAN DRAFT AND GOOD COPY

The use of storyboarding and oral storytelling as pre-writing activities to enhance fluency and description in elementary students' narrative writing

Stories happen all the time, all around us. All we need to do is open our eyes and tell what we witness, or close our eyes and tell what we imagine.

When I first started this journey to pursue a masters' degree, I had no idea what to expect. I was somewhat fearful that it would involve a lot of statistics and quantitative analysis of data. I've always been somewhat skeptical of data analysis as there are always a multitude of variables that come into play during assessment. I worried that the collected data might not be accurate and the research might be faulty. I was relieved to learn, however, that in all probability, there is no such thing as 'pure data' (Pepper, 1942). I discovered that it was acceptable to conduct research that wasn't quantitative in nature, and I was encouraged to investigate a topic of interest based on personal reflections on how I observed and interpreted student learning. I was told to 'trust the process' (McNiff, 1998), to "trust that the creative intelligence [would] find its way" (Csikzmentmihalyi, p. 3), that everything would eventually become clear, and that my topic would present itself to me. I wondered comically to myself if this was going to be possible when I didn't even know what the 'process' was! Eventually, however, it all became clear. I came to understand that 'the process' that I was supposed to 'trust' was one of self-discovery and whatever it took for me to get there. My masters' journey, then, was 'the process.' The goal was not about writing a final research paper; rather, it was about the journey of finding myself, and of becoming a better teacher. As a result of working with dedicated teachers and the fellow graduate students in my cohort, I have come to embrace this awareness. They have enabled me to think, to reflect, and to be artful in both my research and my teaching.

I took many courses with my graduate studies advisor, who graciously held my hand while I encountered big words like hermeneutic and epistemology, and who helped me to peel back the layers of the creative process through the writing of Ted Aoki and Mihaly Csikzmentmihalyi. I figured if I could learn to say Mihaly's last name correctly, I could accomplish anything. I learned that 'flow' occurred when there was the right combination of interest and ability, provided the setting was neither too taxing nor too boring. Flow is a journey, a developmental journey, sometimes a trickling stream, and sometimes a raging river. It is during flow that creativity flourishes. I wondered how I could best set up the circumstances for creativity to occur, both for myself as artistresearcherteacher (Gouzouasis, 2008) and for my Grade 3 students.

P. Gouzouasis (ed.), Pedagogy in a New Tonality: Teacher Inquiries on Creative Tactics, Strategies, Graphics Organizers, and Visual Journals in the K-12 Classroom, 185–202.

I took a course with Carl Leggo and my questions were partially answered. He managed to wring every emotion out of me that I had previously kept under tight lock and key. He taught me that it was necessary to visit our own backyards in order to see and understand our world more clearly. Childhood memories can be exhilarating and they can be extremely painful. These emotional memories are usually tagged with some sort of visual cue, like a little clay pot made with child's hands or family photographs. I found myself remembering emotions about things that had been long buried. I learned we all "write from a private place: a nation or country in the mind, whose landscape and whose climate are made up of what has been seized and hoarded from the real world" (Birks, p. 1). Although it hurt to remember them, it was through these thought processes that I began viewing my life as a series of stories. While I shared some stories with others, I chose to keep others for myself.

Alex de Cosson led me into the world of visual journaling. Images became a representation of who I perceived myself to be, and my life gradually unfolded page by page in my journal. It was a cathartic experience to be so absorbed in myself. We seldom afford ourselves the time to think about ourselves, to pause and reflect. We seldom stop in the middle of the bridge to simply enjoy the view because we're always to busy in our teaching lives going to and fro. The busy highway of home life and school life leaves us with precious little if any time to just sit and reflect on our practice and on ourselves. Taking the time through visual journaling gave me this opportunity. I was reminded of when I was a little girl who drew pictures and wrote stories and poems. As an only child, I had no distractions from such hobbies. It also led me to remember my childhood wish to be a writer. Somehow, along the busy road of life, I had forgotten this dream. I realized that my aspiration to bring writing to the forefront with my students came, in part, from the sheer joy that I receive when I put pen to paper. Perhaps it would be possible for me to engage the artist in me by empowering my students to become better writers. I wondered if my rediscovered passion for writing, drawing, and telling stories could be useful in teaching narrative writing to my students.

During the summers of 2008 and 2009, I registered in the VAG Art Institutes taught by UBC professor Kit Grauer. Naturally, many of our assignments dealt with visual images. As students, we were asked to reflect on pieces of art and to use them as a springboard for our own creative endeavors. I thoroughly enjoyed both of these institutes and learned a great deal from them. "How perfect!" I thought to myself, "I could learn how to teach my students by actually doing the activities myself." I became hooked on this medium of expression and began to formulate a plan for implementing visual images as a springboard for narrative writing.

I then took an arts-based technology course with Anne Marie LaMonde. Until this time I had been self-conscious about sharing what I had written with anyone other than close family and the other students in my cohort. Since childhood I had saved my writing, mostly a collection of poems written on everything from restaurant napkins to old newspapers, or whatever happened to be handy, when words started to flow through me. I dug out the cardboard box that housed my bits of scribbling and began word-processing them. Anne Marie convinced me to create a personal blog at Blogger.com so I would have a permanent home for my writing. In fact, she showed me how to do this by patiently sitting beside me until the page was constructed. For the longest time, I used it as a safe haven for my words. It was my fortress, a castle that safely contained all that I had ever written. Eventually, she encouraged me to let my castle's drawbridge down and invite other folks to come on in. I would not have had the courage to share my writing had it not been for Anne Marie. She, and the other teachers previously mentioned, have inspired and encouraged me to not only be a teacher and a researcher, but also to be an artist. I hoped to offer my students a similar journey, where they could find and situate themselves, and share their world (whether real or imagined) through art, oral storytelling, and narrative writing. I began to seriously think about how I would implement this three-part writing process with my students.

Reviewing the Literature

Once I had decided on my research topic, I began to investigate journal articles and books that discussed the use of visual images to assist storytelling and narrative writing. I hoped to find a way to bring creativity and excitement to the teaching of narrative writing. I wished to design artful learning experiences that would awaken the sleeping literary giants housed within my students. Moriarty claims, "through their symbolic expressions children may be enabled to explore meaning in their lives" (p. 47). Children construct meaning in their lives by trying out new things, figuring out what worked and what doesn't, then moving forward. I quickly realized that I was a part of this meaning making. For my students to make meaning in their lives, I needed to make meaning in mine.

In *Beyond Monet*, Barrie Bennett & Carol Rolheiser (2001) take a long, hard look at teaching pedagogy. I learned that the best way to improve student achievement was to improve my own instructional practice. Teaching is incredibly complex, but our practice can be improved by involving the notion of "instructional intelligence[s]" (p. 56). Instructional intelligence blends curriculum, assessment, instruction, knowledge of how students learn, and theories of change and systemic change, while at the same time honoring teacher autonomy; acknowledging that there is no one best way to teach. Bennett & Rolheiser believe that each teacher must find their own way. They must 'trust the process' of their own artful reflections on both how they teach and how their students learn. "Like scientists, we research better ways, we test, we experiment; like artists we communicate, tell our stories, interpret, deconstruct, and reconstruct, keeping an open mind to new possibilities" (p. 68).

On the basis of this guessing, testing, thinking and communicating I began to investigate the connection between visual images, storytelling and narrative writing. I was convinced there was a connection between those three modes of expression. I hypothesized that when my students draw a story then orally share their stories, they write better stories. Hoyt (1992) concurs saying, "artistic expression focused on a learning experience can help [students] to organize thinking and rehearse for more traditional means of expression" (p. 583). The key word in this quote is 'rehearse.' Storyboards and subsequent oral storytelling are, in fact, rehearsals for the narrative writing that follows. I hypothesized that by the time that students have storyboarded their stories and orally shared them with their peers, the process of writing is rather simple. They'd scribe their story onto paper, more fluently and with improved descriptiveness because they'd have rehearsed it orally many times with their fellow classmates. While I decided to take this approach, a part of me feared that I wasn't doing due diligence with the teaching of writing by simply handing students a blank piece of paper and telling them to draw a story with a logical beginning, middle, and end. However, Shaun McNiff (1998) tells us to not fear change, for "the discipline of art requires constant experimentation, wherein errors are harbingers of original ideas because they introduce new directions for expression" (p. 41). I hoped to discover a multidisciplinary instructional practice that enabled my students to use their storyboards to enhance fluency and to be more descriptive in their narrative writing.

Tracie Constantino discussed the work of an elementary art teacher, Carl Connelly, "who provided both verbal and visual means for students to respond to art" (p. 1). The article gave me ideas about using visual images to enhance my students' narrative writing experiences. Constantino maintains, "visual thinking [...] is the process of identifying, categorizing, and generating images that are the foundation of all thinking" (p. 6). When a child thinks and composes visually, either using images from things they are directly looking at, or from their imagination, they are often using metaphor and analogies, which are examples of higher order thinking. I found this notion fascinating.

This prompted further investigation on what other authors thought about the importance of artistic expression. I came across the ideas of John Dewey (1934). Dewey was remarkably ahead of his time when it came to ideas on the importance of an arts-based education. When talking about image making and how this relates to cognition and fluency, he describes thinking in terms of "qualities, which occur during art making and result in artistic expression of ideas, as one of the most sophisticated modes of thought" (p. 54). I became more interested than ever in how the use of visual art might increase my students' linguistic fluency and also encourage creativity and higher level thinking skills.

It was my hope that my students would become more fluent and more descriptive in their narrative writing as a result of this approach. I am not alone in this thinking. "There is a substantial body of research and theoretical literation explicating the cognitive sophistication of visual thinking-that is, the intelligence of perception and the role of images in concept formation" (Andrzejczak, Trainin, & Poldberg, p. 2).

The process of storytelling is a lot more than putting words on to paper. As Andrzejczak et al state, "Artwork facilitates the writing process, resulting in a text that is richer in sensory detail and more intricate than the more traditional writing-first, crayon drawing-second approach" (p. 2). The authors assert that students who use visual images as a pre-writing activity increase their written output and are more creative. "As art developed (at times accidentally), students transformed and extended their ideas. For example, a drip of paint became an octopus and an ocean story emerged" (p. 6). When students drew their stories first, they drew from the right sides of their brain, thus engaging a whole new realm of thought processing, the more creative side.

Phillips's (2000) briefing paper outlines a multi-intelligence approach. She details an encapsulated view of the past few decades in art education and its relationship to written literacy. In the 1980's, teachers studied the positive correlation between the arts and specific school curriculum. Gardner postulated that students learned better when more of their senses were involved. Phillips discussed how Eisner "began studying how language speaking, listening, writing, and reading could aid in understanding art" (p. 3) in his discipline-based art education or standards-based art education. Lately, others have turned this idea inside out to investigate how art can improve literacy. Many of the children in our classes are visual learners, so "for these children, initiating assignments with the image instead of the word may promote language skills" (Phillips, p. 3). She outlined an approach that incorporated "students' experiences, powers of observation, and desire for communication into a learning process that develop[ed] language skills (listening, speaking, reading, and writing)" (p. 6). Her students developed their skills to express themselves in an artistic way.

Janet Olson (1992) investigated how drawing could be used as a means to enhance writing. Her students used individual and sequential drawings that communicated stories. She found that "pictures [could] provide additional information to words for the visual learner, and words [could] provide additional information to pictures for the verbal learner. [...] When children are educated in both modes of learning, they can move back and forth between these domains without effort" (p. 51). They become multidimensional learners with fluid thought-processing capabilities.

Reading Phil Moore's (1994) work caused me to reflect on the importance of embracing changes in the ways we teach literacy. Rather than asking our students to write largely through the medium of words, he stressed the need to redefine the word 'text' to include "words, numbers, images and sounds-anything, in fact, which is created to convey meaning" (p. 11). We live in an age where words, sounds, and pictures are often combined in one presentation. Children, better than adults, perceive the relationships between image, word, and sound as complex and interdependent. On a daily basis, we multi-task, combine, and reuse words and images at a lightning speed across a global communication network. We need to "re-examine notions of writing and [. . .] being a writer which exist within a culture which is still predominantly print-based" (p. 11).

Connelly & Clandinin (1990), remind us, "humans are storytelling organisms who, individually and socially, lead storied lives" (p. 2). They discuss that by simply living our lives, we are continuing the process of narrative inquiry. The authors spin fascinating webs describing how "people are both living their stories in an ongoing experiential text, and telling their stories in words as they reflect upon life and explain themselves to others" (p. 4). Likewise, Hodgins (1993) asks, "What is this world if not an organism that lives by the endless interweaving of stories?" (p. 24). I thoroughly enjoyed this book and immersed myself in his vision of how one tells a good story.

I read Doonan's (2005) work and was delighted to find further validation for my hypothesis. She wrote, "[P]ictures are a means to an end. They aid literacy and language development and as such are valued for providing a verbal and written experience" (p. 7). She believed that image making offered many possibilities for the development of creativity and fluency in written expression. She encouraged her students to make pictures that told stories. Doonan felt when the inner artists were encouraged to "play with ideas provoked by images, [they] create[d] something of [their] own through it" (p. 7). The findings of her study supported my hypothesis that students' narrative writing can be enhanced in fluency and in descriptiveness through the use of image making as a pre-writing activity.

A thorough investigation of the literature involving the connection between visual media and writing proved fruitful. Many professionals, whether they are teachers in the field or researchers, are attempting to find new ways to teach narrative writing for "[m]aking sense of prior and current experiences while making connections between personal and professional life worlds is foundational in continual professional development" (Kalin, 2007, p. 77).

Research Questions

I narrowed down the research questions that I wished to investigate. I hypothesized that a three-part writing process including storyboarding, and a repeated oral storytelling of their stories, would enhance fluency and descriptiveness in their narrative writing. After all, stories happen around us all the time. McNiff (1998) feels, "Everything significant about the soul's ultimate journey is imprinted in its childhood formation" (p. 159). Sometimes these stories are what we actually perceive in the world around us, sometimes they are 'backyard stories' from our own lives, sometimes they are totally imagined and sometimes they are a combination of the above. Visual images play a huge role in our perception of the world. The questions I hoped to answer through my research were as follow: 1) Does student storyboarding and subsequent oral storytelling enhance fluency and descriptiveness in my Grade 3 students' narrative writing? 2) Does overall enjoyment of writing improve as a result of these kinds of writing experiences? 3) Would I be able to produce a work of art that somehow represents what my students and I have learned as a result of this study?

The Setting and Research Design

This study was conducted in my Grade 3 classroom. My elementary school is situated in a lovely forest environment. Families living in the area possess middle to high socioeconomic status. Homes in the area sell, on average, for one million dollars. Families have the money to do many extracurricular activities such as theatre and sports activities. The children are involved in many after school activities such as music and art lessons, and sports activities such as soccer, baseball, and karate. The school families and the community as a whole are very supportive of the children in our school. As a result of this enrichment, children are able to bring these outside experiences into their narrative writing, making it unique and worldly.

Our school has many play areas—a large soccer field, an upper forest, an upper climbing apparatus, a garden and outdoor reading area, a lower forest with our own troll's head rising out of the ground, and a frog slide which was hand carved by local artist, Eric Neighbour, with help from 250 of our students in 2007. We have a number of planters that display a variety of West Coast natural vegetation and planters of annual flowers. A great deal of effort has gone into making the outdoor environment of our school as aesthetically pleasing as possible. During my research, I took the children outside, allowing them to engage with these great learning environments. These environments were a great source of inspiration for the students' storyboarding, oral storytelling, and narrative writing.

Our classroom is a bright one that is filled with student work and a multitude of books; some picture books and some chapter books. There is wide range of reading material in the classroom. We always have art materials on hand that the students are encouraged to use at any time. It is a welcoming room that has been my home away from home for the past seven years. Although there are, most assuredly, expectations regarding their work, the children know that I love them and that *they* are my first priority, not the curriculum.

In total, seven girls and twelve boys, all either eight or nine years of age participated in the study. Like most Canadian schools, Queensbury Elementary has a culturally and linguistically diverse group of students. Of the 19 students taking part in this journey, eight spoke English as a second language. Of those eight, four spoke Korean, one spoke Chinese, one spoke Romanian, and two spoke Farsi in their homes. All eight were designated ESL students; two designated direct and six designated indirect. They were all Level 2 or higher, meaning that they had enough basic mastery of the English language that they could orally tell their stories in English. Two students in the class were designated as Gifted, as a result of the CCAT (Canadian Cognitive Abilities Test), that had been administered to the entire class in February 2010. One child was designed Special Needs and was assisted with the activities in this study by a full- time special education aide. All students were included in research study and participated in the four activities outlined below.

The data of the study involved the following components: 1) two, simple self-assessments, one at the beginning and one at the end of the study, and 2) four writing assignments that followed the three-part writing process with student storyboarding, oral storytelling, and rough and good copies of their writing.

During the period of this research study, I asked the students to complete a minimum of four writing assignments. These activities were sandwiched by a student self-evaluation pre-test and a student post-test to record the level of their overall enjoyment of writing. Even before I started this study, I knew my students were very creative and loved to write. My reasoning for administering the pre-writing assessment and post-assessment was to ensure that their love of writing didn't diminish as a result of my study.

The only question asked on the pre-assessment and post-assessment was, 'How do you feel about your writing?' There were three faces—a face with a sad smile, a face with a straight-line mouth, and a face with a smile—which represented, 'I don't feel good about my writing,' 'I am indifferent about my writing,' and 'I really like my writing.' The students merely circled one of the faces to describe their feelings. These self-assessments took approximately two minutes to accomplish and were done during regular class time. The students were not asked to commit any additional time outside the regular school schedule to the project.

These self-assessments, along with their storyboards, oral storytelling and narrative writing samples provided data about how improvement manifested itself in my students' narrative writing. This classroom-based project was part of the regular curriculum and was assessed according to BC provincially mandated curriculum PLOs (Prescribed Learning Outcomes). I assessed their writing samples using the year-end narrative writing rubric that I obtained from the BC Ministry of Education website. Storyboarding, oral storytelling, and the emphasis on narrative writing is emerging as common practice K-7 in NVSD schools and in the province of BC as a whole.

There were no known risks with the proposed research and all the parents gave consent for participation. Some of the activities required students to work together. When they did this, any so called 'risk' involved was part of their everyday school experience. Collaborative learning was encouraged in the class; however, students that expressed a wish to work on their own were allowed to do so. We went outside our school boundary, crossing a road, to do a writing activity in a local park named Kealy Woods. Naturally, there was a slightly elevated risk involving leaving the school grounds and going to a wooded area. All the children had letters of permission to go on a walking field trip on file, so this legal issue was addressed.

Implementing the Approach

At the beginning of the study, I gave my students their initial self-assessment. I knew that my students were good writers who enjoyed writing from previous activities that we had done throughout the year. It was no surprise that all participants in the study said they were either indifferent to or enjoyed writing, as nine students circled the straight face and ten circled the smiling face on their initial self-assessments.

I began the first activity by encouraging my students to develop original narrative stories through storyboarding and oral storytelling. This strategy engaged all students, as everyone was able to tell a story through drawing. I told the students to not worry about being a perfect artist, but to try and add as much detail as they could into their storyboards, as they would have more interesting things to eventually talk and write about. They were surprised to learn that the framework for good story writing actually started long ago, with a Greek philosopher named Aristotle. The students were taught their stories should be interesting to the listener or reader. They should make sense, and they should have a logical beginning, middle and end. I reminded them that the beginning of a story usually introduced the main characters and located the story in a specific time and place. The middle part usually had the main characters having an incident of some kind that draws the reader in even further. Sometimes there is more than one incident that leads to a rising in the action that comes to the climax (the most intense culmination), followed by the denouement, or falling action coming to the end or conclusion.

I purposely did not give the students a topic, word banks, or any similar writing tools, as I wanted the story to come from them alone. I wanted the students to think creatively about possible story lines. "Contemporary trends in education reflect a shift from traditional teacher-centered approaches to more student-centered approaches to learning" (Douville, 2004, p. 36). My students were really excited to get going. While they wanted to share their ideas for their story while drawing, I asked them to be silent, assuring them that there would be ample opportunity to share with their peers once their drawing was done. It was interesting to see how students became totally absorbed in their drawing. They didn't need to "labo[u]r through the word[s] to come to the mental picture of meaning, but [they] use[d] imagery [...] to mentally visualize the word's meaning as the word is holistically approached" (Sinatra & Stahl-Gemake, 1983, p. 4).

I encouraged the children to *go with the flow*. This meant, "holding on to [their stories] lightly (even though they may seem very important) and being willing to change them if something else more appropriate and satisfying [came] along" (Gawain, 1978, pp. 59-60). It is generally proposed that written expression is primarily a left-brained activity, whereas drawing is a right-brained activity. From that perspective, storyboarding encourages "the use of thinking inherent in analogy, metaphor, synthesis, and imagery" (Sinatra & Stahl-Gemake, p. 4). I hoped that this type of thinking would foster creativity in my students and enable them to be more fluent and descriptive in their narrative writing. Also, "through their symbolic expressions children [were able to] explore meaning in their lives" (Moriarty, 2010,p. 47). "[T]eachers who use this approach have discovered [. .] children seem to learn with more engagement when they have a chance to combine their understanding in art and language arts" (Grauer, 2006, p. 113).

True to the research literature, the children loved this activity. "Art is not about thinking something up. It is about the opposite-getting something down [...] there is no strain" (Cameron, 2002, p. 117). They couldn't wait to share their stories with their classmates. I had originally intended the activity to last for forty minutes, but they were so keen to add more details to their drawings that I extended it to two forty-minute periods.

Once their storyboards were completed to their satisfaction and mine, we began the process of orally sharing their stories. I used a sharing technique that our advisor shared in our master's classes where I lined up my 19 students knee to knee sitting opposite each other in their chairs, so that they were, in effect, pair-sharing in close quarters. I told the students that I would allow two minutes for oral sharing with their first partner. I asked them to use their storyboards as a guide in order to be descriptive in their storytelling. I used prompts such as 'What color were the leaves on the tree in your picture?' 'Were there clouds in the sky?' 'What were the characters wearing?' 'Describe the animals in your picture?' to begin. All the students in one of the lines were the storytellers for the first run through. The job of their partners was to be attentive listeners to the stories. If there was something in the story that didn't make sense, it was their job to ask for clarification and perhaps to offer suggestions as to how to improve the story. The listeners responded in an "authentic way, and then, by routine or by author choice, they [offered] comments and ask[ed] questions that might help […] [the] writer" (Dyson, 1994, p. 4). The listeners had one minute to respond to the story they had just heard. The storyteller would take this response from their peer into account before moving on to the next listener. I simply blew one short blow on my gym whistle to signal that it was time to share stories, two short whistles when it was time for the listeners to give feedback to the storyteller, and three short whistles when it was time to 'shove a bum' one chair to the left, so they faced a new listener. The storyteller at the end of the row got up, walked around to the beginning of the row and sat down. I think the children had fun with this musical chairs variation of think-pair-sharing.

We went through this process a total of three times. At the end of three times, I asked for 'thumbs up' if the storyteller felt they had the story in their head or 'thumbs sideways' if they felt they needed another run through. Seeing a few thumbs pointing sideways, I gave them one more opportunity to share their storyboard. Then, we switched roles, so those that had been listeners now became the storytellers and vice-versa. We used the same method for sharing, providing feedback and 'shoving a bum' as we had for the first row of storytellers. Although it did get a little noisy with 10 storytellers all talking at the same time, the student engagement was powerful. I walked around listening to the stories and the listeners' responses. I followed a storyteller for more than one telling of the story. I wanted to see if the storyteller used any of the suggestions that had been given to them by their peers, and had actually changed their story, or whether they kept to their original story. I found that the storytellers did use the suggestions, resulting in more cohesive stories. The stories came out more fluidly and they became more descriptive the more times they were told. The following is a transcription that shows the changes in the beginning of one of my students' stories during four attempts with their peers.

Storyteller *Listener*

1ST ATTEMPT

Once upon a time there was a creature…

where did this happen?

2ND ATTEMPT

Once upon a time in a magical grassy field with colors of the rainbow on a planet in the far reaches of the solar system, there

why was he fading
in color?

lived a creature who had the ability to fade in color…

3RD ATTEMPT

Once upon a time, on a planet in the far reaches of the solar system, on a grassy field that had all the colors of the rainbow in it, lived a small creature who had the ability to shapeshift and camouflage… *don't tell me this using those words. too direct*

4TH ATTEMPT

Once upon a time, on a planet in the farthest reaches of our solar system, there lived a small creature. As he walked through wide meadows filled with tall grasses that were every shade of the rainbow, he changed color to match his surroundings. When predators flew overhead, he made himself as small as a pebble so they wouldn't see him… *wow, that's a great beginning!*

By rehearsing the story four times, this student became a better oral storyteller. Other students did as well. It was fun to see them all communicating with students whom they might have not normally spoken. Seeing girls and boys talking together, sharing a laugh, and helping each other out was encouraging. Similar to Dyson's (1994) findings, they engaged in "artful performances, through which [they] hoped to gain others' attention and respect" (p. 10). In doing so, important social connections were made whereby students made meaning of their worlds. Reaching out to their peers through "verbal art […] highlight[ed] the musical and image-creating properties of language" (p. 10).

Next, I handed out lined paper so the students could transcribe a rough draft of their story using written words. They had already rehearsed their story four times orally and as a result of listener input, had modified them. Fluency was definitely increased and the descriptive quality of their drafts was exemplary. They could hardly wait to write down their stories. Instead of having children say, 'I don't know what to write' or 'What should I write about, Mrs. Karr?' when asked to write a story, their words flowed out. Following their draft writing, I asked the students to get another student to peer edit their story prior to requesting me to edit them. I used this approach because researchers have shown that peer editing can improve achievement (Fuchs and Fuchs, 2001; Topping, 1987).

The second activity refined the learning that had occurred during the first writing activity. I reminded the students about the overall structure of a good narrative story and led them through a 'gallery walk' of the storyboards from our first experience to get them prepared for our second activity. We discussed the need to situate the characters in an interesting setting, as this was a weakness that listeners had pointed out in our first experience. Some of the characters in the first storyboards appeared to exist in a vacuum of white background space. They were not located in any specific setting. Providing a setting enabled the storytellers to discuss so much more in their stories. Before handing out the blank pieces of paper, I encouraged the students to close their eyes and to think of a story in their heads. I asked them to think about their characters and to give more thought to the setting of their story. I asked them, 'Does the setting remain the same throughout the story or does it change?' They had learned from their stories in their previous activity that the best stories were those that were complex and had a lot of interesting details.

Figure 1. The storyboard for "Space Travel".

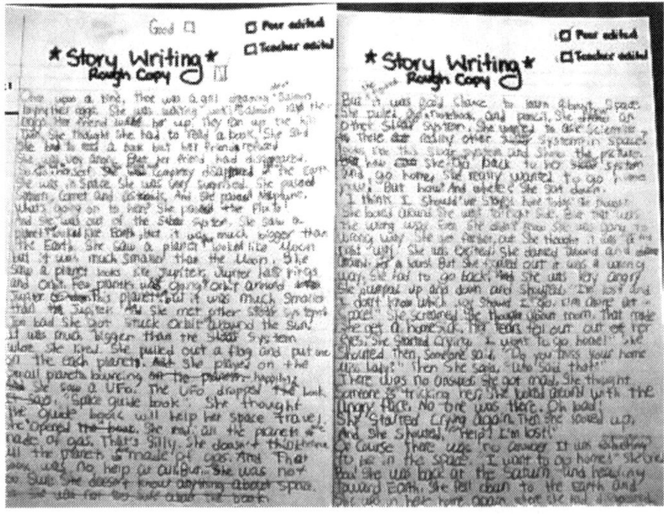

Figure 2. The first two drafts for the story, "Space Travel".

The storyboards for this second activity improved in overall appearance and attention to detail. They also situated their characters in interesting and varied settings, which added to the details that they were able to put into their oral and written stories. Of particular note, was the second storyboard of my special needs student. He was so involved with his storyboarding that he didn't lift his head up from his paper for over an hour. When I asked him to tell me about his story, he said, 'Not now, if I stop thinking about it, my story will go away.' When he was finished with his storyboard, he literally hopped across the room to my desk. He was so excited to share his story with me. When I told him that I liked his 'big head' character the best because he made me laugh, he actually laughed himself and said, "That makes *me* happy." This laughter and interaction was the most positive interaction that I'd had all year with this student. His excitement and laughter made me rethink some of the behavior modifications that I had employed with him during the year. I realized that I should have been communicating with this child through his strengths rather than his weaknesses. I should have asked him draw to storyboards and write narrative stories all year long.

Figure 3. Final draft of "Space Travel".

The other student that comes to mind when I reflect on this second activity was one of my ESL students. While her command of the English language was very basic, she possessed excellent artistic skills. Beginning writers who come to our classes from different countries, and possess a home language other than English, often experience difficulties with written expression. It is much easier for them to draw an image and then extract a story idea from the drawing than to construct the words directly from brain to paper. She was able to share her storyboard with her peers and they were able to assist her with unknown words because they were able to recognize things in her drawings. The more she told her story, the more she improved her ability to use the correct English words to describe the details in her story. By the time she wrote it down, she had practiced her story orally many times and it was much easier for her to do.

For the third activity, I decided to give my students a change from totally open-ended narrative writing. I told them that they would be writing a story that had a common thread. Armed with paper, clipboards and pencils, I took my students outside to a forested area in our school playground. I sat them in a circular fashion around a sculpture that school district personnel had created in our forest–a giant troll head rising out of the ground. Like the first two activities, they were encouraged to think and draw in silence. I asked them to visualize the story, and then sketch it with their pencils. I encouraged the students to be brave, to not worry about making mistakes, to just allow a creative storyline to happen in their heads, and to draw this story with a logical beginning, middle, and end. I reminded the students about structure and the need to situate the main character(s) in a setting. Logically, the setting would begin in the forest, but it didn't necessarily have to stay there. The floodgates opened once again. This activity was most rewarding for the students and myself. They loved being outdoors in the forest.

Rather than taking them back to our classroom to share their stories, we simply formed two lines facing each other, sitting cross-legged on the forest floor. I used the familiar whistle prompt to let the students know then they should either be sharing their story, giving input to the storyteller or 'shoving a bum' to the next listener. We 'shoved a bum' three times then I asked for the 'thumbs up' if they felt they had the story in their heads. This time, they all felt confident and another retelling of the story wasn't necessary. They were very anxious to get to their writing. We ventured back into our classroom to begin our rough drafts. The results were super. I was pleased with the improvement in their storyboards, oral storytelling, and narrative writing rubric assessments for this activity. They all included the giant troll in some way, but all of their stories were unique and creative.

The children had so much fun writing outdoors for activity three that I decided to get them out into the environment once again for their fourth and final activity. Sometimes we need to go outside our ordinary "s/p(l)ace" (de Cosson, 2007, p. 130) to "relocate inquiry within the realm of local, personal, everyday places and events" (Finley, 2008, p. 72). "In critical arts-based inquiry, the location of research changes from the isolated sanctuaries of the […] school […] [as] socially responsible research for and by the people cannot reside inside the lonely walls of [the classroom]" (p. 74). Being outdoors in nature opens up many possibilities for instruction. I loved how my students were able to write about nature with the light and love that it deserves.

For our last activity in this study we walked to Kealy Woods Park, adjacent to our school. We hiked up to a rock bluff in the middle of the park overlooking the forest and the local mountains of North Vancouver. I asked my students to sit in a circle with their backs almost touching. I handed them a clipboard that I had prepared prior to the lesson; each having a piece of water color paper on it that had been taped down on all four sides to prevent shrinkage. I had numbered the clipboards one through 19, so I would be able to (re)construct the view of what they saw in front of them once their paintings were finished. We discussed framing a view with their fingers and I pointed out how their view would differ from their neighbor's because they were seated in a circle. I encouraged them to add as many details as they could.

We all had a great morning in Kealy Woods Park. Some of the remarks I remember were, 'Beats reading about nature in a textbook,' 'Boy, that morning went fast,' 'Can we do this every morning, Mrs. Karr?' and 'I love learning about things by being a part of them.' That last remark really struck home.

Eventually, we had to go back to the classroom, where I handed out watercolor pencil crayons and asked the students to shade in their pencil sketches with a lot of color. I encouraged them to use as many different types of green as they could, because Kealy Woods Park didn't just have one type of green in it. I have many great artists in my class this year and they jumped into this part of the assignment with great flourish. Once they had shaded their sketches using watercolor pencil crayons, they added a bit of water to create their paintings.

I asked my students to use their paintings to write a narrative poem that described a journey about 'becoming.' I remembered reading Ted Aoki papers that investigated a grey area or "in-between spaces that [were] neither this nor that but this and that" (Pinar, 2004, p. 9). I realized that this activity might be expecting a lot from the children, but I was confident that this particular class would be able to accomplish it. To begin, I put up an overhead that showed many concentric circles. 'Me' was the only word in the center of the circles. In the subsequent larger circles I wrote these words in this order: my family, my community, my province, my country, my world, my universe, and my infinity. I took them on a mental journey going out from their bodies to infinity in order for them to get a different perspective of *being*. Next, I asked them to close their eyes, and asked them to go back in their minds to Kealy Woods Park. I asked them to imagine sitting on the rock, then imagine going out of themselves to the forest, then going further out to the sky, then going further out to space, then going further out to infinity. When I asked them to open their eyes, one of my students said, "Whoa, what a rush!" I asked them if they found any connection between the imaginary journeys they had just taken prompted by the concentric circles overhead transparency with the imaginary journey they had taken from Kealy Woods Park. After a bit of thinking, students commented that, 'Well, they're kind of alike,' 'they were both journeys out of ourselves,' 'both activities caused me to think of other people, not just myself,' and 'I'm part of something much bigger than myself.' With these freshly minted ideas in their minds, I asked them to sit knee to knee to share some of their thoughts and ideas with their peers. They used their paintings to tell their personal journey stories. Once we had pair-shared three times, they were ready to put pen to paper. The narrative poems were simply amazing. Samuel Johnson once said, "Poetry is the art of uniting pleasure with truth." Moriarty adds, "Through imagination a poet expresses a symbolic relationship with the world in a new way" (p. 50). Halstead (1995) suggests that the "process of exploring abstract ideas through metaphor emerges from the fusion of the imagination and embodied experience" (p. 140).

I think fondly of one of my students' poems, who by his admonition,' dug deep' but came up 'short.' He wasn't implying that he didn't understand the topic, only that he wrote a short poem. This reminded me of a comment that Carl Leggo made about one of his poems saying, "at times I say very little, not because I don't want to say more, but simply because I don't know what I mean" (Schwarz, 2006, p. 66). How wonderful it is that poets feel comfortable dwelling in grey areas, were they "come close to … instability, [where] impossibility and playfulness [are] involved" (p. 66).

Another student described her poem as a 'gift from someone she didn't know.' When I asked her to elaborate on this, she said that she didn't actually write her poem. She said, 'Someone said the words in my head and I just wrote them down […] after all Mrs. Karr, this is way too good writing for me, don't you think?' I was fascinated with her insight.

Natalie Goldberg described her writing in a similar fashion. She said her writing was like a "divine structure had just whipped through. That which manifests from nothing changes everything and then is gone" (p. 23). I too, feel like a fraudster when it comes to my own writing. I feel like others are dictating words to me; that I'm merely the messenger. It was very special to share some of these insights with my students. The beauty of poetry is that we can reflect, on our living and on our life lessons. We don't need to make sense; we don't need to make sure that the commas are in the right place. All we need to do is express our feelings and emotions in a way that reaches out to others.

I was hesitant to leave this "s/p(l)ace" (de Cosson, p. 130), as we were all having so much fun with the process of creating poetry, but I knew the children had one final task to complete. I handed out the self-assessment post-test of their writing. I was pleased to see that the activities in this study had not deterred my students from the enjoyment of writing. In fact, all 19 children circled the smiling face in their post-tests, opposed to only 10 at the beginning of the study. I was pleased to see this final result.

Once my students had completed all four activities, my thoughts turned to creating a piece of art that would culminate this study and be a tribute to my students for all the hard work that they had done. I decided to (re)use/(re)cycle a project that I had done for one of my previous courses. A fellow student in my graduate cohort had created a mask of my face that I had painted a bright golden yellow. I had mounted this mask on a little stump of wood causing it to resemble a beautiful little golden mushroom. This toadstool became a representation of me. I placed this mask in the center of two concentric circles created with my students' paintings and poems.

I came up with the concentric circle idea after studying the work of Andy Goldsworthy, an artist who used items of nature to create his art. Watching a DVD about him and his art in one of my graduate classes taught me so much about what it truly meant to be an artist. I learned that it was possible for me to be an artist, a researcher and a teacher. It was an enriching experience for me to integrate "lived experiences as mother, teacher, scholar, and artist" (Wilson, 2004, p. 48). When viewed from outside the two concentric circles, one could see the entire panorama of 360 degrees that my students had painted and one could read the poems that they had written. Their paintings, backed by green construction paper symbolizing the forest, were placed in the inner circle. Their poems, backed by blue construction paper symbolizing the sky, were placed in the outer circle. I asked each student to find two rocks from our school playground, one that was dark in color and one that was light in color. The darker colored rocks were placed on top of their paintings and the lighter colored rocks were placed on top of their poems.

By handling the rocks, their energy was in them and they anchored the paintings and poems to the earth. They loved the idea of being a part of my art. I liked this idea, too. I constructed the art in the school gym and invited my students and their parents to come down and walk around it.

It was fun to share this art piece with my students and their parents. I think they were delighted that I had to do 'work' as well as them. Its creation provided us with tremendous opportunities for personal growth. We learned a great deal about us and about our place in the world—that it's important to be connected with our planet. We learned that reflecting about our place in the world wasn't a one-shot deal.

Going on from Here

Throughout this research, I found my "s/p(l)ace" (de Cosson, p. 130) "where my meaning becomes and belongs in its progression forward on the journey to anticipate meaning out of the curriculum of being that finds itself doing what it is called to do" (p. 128). My students tried new techniques and became more fluent and more descriptive in their narrative writing. Through practice they improved their storyboarding, their oral storytelling, and their narrative writing. We have grown as a result of this journey and we had fun in the process. What more could I have hoped for?

I don't pretend that this study provides scientific proof that using storyboarding and oral storytelling as pre-writing activities increases fluency and descriptive writing in children's' narrative writing. After all, this study only involved 19 children and it only lasted for three months. In thirty-four years of teaching, however, I can honestly say that no pre-writing strategies worked as effectively as my 3-part writing process. I would enjoy being involved in a longitudinal study on a district level to determine if the perspectives presented in this study holds true over a longer period of time with a larger sample of participants. I have shared my process with a number of other teachers, both in my master's cohort and with other teachers in my school, and have heard positive feedback from my colleagues. Also, although this study was done with Grade 3 students, I believe it could successfully be tried with writers of any age.

My students found it easier to create storyboards and orally tell their stories prior to writing them. It was important for me to just get out of their way, so they could find their own voices, look at their world through different lenses, and make meaning of it all. I learned that it was important to "ask students to describe what they have created in their art … let[ting] students know that their ideas and ways of expressing themselves [was] important" (Marchisan & Alber, 2001, p. 159).

I firmly believe that many of today's current accepted, traditional instructional practices are to blame for the lack of fluency and descriptiveness in students' narrative writing. It is up to us as educators to embrace change, to alter these practices and to open up and play with the 'box.' It is not an easy task to rethink the teaching of narrative writing, diverting it from the normal "parallel, analogic, and imagistic strategies" (Sinatra, p. 5). We need to acknowledge that creative thought is not reserved for gifted students, but rather, it is a quality that all children possess. It only needs to be nurtured to flourish. We need to redefine writing to include "images…[in order to] convey meaning" (Moore, p. 11). Grauer (1984) agrees stating, "Discretion to adapt and modify the linking of art and writing processes [is] an essential ingredient in evolution of the curriculum and its implementation" (p. 32). Using my 3-part process for narrative writing with storyboarding and oral storytelling as pre-writing activities to enhance fluency and descriptiveness is definitely a step in the right direction. I've learned that there are many ways to "see." Telling stories through images, then retelling them through oral storytelling, then finally writing them out with words enables students to use many perspectives, or "multiple intelligences," thus experiencing more than one way to make meaning (Gardner, p. 3). My students and I learned how to live the curriculum as a result of this study. "This lived curriculum, of course, is not the curriculum as laid out in a plan, but a plan more or less lived out" (Aoki, 2005, p. 201). We were "knowing, perceiving, teaching and being" (de Cosson, p.139); moreover, throughout this study we were constantly negotiated and transformed ourselves (Dyson, p. 17).

At varying times, during the past three years, I was challenged, frustrated, humbled, elated, and transformed. My personal and professional life have been blessed by this journey and I feel that I am more "consciously skilled" (Bennett & Rolheiser, p. 14). I feel that growth has occurred as a result in both "my body and mind" (Wilson, p. 43). I learned that I have the right to nurture myself and be concerned with "caring, of sharing of self" (p. 43). Finally, credit must be given to my students, for they played a large part in guiding my journey. I can't tell you how many times my students have come up to me over the years and asked, 'Mrs. Karr, can I tell you about the story in my picture?' It is so important to "acknowledge the competence of young children […] to listen closely to their conversations and collaborate with them in realizing their ideas" (Fraser, 2006, xviii). With this research study, I hope to follow my students' lead and investigate their wonderful stories.

When we create, we are connected with the oneness that exists in all there is. We are complete. Touching creation brings the vibrations of our souls back in tune with others and we find ourselves in a happier and healthier 's/p(l)ace.'

Tapestry

the universe is woven
in delicate strands
too fine to see
but whispers detect
its presence
our breath
bounces back to us
when we speak
our thoughts
out loud

Gerri Karr
North Vancouver School District 44
gkarr@nvsd44.bc.ca

CATHERINE KIERANS

VISUAL JOURNALING IN AN ALTERNATIVE MATHEMATICS CLASSROOM

Introduction

Some students at my alternative secondary school have had a long-term dislike of mathematics that has negatively affected their attendance, progress, marks, and engagement throughout most of their experiences in mathematics courses. I have noticed that many of these same students have been enthusiastically involved in artistic endeavours, especially in art therapy classes and graffiti artwork projects. In consideration of those factors, the purpose of this study was to determine the efficacy of using visual journals in secondary mathematics classroom (Grades 8 – 10) composed of reluctant and discouraged learners. I explored the affect of using visual journals on improving attitude, attendance, and comprehension of students who are disengaged learners in an alternative mathematics classroom. I hoped to tie into students' natural interests and visual capabilities to make math more accessible, meaningful, and fun. Based on my personal experiences with visual journaling, I projected that students would (1) attend classes on a more regular basis, (2) possess a more positive attitude toward mathematics that allows them to be more willing to learn, and (3) increase their engagement in mathematics classroom work and assignments.

My students are not alone in their dislike of math. When I identify myself as a mathematics teacher, many adults often volunteer that they have never liked math. Even in the press, mathematics has been reported as being a challenging subject, as evidenced recently by a headline in the *Calgary Herald* (McGinnis, 2010) newspaper, "Mathematics is the most 'catastrophic' subject for students, and even induces panic in many adults." The article contains comments many of us mathematics teachers have heard, quips like "I shouldn't be allowed to do math!" or "The subject we love to hate."

While math is perhaps the least liked subject at my alternative secondary school, most students have openly expressed their enjoyment of art. Our hallways are decorated with artwork that clearly demonstrates the creative and emerging talents of our young students. In addition to the regularly scheduled art course, art therapy classes began several years ago as an infrequent pullout with an external art therapist. The popularity of the program expanded into what we have today, with a full-time art therapist who has developed an inspiring, innovative, phenomenal program that now consists of at least ninety student participants, approximately 75% of our school population. Although students enter the pullout program initially to participate in extra artistic activities, they usually benefit personally,

P. Gouzouasis (ed.), Pedagogy in a New Tonality: Teacher Inquiries on Creative Tactics, Strategies, Graphics Organizers, and Visual Journals in the K-12 Classroom, 203–218.

emotionally, and socially from the opportunities to express themselves in a safe learning environment. Students may enter the art room stressed and flustered, and usually leave in an elevated and calm mood. Thorsen (2010) believes in the therapeutic power of art and says her role in the art therapy program is to "facilitate artistic expression thereby empowering the student and lifting mood" (p. 1). This change in mood often does not happen in a math classroom without a great deal of staff intervention and creative problem solving. That is why I considered how bringing art into the mathematics curriculum may help with this considerable concern.

I first became involved with visual journaling through two recent summer courses, and found the experiences challenging as I adjusted to the new approach of expressing myself and my learning through art and journaling. Yet the process was thoroughly enjoyable and the results were surprisingly satisfying. I was especially impressed with the unanimous positive responses from my fellow graduate students. The pages of our journals gave evidence to the effect that visual journaling had on our engagement and our learning. I considered the potential for using a visual journal in a mathematics classroom and the thought became reality through the present research project at the end of the 2009-2010 school year.

My School

The Alternate Secondary School in which I teach was established in 1974 to provide an educational program for those students who were not able to meet the expectations of North Vancouver mainstream schools. It started out as a small program for 12 potential dropouts between Grades 8 through 10, and has gradually expanded to include students from Grades 8 through 12. Our enrolment now averages around 150 students, with about 55% boys and 45% girls, aged between 13 to 19 years old. Most of the students (96) are registered in our main program for Grades 8 through 10.

Students who enter the main program are considered at-risk for school failure for complex reasons that include academic, behavioural, mental health, and social concerns. Entrance into our main program is also recommended for those students who would benefit from a more individualized, supportive program. Students can enrol at any time of the year and are placed in one of eight homeroom groups composed of twelve students in Grades 8 through 10. Along with small-sized classes and teacher to student ratios of 1:6, we offer core subjects on a daily basis (Math, English, Social Studies and Science) and some electives every other day (PE, Art, Information Technology) or once a week (Planning and Woodworking).

I am currently one of the two math teachers. Students in our classes work in individualized programs following grade-level mathematics curriculum, which have been modified and adapted to meet their learning needs. Unlike mainstream schools' evaluation processes, students earn marks based on their attendance and effort. There is less emphasis on the usual assessment strategies such as test results and homework completion, as those approaches have not worked for these at-risk youth in their previous educational experiences. At our school, students progress at their own pace through the curriculum, and many students seem to benefit from having their own personal tutor (i.e., me) guide them through their mathematics assignments. Lessons are introduced one-on-one in a variety of ways, from examining a problem and looking for patterns and solutions, to working through hands-on activities that evolve toward an understanding of the concepts.

The Research Problem

Our individualized approach to learning mathematics has produced positive results for some students who have experienced failure in previous mathematics courses in mainstream school settings. Many students mention that they like learning at their own pace and that they appreciate having their lessons tailored specifically to their learning needs. I like working with the students one-on-one and enjoy the dialogue that spontaneously develops into a unique lesson. Students receive immediate feedback on how well they are demonstrating their understanding. Through this process, I learn from them as they learn from me—a reciprocal benefit. For students who are motivated and focussed on their academic goals, this individualized setting is ideal for their educational goals.

However, the reality is that many students do not possess strong academic skills and some students possess very low skills in mathematics. Some may have been diagnosed with learning disabilities, including written output difficulties, slow processing speeds, and short-term memory concerns. They may be physically and mentally restless and have a difficult time concentrating on their assignments for the full length of a fifty-minute class. They may possess a low tolerance for frustration, and may be resistant or reluctant to get engaged in their lessons. Some may be struggling with emotional or impulse control. Others may be distracted by concerns outside of school that impede on their ability to focus on academic matters. A few have mental health concerns that make participating in class activities challenging.

With the individualized atmosphere of the math class, it is difficult for me to get a real feel for how well students understand the math that they are learning. I make sure that the students discuss with me what they are doing and how their lessons are progressing. When asked to explain what they are studying in math, many students have a difficult time giving details or speaking mathematically about their learning.

Attendance has a significant impact on the progress of student learning at our school. As in mainstream schools, regular attendance helps to maintain and enrich the continuity in the students' individualized learning program. However, there are several students who frequently skip school, or they may have average attendance but choose to selectively skip their mathematics classes because they do not like mathematics or they do not feel up to handling the expectations required to learn mathematics. There are other students who schedule their pullout activities specifically during their mathematics classes, usually to attend art therapy classes.

Generally there are two challenging times in settling the class: (1) at the start of class getting students engaged in their lessons, and (2) at the last ten-fifteen minutes of class encouraging students to work to the bell and not pack up their work early. Most students spend about thirty minutes of quality time on their math assignments; the more committed and academically capable can work and stay focused for the full fifty minutes. Many students enter the classroom groaning and commenting that they hate math and ask if they could do something fun instead of doing math. As a teacher, it is difficult to hear these negative comments. At the end of class, during the last ten to fifteen minutes, students feel like they have worked very hard and have earned a break. Their off-task behaviour disrupts the class focus and very few students are able to work through this unstructured time to the bell.

In consideration of those factors, and in an attempt to frame my research problems, I have questioned how can I engage my students for longer periods of time in their mathematics class through the use of an activity that can lift their mood and their attitudes toward math, and that will fit into their different individualized mathematics programs. I have also tried to imagine the type of activity that could bring some requested "fun" into the classroom, while at the same time strengthen and reinforce their learning, appreciation, and understanding of math.

Refining the Problems: Math Anxiety and Negative Attitudes Toward Mathematics

Most of my students mention that they have never been good at math. Hekimoglu & Kittrell (2010) suggest that the "repeated recollection of uncomfortable and often underlying traumas can strongly influence students' abilities to learn mathematics and can foster a *learned helplessness syndrome*" (p. 301). They believe that students' chronic failures and frustrations may lead to feeling that mathematics is impossible and create a sense of math anxiety, boredom, resistance, reluctance, anger, and disengagement.

One of the reasons I decided to use visual journals was to help students make the transition from negative, perhaps math-anxiety related attitudes, at the start of class to a more relaxed, comfortable, accepting disposition. My concern has been that students' negative attitudes when they enter the classroom significantly affect their progress and engagement in their programs. Bower (2001) states, "by about age 12, students who feel threatened by mathematics start to avoid math courses, do poorly in the few math classes they do take, and earn low scores on math-achievement tests" (p. 405). Ashcraft & Kirk's (2001) integrated research on the relationship between math anxiety and math cognition produced results that suggest math anxiety can compromise and reduce the working memory capacity needed for learning and mastery. They conclude, "Math anxiety disrupts the on-going, task-relevant activities of working memory, slowing down performance and degrading its accuracy" (p. 236). In a study that examines the effects of students' mathematics-related beliefs on their learning, Op't Eynde, De Corte, & Verschaffel (2002) state, "In a similar way, self-confidence and positive emotions (affective factors) are no longer considered as just positive side effects of learning, but become important constituent elements of learning and problem-solving" (p. 14). With those studies in mind, perhaps by implementing an enjoyable, non-threatening activity like visual journaling into the curriculum, stressful, anxious, and negative attitudes would be reduced and alleviated, which could improve students' performance and understanding.

The BC Ministry of Education *Integrated Resource Package (IRP) for Mathematics 8–9* (2008) concurs that students' attitudes have a significant impact on their learning. "Students with positive attitudes toward learning mathematics are likely to be motivated and prepared to learn, participate willingly in classroom activities, persist in challenging situations, and engage in reflective practices" (p. 12). My project on visual journaling will also tie into the new emphasis of visual learning, that "students are expected to … develop visualization skills to assist in processing information, making connections and solving problems." (p. 6). In the *Common Curriculum Framework 2008 for Grades 10–12*, visualization is stressed as an important process for older students as well: "The use of visualization in the study of mathematics provides students with opportunities to understand mathematical concepts and make connections among them" (p. 9).

Journaling in Mathematics Classes

Teachers who have used journaling in their mathematics classrooms have noted the positive effect on students, cognitively and affectively (Lim & Pugalee, 2006), and on increasing the retention of information (Hanson, 2002) in an enjoyable manner. A common recommendation has been the continued implementation of journaling in their classrooms (Hanson, 2002; Lim & Pugalee, 2006, Pinzker, 2001). Pugalee (1998) acknowledges that many mathematics teachers are now using writing as an effective teaching technique and identifies five areas that writing may enhance and promote: knowledge of mathematics, problem-solving strategies, self-monitoring and reflection, affective issues, and discourse. In particular, writing gives students an opportunity to reflect on their feelings about mathematics and "such perspectives are crucial in moving the student to a frame of mind where they can react positively to these feelings and begin to experience mathematics with heightened confidence" (p. 21).

Communication is an important step in the process of the constructing and learning of mathematics. Often communication in the classroom is in the form of discussion to enable students to demonstrate their reasoning and thinking processes. Baxter, Woodward, & Olson (2005) used journaling in a low-track Grade 7 math class composed of low-achieving students to supplement small and large group class discussions and "to include all students in mathematically meaningful communication" (p. 120). Their experience with four students suggests that students' journals are a valuable alternative means for those students who do not engage in or feel comfortable with oral-based communication. Perhaps journals could also achieve similar results in less discourse-based classrooms such as mine to help marginalized students communicate their learning.

Art Journaling and Visual Journals in Mathematics Classrooms

A few teachers have reported on the positive effects that art has had on student learning. Chapman (1998) explains that integrating art into core curriculum subjects boosts student's academic performance. He suggests that art instruction could be the bridge to help stimulate creativity and promote critical thinking skills in a number of subjects. Hanson (2002) agrees, as her intervention project noted that incorporating visual arts into mathematics and science classes improved student learning.

Ernst (2001) believes that when multiple forms of expression are honoured, "the pictures of learning in that wider frame include more children, more success, more learning, and endless possibilities" (p. 367). Ernst (1997) encourages the use of student journals, often referred to as "observation journals," as a strategy for students to connect their drawing and writing with learning, for she feels there is a strong connection between those three areas. I noted that in her studies, the student journals were implemented in science, social studies, art, and reading in Grade 4 classes, but not in their mathematics classrooms.

Stix (1994) promotes the use of Pic-Jour Math in Grades 3 through 8, which uses journal writing, pictures, numbers, symbols and manipulatives to enhance students' thinking and understanding of mathematics. Stix (1994) states, "the results are a better understanding and retention of mathematics, a decrease in 'math anxiety,' and a heightened confidence level among students who have really made a lesson 'their own'" (p. 264). Stix (1994) ascertains, "An integrated approach, including pictorial journal writing or note-taking, takes advantage of students' strengths, deepens their understanding, and teaches them to communicate their ideas to others effectively" (p. 268).

I expand on these previous studies in the present inquiry to examine incorporating a visual journal in a mathematics class for at-risk adolescents who have had difficulties in mathematics to create a more successful learning environment.

Description of the Inquiry and Students

I implemented visual journaling in all four of my mathematics classes during the last five weeks of the school year. Every student was required to work in their visual journals during the first ten to fifteen minutes of each class. The daily visual journal prompts were organized as follows. For the first week, students created covers for their visual journals that reflected some aspect of themselves and their beliefs, attitudes, and understandings about mathematics. During the second week, visual journal topics encouraged personal reflections on the mathematics that is all around us. The focus was to emphasize a positive side of mathematics by exploring its usefulness and its connections in our everyday lives. In the third week, students were asked to reflect on their attitudes and feelings about mathematics. Many of the journal prompts encouraged the use of metaphors as a lens to explore students' attitudes and beliefs about mathematics. For the fourth week, topics encouraged students to express their current mathematical learning visually and in writing.

During the last week of the study, students evaluated the effects that visual journaling had on their attitudes and their learning of mathematics.

Joan (all names have been changed for this action research project) is a fifteen-year old girl who entered her Grade 9 program in April 2010. During her elementary school years, she attended six different schools in North Vancouver, Richmond, and Edmonton. Report cards mention that she was adjusting well to her new surroundings, that she was very social in her classes, and that she was working towards meeting the expectations of children in her age range. Academically she struggled to understand and apply concepts, and she received ongoing learning assistance support in Language Arts and Mathematics. In a mainstream secondary school in Richmond, her mathematics teachers noted that her effort and achievement were unsatisfactory, and that she often assumed she was not able to do the work. She earned failing marks in Math 8, Science 8, and English 9, and finally transferred in her Grade 9 year to our alternative school in North Vancouver to catch up and complete her Grade 10.

Joan has had long-term difficulties with mathematics. Her beliefs have been that she cannot do math, that she has never been good at math, and that she has never understood the concepts. I did not realise her feelings toward mathematics until she started working in the visual journal. Her marks with us, based on effort and attendance, have been above 95% in mathematics.

John is a fourteen-year old boy who joined us in April 2010 to complete his Grade 9 and 10 program. John is a quiet student who has been a pleasant and polite member of his homeroom group. In elementary school, teachers commented on his lack of confidence, his difficulties with skill and concept acquisition beginning in Grade 1 (especially in mathematics and language arts), and concerns with behaviour and peer conflicts. Most report cards mention that, with support, John was able to make some progress in his class work, although he struggled to complete assignments and homework. In secondary school, John had difficulties meeting school expectations and was referred to us to receive extra support to help him work toward success personally and academically in a school setting.

John has had long-term difficulties in math and has needed ongoing support to help with completion and focus in his previous schools. I thought the visual journal would be an excellent way for him to express his difficulties and enrich his learning, as he has been too quiet during most of our lessons together. I have been pleased that he has been completing his assignments on his own, but I have also been concerned that he has not been gaining a real understanding of the concepts. His marks have been above 90% in most of his courses with us.

Jack is a sixteen-year old First Nations student who enrolled in October 2007 at the start of his Grade 9 program. From Grades K-5, Jack lived in a foster home, and school reports indicated that he was achieving grade expectations in mathematics and language arts. At the age of ten, Jack was referred for psycho-educational assessment due to concerns that he was not working to his full potential. According to a psycho-educational report, Jack "is a bright boy who tested in the top 5% of students when given an intellectual screening by the North Vancouver School Board" (Bowden, 2004). Due to personal circumstances, his programs in Grades 6–7 were adapted, yet even then he did not complete the work to meet minimum expectations. In Grade 8, he enrolled in a skills development centre and this helped him pass most of his courses (he earned 73% in Math 8). However, in Grade 9, several incidents suggested that Jack would benefit from enrolment in a more supportive program and he was transferred to our school. He has had a few tough years with us, with incidents that include ongoing drug usage concerns and angry, confrontational, defiant behaviour. He recently completed his Grade 9 credit requirements in June 2010.

I was interested in Jack's response to the visual journal because he especially needs time to transition into mathematics. Before the implementation of the visual journaling study, on his own he found an origami book and usually spent the first ten minutes of his mathematics classes creating origami animals. Even the more challenging folded designs did not frustrate him, as he patiently and expertly followed the complicated instructions. He seems to need the visual-kinetic intervention to grab his attention, settle him down, and help set the mood to transition into a learning mode. Jack is a capable student and can achieve good results on quizzes and tests, and often responds to questions with insights and answers that reveal his intelligence. His previous marks at our school have been below 60% in most of his courses due to low attendance and lack of effort.

Josie is a sixteen-year old girl who joined us in November 2008 to complete her Grade 9 program. She has had behavioural and emotional concerns that date back to Grade 3. Academically, Josie has been meeting expectations in her courses until she reached secondary school, where she continues to have attendance issues, health-related absences, drug usage concerns and off-task behaviour that has affected her academic progress. She was referred to us to get caught up in her Grade 8 - 9 programs, which she recently completed in April 2010. Her average grade in mathematics at our school has been below 60% due to poor attendance, low effort and incomplete assignments.

I was interested in Josie's response to the visual journal because she seems disinterested in school, especially in mathematics, despite her obvious capability in the subject area. She has appeared unmotivated and unwilling to get engaged in her individualized program. For various personal and emotional reasons, she has attended several art therapy classes every week, usually during her mathematics classes. As a result, I usually have worked with her about once a week. I felt that she would be someone who could become more engaged in mathematics through the artistic emphasis of the visual journal. Josie recently has had a more positive and mature attitude around the school. She finally earned As in all of her courses in the last term this year, and in the mathematics classroom, better consistency in attendance helped to improve learning and understanding.

The Visual Journals' Impact on Attendance

This was the first time I had integrated visual journals into the mathematics curriculum, and I was very pleased with many aspects of the results. In general, most students made an effort to respond thoughtfully to the journal topics. I was impressed by their insights, their openness, and most surprisingly by their creativity. Some students demonstrated their artistic talents, while others shone through their literary skills.

Students are referred to us for various reasons, although for many, low attendance plays a significant reason for the recommendation to enrol in an alternative school setting. Maintaining regular attendance continues to be a goal for those students who struggle with achieving success in an educational program. In my four classes, I had hoped to encourage learners to improve their attendance by integrating a more accessible component into their mathematics curriculum. The study began during the last five weeks of school, often a difficult time period in which to hold and sustain students' interest and motivation. Yet overall, attendance in the mathematics classes increased slightly above the previous term's attendance, from an average of 74% to 76%. Also on a positive note, 38% of the students increased their marks above their previous reporting period's standings.

When questioned about the impact visual journals had on attendance and their marks, most students commented that the visual journals did not necessarily make a difference. They referred to their own personal goals to achieve better marks and higher attendance as the reasons for their improved results. As Joan explained, "No, the journal didn't make a difference; I would have been here anyway." However, a few students said that the activities did make a difference for them. One student offered, the visual journaling "makes me want to come to math because I hate sitting in class doing a full class of math." Josie, an active participant in the art therapy program, said that the visual journals added a different perspective to the class, that it was more fun, and that she especially enjoyed the project for the opportunities to use "lots of colours in math."

Visual Journals Open Spaces to Reflect on Attitudes and Feelings

Within the pages of their journals, unfortunately most of my students expressed negative and discouraged attitudes toward mathematics. This was a sensitive, delicate undertaking because I did not know how the students would react once I encouraged and promoted an open dialogue about their feelings towards mathematics. The responses could have gone in undesirable directions, thereby further encouraging an atmosphere of resistance and negativity that I was hoping to change. In fact, one student lost her temper within her journal, scribbling so hard that she tore several pages; she wrote, " This didn't help...now I just want to fight" and left the room, too angry to control her emotions. Another student wrote about his disappointment with his progress and extended his journal time to about half of the class, ending with "@#*@ this little ginny pig journal experiment!" He then worked sullenly on his mathematics assignment for rest of the class, until near the bell, when he began to interact with others in a more pleasant manner. When visual journals give space for expressing attitudes and feelings, the results may have a powerful impact on students' emotions and behaviour in the classroom.

Despite having the chance to express negative feelings toward mathematics, most students were able to gently transition into their studies. For some, the novelty of exposing their attitudes promoted closer examinations of their beliefs about themselves as learners and about the nature of mathematics. In particular, a usually quiet student, John began to express his feelings that he never revealed during previous discussions and class lessons. His usual on-task, focused attitude had covered up his long-time dislike of and difficulties with mathematics. In one of his earlier visual journal assignments, when asked to describe mathematics as a colour, he wrote, "black because math for me is really hard and bitter because I don't enjoy it and it is difficult." His picture showed four yellow lemons in a swirling thick black background with the words "bitter lemons in a hurricane." Another drawing titled *Math as a Face* showed a face labelled as "unhappy." These were not the typical emotions that John expressed in the mathematics classroom. In his autobiography reviewing his past experiences with mathematics, he wrote, "I didn't like it because it was so boring cause teachers would spend an hour talking and teaching and when we finally got the worksheet I forgot most of what she was talking about." Yet in one of his later entries, John stated, "My ideal math class would be the one I have now because I enjoy being here. I like the class sizes and the learning ..." For me as his teacher, I felt encouraged to learn of the changes in attitude about himself and his learning abilities that John was experiencing in mathematics. I would not have appreciated this change without the aid of the visual journal activities.

Visual Journaling Meets Emotional Needs of Students and Fosters Positive Learning Atmosphere

Although I engage in daily dialogues with my students, the discussions are usually focused on the mathematics presented in their individualized programs. Students' emotions, attitudes, and personal issues are dealt with separately and sometimes one-on-one outside of class time. There has not been a consistent routine that allowed students the opportunity to address the concerns that were affecting their attitudes, performance, progress, and behaviour in their mathematics class. Yet there has been a real need to connect with these marginalized students in a more individualized manner. The less-personalized atmosphere of mainstream school setting has not helped these students achieve their full potential. One of the key benefits of implementing visual journaling time into the daily schedule has been to offer students a place to express themselves, to validate their thinking and their emotions, and to touch on personal topics not always discussed in a mathematical setting. Creating personal pages that reflected themselves added a new imaginative dimension to the often impersonal, algorithmic focus of their mathematical assignments.

The visual journals opened spaces for reflection, for students to reflect on themselves and their personal concerns, yet also to reflect on their coursework, their learning needs and academic goals. Giving time and place for this kind of dialogue had an impact on the students in my classroom. It seemed that some of their emotional needs were being met through this activity, for there was less complaining and negativity at the start of classes. Students liked working in their journals, and their attitudes in general appeared to be more positive and relaxed, as evidenced by their quiet, focused, and on-task responses. Their moods seemed to actually change during the time spent on visual journaling. This change in the atmosphere at the start of class was one of the first noticeable effects of the visual journal on my students' attitudes. The activities created a better learning environment that helped most of the learners to transition smoothly into their mathematics programs with less resistance, reluctance, and negativity.

Upon reflection of the visual journaling process, I appreciated Josie's comment, "I got almost all of my energy out which is awesome. And now I get to focus." Many students mentioned this beneficial aspect of the visual journal, as affirmed by another student who wrote, "I like doing this - helps me get into the math mind frame." Some liked the opportunities to have a "more positive look at math." Others appreciated that journaling time provided different activities that were fun; as Josie explained, "it made me want to work on my journal all class sometimes." Jack liked the doodling and drawing activities that helped "calm the mind before stressin' it on some math. I felt I did better because there was more stuff to mix in with math instead of thinkin' hard right away."

A More Realistic Purpose for Visual Journals: Better Attitudes Toward Learning

One area that the visual journals helped to separate and define was the attitudes toward mathematics and the attitudes shown in the classroom. Not all engaged and enthusiastic students reported in their visual journaling activities that they liked mathematics. However, most of the disengaged, easily frustrated, and discouraged learners repeatedly indicated their dislike of mathematics. The students who were demonstrating more positive attitudes in the classroom were the ones who were doing well on their assignments, despite their negative feelings about mathematics. Reflecting on this point, perhaps a more realistic, purposeful outcome for this study would be to encourage a better attitude about learning, and perhaps a better attitude toward mathematics might follow. Nardi & Steward (2003) suggest that if students "believe they can do mathematics and engage positively with it, then they actually enjoy the subject more" (p. 363). Through the visual journal activities, there was a noticeable change in the learning environment, and for some students, that was enough for them to appreciate being in the class somewhat more than before.

A common theme reflected in the visual journals was students' negative self-image of their mathematical abilities. Joan was not alone in expressing, "I'm not good at math – never was and never will be." She has experienced long-term feelings of dislike and inadequacy toward mathematics throughout most of her life. Her drawing of *Math as a Face* was labelled "Frustration." On another page, she drew a mango and wrote, "If math were a food it would be a mango because I'm allergic to it." Later she wrote, "Personally I do not like math. It is the hardest subject for me to learn." Yet in the mathematics classroom, despite her feelings toward math, she demonstrated a positive, enthusiastic, engaged attitude. It seems that her positive attitude about learning, and about school in general, has helped her achieve the attitude and successful results that I was hoping students would attain; yet this was done without creating a complete, transformational change in her attitude toward mathematics.

The more positive, willing, and engaged attitudes that emerged during my study may be attributed to the less stressful start to the class. Furthermore, the journals added a change in the usual routine, and that, in itself, seemed to help create a more appealing atmosphere in the classroom. It gave students another activity to work through, which broke up the long focus on their individualized programs that often seems to bore, stress, and discourage learners.

Visual Journals Opened Communication with My Students

Pugalee (1998) says that writing in the mathematics classroom "offers students an outlet through which they can communicate with the teacher... Writing provides students with an opportunity to share affective issues with the teacher...the teacher can use the writing opportunities ...to create a feedback mechanism" (p. 22). It was natural response for me to react to many of the students' entries and to create an ongoing dialogue with them. For example, through the visual journal, Joan revealed her long-time dislike of mathematics. This led to more open discussions with her about those feelings: exploring where they originated, why they have persisted, and how have they affected her progress in mathematics. The discussions have moved onto suggestions for her to reconsider and re-evaluate her beliefs about her abilities, and to slowly refocus her efforts to produce more positive results in mathematics. Joan's visual journal helped me communicate and connect with Joan in ways that were not possible through typical, traditional class procedures, and together we developed more effective learning strategies to help her grow in the mathematics classroom.

John's resistance to using his visual journal space was a surprise at first. However, considering that John was a very quiet student, I should have anticipated the difficulty he encountered when asked to express himself visually and in writing, that this was pushing his naturally private comfort zone even further. His reluctance was gently, yet firmly, eased into compliance with staff interventions and encouragements. In this way, his hesitant results revealed more than had been discovered through our discussions during his mathematics lessons. Even though he at first seemed distressed with the assignments, as he became more engaged in the process, his responses were thoughtful and presented a different kind of person. Perhaps, with time, he will feel more comfortable and more vocal during our mathematics lessons. The visual journal assignments have opened another avenue to reach and engage in better communication with many of my students.

Visual Journals Provide opportunities to Develop Personal Relationships

Hekimoglu & Kittrell (2010) determined that there are several ways to change student attitudes and efficacy toward mathematics. Interestingly, they found that the most effective strategy for promoting substantial beliefs change came through the context of personal relationships. To that end, Hekimoglu & Kittrell encourage teachers to get to know their students so that they can better understand what kind of teaching support and encouragement will enhance students' learning needs. At our school, we strive to build connections with our students, as our motto affirms, "Trust. Respect. Success." For me, the visual journal provided another path to help develop better relationships with some of my students. It was through the pages of the visual journals that students began to open up and communicate themselves in their own ways, using their own special talents, artistically and fluently. This helped me to appreciate their struggles and their concerns, to built on their confidences and to encourage their growth. As their voices and personalities were surfacing through art and reflection, I began to see my students as more extraordinary individuals.

I appreciated and laughed at the cleverness of some of the penetrating insights my students had about mathematics. One student wrote, "Math is like…an old man that won't die, just keeps throwing questions at you," which was written below a pencilled sketch of an old man's face wearing wire-rimmed glasses. Another pasted a picture of a bruised M&M caricature and below described himself as sometimes feeling good about math and other times feeling bruised by it. Their creativity and thoughtful responses created spaces for new dialogues about attitudes, learning, and personal connections to mathematics.

Several of Jack's responses during visual journaling time opened my eyes to students' lives outside of my mathematics classroom. One of his responses, "it helped me get my writing hand ready for work," made me pause and reflect on his previous activities before arriving in my class (PE, computers and woodworking) and I realized that he had not yet held a pencil that day. Some students may need time to get into their handwriting mode before they can be successful with coordinating the many other demands of a mathematics classroom. A simple entry into a visual journal provided that new fresh insight for this experienced teacher, as well as another purposeful teaching strategy for the visual journal – to get students writing hands ready for work.

Summary: Visual Journaling Benefits Students

Mathematics has been one of the least liked classes for many of the adolescents at our alternative school. Students try to avoid the class in different ways, through skipping the class, scheduling pull-out classes like art therapy during math, to disrupting class work and disengaging from assignments. It has been an essential goal of mine to develop activities to overcome the negative, reluctant, and discouraged attitudes at the start of class that hinder progress and achievement in mathematics.

Pugalee (1998) suggests, “In writing about where they are affectively, the student gains a new sense of their own limitations and histories” (p. 21). He believes these perspectives are crucial in helping students move forward to where they can begin to respond positively and see mathematics with a new sense of confidence. Through the pages of their visual journals, students expressed their concerns, attitudes, and learning needs. It allowed their personal voices to be heard and shared. The result was that some students began to address their attitudes and beliefs about themselves as learners and about mathematics in general.

The visual journal encouraged and pushed the students to be creative and insightful about themselves, their learning, and about the nature of mathematics. Stix (1995) suggests, “An integrated approach to teaching mathematics that includes pictorial journal writing … generates an opening for creative expression” (p.12). In my classroom, the emphasis on connecting art, writing and mathematics provided students with opportunities to make meaningful connections within their learning space, within their lives, and within their communities. The visual journal pages contrasted with their everyday workbooks, situating the connections of art/writing/mathematics in a separate, distinct place. Yet, by returning to the journals at the start of every class, the three areas of learning became interwoven and became a creative gateway for entering their work, their explorations of new ideas, and their learning of mathematics with more open, receptive, thoughtful minds.

Stix (1996) believes that “Journal writing gives students the opening they need to become active participants in their own learning” (p. 6). This sense of control over their learning helped some students reach beyond their usual effort and produce work that reflected more patience and focus. It was also noted that perhaps the activities that involved writing and drawing slowed down the thinking and learning process, which helped those learners who struggle with the rapid pace of oral instruction. Lim & Pugalee (2004) maintain, “Writing in mathematics engages students as they manipulate, integrate, and restructure knowledge through using and reflecting on prior knowledge, concepts and beliefs” (p.2). I had hoped that the visual journal assignments would have some impact on improving students’ competence and comprehension of their mathematics lessons. However, unlike the benefits mentioned in research, the assignments in my study that asked students to draw and write about their mathematical learning proved to be the weakest responses in their visual journals. Their entries were minimal and sparse, and they often relied on copying examples from their textbooks. During discussions about their lessons, students’ responses did not display better understandings of their mathematics topics, nor demonstrate more fluent mathematical literacy. Students need time and more opportunities to develop their skills in thinking and expressing themselves mathematically, visually, and in writing. However, there was limited time spent on these activities in my study, and it will be one area that I would like to explore further in future visual journaling projects.

Visual Journaling Benefits the Teacher

I agree with Powell & Lopez's (1989) findings that journal writing "proved to be a powerful vehicle for dialogue between student and instructor" (p. 167). The visual journals presented opportunities to create ongoing discourse with my students in a private, safe environment. I felt that I reached and connected with more learners, especially the quiet, reserved, and disengaged students. As Powell and Lopez (1989) further explain the benefits of journal writing for the teacher, "The revelatory nature of students' expressive writings provides instructors with feedback on important dimensions of their pedagogy" (p. 173). Lim & Pugalee (2006) see writing as an essential component of classroom practice. They emphasize the importance of the writing process for teachers, who may find that they teach by addressing "students' needs, rather that just 'covering' the curriculum" (p. 18). As I became more aware of my students' learning strengths, I became a more effective teacher. Some students commented that they felt that I seemed to connect with them better, as Joan wrote, " it's kinda like she knows how I learn and how I like to learn."

During the five-week study, students were more comfortable with visual journal topics that focused on the personal side of their learning and their attitudes about mathematics. These topics engaged the students with minimal questions and encouragement from staff. Perhaps this was a natural outcome for journaling activities. When Koirala (2002) gave 'write what you think' topics for journal entries, "more than 80% of the students simply chose to express their beliefs about mathematics" (p. 219) instead of mentioning and demonstrating their mathematical learning or understanding. I concur with Powell & Lopez (1989) who talked of the process-product style of journal writing, "where writing is used first to focus on learners and then as a means to have learners reflect on mathematics" (p. 159). Because of the limited time frame of a five-week study, the focus for me was to provide students the space to become comfortable talking and drawing about their attitudes and feelings about mathematics. There was less emphasis on mathematics achievement and more on the learning process and learners. As a result, the visual journals allowed me to become more aware of students' struggles and hopes, their strengths and their weaknesses. I became a more empathetic teacher in response to the opportunities to foster better relationships with my students.

By incorporating the visual journaling within my mathematics program, students were challenged to take more control of their learning. The assignments encouraged them to work toward developing more extensive mathematical skills beyond manipulating numbers and symbols by the integration of drawing, writing and thinking mathematically into their mathematics programs. Through continued implementation of visual journals in the classroom, I believe students will become more mathematically competent, resulting in a more successful program for my students.

Visual Journaling Benefits the Learning Environment

> Writing and mathematics can be effectively linked to provide a vibrant and constructive learning environment. (Pugalee, 1998, p. 22)

The most encouraging result of the visual journaling program has been to create a more nurturing and pleasant learning environment. The amount of negative comments that usually preceded students through the door at the start of class has decreased. By gently doing something that they like, reluctant learners are building up to being less resistant to doing mathematics. The relaxed, positive attitudes that are evident at the start of the class have helped to overcome the negative feelings that have hindered many of my students in their progress and achievement. With a more welcoming and encouraging atmosphere, students have a better chance to become more successful learners in their mathematics programs.

Catherine Kierans
North Vancouver School District 44
CKierans@nvsd44.bc.ca

MARSHA B. THOMPSON

DEVELOPING CONFIDENCE AND COMPREHENSION

The use of visual journals in a Grade Eight mathematics classroom

Introduction

Marvelous, malicious, monstrous, mind-boggling, magical, miserable, magnificent, morbid. These words were amongst numerous positive and negative adjectives playfully brainstormed by my Grade 8 students to describe their feelings and responses when presented with the general topic of mathematics. As my students contributed ideas during our word gathering session, I noticed a great deal of emotion, especially with the addition of the more negative words, and I had to energetically encourage the addition of positive descriptors.

I have taught numerous grade levels and subjects in my many years of teaching in Richmond, BC. However, I continue to be amazed and frustrated by the degree of highly negative emotions upon entering the classroom in September 2009 with my Grade 8 mathematics students. Unfortunately, I also recall experiencing similar feelings of trepidation as a young teenager, and it wasn't until my later years that I truly began to experience and appreciate the fun and beauty of math.

Why do so many students appear to "hate" math? Why do such a number of my new high school students feel intimidated by this subject? Why do students who enjoy mathematics and do well in this area remain quiet, almost shy about their skills and preferences? What can I, a Grade 8 mathematics teacher, do to improve students' feelings and understandings in this area of study?

As a student myself, while pursuing my Master's degree in Curriculum Leadership at the University of British Columbia, I was given the opportunity to use what we now consider an Instructional Intelligence (II) tool, the visual journal, in many of my classes to facilitate and enhance learning. I was initially inspired by the use of visual journals during an action research course. My appreciation for this method was further enhanced during a Teachers' Summer Institute held at the Vancouver Art Gallery and the UBC Museum of Anthropology. In both of those courses, we were encouraged to record notes, develop artistic efforts, find souvenirs, do research, and elaborate our own personal ramblings and ruminations. Although I do not consider myself to be especially artistic in the visual sense, and was somewhat skeptical at first, I grew to value this educational approach. Would it be a tool that could help my young students to improve both their self- esteem and confidence in mathematics, and also contribute to the development of greater comprehension of the math concepts taught at this grade level? It was that question, as well as the others I previously presented, along with a burning desire

P. Gouzouasis (ed.), Pedagogy in a New Tonality: Teacher Inquiries on Creative Tactics, Strategies, Graphics Organizers, and Visual Journals in the K-12 Classroom, 219–226.

to improve my students' attitudes toward mathematics, that provided the spark for my current inquiry through the implementation of (visual) mathematics journals as a tool in my classroom.

Narrative inquiry, with its focus on the ways humans experience the world, provided me with a powerful and meaningful way to represent both my students' and my own experience with visual journaling in mathematics. As I learned from Carl Leggo, narrative inquiry speaks to the heart, the mind, and the whole. At its heart is meaning making, the intention to find some wisdom through the interaction between reader, text, and author. Connelly & Clandinin (1990) theorize that "education is the construction and reconstruction of personal and social stories; learners, teachers, and researchers are storytellers and characters in their own and other's stories" (p. 2). It is my hope that my use of narrative inquiry enables the reader to get inside the 'data' in a more meaningful manner, to hear our stories, just as visual journals were my alternative form of representing meaning and understanding for my students and me.

Theoretical Considerations and the Research Problem

Kaline, Grauer, Baird & Meszaro's (2007) theory with reference to the use of visual journals suggest that "the very nature of visual journaling facilitates the generation of first-person voices leading to a more holistic and personal way of coming to know" (p. 202). Visual journals are records of process, and also a new area of focus that are part of the new Grade 8 provincial math curriculum (2008), where it is stated that students are expected to "demonstrate an understanding of their learning, concretely, pictorially, and symbolically" (p. 42). Journals can provide visual/linguistic evidence of how our thinking changes and develops over time. As such they are rich sources of assessment. Visual journaling within the mathematics classroom invites students to personalize their meaning making in more non-textual ways that go beyond merely taking notes from a lecture or completing assignments from textbooks.

Arcavi (2003) notes that the "centrality of visualization in learning and doing mathematics seems to be widely acknowledged. Visualization is no longer related to the illustrative purposes only, but is also being recognized as a key component of reasoning and problem solving" (p. 235). Hershkowitz, Arcavi, & Bruckheimer (1999) believe that "visualization can be central not only in areas which are obviously associated with visual images (such as geometry), but also in formal symbolic arguments (such as high school algebra)" (p. 255).

As it is well known, Howard Gardner (1993), developed a theory based on multiple skills and abilities known as Multiple Intelligences. He postulated that there are many different types of talents or knowledge that could help to enrich one's life and respond effectively to one's environment. Of the eight intelligences he recognized in his initial theoretical stance, two intelligences (1) *visual-spatial*, the capacity to perceive the visual-spatial world accurately and to modify or manipulate one's initial perceptions, and (2) *intrapersonal*, knowledge of one's own feelings, strengths, weaknesses, desires, and the ability to draw on this knowledge to guide behavior, appear to support the idea of using visual journals in the classroom. In Gardner's foreword to David Lazear's (1991) book, *Seven Ways of Knowing,* he writes, "I especially applaud the use of journals in which one can reflect about the use and evolution of one's intelligences" (p. v). Building on the ideas of Gardner, Lazear states, "the human brain naturally thinks in images. In fact, its capacity to form images or to visualize is one of its most basic mental processes" (p. 51).

Blecher & Jaffee (1998) suggest that sketchbooks (i.e., visual journals) can become tools for widening the learning circle to include learners who are often marginalized. They believe that disciplinary boundaries are crossed, encouraging conceptual development, and fostering creative and critical inquiry. That idea was further elaborated by Tomlinson (1999), as she states, "the brain learns best when it can come to understand by making its own sense out of information rather than when information is imposed upon it … brain research tells us that each learner's brain is unique, and educators must provide many opportunities for varied learners to make sense of ideas and information" (p. 19). I was particularly interested in these ideas as our school, and my math classes in particular, have students who possess a wide range of abilities and skills, as well as an inordinately large population of challenged learners who require adaptations and modifications to their curriculum and learning patterns.

Douglas, Smith Burton, & Reese-Durham, (2008) have reported research results that suggest "performance on a post mathematics assessment for students exposed to Multiple Intelligence Instruction (MI) will show considerable increase when compared to those taught using Direct Instruction (DI)"(p. 182). Burns (2010) concluded, "sometimes pictorial representations of problems can help" (p. 4) when solving mathematical questions.

With the considerations unearthed in this literature review in mind, my research task was to explore whether the use of visual journals in the Grade 8 mathematics classroom would help to counter this math phobia, increase self-esteem in mathematical areas, and at the same time guide and help students toward better comprehension and the development of a deeper understanding of the math curriculum concepts presented at this level.

The Inquiry

My research centered on my two eighth grade classes at a secondary school, in Richmond, BC, considered by many local administrators to be an "inner-city" high school. Census findings indicate that the students come from the lowest socioeconomic family levels in Richmond. Although Asian backgrounds predominate, our students come from a number of diverse cultures. Many immigrants from China initially come to Richmond for the comfort of being able to function in their native language, and due to many low cost rental units in our neighborhood, our school comprises a large itinerant ESL population. Of our 953 total student population, 257 are ministry recognized ESL students. Twenty-six international students reside in our catchment area, either with relatives or in host families, and many young people live in situations without a parent or responsible adult figure present. There exists an extreme range of economic circumstances, and varying elementary educational experiences. Of the 55 students in my two math classes, five are identified as ESL level one or two, eight have adaptations to their learning in math, and one 'modified' student follows his own highly personalized curriculum.

Our visual journal adventure began with asking the students to obtain a notebook that could be used as a visual journal. I did not set tight guidelines as to size or quality of this notebook, but I did tell them we would be doing a lot of drawing and coloring in the book, and that it needed to be sturdy and have enough pages to last a school year. Initially, I wasn't sure how this request might be received, but as it was included in their formal supplies list, it was not a problem. It was helpful to have some examples on hand so that the students could describe what was needed to their parents and shop accordingly. Several of my students have since suggested that it might be a good idea for me to purchase a quantity of journals for sale in the classroom.

We started the book off with the question, if math was a color, what color would it be for you, and why? They were encouraged to use art, and words to respond. The results gave me a wonderful springboard to laugh with the students, allow and acknowledge their various feelings and fears, and it served as an icebreaker to our year, and to introduce the idea of a visual journal.

At my school, our week is divided into Day One and Day Two, with Wednesdays being an early dismissal day with shortened classes, 50 minutes instead of our usual 75. It was my intention to use the visual journal on the regular hour days only. It is my personal belief that 75 minutes is too long for any class in Grade 8, except perhaps science labs, and I thought 15 minutes of in-class visual journaling would be a welcome and useful break from "normal" routines of mathematics. As the term progressed, however, my concerns about covering the curriculum, a great deal of time spent explaining and taking up student questions and problems, and the many interruptions we have in a usual school day, meant that I often assigned the visual journal as homework. I did use it as a note taking location, from which the students were asked to use color and optional pictures to further elaborate their learning and express their feelings. I assigned completion marks to this activity, especially as pictorial representation is a part of our new curriculum. My original assessment criteria was that students date their work, address the topic of the lesson in some obvious manner, show at least one example of the concept being taught, add color, and pictorially represent their learning. Visual journal comprised approximately fifteen percent of their final grade.

Many mathematics curriculum areas lent themselves favorably to visual journaling. Studies of surface area and volume in particular, because of their inherent visual nature, provided the students with numerous ideas for drawing and coloring as they personalized their learning. However, other mathematical areas of study were less compatible with this approach. I found that I often had to guide my students to word problems they could illustrate or use as examples in order to fulfill my criteria. The students quickly learned how to do this independently.

I used several strategies of ensuring completion and quality of the visual journals. Initially, I did a quick walk around the classroom, checking for the key points of my criteria. In this way I was able to see who had actually competed their journaling and whether the criteria had been met, but I wasn't able to personally respond to the students' work in a meaningful manner. After the first month, or introductory period, I started to collect their journals after five or six entries. I found that this was a positive and timely progression in my assessment process. I could respond with pictures and words of my own, and I also had more time to obtain a much clearer picture of their understanding of the unit areas they had been taught. Many of my more reluctant students responded favorably to this more personalized approach, and I noticed dramatic improvement in their subsequent visual journals. Other students appeared to enjoy my general and anonymous classroom references to their comments, cartoon characters, artwork, color-coding, and often, humorous expressions of their feelings towards mathematics. For example, one student who insisted she "hated math" in every page of her visual journal, was often smiling and laughing during class, as we bantered back and forth on this topic. I was thrilled to see her grades improve as the year progressed; moreover, she gained enough confidence to ask questions out loud in class.

As the term progressed, in addition to sporadic walk around checks, I formally collected visual journals towards the end of each unit of study, ensuring that they were returned prior to their unit assessment tests. In this way I was able to note where a student might need extra help prior to an exam, intervene in a timely manner, and hopefully improve their comprehension and confidence prior to "the big test."

Learning Outcomes

In response to my informal questioning of students, and an anonymous written response questionnaire, administered in May, it appears that an overwhelming number of my students enjoyed the visual journaling process this year. The main reasons given for this enjoyment were that the visual journals were "fun," "bumped up marks," "helped study," "helped to express feelings about math," and "helped me remember easier." The following are some of the more memorable quotes.

> "I enjoyed using visual journals because it helped me reflect on what we learned on that math class or how we are feeling about an upcoming test."
>
> "I think that the use of pictures and colour in any subject especially math helps me more because I'm very visual, in order for me to remember something, pictures are easier than notes."
>
> "I like the idea of being able to express your feelings about math through the journal too."
>
> "I got to think of math as a bigger topic than just numbers and I got to show my creative side."
>
> "It gives me a break from the old-fashioned textbook math."

The more negative comments reflected a few students' feelings of lack of artistic ability. This was frustrating to me in that I thought I had gone out of my way to explain that the quality of their art had nothing to do with how the journal would be evaluated. Numerous students pointed out that on a heavy homework day, the visual journal added to their workload. They definitely wanted more in class time, and less of a homework approach for this activity.

In response to questioning as to whether the visual journal helped to develop and improve self-confidence or self-esteem in the area of math, the response was mixed. Several students found that the examples helped them study and remember, and that drawing was a new way to approach problems, therefore their confidence improved. They appreciated my written responses and happy faces, and the fact that it was all right for them to show work with no judgment as to whether it was right or wrong. A few students, who chronically did not do homework of any sort, blamed the visual journal for a drop in their math grades. Others stated that they were already confident and that journaling did not affect them in either a positive or a negative manner. Some telling comments were as follow.

> "I think it helped my self-confidence a little. It helped my brain organize the rules for each unit so I could comprehend the work better. Which lead to a better mark on tests because I understood what I was doing."

> "I think it did help me basically laying out and organizing the math. Therefore now when I want to work on math, I am actually excited about it because I will know that I understand it."

> "Not really, because I am not a very visual person."

A majority of students found that the visual journal helped them to personalize their learning.

> "The visual journal was like basically teaching yourself math, with the way you're comfortable with yourself."

> "The visual journal gave me time to stop and think about what I was really learning and put what I was learning into pictures and doodles."

> "It took away the dark, gloomy side of math bringing it to a whole new level to the point where I started to enjoy math."

> "I had my own custom study material."

As I read the students' comments, and informally spoke with them with regard to their visual journaling experiences, the levels of self-awareness they possessed encouraged me. Most students appeared to have at least a basic understanding of their strengths and weaknesses as learners. One student wrote, "When I don't understand about a subject and can't give an example in my journal, that's when I know what I need help on, and can look back and understand not to make the same mistake on a test." In my teaching, I often refer to the multiple intelligences and I also attempt to outline various ways of studying to facilitate and accommodate different learning styles. However, these ideas didn't appear to have been new to many of my students, especially the ones who received their primary and intermediate schooling in Richmond. On that level, I was encouraged, as it gives students another valuable tool for their personal learning toolbox.

An overwhelming number of my students liked the fact that marks were allocated to visual journal completion. Although a few felt they were being penalized because they weren't artists, most felt the criteria gave room for those who chose only to highlight with color only, as well as to those who were indeed totally and amazingly creative and artistic. Undoubtedly, the fact that the mere completion of the visual journal could boost marks was a reason for many to applaud this aspect of their math class. One suggestion from the students was that I allow them to pick one entry per concept or unit for evaluation, rather than counting every entry, similar to establishing a portfolio from which your best work is drawn for presentation.

When I asked the class if they were doing better, worse, or the same as in their Grade 7 experiences in mathematics, the most common response was that they were definitely doing better. Many credited the visual journal, which was a gratifying experience, but others stated reasons such as, the different teaching style I employed as compared to their previous teachers, their own more mature study habits, as well as the fact that they had seen some of the material before. Some of the students who complained about their lack of artistry did acknowledge that it was really their tendency to procrastinate and not do homework at all that had led to their lower grades. A majority wanted to see visual journal continued into grade nine, but with one major alteration. They felt much more class time was needed for this activity. They did not want it as an extra math assignment on top of the actual textbook and workbook exercises, especially as they anticipate a heavier year for homework in all subject areas next year in general.

Summary and Recommendations

I have learned a lot from my students, both during the actual class working on and with their journals, but mainly through their candid thoughts when informally interviewed. I will incorporate many of their suggestions into practice. I particularly liked the suggestion to share their journals with each other in a more formal manner. I can envision the use of the Gallery Walk, a creative teaching and learning strategy that I personally experienced in my learning during the graduate program. I would like to try this collaborative, sharing idea next year, however, I would like the students to know in advance that this was likely to happen. I do question, however, if it will affect their input if they thought other students would be looking at their class work.

From a teaching standpoint I found the use of the visual journal to be a most positive experience. In the past, as a mathematics teacher, I have not generally been able to get to know students in such a well-rounded way. Through the use of the visual journals, I was able to observe and respond to student writing and drawing on a more personal level, and I believe it enabled me to develop a better, deeper rapport with many students as a result of their honesty, sense of humor, and frank expressions of frustration at times. I loved the insights into personality and self-awareness that I was afforded, as evidenced by previous quotations.

With only one exception, my students have been very successful in math this year. Only one student will be repeating this subject, and interestingly enough, he chose not to do visual journal after the first week, and seemed fixated on blaming the art concept of the journal for his overall lack of competence in math. Where students did lose an appreciable amount of marks due to lack of use of the visual journal, it was almost entirely due to the more organizational aspect of just bringing it to class.

In conclusion, as a result of my research project on the use of visual journals in a Grade 8 mathematics classroom, I can confidently suggest the following ideas for other teachers who are interested in implementing this approach in their practice.

- Grade 8 students respond positively to the use of visual journals and seem to enjoy the inclusion of this educational tool in their mathematical education.
- Grade 8 students value the visual journal as a study and memory aid.
- Grade 8 students enjoy the opportunity to reflect on and freely comment on their mathematical experiences.
- This educational tool appears to be an aid in terms of student comprehension of the mathematical concepts presented in Grade 8.
- In some cases, the use of a mathematics visual journal appears to help with student self-esteem and confidence.
- The incorporation of the visual journal in mathematics creates a positive, personal and insightful link between teacher and student in a way that is not usually experienced in this subject.

I thoroughly enjoyed using visual journals in my math classes this year. When I think about the various mathematical entries, and the thoughts and images included in the journals, I smile. I feel I was given the gift of a novel and refreshing insight into the humor, feelings, frustrations, and joys of my students. The journals offered me a place where I could respond personally and somewhat privately, to each adolescent in my classroom. I will most definitely use this educational tool in the years to come.

Marsha B. Thompson
Richmond School District 38
MBThompson@sd38.bc.ca

STEPHANIE STRANDT

SCIENCE NARRATIVES FOR TEACHING AND LEARNING

Beginning the Story

In this paper I present a case for the use of narratives in teaching and learning science. I will explore the ideas of (1) why there is a need to change current teaching practices (2) why teachers would want to include this method of instruction into their current teaching practices, and (3) the types of narratives that are useful in teaching and learning science.

First, I will address the question of why we need to change current instructional practices. Science education has been criticized regarding the way it is taught in schools (American Association for the Advancement of Science, 1993; National Research Council, 2000). Avraamidou & Osborne (2009) state that there is a need to explore new modes of communicating science. The delivery of science has been described by Lemke (1990) from the perspective that "Science education sometimes unwittingly, perpetuates a certain harmful mystique of science. That mystique tends to make science seem dogmatic, authoritarian, impersonal and even inhuman to many students. It alienates students from science" (p. xi). With this in mind, it seemed to be a good time to explore the use of narrative to bring a more personal sense of connection to the science curriculum.

The Literature on Narratives in Teaching Science

Anyone browsing through high school science textbooks will notice large amounts of expository text with little or no mention of personal insights or real life experiences. Wellington & Osborne (2001) describe the features of an expository text as univocal, non-dialectic; moreover, its major focus is either descriptive or explanatory. Such texts commonly deploy the genres, language, and grammar of science and are difficult to read. That type of text reinforces the inhuman and impersonal features mentioned by Lemke (1990) and provides further evidence why incorporating narratives into the science curriculum is a worthy endeavour.

As the primary focus of the present inquiry, I consider narratives as the language that students use everyday, either though the telling of their own stories or listening to others. If science is to play a role in their everyday experiences and not merely seen as something learned and discussed in a classroom, it needs to be communicated in a meaningful way to the student. Science should not be disconnected from a student's everyday experiences. The extensive use of new

P. Gouzouasis (ed.), Pedagogy in a New Tonality: Teacher Inquiries on Creative Tactics, Strategies, Graphics Organizers, and Visual Journals in the K-12 Classroom, 227–234.

vocabulary excludes students from conversing in the language of science, therefore, science becomes something external to their personal experiences.

The use of narrative is an important aspect of student's everyday lives. They speak with friends in narratives and it is a natural way for them to gather information. If science educators can use this natural mode of communication to share scientific concepts and insights, they would have a very powerful tool to increase students' understandings and more importantly, increase interest in science. Narrative stories may then become a vehicle through which experiences are learned, shared, and communicated amongst people. Schank & Berman (2002) go on to say that for communication, memory, and learning purposes, stories are likely to be richer, more compelling, and more memorable than the abstracted points we ultimately intend to convey or learn when we converse with others. In further agreement with the idea that narratives have a place in science education, Gough (1993) states that science fictional texts should be integral to both science and environmental education, and narrative strategies of fiction may be more appropriate for representing science than the expository textual practices that have dominated science and environmental education to date.

Unfortunately the current emphasis on assessment as a measure of the performance of schools has led to the elimination of any material that is seen as extraneous to the core of examinable content (Watts & McGrath 1998). Thus, science curricula are dominated by factual knowledge that fails to provide students an overview of the major themes, and it doesn't enable them to see connections to the world around them. Yet stories are used every day as a way of making sense of and communicating events in the world. Movies, books, television programs, and everyday conversations are filled with the telling of stories (Schank & Berman, 2002). Thus, it seems reasonable to suggest that if we are to foster an appreciation and understanding of science then there is a need to determine which aspects of science pupils value and use in their everyday lives.

Osbourne & Collins (2000) researched pupil's views of the roles and value of the science curriculum and found pupils complained that unlike other subjects in which one can use their imagination, in science, there's no room to put anything of *you* into it. Everything else is more creative, even history. Wray & Lewis (1997) suggest that part of the problem for science is the genres of writing it uses—the explanation, the experimental report, or description—all unfamiliar genres that students find both alien and alienating. If we are to respect what students are telling us, we must carefully structure the writing in science to avoid generating such negative reactions. So what does this mean for our teaching practices and for learning, and where do we find these narratives to use in our classroom?

Having established the need for a change in science education the second question I will address is why teachers would want to include this specific approach of instruction, namely narratives, in their current teaching practices. For teachers to change or incorporate an instructional strategy that is not part of their instructional repertoire, there must be a perceived advantage to either the student, the teacher, or both. I believe that the use of narratives is an advantage for both. As Gough (1993) found,

> Two components were mentioned in comments about science educations disjointed nature: first the disparate nature of biology, physics and chemistry and a failure to see any commonality or unity between the subjects, pupils found themselves constantly chopping and changing between doing one thing one day and something very different the next day... this made science less coherent and therefore harder to understand. (p. 610)

Another area of science education that is criticized is the fragmentation of disciplines. Students chose to study chemistry, which is separate from physics, which is again separate from biology. This compartmentalisation of disciplines further places science into smaller and smaller boxes that are not only seen as separate from a students' natural world but separate within science itself. Inherently speaking, narratives do not possess boundaries that box science disciplines into discrete areas. Rather, they may help make bridges between scientific disciplines. This bridging embodies science as one entity that can be learned, experienced, and enjoyed in a way that engages the learner.

Narratives may help students see the connections between these seemingly separate disciplines and make sense of science as a whole. This is an important step for students because it aids in their ability to identify when, where, and how science plays a role in their lives. Science may then become a natural part of them instead of something outside of their experiences. One may reasonably hypothesize that when students make this personal connection they will naturally accept science instruction which will in turn foster a sense of curiosity that leads to a desire for a deeper understanding.

Additional studies that compare the effects of narratives on learning provide evidence that narratives enhance retention and comprehension (Englert & Heibert, 1984). This increase in retention is confirmed by Sparkes (2002) when he says that narrative information is retained for longer periods than factual information in long term memory and that narratives constitute an important means for science communication to transmit information in an accurate, memorable, and enjoyable way. When students are engaged in science, they enjoy the learning process and learning may become secondary to the task at hand. A well written narrative is both engaging, informative, gets the student's interest, and holds it for longer than traditional teaching methods. Eleven years ago, Osbourne & Collins (2000) stated that the use of note taking or undemanding writing activities are still predominant in education and are the least effective in helping pupils to attain knowledge and understanding of the subject. Wallace (1996) further enforces that notion when he describes note taking as boring writing where little active processing and participation is required by the learner. Such work offers pupils little control over their own learning, and ultimately leads to boredom, disenchantment, and alienation. We all know that the lecture style of teaching is a quick, simple technique used to communicate large amounts of information in a relative short amount of time compared to student centered ways of teaching. With the increase in content that must be covered during the course of the academic year, it is no wonder why many teachers feel this single strategy is necessary and easier to implement than other tactics and strategies. The down side of this approach is that students that are left feeling unengaged and seeing little value in the information they have written down except for regurgitation for the purposes of assessment. It seems reasonable to suggest that if we can somehow interweave factual, detailed knowledge with meaningful stories about the impact the science may have on people's lives, students may develop an appreciation for what was once seemly unimportant information and embrace it with an understanding that was not initially present.

Science education is also heavily weighted toward simple recall of facts and lacks the opportunity for students to use the higher reasoning skills of analyzing, interpreting, and constructing meaning. Apple (1992) believes that another area of criticism is that science curricula are dominated by factual knowledge, which is readily assessed in traditional ways (e.g., multiple choice tests) rather than material that seeks to imbue a critical understanding of science reasoning or science practice. Narratives used in conjunction with other modes of communicating curriculum content may help students see science in practice and open up points for discussion. That may aid in students' development of critical thinking skills and provide them a way to communicate science in a language that is understood.

Finally, Sutton (1992) points out that there is a lack of time to diverge, that there is no opportunity for the pupils to set the agenda themselves and to pursue topics of particular interest and, most importantly, there is no time for discussion. Narratives provide the foundation for discussion around the impact on the characters' lives and of the science itself. These kinds of discussions engage students and provide them with the opportunity to voice their own opinions, to use language that is familiar to them, and to see science as part of their lived experiences. Sparkes (2002) sums up these ideas in the following paragraph.

> Textbooks are not natural ways of writing about the social world, nor are they a clear form of communication to all audiences. As Plummer (2001) points out, one consequence of scientific writing is to render the majority of such texts unreadable to all but the smallest of like minded group. As Golden-Biddle and Locke (1997) emphasize, scientific writing is not a natural way of writing; it has to be learned . . . if the writing of scientific style does not come naturally, then neither does the reading of it." The results of this study as a whole suggest that science can be learned though literary stories and that this represents a more enjoyable way of learning compared to traditional texts. (p. 29).

It is generally accepted knowledge that students who are actively engaged in the classroom environment make it a more enjoyable s/p/lace (deCosson, 2004) of learning for both the student and the teacher. This sense of a shared learning community—where students have a place to discuss and share ideas, where science can be spoken about in a way that makes sense and where the teacher can connect with students in a more meaningful way—benefits the students and teacher alike.

Since I understood the possible benefits of using narratives, to both student and teacher, I had to decide which narratives should be used. Sutton (1992) describes features of narratives that are most effective for teaching and learning when he describes them as not an account of fact, but as an expression of thought by some person who can be identified or at least envisaged. It offers a point of view, a kind of explanation, a way of talking about the topic. Negrete (2003) provides further insight when he explains that when analysing the scientific information in terms of its role in the story, a suggestion arises that there is a relationship between how central to the development of the story the scientific information is, to how memorable it becomes. In other words, the closer the scientific information is to the important moments of the narration, for example, higher in hierarchy with respect to plot; it is more likely to succeed in communicating and making such knowledge memorable. This research has helped establish criteria for deciding which narratives will be used in the classroom. Criteria were set out to choose which narratives would be used, which would be given as further readings, and which would not be suitable altogether. The following lists, in no particular order, the criteria used (1) narratives that could be read within a class or two; time constraints in the course prevent the use of entire novels and where novels were chosen only selected parts were required by the students for reading, (2) topics had to directly link to the course learning outcomes, (3) stories had to be personal and sufficient in length to make a connection to the characters, and (4) the science in the story had to be central to the plot without oversimplifying science concepts and ideas since the narrative is only useful if the student gains some scientific insights as well as gaining an understanding of the social aspects as well.

Using Narratives in My Biology 12 Classes

I chose Biology 12 to pilot this strategy and find resources, because it contains a curriculum that easily lends itself to people's stories around disease. The course is entirely devoted to human anatomy and physiology. I specifically chose to focus on the circulation and nervous system units. Regarding circulation, I looked at heart attacks and strokes; for the nervous system, I focused on Alzheimer's. My reasoning for selecting these specific areas is that they are common occurrences in an aging population, which increases the likelihood that the students not only have heard of these conditions but have experienced them on a more personal level through parents and grandparents. When I polled the two classes, over 50% of the students had some experience with one of the conditions mentioned above. I speculated that if the students had a personal connection to the condition they would be more interested in learning about it than a more obscure disease or illness.

For the unit on heart attacks and strokes I chose *My stroke of insight* (Bolte-Taylor, 2006) and *The diving bell and the butterfly* (Bauby, 1997). Jill Bolte-Taylor was a recent speaker at the Ted Talks conference in California. After reading excerpts from her book, the class watched the video of her relating her experiences. This helped bring the story to life for the students as they watched her emotional, heartfelt description about the morning of her stroke and the years of recovery that followed. *The diving bell and the butterfly* is also a personal account of living through a stroke that has been made into a major motion picture and we watched segments of this movie in class. Being able to provide the two stories in both written and visual mediums further aided in the students' understandings of the ideas being presented. The unit on the nervous system included parts of the brain, and I chose the story *Still Alice* (Genova, 2009) to elaborate this topic. It is a full length novel from which the students only read sections. The story involves a woman in her fifties that develops early onset Alzheimer's disease. Students were given a set of questions along with the readings and they were expected to be able to discuss them. Instead of collecting answers to the questions, I split the class into smaller groups and assigned each group a question that they were responsible to delve into; they were required to lead the discussion for that question. I gave the student's participation marks during the discussion, and that encouraged them to share their ideas with the class.

Some Discoveries Along the Way

Introducing the use of narratives to the Biology 12 class was at first discouraging. Some very vocal students expressed their displeasure at this activity because it seemed like a task they should encounter in an English class and not a science class. At first, they did not see the relevance of the reading and therefore they resented the assignment. The majority of the students had enough trust in me as the teacher to go along with any assignment I chose for them and read the story without incident. After the first reading and the discussion groups that followed, all students began to see the connection to the science content and enjoyed an opportunity to discuss the ideas as a group. The students commented that they had never read stories in science and they enjoyed reading about things they were learning. Moreover, students mentioned that it was nice to read about science and understand what they were reading. This comment illustrates that only using narrative would provide an incomplete educational experience—that the background knowledge that comes from more traditional ways of teaching and learning science made the stories more meaningful and more enlightening.

The most successful readings were about strokes. Many of the students had experiences with strokes—they recognized the symptoms in a story through experiences with a grandparent. One narrative that the majority of the students enjoyed the most was the heart and stroke survivor story. Students were asked to search through the survivor stories that are linked from the Heart and Stroke Foundation website and choose a story that resonated for them. Students then wrote about why they had chosen a particular story, what they learned from it, and what personal connection they made with the person in the story. Students liked the freedom of choosing their own story. Many chose stories that were similar to their own experiences while others selected stories that illustrated great courage and a determination to recover. The responses from the students were insightful and demonstrated a connection with the survivor.

One story that was chosen by a number of male students was one of a young man in his mid-twenties. The lead character was active, led a healthy life style, and was not over weight. He felt symptoms early one morning but dismissed them and continued his daily activity. The symptoms became increasingly worse, and when he was at work a colleague noticed the young man slurring his words and acting strange, so he called 911. Subsequent to the reading, students commented on how young this person was, how they had considered strokes as an old person's disease, and how they felt that they too would dismiss the early signs of a stroke in this situation. This turned into an investigation and discussion regarding what to look for at the onset of a stroke. I believe that without identifying with someone who had experienced a stroke my students would not have been so eager to discover the early signs and symptoms. They quickly discovered a clear understanding how important early recognition and immediate help is for someone having a stroke, and this will have lasting benefits to them and those around them.

Another story that was chosen by a couple of girls from each class was that of a young mother of three who had a slim chance of a full recovery after a stroke left her with partial paralysis of her arm and without the ability to talk. The young mother worked very hard and expressed her determination that she would recover regardless of what others were telling her. My students were inspired by this young woman's courage and faith in herself. I hope this is a story that will stay with them when they face difficulties of their own.

Summary and Suggestions

This project was not without its challenges. One challenge was finding narratives that not only fit into the curriculum, but complemented it; narratives that at the same time possessed enough science content to make them useful to the course. I have found other suitable narratives that could be worked into other areas of the Biology 12 curriculum but it remains a difficult search. The task of finding appropriate, rich narratives will be a life-long pursuit. Although there are many non-fiction stories that have very good science content, they are missing that individual connection that helps students relate to them on a personal level and see how science operates in their everyday lives.

The class discussions, after the readings were completed, were anther challenge for me as a teacher. In conversations with my science teacher peers, I have discovered that science teachers in general don't often hold discussions around empathy with people, trying to discover how it would feel for someone to be going through a disease being studied. Before my first discussion, I sat in on an English class and observed how the teacher led the students, used quality follow up questions, and kept them on topic. Questioning is a skill that takes time to master, and it felt awkward the first time. With practice this will become easier but at the moment it is still a work in progress.

I believe that I have confirmed my ideas that a person's (i.e., student's) identification to a character in a story is of greater interest than the actual disease the character is living with or fighting against. I believe this is why I found narratives a more enjoyable and engaging addition to the science curriculum than the non-fiction stories I have used in the past.

Coda

Throughout my inquiry, I have tried to find evidence to support the notion that narratives can be a useful tool in science education. I began with offering reasons for a change to current teaching practices and a need to help students make more personal connections to the science material being taught. I have found narratives that fit into the Biology 12 curriculum and explored their applications in the classroom. I neither propose that narratives are the only way science should be taught, nor do I suggest that there is no place for expository texts. I do, however, see a gap between a sterile discipline that is removed from student's everyday life and a science that is alive and may be recognized in themselves and those around them.

Negrete (2003) summarizes the ideas expressed in the present inquiry when he says that the challenge to science communication is to establish a bridge between science and the general public. To this end, it seems necessary to translate science into a common language that enables the reader to become interested and excited about scientific information. Science communication is not original in the scientific content that it conveys, but in the way that it presents the information, and this is precisely what creates an important challenge for this discipline. I suggest that while literature is an alternative and effective medium to teach science, it does not wholly replace current models of instruction. It functions as a complementary companion. A companion, that if chosen well, can enhance student interest, engagement, and understanding of science. In a broader sense, narratives represent an important means of communication to transmit and recreate information in an accurate, memorable, and enjoyable way. We must continue to search for those narratives that instil the sense of awe and wonder that is deserving of nurturing a lasting, lifelong science education.

Stephanie Strandt
North Vancouver School District
sstrandt@nvsd44.bc.ca

WENDY MCNAUGHTON

THE IMPACT OF CONCEPT ATTAINMENT LESSONS ON THE METACOGNITIVE SKILLS OF YOUNG CHILDREN

> Brains are born and minds are made, and one of the privileges of the teaching profession is to have an important part to play in the shaping of minds.
>
> (Eisner, 2005, p. 106).

Introduction

Metacognition. What is it? Why is it important? What does research have to say about it? How is it relevant to learning and teaching? How did I come to investigate metacognition and concept attainment?

Initially, when I was selecting a topic for my research project, I was interested in determining which teaching strategies and tactics were best suited to early primary students. As I participated in workshops and summer institutes and learned more about teaching tactics and strategies, I was always left wondering, "How will this work with the young students that I teach?"

Many of the strategies and tactics presented in the workshops seemed very promising, yet I was unsure of how or if they would work at the Kindergarten and Grade 1 level. Four- to six-year-old children are at a different place, both academically and developmentally, than the students for whom many of the presented strategies and tactics were designed. With this disconnect in mind, I initially wanted to figure out how to select, modify, and adapt the strategies and tactics I had been given so that they would become a good fit for young learners. After talking to a colleague who taught at a similar grade level to my own, and who had been through a graduate program, it seemed that the scope of my original project was too broad. After further discussion, I opted to investigate a single teaching strategy (i.e., Concept Attainment) to see if I could determine whether it might have an impact on students' metacognition. That is how my project was conceived.

Given those perspectives, the intent of my study was to find out how students' "thinking about their thinking" (i.e., metacognition) might be developed over time through the use of the teaching strategy known as *concept attainment*. This teaching strategy was introduced early on in my master's program, as we looked at the various teaching tactics and strategies presented in *Beyond Monet: The Artful Science of Instructional Integration* (Bennett & Rolheiser, 2001). Concept attainment lessons are a powerful way of getting students engaged in thinking, and,

P. Gouzouasis (ed.), Pedagogy in a New Tonality: Teacher Inquiries on Creative Tactics, Strategies, Graphics Organizers, and Visual Journals in the K-12 Classroom, 235–254.

as I had discovered when trying out this teaching strategy in my Grade 1 class the year before, they can be successfully used with younger students. Because the concept attainment strategy encourages students to think and reflect on their thinking as they proceed through the examples in the lesson, it connected very well with my study of metacognition.

Looking at the development of students' metacognition seemed worthy of research, in part because the British Columbia Ministry of Education (2000) specifically discusses metacognition in the area of intellectual development. In *The Primary Program: A Framework for Teaching*, 'learning through reflection' is considered one of the ways that students learn.

> Children need to understand what it means to learn, who they are as learners, and how to go about planning, monitoring, and revising, to reflect upon their learning and that of others, and to learn to determine for themselves if they understand. These skills of metacognition provide strategic competence for learning. (National Research Council, as cited in British Columbia Ministry of Education, 2000, p.36)

Thus, the development of metacognitive skills is foundational to becoming a life-long learner. Based on that, I believed that anything I could learn about developing students' metacognition would be of significance in my praxis.

Looking Back

Metacognition. A word I recall first hearing at a keynote address in a high school gymnasium one professional development day many years ago. The simple definition given at that keynote address was "thinking about your thinking." This caught my attention, perhaps because I often seem to catch myself thinking about my thinking. I believe that address, in some way, planted the seed that would lead me to delve further into this topic.

As well as being personally interested, I was curious about how research in the recent past had added to our knowledge of metacognition and its relevance to teaching students in the early primary years. Those considerations led me to investigate the relationship between particular teaching strategies, such as concept attainment lessons, and the development of early primary students' metacognition.

My teaching career started in North Vancouver in 1976. Over the years I have taught at five different elementary schools in the district. Although I have taught all grades from Kindergarten to Grade 7, the vast majority of my experience has been at the Kindergarten and Grade 1 levels. This is where my heart is as a teacher and where I am most passionate about learning more about the art of teaching and learning—about pedagogy.

Over the years I have delved into specific areas of interest as part of my professional development. In particular, I have explored gifted education, teaching and learning through the arts, and students with special needs. Each of these fields has led me to develop a better understanding of multiple intelligences, learning styles, and reaching a diversity of students.

When the North Vancouver School District began to work with Barrie Bennett, and promote the ideas explored in his text (Bennett & Rolheiser, 2001), I was quick to get involved by attending workshops and taking in-service opportunities. I have always enjoyed discovering new ways to reach and teach learners through engaging experiences. Something that struck me as I read through *Beyond Monet* and participated in instructional institutes led by Barrie Bennett, was that many of the ideas seemed too advanced for the development of students at the Kindergarten or Grade 1 level. Through meeting and talking with colleagues, I discovered some of the ways that they were either adapting or modifying strategies or tactics for younger students. I was especially encouraged by some of the organization and management ideas I saw in works by Lorna Curran (1998, 2000). Keeping in mind the developmental issues associated with early primary students, what intrigued me most are the instructional intelligence ideas that are possible to use with this age group.

With an interest in how instructional intelligence strategies and tactics can be selected, modified, and adapted to best suit the learning needs of a diversity of early primary students, it seemed a natural fit to see how this connected specifically to the development of students' metacognitive skills. It is from this connection of teaching strategies and the development of thinking skills that my project grew.

The British Columbia Ministry of Education (2000) has stated that there is a need for students to actively participate in their learning, and one of the ways students learn is through reflection. Thus, the purpose of my study was to determine if using concept attainment teaching strategies would help develop metacognitive skills over time. From that perspective, the specific research question that arose was, what teaching strategies or tactics would encourage and enable young students to reflect on their thinking?

Review of the Literature

In the thirty-five years since John H. Flavell coined the term, there has been considerable growth in the study of *metacognition.* My search of the literature led me through a timeline of developments. Metacognition has been defined as "any knowledge or cognitive activity that takes as its object, or regulates, any aspect of any cognitive activity" (Flavell, 2004, p. 275). Work in this area began in the early 1970s, and since then a proliferation of metacognitive terms has evolved. As I reviewed the literature I became aware of many of these terms, including *metacognitive awareness*, *metacognitive experience*, *metacognitive knowledge*, *metacognitive skills*, *theory of mind*, and *self-regulation.* As I sifted through the literature it also became apparent that there is still debate about the meaning and scope of the term metacognition (see for example Corkill, 1996; Livingston, 1997; Pintrich, 2002; Reder, 1996; Schraw & Moshman, 1995; Veenman, Van Hout-Wolters, & Afflerbach, 2006). These discrepancies come in part because researchers have had different foci for their studies. Some have taken a more general perspective while others have been more specific in looking at certain age groups, tasks, and processes. Metacognition relates to the fields of cognitive psychology, developmental psychology, social psychology, and educational psychology. Depending on which of these areas one focuses upon, one may define the term somewhat differently. For my purposes, I have stuck with the simple overarching definition of "thinking about thinking."

To develop an understanding of how research and theory in the general area of metacognition evolved, it was helpful to take a historical look at the fields of cognitive and developmental psychology. The work of Jean Piaget greatly influenced these areas of study (Siegler & Ellis, 1996). Piaget was a developmental psychologist who was well known for his Cognitive Development Theory, a global theory outlining four age-related stages of cognitive development through which individuals progress. Fundamentally speaking, from Piaget's interest in studying human thinking (cognition), many individuals began to pursue research in studying individuals' thinking about their thinking (metacognition).

John H. Flavell, an early North American Piagetian, is the researcher most often associated with early developments in the field of metacognition. According to Flavell (1979), metacognition consists of two sub-categories namely *metacognitive knowledge* and *metacognitive experience,* sometimes referred to as *metacognitive awareness* and *metacognitive skills*. Flavell further sub-divided metacognitive knowledge into three categories: knowledge of *person, task*, or *strategy*. The person category includes "everything that you could come to believe about the nature of yourself and other people as cognitive processors" (Flavell, 1979, p. 907). This knowledge of person category could then be subcategorized into beliefs about ones' own thinking (intra-individual), beliefs about others' thinking (inter-individual), and knowledge of universals of cognition. The task category includes information about the task and the potential implications of variations in the information. The strategy category involves knowledge of both cognitive and metacognitive strategies and the appropriate conditions in which to use a given strategy. Flavell stated, "Although metacognitive knowledge can undoubtedly undergo at least some modification without metacognitive experiences, I suspect that these experiences play a major role in its development during childhood and adolescence" (1979, p. 908). Metacognitive experiences may vary greatly in duration or complexity. They are sequential processes that involve planning, monitoring, and reviewing cognitive goals. These are all skills that are relevant to teaching and learning.

As I read through Flavell's work, I considered how these categories of knowledge are relevant to teachers. Teachers need to be aware of (a) our students' ability to learn and process information (person variable), (b) the skills or concepts to be learned and how demanding they will be (task variable), and (c) the various teaching strategies that are available and which strategy would be appropriate (strategy variable). Taking all of that information into account, teachers then have to act using past experiences to help plan, monitor, and review lessons. This is central to what Bennett & Rolheiser (2001) have referred to as the art and science of teaching.

Twenty years after the work in the area of metacognition began, Schraw & Moshman (1995) presented a review of metacognitive theories. Much of what they described paralleled the findings of Flavell. However, what stood out for me were their findings as they related to developmental differences and age. The following are some of the excerpts I found to be relevant to my work with Kindergarten and Grade 1 students.

- Many theorists believe that metacognitive knowledge appears early and continues to develop at least through adolescence. (Schraw & Moshman, 1995, p. 354)
- Children routinely demonstrate and use knowledge without being able to express that knowledge. (*ibid.*, p. 354)
- [A]lthough children as young as four possess metacognitive *knowledge*, individuals differ greatly in the nature and extent of their metacognitive *theories*. (*ibid.*, p. 356)
- [T]heories change gradually over time given personal experience and self-reflection. (*ibid.*, p. 358)
- At the age of six, children also begin to develop an awareness that knowledge and understanding are constructed and that they have some degree of control over this process. (*ibid.*, p. 360)
- Socially shared conceptions about the nature of cognition are transmitted to children via informal experience and formal education. (*ibid.*, p. 362)
- Paris & Byrnes have suggested that self-directed reflection develops in young children as part of self-correction and takes on increasing importance as children grow older. (as cited in *ibid.*, p. 364)
- [M]ost children are able to theorize about their own cognition by the age of four even though the depth and breadth of their theorizing continues to develop throughout their school careers. (*ibid.*, p. 368)

This information about the developing theories of metacognition prompted me to delve further into what was happening with children between the ages of four and seven, the age range of students whom I teach.

It was at this point in my inquiry that I began to explore the field known as theory of mind. Whereas most studies interested in studying the development of metacognition involve older children and adolescents, most studies concerning the development of theory of mind involve infants, toddlers, and preschoolers. Lockl & Schneider (2006) said theory of mind "refers to children's ability to attribute mental states, such as beliefs, desires and intentions, to self and others and includes their knowledge that mental representations of events need not correspond to reality" (p. 16). In their discussion of theory of mind and metacognition, Lockl and Schneider point out that theory of mind studies are generally concerned with what the individual knows about another person's mind, whereas metacognition studies are more concerned with what an individual knows about their own thinking. Bartsch & Estes (1996) suggested, "children's initial acquisition of mental state concepts provides a foundation for later metacognition" (p. 281). They reasoned that one must first of all have a concept of cognition before beginning to engage in thinking about or regulating their own thinking. Similarly Lockl & Schneider (2006) proposed, "children have to acquire an understanding of mental states as representational before they can reflect on their own or other people's memories" (p. 17). As an early primary teacher I found this fascinating because it seems that much of the research supports the notion that children, up until approximately the age of four, are still developing a theory of mind. If, as Bartsch & Estes claim, theory of mind were a prerequisite for metacognition, it would seem reasonable to postulate that most Kindergarten or Grade 1 children are in somewhat of a transition phase.

I found the work of Pillow (2008) very interesting, particularly because of what he had to say about the cognitive development of young children. He stated, "[T]he emergence and elaboration of children's concepts of cognitive abilities may function as a developmental bridge between young children's understanding of mental states and adolescents' and adults' epistemological thought" (p. 297). He went on to describe three levels of conceptual understanding. The first, *occurrence knowledge,* refers to knowledge that certain cognitive activities occur. The second, *organizational knowledge* refers to knowledge of relations among cognitive activities. The final level is *epistemological thought*, which refers to "reflection on the nature of knowledge and relation between knowledge and reality" (p. 299). Pillow found that much of children's occurrence knowledge, or understanding of multiple cognitive activities, began to appear as they transitioned from early to middle childhood, roughly between the ages of five and seven. Organizational knowledge and epistemological thought developed later. Children as young as three and four possess some understanding of mental states—as demonstrated in theory of mind studies (see Bartsch & Estes, 1996; Flavell, 2004; Lockl & Schneider, 2006)—however, they are less aware of the cognitive processes that influence those mental states.

Pillow (2008) also examined the role of memory, attention, inference, and stream of consciousness in cognitive activities. It was interesting to note that in the studies involving memory tasks, kindergarten children showed no preference between four strategies (e.g., looking, naming, rehearsing, categorizing), whereas third grade children chose an appropriate strategy to aid them in remembering.

With regard to attention, it would seem that at around five years of age children become aware of the fact that if you are attending to one message or task it is difficult to attend to another. An understanding of inferential knowledge is something that appears to develop a little later. Most three and four year olds would not recognize inference as a source of knowledge whereas six and seven year olds are gaining a rudimentary understanding of inferential knowledge.

Pillow's (2008) research, which indicates significant growth in children's understanding of activities between the ages of four and eight, echoes the findings of Schraw & Moshman (1995). In fact, most of the literature that I reviewed indicated that development of metacognitive awareness may arise as early as four to six years of age with a gradual increase in metacognitive knowledge occurring in the following years (Bartsch, Horvath, & Estes, 2003; Flavell, Green, Flavell, & Grossman, 1997; Pillow, 2008; Veenman & Spaans, 2005; Veenman, Van Hout-Wolters, & Afflerbach, 2006). However, some studies seemed to indicate that the development of metacognitive skills should not be expected to happen before the age of eight (Pillow, 2008; Veenman & Spaans, 2005; Veenman, Van Hout-Woulters, & Afflerbach, 2006; Desoete & Roeyers, 2002).

Another field of research directly related to that of metacognitive skills is *self-regulated learning*. "Self-regulation refers to self-generated thoughts, feelings, and behaviors that are oriented to attaining goals" (Zimmerman, 2002, p. 65). Self-regulated learners employ metacognitive skills as they plan, monitor, review, and adapt their activities. Some researchers use the words self-regulation and metacognitive skills interchangeably (see for instance Krasiejko, 2010). As I see it, self-regulated learners, in addition to using their metacognitive skills, must also understand what motivates them.

Dignath & Büttner (2008) performed a meta-analysis examining research on fostering self-regulated learning in both primary and secondary students. One of the findings of their study was that "self-regulated learning can be fostered effectively at both primary and secondary school level" (p. 231). The authors also indicated that the research suggested a need to give encouragement and motivational support to younger students. For both age groups, it was important to provide ample opportunities to practice and become fluent with a skill in order to facilitate the transference of the skill to a new situation. Because young children are still developing their metacognitive knowledge and skills, Dignath & Büttner suggested that these children "might therefore benefit more from pure instruction of metacognitive strategies in order to broaden their strategy repertoire" (p. 253). Clearly this research has implications for teaching practice. I am interested to see what develops next in the field, particularly as it relates to early primary education.

Although there is not total agreement on whether metacognitive knowledge and skills need to be taught explicitly, the majority of the research I found indicated the importance of specifically incorporating these elements into lessons (Blakey & Spence, 1990; Dignath & Büttner, 2008; Livingston, 1997; Pintrich, 2002; Scruggs, Mastropieri, Monson, & Jorgensen, 1985; Swartz). Arthur L. Costa (1984), an educator who has had an ongoing interest in the development of children's thinking skills, suggested, "*direct* instruction in metacognition may *not* be beneficial" (p. 58, original emphasis). He stated, "when students experience the need for problem-solving strategies, induce their own, discuss them, and practice them to the degree that they become spontaneous and unconscious, their metacognition seems to improve" (p. 58). All researchers seem to agree that strategies to improve metacognition not only need to be taught, but should be infused into lessons in a variety of subject areas, rather than being taught as stand alone lessons.

Costa (1984) outlined twelve strategies that can be used to enhance metacognition. He referred to them as planning strategy, generating questions, choosing consciously, evaluating with multiple criteria, taking credit, outlawing "I can't," paraphrasing or reflecting back students' ideas, labeling students' behaviors, clarifying students' terminology, role playing and simulations, journal keeping, and modeling. Of all of these strategies, teacher modeling is the one he felt has the greatest impact. Because students often learn through imitation, it is beneficial when a teacher explicitly demonstrates metacognition through sharing aloud their thinking processes. This may in turn enable students to describe what is going on in their heads and give us a glimpse into their metacognitive knowledge or skills.

Two other researchers who have written about developing metacognition in the classroom are Blakey & Spence (1990). They suggest six strategies for developing metacognitive behaviors. There is considerable overlap between the six strategies they set out and the twelve put forth by Costa. Blakey & Spence's first strategy *identifying "what you know" and "what you don't know"* is similar to Costa's strategy of *generating questions.* Their second strategy, *talking and thinking,* encompasses much of what Costa describes as *paraphrasing or reflecting back students' ideas, labeling students' behaviors, clarifying students' terminology*, and *modeling.* The third strategy Blakey & Spence suggest is *keeping a thinking journal,* which corresponds directly to Costa's *journal keeping.* A fourth strategy *planning and self-regulation* matches up with Costa's *planning strategy* and *outlawing "I can't."* Their fifth strategy *debriefing the thinking process* is similar to Costa's *choosing consciously* and *evaluating with multiple criteria.* Blakey & Spence's final strategy, *self-evaluation,* has components similar to Costa's *taking credit* and *evaluating with multiple criteria strategies.*

Ann Epstein (2008) suggests five strategies for developing metacognitive knowledge that are particularly well suited to young learners. Firstly, for young learners it is important to provide opportunities to plan and reflect on a regular basis. Secondly, it is beneficial to wonder with them, asking children questions that cause them to explore alternatives. Thirdly, teachers need to encourage their students to elaborate on their ideas by asking prompting questions, such as "How do you know?" Fourthly, teachers need to encourage students to be problem solvers by helping them to recognize a problem, generate solutions, and then try out their ideas. Finally, Epstein suggests that it is important to give encouragement rather than praise. As I look forward to teaching full day Kindergarten in the coming year, I feel these five guidelines will be most helpful in creating an environment that encourages this kind of thinking.

As a result of my review of literature, I feel far more knowledgeable about the topic of metacognition than when I first began my research. Some days I feel like I have just scratched the surface and have so much more to learn. There is a wealth of information on the topic with ongoing research continually emerging. It has taken time to consider and figure out how the various studies, theories, and research all fit together. That said, on the whole I think I have built a good foundation of knowledge, and have gleaned information that will have a positive impact on my teaching practice.

The Research Setting

My research involved a class of Grade 1 students at an elementary school in NVSD44. There are approximately 360 students in the school from Kindergarten through Grade 7. The population is quite stable with few transfers in or out during a typical school year. The school is situated in a predominantly single family residential area with a green belt surrounding the school. It has been a "school of choice" for several years, due to location, ranking by Foundation Skills Assessment (NB: the FSA is administered to Grade 4 and 7 students across British Columbia) results, parent satisfaction, and word of mouth. The school has a reputation for welcoming and accommodating Special Needs students at every grade level. Less than ten percent of the students are an English as a Second Language (ESL) learner, with several international students attending the school. It is composed of a diverse cross-section of students.

Parents at the school are very involved. They volunteer in the classrooms, and fundraise to provide financial support. Most parents have completed post secondary education and are employed in white-collar jobs. The majority of students come from a two-parent family with all their basic needs met. Parents are knowledgeable and have high expectations of the students and the school.

There were 24 students in the Grade 1 class that composed my study group—sixteen girls and eight boys. Two of the students received ongoing support from a learning assistance teacher because of initial testing indicating that they were at risk in reading. Two students were English as a Second Language learners—one of them was an international student. Like any class, there was a diversity of learners.

I was in a job share position in which I taught Wednesday through Friday and my teaching partner taught on Mondays and Tuesdays. We taught in a self-contained classroom with desks arranged in groups to facilitate partner or group work. The space was organized so that the whole class could come together at the carpet.

After teaching at the Kindergarten and Grade 1 level for over two decades, I have gained considerable experience with this age group. Just as no two students are the same, neither are two classes. They all have their own characteristics and peculiarities. Despite the diversity of students and classes, there are some common developmental milestones. It is with the early primary student in mind that I approached my research.

Planning

Once I had the idea for my research project, there was a lot of work to do before proceeding. Because the study involved students in my class, I had to first obtain approval from the UBC Behavioral Research Ethics Board (BREB). The application form for the BREB review included a section where I had to summarize my research proposal. This helped me to think through the various components of my research and clarify the processes I would use. Although it was considered a "minimal risk" proposal there were still various levels of consent that I had to obtain. I sent an outline of my proposal to the superintendant of the North Vancouver Board of Education and he gave permission for me to conduct the research in my classroom. The parents of the students in my class were then informed of my research proposal and completed a consent form which was returned to the school principal, and held until reports were written so that there could be no possibility of lack of consent effecting the student reports. Twenty-four parental consent forms were sent home and twenty were returned. Getting one hundred percent return of forms is a challenge. In this instance it was especially difficult because I was not receiving the forms and could not therefore remind parents to return them. All of the forms that were returned gave consent for their child to participate in the study. One of the trickiest consents to handle was the student assent. It was challenging to inform the students about the research in language they would understand. My teaching partner asked each of the students individually for their oral consent. I was pleased to be informed that all of the students were willing to be included in the study. Once these hurdles were overcome I was able to proceed with my inquiry.

Implementation

At the onset of the study I asked the students some questions to engage them in reflecting about their thinking and to collect information about what six-year-olds at this stage believe and express about their thinking. The students were asked these same questions again at the end of the study to see how their responses might differ.

Lessons using concept attainment teaching strategies were incorporated into regular class activities. An advantage of using this teaching strategy is that it is well suited for use in various subject areas such as mathematics, social studies, and language arts. To collect some data about student thinking during the concept attainment lessons, I designed a work sheet divided into eight numbered boxes. As we went through the examples, students could either write about or draw what they were thinking in each of the boxes. Each box also contained picture symbols they could circle that would indicate "I'm still thinking," "I've got it," or "My thinking is the same." The purpose of this was to try to track changes or developments in their thinking about their thinking.

Because five and six year olds' reading and writing skills are just emerging, it was important to take this into account both for planning activities and collecting data. Initial and final questions were asked of each student individually, with me transcribing their oral responses. Many of the class activities involved verbal components, particularly with students sharing their thinking at the end of a lesson. I considered how to use visuals instead of print. This involved adapting activities to allow them to record their ideas through drawing rather than writing. Tishman & Palmer (2005) have discussed the value of what they term *visible thinking*: any representations that in some way document the learner's unfolding ideas as they work through an activity. The examples for the concept attainment lessons often used objects or pictures rather than text. Each of the concept attainment lessons had a strong visual component in keeping with the emerging reading and writing skills of the students.

Off and on since the beginning of the school year, the class had participated in a few concept attainment type lessons, so the strategy was not entirely new to the children. The children had often engaged in an activity called "What's My Rule?" In this activity items are sorted into two or more groups and the students must try to figure out what the rule is for sorting the objects. This ties directly into the sorting activities that are part of the mathematics curriculum, as students begin to look at and recognize different attributes of objects. This kind of attending to similarities and differences is key to concept attainment.

In all of the lessons preceding the study the students had shared their responses orally. Knowing that the students would engage in the concept attainment lessons, I next had to introduce the recording sheet that they would use to record their thinking during each of the concept attainment lessons. I showed them an enlarged version of the two symbols that would represent notions of "I'm still thinking" and "I've got it." It was reassuring to me that I had chosen symbols that were meaningful to the students—when I showed them the pictures the students were able to explain what they represented. The first picture was a puzzled looking face with question marks; the second was a light bulb with lines indicating the bulb was shining. The students were able to connect the light bulb idea to cartoon or comic drawings where this symbol had been used. Discussion by the class demonstrated their understanding of the symbols.

After determining that they understood the symbols I proceeded to show them the work sheet, entitled 'Great Thinking' (see Figure 1 below) that we would use to record their ideas. I explained to them that they could either write or draw a picture to show me what they thought the rule was for all the things that were in the 'yes' group. All the objects in the 'yes' group started with the /b/ sound (see Figure 1 below). So that there was no misnaming of the items, I had been sure to name each object aloud as I placed it in either the 'yes' or 'no' group. The first time the students used the sheet I guided them by having them locate the box number so that they proceeded through the boxes in numerical order. After the first set of 'yes' and 'no' examples were added, I asked them to circle either the puzzled face or light bulb and to draw or write about what they thought the rule might be. As we proceeded through subsequent examples they continued to do the same but they had the additional option of circling the word 'same' to indicate that they had not changed their thinking. I had the students use a felt tip marker so that they could not go back and erase what they had done.

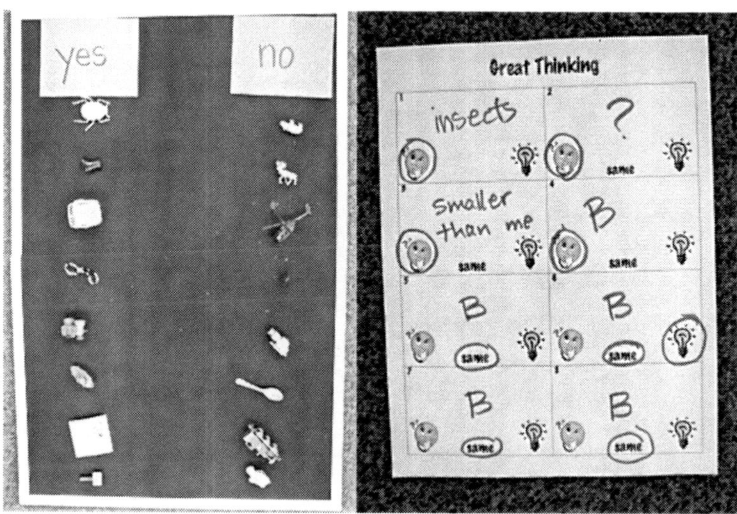

Figure 1. Sorting the "yes" and "no" objects and the "Great Thinking" sheet that I filled out to share my thought processes with the children.

Once we had gone through all the examples I collected the papers. This was done so that the students would not make changes. With the papers collected we then discussed the sorting of the objects and what was the same about all the items in the 'yes' group. I felt it was important for the students to talk about and openly share what they had been thinking during the activity. I noticed in the discussion that there seemed to be a need for the students to have gotten the rule 'right;' moreover, if they had thought something differently at the start, the students were not so eager to share that part of the process of figuring out the concept. I then went through the examples again and talked openly about the thoughts that might have gone through my head. As I thought aloud, I also filled out one of the Great Thinking sheets to reflect and describe my thought processes (see Figure 1 above). I think this modeling was an important step in furthering their understanding of the activity. I wanted the students to develop the understanding that we often change our minds as we are given additional information and that we need to continue to check our ideas to see if those ideas still fit with new examples.

The next day when we did the concept attainment activity with the Great Thinking sheets I made it a little more challenging to determine what was the same about the items in the 'yes' group. Everything in the 'yes' group had an AB pattern, but the initial examples also used just yellow and blue materials (see Figure 2). As more examples were added color was no longer a common trait. I had done this purposely so that it would cause some of them to rethink their original position and make changes to their thinking. Unlike the first time we used the sheets, I found this time students were less tempted to go back and change what they had put in the boxes.

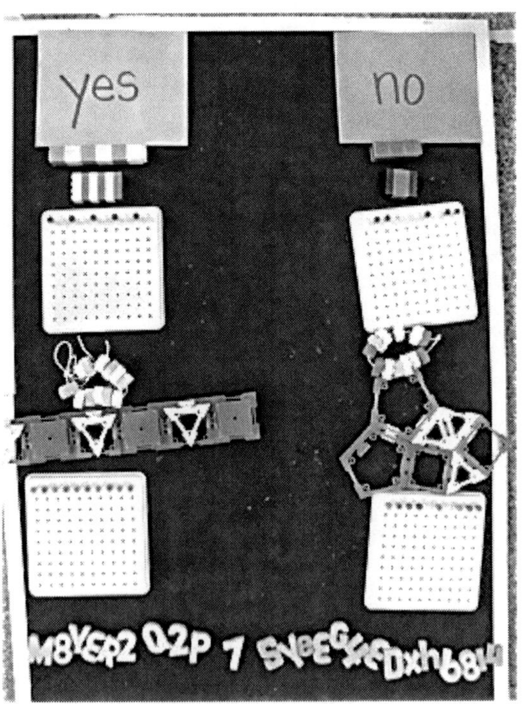

Figure 2. AB pattern in the "yes" group.

The third session tied into our Social Studies theme of community helpers. This time the objects in the 'yes' category were all tools (see Figure 3). As I was setting up the activity and handing out the Great Thinking papers, I overheard a student say, "Oh good, I love this!" It was encouraging to hear the spontaneous enthusiasm after not doing these lessons for almost three weeks due to spring break and report conferences. Students were engaged. Most of them were able to get their ideas on paper without blurting out their ideas. There was a lot of good sharing at the end of the activity. Students described that they thought the rule was (e.g., flat and fat, metal/not metal, or sharp/not sharp), but then changed their thinking with additional examples. The students seemed to be more aware of their thinking, which I connect to a statement from Costa (1988).

> We must convey to students that the goal of their education is intelligent behavior—that the responsibility for thinking is theirs, that it is desirable to have more than one solution, that it is commendable when they take time to plan and reflect on an answer rather than responding rapidly or impulsively, and that it is desirable to change an answer with additional information. (p. 28)

Figure 3. The third session, sorting tools.

As I had set up each of the concept attainment lessons I had always planned the "yes" and "no" examples so that there was more than one solution at the start. This was done purposefully in an effort to encourage divergent thinking. I was pleased that students with time seemed to be more reflective and open to changing their ideas.

Two weeks later, the fourth and final concept attainment lesson that used the Great Thinking sheets was math related. The objects in the 'yes' group were all circles. This was a relatively easy concept for them to identify. It struck me as I reflected on this lesson that the students often look at shape or color first when trying to process information. I wanted them to expand their thinking and consider other attributes, such as function. As part of our co-operative library time we did concept attainment lessons on maps, and Canadian symbols, but due to time restrictions we did not use the Great Thinking sheets. Upon reflecting on my concept attainment lessons, I felt there was a need to further develop the students' ability to compare items.

Identifying similarities and differences is one of the best research-based strategies for improving student achievement (Marzano, Pickering, & Pollock, 2005). One of the graphic organizers suggested by Marzano et al. for comparison of items is the Venn diagram. I decided to introduce the Venn diagram to the students as another concept attainment type of lesson. To do this, I used two hula-hoops on the floor and placed red objects into one hoop and round objects into the other. I then described for the students how there were some objects that were both red and round, and that we could overlap the hoops and put the red round objects in the intersecting space.

Figure 4. Venn diagram with rectangular (on right) and blue objects.

We tried the activity again with blue and rectangular objects (see Figure 4 above). They had a lot of fun finding objects within our classroom space to add to the Venn diagram. Once the students had this new way of organizing items we could move onto more challenging sets of objects or pictures to compare. On another day we sorted different modes of transportation. Our most interesting comparing and sorting involved magazine photos of urban and rural settings. This set of photographs generated lots of discussion. The children were eager to talk about the thinking that had gone on during the activity.

Although I had the four sets of Great Thinking record sheets, I began to reflect and wonder if this was going to be enough for me to get a good picture of the students' thinking and metacognition. The Ministry of Education (1991) suggested having students keep a thinking log to help them reflect on their thinking. This seemed like a perfect way to get students to think about their thinking, as well as giving me some more information about their metacognition. I set up a thinking log that had the sentence starter: "Today I was thinking when ________." That was followed by the sentence stem: "It was ______ because I _________." I put a list of eighteen adjectives (e.g., confusing, fun, new, tricky) at the front of their booklets to help them describe their thinking. Some students found it challenging to record something in their booklet, while others were quick to think of something to record. It certainly was a great tool to get students reflecting on their thinking and learning throughout the day.

After the students had made a couple of entries in their Thinking Logs I noticed that their entries were somewhat simple and repetitive. In an effort to broaden their knowledge I introduced them to Edward de Bono's (1991) *Six Thinking Hats*. Using foam visors in the six colors that de Bono describes, I gave examples of how I could think about something differently depending on which hat I was wearing. I left the visors hanging in the classroom as a visual reminder of the lesson. In the days following I would often point out how our thinking fell into one of the categories described by the Six Thinking Hats. After introducing the Six Thinking Hats, one student drew a green hat in her Thinking Log as a way to describe her thinking. I thought this was a great addition to her reflection and showed the rest of the class that they too could use this as another means of describing their thinking. In the journal entries that followed other students added colored hats, or indicated how they were feeling during their thinking, which provided some evidence of transference of knowledge about the different types of thinking described by de Bono.

When I began my research I wanted to discover if concept attainment lessons might help develop students' metacognitive skills. As I worked with the students over the course of my study, I adjusted some of my teaching and plans. Although not in the original outline of my study, the introduction of Venn diagrams, Thinking Logs, and the Six Thinking Hats seemed appropriate to expand students' knowledge and skills relating to thinking and metacognition. As the study progressed, each of these was purposefully introduced with the goal of getting the students to think more and differently about their thinking.

In addition to the concept attainment lessons, Venn diagrams, thinking logs, and Six Thinking Hats, I realized that something I had not considered part of my research was impacting students' metacognition. The unplanned variable was the book *The 7 Habits of Happy Kids,* by Sean Covey (2008). This book contains several stories about animal characters that encounter problems and learn important life lessons about how to deal with them. When first reading the book in class, I had read a description of each of the characters and the students quickly started to identify with one or more of these figures. This initial bonding with the characters was key, I think, to the students' continued identification with them and their connection of situations in the book to things that were happening in the classroom. I would hear students saying, "Oh, that's like Goob Bear when he made a list. He had a plan." As I reflected on what the students were saying, I could see that the characters and situations in this book had actually helped the children identify many metacognitive skills through their examples.

I also wanted to find out from the students' perspective what had helped them think about their thinking. At our weekly class meetings we often did a check-in, rating our day from 1 to 10. I decided to use this same 1 to 10 rating scale to get feedback from the students about concept attainment activities, Venn diagrams, Six Hat Thinking, and Thinking Logs. As I conferred with each student at the end of data collection, in addition to asking him or her the questions from the outset of the study, I also had them complete a 10-point rating scale. The rating scale gave me valuable information about how the students viewed the concept attainment lessons.

Findings

THE QUESTIONNAIRE

Upon looking carefully through the student responses to the questionnaire I had used at both the beginning and end of my study, I was able to draw some conclusions. As I considered the responses, I looked at changes between initial and final responses. I also looked at similarities and differences in individual responses to each of the questions. From all of this I tried to determine what could be learned about the students' metacognition.

The first question, "What can you tell me about thinking?" elicited a variety of responses. The sample responses to this question illustrate that many initial responses were quite simple. Students would say things such as, "I don't know" or "You use your brain." Some of the responses toward the end of the data collection seem to indicate greater metacognitive awareness. The students were able to talk about their thinking in more detail. Their responses show metacognitive awareness of problem solving, organizing information, planning, sorting, making connections, and evaluating and making choices.

"When do you use thinking?" was the next question. It was interesting to note that math came up frequently in their responses on both the initial and final questionnaire. I wondered if this was related in any way to Dignath & Büttner's (2008) research indicating primary students acquire math strategies earlier than reading comprehension strategies. In math, students start to recognize different strategies they can use for problem solving. Some rely on using their fingers, others use counters, while some have learned to *count on*, or use a number line to solve equations. Recognizing that they use these strategies indicates some level of metacognitive awareness.

Another common theme that appeared in student responses to the second question was thinking occurred when making choices. Frequently, students mentioned a situation where they had to think about whether or not an activity would be safe (e.g., going in the deep end of the pool, doing a trick on the monkey bars). Again, recognizing that they can use their thinking to evaluate a situation indicates some metacognitive skills.

While the students' responses to the question "What helps you to think?" seem to demonstrate the development of theory of mind, comparing initial and final responses for the most part did not indicate metacognitive development. The students frequently stated that their brain helps them with their thinking, but made little mention of *strategies* that could help them with their thinking.

When asked, "What helps you to learn?" students indicated some awareness of useful thinking strategies. The strategy that students most often brought up as helpful to learning was *attending*. They recognized the importance of looking and listening. Some showed awareness of the need to attend to one thing at a time rather than trying to focus on two things at once. One student mentioned practice or repeating an activity until you got it right as a strategy to help with learning. The most interesting response to this question was "By your brain…your brain is watching a …whatever you're thinking is on your brain's TV." Research shows that we often use private speech as a strategy to help us with our thinking (Annevirta & Vauras, 2006; Flavell et al. 1997; Schunk, 1986), but I think this comment demonstrates that there are some who cognitively picture (i.e., image, imagine) what is going on to help them learn (Grossman, 2009).

Interestingly, at the end of the study when students were asked, "What helps you to learn?" one-quarter of them responded "math." I wondered why this response was given by so many of the students. Upon reflection I speculated that it was because the students had been introduced to several strategies for solving mathematical problems and were actively engaged in using those strategies as they worked independently.

Many responses to the question "How do you learn?" seemed to indicate that students feel others are involved in their learning. They describe teachers, friends, parents, or other family members as helping them to learn. As well, the students mentioned that learning happens when you are engaged in an activity or doing something. One student demonstrated awareness that learning can take place in different settings. It would seem children of this age are becoming more aware of strategies they can use to help them with their learning.

What stood out in the responses to the question "How do you figure out how to do things?" was that in the final responses approximately one third of the students said they figured out how to do something by trying. This may indicate that they have realized that by trying to do something they are more likely to have some success than if they did not make any attempt. It may also suggest that they have learned that you can try something, and modify your strategy until you achieve success. A willingness to attempt something new or challenging is an attribute of a self-directed learner.

The last question "What do you do if you don't understand?" elicited responses similar to the question "How do you learn?" The main strategy students shared was seeking help. Annevirta & Vaurus (2006), in their discussion of help seeking-behavior reported that "[a] young learner who asks questions and obtains needed assistance from teachers and peers not only alleviates immediate academic difficulties but also acquires knowledge, skills, and strategies that can in turn be used for self-help to regulate one's performance" (p. 202). In my study, students most often reported seeking help from the teacher, but said they would also ask friends or others. Their responses also indicate an awareness of the value of asking to have something repeated, clarified, or explained. Seeking help is a strategy that appears to be learned early.

CONCEPT ATTAINMENT STUDENT RESPONSE SHEETS

The Great Thinking sheets that students used to record their thinking as we went through the concept attainment lessons were useful so far as they encouraged the children to try to put their thinking into words or pictures. They also raised awareness about how thinking can change. However, it is difficult to draw any conclusions about students' metacognition from the data sheets. Nevertheless, it does seem apparent that there are those students who *don't know they don't know*, those who *know they don't know*, and those who *know they know*.

THINKING LOGS

Like the student response sheets, the thinking logs certainly got the students to reflect on their thinking. Some of the students were able to easily write about their thinking, whereas others really struggled with this. Research has indicated that it is difficult for young students to report on their own mental activity. For instance, Flavell (1999) stated that preschoolers "tend to be very poor at recalling or reconstructing both the fact and the content of their own recent or present thinking" (p. 39). I believe this difficulty with putting thoughts into words was reflected in the thinking log entries. Because the student entries were somewhat limited, I found it hard to draw any real conclusions. I would, however, try this activity again because I think it really did get the students to start reflecting more on their thinking.

THE RATING SCALE

The students were asked to rate the four strategies (Yes/No Examples-concept attainment, Venn diagrams, Six Hat Thinking, and Thinking Logs) on a scale of 1 to 10 as to how much the activity helped them to think about their thinking. Most students rated each of the items at a 5 or higher. In the end, the students rated My Thinking Log as the most helpful, with eleven of the twenty students who participated in the study giving it a 10. Second highest rated was Six Hat Thinking followed very closely by Yes/No Examples. The activity that they rated the lowest was Venn diagrams although only one student rated it as low as a 4.

In addition to having them rate the four activities, I asked the students if there was anything else that had helped them think about their thinking. I also asked them what helped them the most to think about their thinking. These questions resulted in some interesting answers. Five of the students responded that math was the thing that helped them to think about their thinking. These oral responses correlate with the responses on the questionnaire, with one quarter of the student responses specifically mentioning math. I think it is worth further investigation to see why students connect mathematics so strongly with their thinking (for a related study, see Desoete & Roeyers, 2002).

Perspectives and Suggestions for Praxis

Assessing metacognitive development is a challenge. Definitively determining metacognitive development over the short time period of the present inquiry would be nearly impossible. However, as a result of the activities engaged in throughout my research project, I believe most students developed a greater awareness of their own thinking and metacognition. My inquiry has led me to understand more about the development of metacognitive awareness and metacognitive skills in young children. As a result of this, I can confidently recommend that teachers implement a variety of instructional tactics, strategies, and graphics organizers to further develop students' cognitive and metacognitive abilities.

Another recommendation would be to have lots of opportunities for dialogue. Establishing a classroom where discussion is encouraged is important. Ideally, there would be conversations with self, peers, teachers, or others. Children should be allowed to talk to themselves as they work through tasks. This self-talk allows them to think out loud. As children are playing at the dramatic play centre, working in the block corner, or engaged in other small group activities it will be natural for them to talk about what they are doing with their peers. These are instances where they can learn from each other. As Costa (2008) reported, "Learning is a reciprocal process; the individual influences the group's thinking, and the group influences the individual's thinking" (p. 22). Whether students are engaged in solitary or group activities, it would be valuable for the teacher to use questions to help students to extend their thinking, or to reconstruct or elaborate on their ideas.

In addition to encouraging conversation in the classroom, I would suggest other strategies be used to promote metacognitive awareness and skills. Lessons that use tactics such as 'brainstorming,' 'think, pair, share,' or 'wonder, puzzle, explore' would allow students to share their thinking publicly. Providing such sharing opportunities would introduce new ideas, as well as let the students know that their thinking is valued. I also think it is important for the teacher to openly communicate his or her thinking, as this modelling is helpful for students. I would recommend establishing a routine of planning and reflecting together, as outlined by Epstein (2003), as a way to enable students to set goals and evaluate their work. Recording their thoughts, plans, or strategies and making their thinking visible is another tactic I would suggest based on my own experience in the classroom and the work of Ritchart and Perkins (2008). This recording of thoughts could be done as a group, or individually, through drawing, writing, or photographs. As well, I would recommend regularly incorporating key vocabulary (e.g., think, know, wonder, and learn) into activities. My research has led me to believe that strategies and tactics such as these, that cause students to reflect on their thinking, should be implemented on a regular basis.

As a final recommendation, I would suggest using picture books as a way to further develop students' metacognitive awareness. Choosing books that allow for discussion of what characters may be thinking, or predicting what a character may do would provide another opportunity to talk about students' own thinking and the thinking of others. Relating to the experiences of characters in a story may add to the students' metacognitive knowledge without them having the experience firsthand. As was the case in my class, students started to relate to the characters in *The 7 Habits of Happy Kids* (Covey, 2008) and would relate events in the book to situations in the classroom. The students started to show signs of connecting strategies portrayed in the book to real life situations. The imaginary world of books seems like a safe place for students to explore new thinking and reflect on their own thinking.

Building on existing research, I found that teaching tactics and strategies that I designed can be effectively adapted for use with young children to encourage metacognition. Moreover, reflecting on my own and others' research, it seems that the primary years are an important time to stimulate this type of self-reflection. Hopefully future studies of metacognition can be tied in with research on teaching strategies appropriate for children in this early transitional stage. The acquisition of metacognitive knowledge and skills is ongoing. Planning and reflection, when they bracket active learning, are part of an ongoing cycle of deeper thought and thoughtful application (Epstein, 2003, p. 29). As educators, it is vital that we acknowledge the importance of metacognition to learning, and provide the kind of support and experiences that will facilitate further development.

Wendy McNaughton
North Vancouver School District

PART 4

STORIES OF CURRICULUM DEVELOPMENT PROJECTS

BRIGITTE GERANDOL

THE JOURNEY FROM STUDENT TO TEACHER AND BACK AGAIN

An Evolving Understanding of Curriculum Design

Once Upon a Time

When I was a high school student, I imagined that teachers had a big black binder filled with every possible lesson, worksheet, quiz, and test required to teach any class. Teaching, as I conceived it from a student's perspective, was as easy as turning the page in the binder and following the instructions. However, as a teacher, I discovered that there isn't a magic binder. Rather, it is up to the teacher to design, implement, and adapt the curriculum to meet the needs of all students. This process of curriculum design and redesign, from an outside perspective, does not reveal the breadth or depth of the process involved to 'get it right.' How do I design curriculum and what effects do my choices have on the students' abilities to achieve the goals that I set? Wiggins & McTighe (2005), suggest that curriculum is a blueprint for a plan to conduct effective and engaging teaching and learning (p. 5). In the present inquiry, I attempt to work through the process of understanding curriculum design that accomplishes 'best practice.' As a reflexive-reflective practitioner, I require myself to look at past, present, and current curriculum design practices to become a better user of curriculum in the future.

The significance of curriculum design became apparent to me while teaching at an inner-city high school in England. The teacher education program did not prepare me to stand in front of thirty-four British students who *ate me alive* in my first year—they wouldn't listen, stop talking, or sit down. I neither had a lesson plan for teaching defiant, disinterested students nor did I know how to change my approach to engage these students. Marzano (2007) reports that student engagement enhances students' knowledge of academic content, but I neither knew of nor fully understood the implications of that perspective seven years ago. During my Canadian student-teaching experiences, standing at the front of the room was enough to quiet a room and start the lesson. I was at a complete loss in terms of "teaching." I discovered that I simply didn't know how to teach students who weren't eager to learn. So, with determination, I struggled to define myself as a teacher and find my teaching voice. Over time, I began to dabble in creative teaching strategies such as hosting "The Weakest Link" as a review activity with my students. I didn't have sound pedagogical reasons for the success of games in instruction. However, I now know as Marzano (2007) explains, the use of games increases students' sense of anticipation and curiosity (p. 101). Suddenly, my

P. Gouzouasis (ed.), Pedagogy in a New Tonality: Teacher Inquiries on Creative Tactics, Strategies, Graphics Organizers, and Visual Journals in the K-12 Classroom, 257–266.

classes exploded with hives of activity as students designed questions from the course material and challenged each other to learn the information through play. As I developed more student-centered activities, both student engagement and behavior issues improved.

While teaching in England, I experienced the pressures—for both teachers and students—with the quarterly scheduled national exams. Initially, my test scores were low, in part, due to the streaming that occurs in the school system (i.e., I taught the lowest academically achieving streamed groups), and my own challenges as a teacher. However, my overall class scores continually improved as my teaching approaches became more varied and creative, much to the surprise of the senior teachers on staff. The eventual success I achieved in England spurred me on to learn how to design creative lesson plans to engage students at a higher level.

Upon my return from England, I committed to becoming a better teacher—learning the teaching skills that would have enabled me to be even more successful abroad. Teaching overseas started me on the path of understanding best practices of curriculum design and implementation. My 'teaching self' began as a gradual and ongoing metamorphosis, and as Bennett states, "becoming an expert teacher involves continual practice and reflection over time" (Bennett & Rohlheiser, p. 6). This challenging and relentless task requires ongoing commitment to expand one's pedagogical repertoire and try new activities while understanding how each new strategy improves student engagement and understanding. One's first attempt at a new activity will no doubt send us tumbling into an "implementation dip," the term coined by Michael Fullan (2002), to describe the bumpy road it takes to learn and implement a new educational objective. As Wiggins & McTighe (2005) suggest, the cyclic nature of change, as a teacher collects feedback and makes adjustments to any design (p. 271) and repeats until fluency with a new approach is reached. Csikszentmihalyi (p. 152) believes that jobs with variety, challenges, goals, and immediate feedback are enjoyable regardless of the worker's level of development. However, teachers often struggle with the implementation of a new teaching strategy. As teachers, I believe that we must acknowledge that failure is possible. In fact, I considered my first teaching year in England to be a disaster. My second year of teaching helped to dig me out of giving up on teaching altogether; in fact, curriculum design provided me with the hope I needed to continue.

My experiences have led me to believe that the relationships across and amongst curriculum, student, and teacher are intertwined in a complex manner like a twisted, knotted ball of string. What appeared simple in the textbook during my teacher preparation coursework actually required a great deal of thought and preparation to mesh the three aspects together. This is no simple task. As Aoki (1993) suggests, education represents a '*lived curriculum*' whereby all aspects of teaching and learning create meaning for each student (p. 204). The complexity of the relationship between curriculum, teacher, and student increases as we reflect upon our daily practices. From that perspective, one may question how we find a balance between the many variables associated with creating interwoven connections amongst those three aspects of our praxis, the demands of finding the ways of curriculum, student and teacher becoming one.

Becoming Pedagogical: From User to Tinkerer

When do we, as teachers, feel that we have achieved mastery of our teaching? Presently, after seven years of teaching on two continents, I understand that teaching is an endless cycle doing and re-doing, of regeneration and growth, and I may never feel that I have "arrived." When we decide to become reflective-reflexive practitioners, we begin a lifelong journey of questioning our own practices and seeking solutions to the problems that we pose or discover. In addition to our own practices, we often compare ourselves to other master teachers. However, we need to consider what Bennett (p. 15) refers to as the *art of teaching* (i.e., pedagogy) as informed both by art and "science," as well as teaching experiences, as a unique characteristic of each teacher.

From that perspective, the challenge seems to call the reflective-reflexive practitioner to design and implement content in a way that meets the diverse needs of students. The teacher component of the relationship requires us to be self-critical of our own practices. Bennett suggests that is one critical step to increase our implementation of a variety of instruction methods (Bennett & Rohlheiser, p. 80). We must first assess the teacher's use of teaching innovations before we can assess the students' use of that same innovation (p. 80). We need to place ourselves on the continuum between non-use of an innovation and a refocusing use of an innovation (p. 81). We must also be willing to take responsibility of our professional development and provide rich learning environments for our students.

For example, I started working with Bennett's Teams Game Tournament (p. 179) strategy several years ago as a fledgling user of the innovation. After several years of repeated implementation with my math classes, I became a refined user of that strategy. I felt confident presenting a workshop to other teachers in the district to enable the teachers to be involved in the process of the innovation. In retrospect, this particular strategy, although a more complex strategy by Bennett's definition, may have been particularly successful in England for reviewing material for the ongoing national assessments.

As a mathematics teacher, one aspect of teaching that appears trivial is the selection of examples to share with students. Why does it matter which equation I factor? Watson & Matson (2006) suggest using and developing examples that provide students with an opportunity to work out a solution. This approach requires the teacher to select exemplars that will provide students with the opportunity to create their own meaning through patterns and exploration. For example, when developing a lesson about similar triangles, the teacher should provide students with examples that show all the rules so that students can develop their own understanding of the topic. As teachers, we also need to be 'tinkerers' of curriculum (Cuoco, Goldenberg, & Mark, 1996, p. 5; Fullan, 2002; Kruse, n.d.) to provide students with more student-directed lessons that engage student learners. More thought is required of us as we select examples for our classes and for homework assignments. To become a tinkerer, a teacher requires a strong foundational knowledge of the topic. Unfortunately, I realize that while in England, I lacked critical knowledge of unfamiliar terms and concepts unique to the national curriculum.

That said, while in England, I discovered the importance of building presence in a classroom. The 'behavior support expert' suggested the importance of self-awareness of posture, voice intonation, hand movements, and movement throughout the room. In addition, I learned how to use a variety of behavior intervention strategies, from low incidence (e.g., proximity) to high incidence (e.g., remove student from room); however, very little discussion occurred about teaching strategies to improve behavior. Marzano (2007) suggests using a series of graduated actions to get students back on track that reflects the training I received in England (p. 142).

Years later, as I discovered Barrie Bennett's work, I felt that he also provided strategies that would work with, as well as in addition to, the classroom management approach I had learned in England. For example, Bennett suggests that teachers require a diverse number of skills, tactics, and strategies to engage student learners. One strategy suggested is Think/Pair/Share' (T/P/S; Bennett, p. 94). Adding this one tactic to my toolbox has provided all my students with the opportunity to think about, discuss with, and share with the class. In England, this skill may have allowed me to facilitate student conversation rather than to discipline students engaged with off-task discussions. A teacher could then implement a second strategy such as No Hands Up and use Numbered Heads to select student responders. That strategy keeps students alert, and as Marzano (2007) predicts, will raise the level of attention as students wait to be called upon by the teacher (p. 103). The teacher may also use a *thumbs-up* or *thumbs-down* (assessment for learning) approach to get immediate feedback from the students about their abilities to factor trinomials. In retrospect, I have acquired knowledge from both continents and both teaching experiences, to help bring a sense of balance to my understanding of teaching, learning, and curriculum design.

For me, curriculum is always at the heart of teaching. I defer to the "experts" to help guide me on the journey of curriculum design and instruction. From Bennett, I embrace his approach to instruction by becoming knowledgeable with a variety of skills, tactics, and strategies. Most recently, I experimented with Academic Controversy and rejoin in the notion that *Beyond Monet* holds years of teaching inspiration. I am excited by Marzano's (2007, p. 21) four-point rubric, and the approach to breaking down prescribed learning outcomes and assessing all student work using the same rubric. I appreciate that Marzano's work is based on research (i.e., meta-analysis) and I continue to re-read his work and gain additional motivation.

Swan (2007) presents a thoughtful approach to creating and designing matching tasks that engage students at the highest level of thinking. After working with his approach to task design for several months, I discovered an advantage to allowing students to enter a mathematics activity at a variety of access points and experience their own levels of success. Zaslavasky (2008) and Swan (2007) suggest methods to design tasks that allow students to enter the task at a variety of access points. The ideas of those instructional experts are with me, day in and day out, as I attempt to design meaningful teaching and learning experiences for and with my students.

The Unit Plan

After a variety of experiences working with and trying to understand the complex relationships that exist amongst teacher, learner, and curriculum, I challenged myself to design a unit plan that reflects 'good' pedagogical practices. In no way is this unit plan deemed to be the 'best,' or the 'only,' unit plan for this organizer. Rather, this unit plan reflects my journey with curriculum, instruction, and design. This unit plan is intended to show my personal journey of growth and reflection.

For this unit, I selected the curriculum organizer Number from the *Western and Northern Canadian Protocol K-9 Mathematics* (2006) curriculum document. I have taught this unit many times before, however, I had not put this amount of depth or thought into the design of the lessons. What follows, is an overview of the activities I selected, designed, and modified as well as an explanation of how each activity can enhance student learning and understanding of the topic.

The first question students always ask is "Why do we have to learn (*fill in the topic*)?" In this particular unit, the curriculum organizer Number includes learning outcomes that demonstrate a variety of tasks involving exponents. The big question for this organizer is to internalize the importance of exponents by answering the question before the students ask, "Why do we need to learn about exponents?" At times, mathematical ideas and applications can be very abstract rather than practical. However, exponents are important mathematical concepts that arise in numerous applications such as exponential growth (e.g., how fast will the HINI virus spread and interest calculations; how can I calculate how many payments it will take to pay off my credit card paying only minimum payments at twenty percent interest?). Across the unit, this construct is developed throughout the activities in an effort to demonstrate some of the practical applications of exponents in the real world.

Unlike other topics, not all mathematical concepts are applicable to the every day life of a Grade 9 student. Wiggins & McTighe (2005) challenge me to answer the 'big questions' about math: Why do I teach a topic and how does it relate to enduring learning? This is a challenging question for me and it must also be a challenging question for students to comprehend. In the process of designing the Exponent unit plan, I encountered the topic of exponents with negative bases. In an effort to find the relevancy of this topic, I searched for applications at the high school level. After much reading and many discussions with physics teachers, I determined that there is no application that I could teach to my Grade 9 students. I can join my students in questioning how to make all math topics relevant to them at their level. I also realize that unfortunately, the 'big idea' may not be relevant for all math topics.

Recently, I had the opportunity to hear Barrie Bennett speak about the development of learning outcomes into lesson plans. Bennett suggests that to understand how to plan units starting with prescribed learning outcomes, we must understand the language that the Ministry of Education uses to communicate what they would like us to teach. Bennett suggests that the key to learning how to read and interpret learning outcomes includes an in-depth understanding of Bloom's Taxonomy (Bloom, 1956, pp. 201-207; 1984). Wiggins & McTighe (2005) suggest that the taxonomy classifies objectives from the cognitively easy to those that are more difficult (p. 339). Often, educators can interpret the language of the objectives in vastly different ways. A firm understanding of the six levels of Bloom's Taxonomy—recall, comprehension, application, analysis, synthesis, and evaluation—may help to provide more consistency in the interpretation of the learning outcomes.

In addition to Bennett's approach to deconstructing learning outcomes, I studied and applying the work of Robert Marzano (2009), who provides an approach to develop a learning objective into four levels of difficulty using a four-point rubric design. The Marzano (2009b, p. 28) approach develops each learning objective into four levels of difficulty.

Level 4: Knowledge Utilization, (Decision making, problem solving, experimenting, investigating)

Level 3: Analysis, (Matching, classifying, analyzing errors, generalizing, specifying)

Level 2: Comprehension, (Integrating, symbolizing)

Level 1: Retrieval, (Recognizing, Recalling and executing)

In my experiences with this approach, I have taken the time to deconstruct a learning organizer to determine (1) what skills I may require of each level, and (2) how I may be able to assess a particular learning outcome. Marzano (2009) suggests that each learning outcome be handled in this same way followed by assessment tasks that match each of the learning outcomes. Each assignment, quiz, and test can be created with levels. Teachers can quickly and efficiently identify if students are working at a particular level within each topic. Marzano (2009b) uses a four-point marking scale for all his assessment practices. He suggests that students have an opportunity to rewrite the goals in their own language (Marzano, 2007) to become part of the teaching-learning process.

As an example, the following learning outcome is included in the Number organizer (see Table 1 on the following page for the Marzano influenced rubric). Marzano's rubric starts with the learning goals, in my case the Prescribed Learning Outcomes (PLOs) as outlined in the British Columbia Ministry of Education Mathematics 8 - 9 Resource Package (2008). For example, the PLO A1 states, "It is expected that students will demonstrate an understanding of powers with integral bases (excluding base 0) and whole number exponents by (1) representing repeated multiplication using powers, (2) using patterns to show that a power with an exponent of zero is equal to one, (3) solving problems involving powers, and (4) a clear understanding of the task design and analysis of the difficulty levels provides an opportunity to help students self-assess their own understanding of their learning (2007, p. 21).

I have discovered that the process of deconstructing each learning objective into four levels of difficulty provides an opportunity to create rich learning tasks. For this particular outcome, I elected to use a *multiple representation* task as suggested by Swan (2007). Throughout all the research, including Bennett (2001, 2009),

Marzano (2007, 2009, 2009b), and now Swan (2007), the concept of developing tasks based on Bloom's Taxonomy (Krathwohl, 2002) continues. Swan suggests that tasks be developed to classify, interpret, evaluate, create, and analyze mathematical objectives (p. 2). I have used this approach in the past; however, Swan develops task analysis into a deeper and richer experience for students. One addition to this *matching activity* is to remove some of the matched items and replace the items with blank pieces of paper to challenge the students to determine and write out the missing pieces of the puzzle. I participated in such an activity at a workshop, and I was intrigued by my feelings of challenge to fill in all the tasks. My experience with this activity is that it allows all students to find a level of success. This task has been very successful, especially when working with an adapted group of Grade 9 math students.

Table 1. Sample of a Marzano-influenced rubric

Level of Difficulty	*Learning Goal*	*Task*
Level 4: Knowledge Utilization	Students will be able to match questions expressed in words, exponential form, standard form.	Students will be able to match questions expressed in words, exponential form, standard form. In addition to matching, students will be able to fill in missing gaps and create their own exponent sets. Students can create analogies to define exponents.
Level 3: Analysis	Students will be able to match questions expressed in words, exponential form, standard form, area, volume.	Students are provided with a matching activity and match the different forms.
Level 2: Comprehension	Students will be able to change exponent form to standard form and standard form to exponent form. Students will be able to identity the base and the exponent in each scenario.	Students will create area models for given exponent questions using grid paper such as 5^2
Level 1: Retrieval	Students will be able to distinguish between a base and an exponent. Students will be able to recognize repeated multiplication questions.	Use area/volume models to demonstrate area/volume. Convert the formula for area of a square into exponential form.

For students who possess a Level 1 or Level 2 knowledge of a topic, they can match up a few of the basic forms of the concept. For Level 3 students, they may match up all the clues provided and fill in some of the missing pieces. Level 4 students may match up all of the provided clues, fill in all the blanks, and create their own complete entries for the activities. In that manner, each student is provided an entry point into the activity. It is an activity that allows for students to differentiate their own learning based on their present level. Developing the matching activities so that students at all levels can access them (i.e., accommodating individual differences) is one critical aspect for this task design. Again, starting with the Marzano approach to deconstructing learning outcomes provides teachers with possibilities and opportunities to design rich learning tasks.

Further to Marzano's approach to learning outcomes, Keeley (2005) provides a template for writing learning outcomes in student-centered language.

> Knowledge Targets: "What I need to know."
>
> Reasoning Targets: "What can I do with what I know."
>
> Skill Targets: "What can I demonstrate."
>
> Product Targets: "What I can make to show my learning."

These four questions can be used to continue the discussion about learning outcomes as well as providing opportunities for students to develop student-centered assessment tasks in addition to those specified by the teacher.

Throughout the unit, Bennett's *Beyond Monet* (2001) provides rich activities to develop student learning. One skill that I find to be critical for designing effective lessons is that of framing questions. Bennett suggests that Think/Pair/Share (T/P/S; p. 94) provides each student with the opportunity to discuss each concept. That is because in a typical, traditional setting, as soon as the first student calls out the correct answer, it stops the remaining students from thinking through the problem. It takes practice and persistence to create a classroom climate where students are allowed private thinking time and the opportunity to share with a partner prior to the sharing with the larger audience of the class. My objective in designing questions and activities is to provide many opportunities for students to answer questions in partners as well as in small groups. There are opportunities for students to answer questions with a raised hand, but usually after students have been through the process of shared discussion.

For example, in the Exponent unit provides an opportunity to discover the rule when any base (except zero) is raised to a zero the answer is one. After completing an example where a pattern is followed, I ask the students to think individually about the next line in the pattern and then have the partners discuss this with a partner prior to sharing it with the class. Each partner has the opportunity to predict that the next line will be that all bases with a zero exponent equals one. The T/P/S tactic can be used throughout the unit (or any unit) to engage all learners in the activity.

One particularly useful strategy to incorporate into a 'tool box' is that of Concept Attainment. Concept Attainment is a strategy that we use in our daily lives by being particular about our choices—it enables us to recognize and identify those things that are related and those things that are not related. In a classroom, we can develop this sense of discrimination (i.e., learned by rote or with familiar material and familiar contexts) and identification (i.e., learned by inference or with unfamiliar material or unfamiliar contexts) by creating an environment where guessing (e.g., right or wrong, yes or no, same or different) is encouraged. Gagne's (1965) work with learning objectives further develops the idea that teaching and learning objectives move the learner through nine stages starting with initiating interest in a topic to the final stage where the learner can apply the knowledge (Kruse, n.d.). In this unit, I use Concept Attainment to derive the rules for multiplying exponents, dividing exponents, and the power law. Prior to using this strategy in teaching a mathematics concept, I would have developed the concept by playing sorting games with my class.

Watson & Mason (2006) have researched the use of similar examples and not-quite similar examples to shift students to thinking at a higher level—becoming pattern hunters (p. 97). Their approach is similar to Bennett's approach of Concept Attainment using data sets. Data sets also need to provide students with the opportunity to see patterns with the 'yes' data set and determine why the data in the 'no' column does not meet the specific criteria. *Beyond Monet* includes a variety of data sets as a warm up to Concept Attainment. A data set is a set of examples that show items or ideas that *are* or *are not* related to one another on a conceptual level '*yes*' examples and '*no*' examples. In addition to using Concept Attainment to develop the exponent laws, I also include a Jigsaw activity so that expert groups return to their home teams to teach each other the exponent laws. Jigsaw is a very effective tool for teaching and or reviewing the exponent laws. I could convey the same information using direct teaching; however, Concept Attainment piques the natural curiosities of students to solve their inquiries and create their own meanings, as Aoki (1993, p. 204) suggests, and that is a crucial component of curriculum. As a refined user of this strategy, I have continued to develop and extend this activity. One creative twist that I have added is that after I have students sort the data set into 'yes' and 'no' piles, a letter assigned to the back of the 'yes' and the back of the 'no' data card will spell a word, related to the topic, if they are correctly organized. This creates a quick way for students to check their own work.

As we progress through the unit, I am always checking in with students to determine their understanding of the content. Checking is a seemingly simple yet overlooked skill that develops over time and is very useful. As I mentioned previously, one of the quickest and most useful gauges of checking student learning is that of *thumbs up* (i.e., 'I get it'), *thumbs down* (i.e., 'I don't get it') and *thumbs sideways* (i.e., 'I'm unsure'). A quick review of thumbs provides me with crucial assessment information as to whether the class is ready to move on to a new topic or more work with the current concept is required. While writing exponent questions, I might also use questions that have answers from the numbers one to five. Using this approach, I can ask students to hold up the number of fingers represented by the exponent in a question and quickly determine if students can discriminate between a base and an exponent. This simple yet effective process also quickly allows me to make a mental note of those students who require additional help.

In addition to the use of formative assessment tactics, I use a secondary study group to assist those students whom I identified through the learning assessment process as requiring further support. In my class, I have created a culture where students feel safe and secure and will work with me in small groups after the main lesson. Once the majority of students are working on an assignment, I call for volunteers who need additional help with the topic. I may work with students at the whiteboard and review the work we did as a whole group with four or five students. Often, after some clarification, students will fill in the missing gaps and they are able to continue to complete the activities. At other times, I will sit down with a group of four and complete a more intensive review of a topic. Throughout the unit, I will provide opportunities for students who need additional help from me to get the small group or one-on-one help they require. My objective is to provide support and opportunities for all students to reach the Level Three learning outcome (see Table 1 above) as identified in the planning stage of the unit. However, at this point of the process of becoming a pedagogically aware teacher and learner, i.e., through reflection on my practice and reflexively applying my research and practical knowledge to the development of the Exponent unit, I raise even more questions about my own praxis.

Overall, I am happy with the growth I have achieved over the last few years. I feel confident when talking to my peers about instruction and curriculum design. I am still curious about the implementation of new ideas and how new ideas develop and change from the paper plan to the classroom. This unit plan is completed. However, as long as I continue to teach, I will be in a state of flux. I conclude that there is no perfect unit plan, rather the goal for me, is to continue along the quest to become a better teacher and tinkerer. Now that I know that the mythical black binder filled with magical lesson plans does not exist, I know that there is at least a road, which seems like the yellow brick road, that will lead me to a better place, a better praxis. As with any good story, there needs be a happy ending. I hope that this curriculum design helps me, and other teachers who use it, navigate the math curriculum in a more engaging and thought provoking manner. The next step in this journey is to work with my district to publish a selection of the lessons created through this process to be included in the 2011 version of Math 44, a NVSD44 published mathematics curriculum manual (NB: The reader may contact the author for information on the curricular materials referred to herein; see http://www.nvsd44.bc.ca/Math44/math44.html).

Brigitte Gerandol
North Vancouver School District 44
bgerandol@nvsd44.bc.ca

SUSAN K. JOHNSTON

ENVIRONMENTAL SUSTAINABILITY AND ECOLOGICAL SYSTEMS

A curriculum project for grade 10 students at the North Vancouver Outdoor School

My Learning Journey

My fondest memories of elementary school were when I went to play outside. Outside time was usually recess or lunch; there wasn't a lot of outdoor teaching or learning taking place. In junior high school, which lasted from Grades 6-9, the only outdoor experience was in Grade 6 when I went to an outdoor school for 5 days. I loved it. We were exploring the outdoors everyday, looking at bugs and animal tracks learning about nature and the environment. That experience lasted less than a week but I remember it better than my other school experiences. After Grade 9 and moving on to high school, there weren't any opportunities to study outside. Most subjects were confined to the classroom; even science where we learned about animals and the environment was in the classroom. In Grade 11, I took an opportunity to head outside; I volunteered to be a camp counselor for the same outdoor education program I participated in during Grade 6. I thoroughly enjoyed going back to the outdoors to see, guide, and assist the younger students. As for my own learning or education about the environment, there was no official program for the high school students, and this is what I would like to change and improve upon.

My personal experiences, as a student in Calgary, seem to parallel the current North Vancouver Outdoor School (NVOS) model of outdoor learning experiences. It is an amazing place with programs for Grades 3, 4, and 6; however, there are no formal curricular programs for high school students. The elementary aged students attend from 3-5 days and experience an outdoor education in ecology, nature, the traditional ways of the First Nations, and outdoor recreation activities. Similar to my adolescent experience, North Vancouver Grade 10 students get the opportunity to be the camp counselors for the younger students but are not necessarily building on their personal knowledge and learning new information, or learning and doing anything that relates to their Science 10 curriculum. The current Grade 10 life science portions of the curriculum focuses directly on ecological topics that could be taught, explored, and investigated in an outdoor environment. My goal is to change this lack of programming for high school students, most specifically Grade 10 students, by creating a curriculum for the life science portion of the course that

P. Gouzouasis (ed.), Pedagogy in a New Tonality: Teacher Inquiries on Creative Tactics, Strategies, Graphics Organizers, and Visual Journals in the K-12 Classroom, 267–273.

will integrate the outdoors and the current district initiative of Instructional Intelligence strategies.

My curriculum development is centered on the problem of how educators need to inspire the next generation of students given the prescribed Grade 10 life science portion of the curriculum. This program will incorporate a hands-on, outdoor approach to the curriculum where the students become immersed in their local environment. The program incorporates the already successful NVOS site and programs, but also the techniques of Instructional Intelligence (II) tactics, strategies, and graphics organizers presented in *Beyond Monet* (Bennett & Rolheiser, 2001). The Instructional Intelligence based activities are designed with specific curricular topics to provide students the opportunity to explore, develop, and reflect on their knowledge. I have named the program *Environmental Sustainability and Ecological Systems*.

Why Outside?

Have you ever tried to explain the sound a dog makes to a deaf person? It seems trivial and irrelevant to do so, since that person will never hear the sound of a dog. It also seems inappropriate to teach someone about the different plants and animals that live in an environment without being able to be in that environment. When I was 18 years old I wanted to be a Marine Biologist, I lived in Calgary Alberta, the only province of Canada that is surrounded by land. I could have taken the degree at the University of Calgary, but it seemed ridiculous to be in a land locked area trying to study the flora and fauna of the ocean. So I made my way out west to UBC to really find out what the ocean was all about. This is the mentality I think of when I teach the life science portions of the science 10 curricula.

Outdoor Connections

Why is connecting with the outdoors important, why is it important to encourage learning in an outdoor environment? From one perspective, “not only is being outdoors pleasant, its richness and novelty stimulate brain development and function” (Rivkin, 2000). However, the “pleasant nature experience” has been fading for today’s youth. Richard Louv, a journalist and child advocate, has written extensively about something he calls the “Nature-Deficit Disorder.” This disorder was named based on research that more and more children are not connected to their environments, thus causing a variety of learning and attention issues. Louv (2006) describes this disorder in his book as “the human costs of alienation from nature, among them: diminished uses of the senses, attention difficulties, and higher rates of physical and emotional illnesses” (p. 34). Louv is not the first person to make connections between the lack of outdoor play and behavioural issues. There is even more documentation that uncovers the fear of the outdoors and the over scheduling of children (Taylor & Kuo, 2006, p. 124). Evidence for the benefits of free, unstructured play and outdoor learning has been shown in improved test scores, and knowledge gained in comparison with indoor learning (p.

128). When children play in the outdoors it can influence their interest and attitudes toward nature and the environment, which can eventually lead to occupations in outdoor environments (Wells & Lekies, 2006). Wells & Lekies demonstrate that play in the outdoor environment can also influence environmental awareness. Through my research I found a quote that really spoke to my underlying reasons for developing a curriculum for the Grade 10 learner, "If a substantial portion of the population has little or no interaction with pristine natural environments as children, how will that affect their lifelong attitudes toward such places?" (Lougheed, 2008, p. 438).

Environmental Education

In this day and age it is nearly impossible to open a newspaper, turn on the television, or even surf the internet without seeing or hearing about the damage happening to our environment. Oil spills, air pollution, pesticides, global warming, and excessive energy use are commonly mentioned in the daily news. "While the media bombard us with images of melting icecaps and rain forest destruction, it is vital to counterbalance this with messages that provide vision of a livable future" (Cramer, 2008, p. 285). Given the prevalence of these issues, there has been a surge toward environmental protection programs, green movements, recycling programs, and a variety of awareness programs to educate society. Most of these programs give hope for the health and sustainability of our global community, and as time goes on each generation seems to be developing more concern for the environment. This concern is promising as long as progress is made, otherwise, environmental degradation will continue. The curriculum for the Grade 10 *"Environmental Sustainability and Ecological Systems"* focuses on engaging the learner to understand sustainability not only as a concept, but also as a starting point to make a difference in their local and global community.

Many environmental education programs aim to build public awareness about environmental issues by providing opportunities so people can acquire the knowledge needed to improve the environmental problem. (Ballentyne & Packer, 2006, p. 1). This acquisition of knowledge is essential to produce meaningful programs to support the environmental cause. In the program I am designing at North Vancouver Outdoor School (NVOS), students will be inspired through activities and lessons that engage them on a variety of levels and will ultimately inspire local environmental action. As stated by Hungerford & Volk (1990) "the ultimate aim of education is shaping human behavior" (p. 8). I believe this to be especially true with respect to the topic of sustainability of ecosystems. As an educator, my goal is to encourage students to understand the changes humanity needs to make. "Environmental education must look outward to the community. It should involve the individual in an active problem-solving process within the context of specific realities, and it should encourage initiative, a sense of responsibility and commitment to build a better tomorrow" (UNESCO, 1980, p. 12). We need to be concerned about the ecological issues that will be tackled by the students using *their* ideas that *they* will implement.

Reasons for the Development of a Curriculum

Not only can outdoor learning provide students with a sense of control over their learning, it can give them a freedom not available in the traditional classroom (Lai, 1999, p. 247). My curriculum is loosely based on the analysis by Monroe, Andrews & Biedenweg (2007), who demonstrated that when developing environmental education programs there are four essential categories for success: "(1) to convey information, (2) to build understanding, (3) to improve skills, and (4) to enable sustainable actions" (p. 205). In my particular situation, the information is conveyed by means of the classroom teacher and NVOS staff; the building of understanding occurs within the Instructional Intelligence Strategies and through visual journaling; the improvement of skills comes with practice and investigation; and the enabling of sustainable action revolves around an action-based project with the student in control, as a leader and designer of their learning.

Most of the research defending the importance of children and their connections with nature has focused on the pre-adolescent. In my opinion, I feel the adolescent age, 13–17, is the group that is often overlooked and that this age group is often stereotyped as an "uncaring age." Throughout my experiences teaching youth aged 12–16, I have noticed the desire of teenagers to want to make a difference. Often, they just need a good, strong, inspiring mentor to lead them in the right direction.

Instructional Intelligence and the Curriculum

In combination with the outdoor environment and use of the outdoor school facilities, creative, student centered, instructional strategies will be implemented into the curriculum I have created. Bennett discusses the rational for using instructional processes from the perspective of teaching as "complex;" he understands that "real world does not work in rows" and that the strategies he describes places "learning in the hands and the minds of the learners" (Bennett & Rolheiser, 2001, p. 28). In the traditional classroom it is easy for a teacher to become the main delivery mode of knowledge. Teachers always struggle with how to engage all learners when we are given a wide variety of students who possess a variety of background knowledge, economic status, and aptitudes. When implementing creative, instructional intelligence strategies the student is in control of their learning. They themselves become the delivery method through their involvement and engagement of the subject matter. I have personally seen this result in my classrooms and have had multiple conversations with other professionals who have also seen the impact creative, student-centered, instructional strategies can make on a classroom environment. The largest impact that I have seen and appreciate is with the engagement of every student in a variety of curricular contexts.

Youth and the Environment

Youth of today are exposed to an increasing amount of facts concerning the environment. Making sense of this complex information is not easy. The amount, let alone the information itself, can be overwhelming. Also, in terms of environmental degradation, it can be somewhat disheartening. When Rachel Carson published *Silent Spring* in 1962, she launched an environmental movement with her in-depth analysis of pesticides and their effects on the environment. In 2011, we continue to face threats to our environment, similar to problems raised by Carson and even more devastating catastrophes that are harming planet Earth. In my experiences, I have found that youth possess an optimism that is different from adult perspectives. As educators, we need to tap into this optimism and use it to inspire youth to become environmentally responsible citizens. Interestingly, Palmberg & Kuru (2000) believe that "responsible environmental behavior is a learned response or action, and that increased awareness and knowledge of environmental action strategies contribute to increased motivation to take action" (p. 35). I personally want to believe that humans naturally care about their environment and want to make a difference. One could say that my thinking is extremely naïve, as it is very apparent that there are many careless people who do not respect the environment. Being an environmentally responsible person is not an innate ability or skill. Therefore, we must inspire our youth to take action, by improving our science curricula, so that they may invoke responsible actions and leadership.

Art and Science Connections: Visual Journaling

Incorporated into the curriculum is the documentation of the student's thoughts and ideas in a visual journal. I have used visual journals in my own studies and find them to be a place of great reflection, idea collecting, and knowledge building. The visual journal is not only a reflective piece but also a questioning piece. Science is a natural setting to ask questions and explore ideas. In the "*Environmental Sustainability and Ecological Systems*" curriculum (Johnston, 2010), students will be encouraged to question and think about the topics and ideas presented during the course. The integration of art with science compliments each other because they share many commonalities, for example " both disciplines are based on observation and experimentation, they both involve problem solving and reexamine theory, they both encourage reflection, assessment and openness to change, they also both respect historical tradition." (Chessin & Zander, 2006, p. 43). Not only are art and science engaging avenues for questioning, but also creativity. In a conversation with Sir Ken Robinson, a recognized leader in the field of creativity, Robinson states, "creativity is a disciplined process that requires skill, knowledge, and control" (Azzam, 2009, p. 24). The discipline of creativity within the visual journal is a place for expression, and a place to build on the students' own personal interests eventually working them into an action-based environmental project.

Educators inadvertently stifle the creative process in the classroom. Between the pressures of standardized testing and the pressures of delivering the prescribed curriculum, creativity can be squelched and lost. "Children have an innate sense of curiosity; unfortunately the school curriculum and focus on test scores draw the science away from investigation and towards memorization." (Smith, 2002, p. 588). Visual journals can be a place of creativity, questioning and curiosity without the added pressure of the students' wondering if they are doing everything right. The ultimate goal of the visual journal is for the student to uncover a topic of passion and develop it into an action-based program that can be created during their stay at Outdoor School and implemented when they return back to school. Most people care about what they know about, and with their keen passion and concern, "student ownership and engagement are much more likely to emerge when the students have had the chance to participate in the creation of their own learning agendas." (Smith, 2002, p.593). Yilmaz et al. found that when students knew more about the scientific concepts there was an increase in positive action towards a variety of environmental issues. (2004, p. 1544) The goal and outcome of the Visual Journal is a "learning agenda" a place to explore, develop and combine their thoughts and "teachings" into a plan of action.

Final Thoughts

I am not only concerned with Louv's "Nature-Deficit Disorder" but also with children's lack of connection with the environment and their lack of knowledge about the natural world in which they depend upon. It is always interesting to question students about where their water comes from, as well as other commonly used planetary resources. The movement toward common outdoor activities can directly impact the participation and attitudes of children as they enter adulthood in a positive way when issues surround environmentalism (Wells & Lekies, 2006). From that perspective, outdoor participation within the curriculum should encourage a respect for the natural environment. "Teachers who incorporate the study of the natural world into their curriculum reap the rich benefits of simply getting students outside the classroom and taking advantage of their curiosity" (Smith, 2002, p. 589).

Throughout my teaching career, I have been able to take both Grade 4 and Grade 6 students to NVOS and each time the students had unique and engaging experiences that could not be mimicked in the classroom. I remember when I had a group of Grade 6 students at the NVOS, a deer had washed up onto the shore of the river. It was frozen solid, and had died from a natural cause. The staff at NVOS dragged the deer into the forest to decompose, a topic of ecology that is discussed but rarely seen. A few days later I took the students to see the deer. It had definitely changed in appearance, and most of the changes were due to other animals scavenging and eating its remains. We could see the tracks of the animals that came to feast on the deer. Teachers often talk about those moments in teaching, those "a-ha moments" where they feel like everything is clicking. This was one was an actual demonstration of the food chain, "the wild taking care of itself." The reactions of the students were also something I will never forget, especially when one student cried because she was a vegetarian. About a week after returning to the classroom, I was emailed the most recent photos of the deer. It was completely stripped and gutted—only the skeleton remained. To me this is an idea demonstration of what outdoor learning can do. It can expose students to the world they are studying by enabling them to experience it as it occurs.

There is evidence that when students are immersed in the environment during an environmental program, their attitudes toward environmental issues are heightened (Ballantyne & Packer, 2006, p. 1). Researchers have also demonstrated that students are more able to come to an understanding through hands-on experiences than just classroom experiences (Smith-Sebasto & Cavern, 2006, p. 14). In the development of the "*Environmental Sustainability and Ecological Systems*" curriculum (Johnston, 2010), a hands-on, experiential outdoor learning environment is essential to the success of the program. The opportunity to be immersed in the "learning" is important not only for the students, but also for teachers to enable them to utilize the environment to suit their educational and instructional needs. So, get out and learn!

Susan K. Johnston
North Vancouver School District 44
SuJohnston@nvsd44.bc.ca

CORRINE REID

THE ART AND SCIENCE OF TEACHING MATHEMATICS

One teacher's creative journey

As a math and science teacher, I am often perplexed by students' dislike of the subjects I teach. Particularly mathematics, where students are reluctant to learn and are often satisfied with not understanding the concepts we cover in the classroom; they attribute their lack of understanding to a deficiency of innate abilities or skills with respect to mathematics. After only a couple of years of experience as an educator in the math classroom, I have realized that there is a shortfall in an inherent enjoyment of math among many students. As a trained science teacher, I find it easy to create a science environment where students are busy learning and exploring, easily relating the concepts we cover to students' everyday lives. As the teacher, I never get bored teaching a subject that instills notions of exploration, such as science. Mathematics, on the other hand, can sometimes be boring and lack opportunities for exploration, often leading to a "chalk and talk" type of environment where the teacher delivers and the students take a passive role in knowledge acquisition. I am not necessarily looking for merely a "fun" environment where learning may or may not occur—my goal is to create a math environment that instills a desire for investigation and exploration where students are engaged in the learning process. This paper explores my journey through a process of creating a mathematics curriculum that "lets students in on the process of creating, inventing, conjecturing, and experimenting" (Cuoco, Goldenberg & Mark, 1996, p. 2).

Teaching for the North Vancouver School District (NVSD44), I took advantage of their forward thinking educational directions where Instructional Intelligence (II) became the heart of the district's teaching philosophy. Although II is not a "new" approach to teaching, "it implies a collective expertise that assures that all teachers and students are actively engaged in challenging, relevant, and interesting learning situations—situations that connect to their past experiences and engage them in constructing new experiences" (Bennett & Roheiser, 2001, p. 4). Through the search for enhancing excellence in education, NVSD44 had set in motion an educational reform whereby teacher directed curricula was being replaced by student-centered classrooms; multiple teaching tactics, strategies, graphics organizers and collaborative learning were used to support the reform toward the creation of classrooms that engage students and promote mastery of learning.

The main premise of II is to provide the teacher with a toolbox of tactics, strategies, and organizers that will help them to become creative, effective

P. Gouzouasis (ed.), Pedagogy in a New Tonality: Teacher Inquiries on Creative Tactics, Strategies, Graphics Organizers, and Visual Journals in the K-12 Classroom, 275–284.

teachers. The district put on many workshops that focused on this adopted philosophy such as a summer institute where teachers in the district presented their trials and tribulations with the teaching strategies and tactics. I also attended keynotes featuring Barrie Bennett speak about how II is a path through which teachers can provide an exciting environment where students experience learning. I was hooked. I connected with this philosophy, an educational system that helps to develop master teachers but also supports the diverse learners that is found in every classroom.

> The quality of the teacher in the classroom is the most important factor in raising student achievement. (Hopkins, 2008, p. 737)

I was fortunate enough to be accepted into a masters program, a collaboration between the University of British Columbia (UBC) and North Vancouver School District (NVSD44), that focuses on Instructional Intelligence and curriculum leadership. Although I was only two years out of teacher's college, I felt that I went into the field unprepared to teach in ways I envisioned. After one year of teacher preparation, I felt that I was left with a lot of unanswered questions and only a very basic understanding of how to create an effective classroom experience. I was impatient and wanted to develop my teaching practice to become an "expert" teacher. The NVSD and UBC provided this opportunity. NVSD also supported teachers to work with other like-minded, passionate teachers within the district to revamp their teaching strategies and their classrooms. This was my opportunity to become an educator who could possess, in Barrie Bennett's words, "a rich and meaningful repertoire of ways to assess learning, a deep knowledge and ability to intersect multiple content areas, an extensive understanding of how students learn, an extensive repertoire of instructional methods that you can integrate in a variety of ways, the ability to wisely go about the process of educational change, [and] a personality that encourages students to walk into your room." (n.d., para. 5). Moreover, this was my chance to learn to become an effective teacher where my "lessons are clear, accurate and rich in examples and demonstrations" (Leinhardt, 1986, p. 52).

As an initiative of the NVSD, the implementation of II has been the genesis of improving the conditions of learning for students across the district. No longer is the teacher-centered classroom the norm in most of our schools, as we are in an era of change where active classrooms and student involvement are fundamental (Farris, 1991, p. 49). However, for this change to occur, we must understand the system through which it is occurring. The success of the initiative "depends on a coordinated "bundle" of innovations—generally affecting several groups of stakeholders—that results in a coherent system after implementation" (Ellsworth, 2001, p. 24). I was to become a part of this "bundle" of innovations, becoming a leader in the district with other teachers so that we could become "change agents [that] are career-long learners, without which [we] would not be able to stimulate students to be continuous learners" (Fullan, 1993, p. 13).

> It is the supreme art of the teacher to awaken joy in creative expression and knowledge. (Albert Einstein, from Longworth, 2003)

According to the British Columbia Ministry of Education, "learning requires the active participation of the student, people learn in a variety of ways and at different rates and learning is both an individual and a group process" (Math 8 & 9 IRP's, p. 11). The ministry has set out a list of Prescribed Learning Outcomes (PLOs) that we as teachers have to meet throughout a year of study. The Grade 8 and 9 mathematics curriculum is divided into eight concept organizers—Number, Patterns, Variables and Equations, Measurement, 3-D Objects and 2-D Shapes, Transformations, Data Analysis and Chance and Uncertainty. Moreover, with recent curricular changes in British Columbia, the Ministry also outlines seven mathematical processes that must be met—Communication, Connections, Mental Mathematics and Estimation, Problem Solving, Reasoning, Technology, and Visualization. This is a tall order that we as educators must meet. The Ministry guidelines are backed by sound research and pedagogy that is beginning to focus on teaching mathematics *for understanding*.

Since 1989, there has been much modernization in the way mathematics is to be presented in the classroom. No longer is mathematics about following arbitrary rules and algorithms as outlined by the teacher, but is about "engaging in the science of pattern and order" (Van de Walle 2005, p 18). As an effective teacher, one has to juggle many roles. Teachers are under pressure to cover the entire curriculum in a short amount of time in classrooms that have a number of students at various levels of cognition and achievement, as well as students who possess behavioral issues. Creating lessons and tasks that support all the situations and issues that a teacher faces in the classroom can be difficult if not impossible at times.

Many mathematics teachers spend hours debating what it means for students to understand mathematics. Pirie & Kieren (1994) have developed a theory that is based on a constructivist model where understanding of the whole is a dynamic process that folds back on itself so that the path of learning is not necessarily linear. Such a model supports many of the students' learning patterns that I have encountered. Learning does not occur in one direction or through one path, thus I believe that understanding students' metacognition of mathematics learning greatly increases an educators' ability to teach mathematics for understanding. The theory proposed by Pirie & Kieren (1994) supports the notion of folding back "which reveals the non-unidirectional nature of coming to understanding mathematics" (p. 173). As teachers, we need to "focus on designing sequences of tasks that invite learners to reflect on the effect of their actions in the hope that they will recognize key relationships" (Watson, 2006, p. 93). Students need to be given the time to explore and to fold back on their continuation of learning. This theory gives educators "a frame for planning and engaging in mathematics lessons and, in addition, to make observations about curriculum development" (Pirie & Kieren, 1994, p. 78).

Task development and design is crucial to a teacher's success in the mathematics classroom. Often, students take a passive and unmotivated approach to learning new concepts. This is often supported by the teacher's assumptions that students have little or no prior knowledge of the content to be covered, relying on a teacher-centered model of instruction. "Often, task designers concentrate on content rather than on the nature of the cognitive activity the tasks generate or on the classroom milieu" (Swan, 2007, p. 219). Teachers need to find tasks that support an active constructivist approach such that the learners can be the experts and use their own prior knowledge to help with the construction of new knowledge. It is important that task design focuses on "multiple entry points, allowing students to take on challenges at different levels" (Swan, 2007, p. 219). Increasing student involvement in the classroom allows students to engage in the discussion process of concepts and to include collaboration in the mathematics classroom, students will gain a better understanding through a constructivist model of learning.

Using the research of Watson & Mason (2006), as well as Swan (2007) and Pirie & Kieren (1994), I was able to gain a better understanding of how to create lessons and activities that supports a constructivist learning environment where students are engaged in "classifying, interpreting, comparing, evaluating, and creating" (Swan, 2007, p. 219). The goal of my project was to provide teachers with a group of lessons that helps them to dig through the PLO's as prescribed by the Ministry of Education and to teach lessons that engages the students in mathematics. Often times, it is not the mathematics teachers who teach Grade 8 and 9 mathematics, it is usually a course left to the administration to fill with an extra teacher. Although mathematics is taught to all students from Grades 8 through 11, Grade 8 always seems to be a minor concern to administration. Prestage & Perks (2007) state that teacher's personal beliefs and characteristics of what it means to be a teacher become apparent when developing and teaching lessons. Often, teachers who do not understand the complexities of math rely on how they learned math, which usually takes the form of a teacher centered classroom where the teacher turned to a formula and applied it. Many teachers think that they simply need to teach the tasks that are illustrated in the textbook, without bringing an awareness of what the students bring. Prestage & Perks (2007) illustrate a model of how teachers should plan for classroom events where the teachers are aware of the learner knowledge, the teacher knowledge, the curriculum knowledge, and pedagogical knowledge (see *Figure 1*). Prestage & Perks "believe that 'good' teachers need to reflect upon these classroom events not simply to consider their success or failure for the pupils but to reconsider their own personal understandings of mathematics, to reflect upon the 'why' not only of teaching but also of mathematics" (pp. 382–383).

As to what part of the curriculum that I was to work on, I asked myself what concepts students struggle with and how I can help them become more successful. I have found that more often than not, it is (1) the basic skill sets that are not well developed and (2) the basic skill sets may be lacking in the students that I teach. Subsequently, students struggle all the way through, hating every minute of math instruction and every second of math homework.

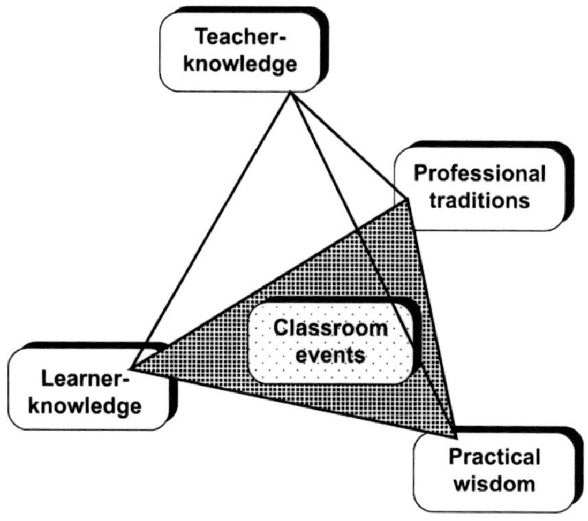

Figure 1. Planning for classroom events (Prestage and Perks, 2007, p. 382).

Teaching is a complex combination of many forms of knowledge.
Pente (2004, p. 92)

For the present inquiry, number sense became my focus of Grade 8 mathematics. Number sense is an enormous and complex topic as it is the underlying basis for all mathematical processes that students encounter. According to Howden (in Van De Walle & Folk, 2005, p. 93), number sense is described as "a good intuition about numbers and their relationships. It develops gradually as a result of exploring numbers, visualizing them in a variety of contexts, and relating them in ways that are not limited by traditional algorithms." Students often lack an understanding of what a number is and how to use that number in operations. Moreover, they lack an inherent skill of working with numbers and playing with numbers. They rarely try to construct their own learning, often turning to the teacher for the "right" answer and for the pattern to be highlighted for them. Many students are very good at following the arbitrary rules for various algorithms—long division, addition and subtraction of numbers. However, do they know why they are doing what they do? Do they understand how it works? Have they had the opportunity to find their own way of doing mathematics that is not "the teacher's way"? Mathematics is founded on complex symbols and abstract concepts; for students to develop and grow in their mathematics skills requires students to be aware of the metacognitive processes.

Rather than being frustrated with the lack of number sense the students possess coming into Grade 8, I decided to take it into my own hands and to work with the Ministry's guidelines and the research behind Instructional Intelligence to develop a hands-on curriculum that removes the teacher from the center of the classroom and focuses on student involvement and engagement in a constructivist environment. It is one thing to prescribe for teachers to teach something, it is another to provide the teachers with the tools to create a student-centered classroom that focuses on math habits of mind.

Each lesson begins with a discussion of the big ideas that will be addressed in the lesson. It is a synopsis of what the students should be able to know and what they should be able to demonstrate at the conclusion of the lesson. This component of the lesson gives the teacher an idea of the concepts that will be taught and link closely to the PLO's. Following the big idea is the focus activity, this is an activity that takes about ten to fifteen minutes at the beginning of the class to get the students thinking about what will be happening during the lesson. These activities are designed to get students minds on math and to allow the teacher to "pay attention to the knowledge, beliefs, attitudes, and skills students bring to the classroom" (Keeley, 2008).

> Sometimes I feel as though I am going around and around in cycles, overlapping, revisiting, coming back to the same questions.
>
> Naths (2004, p. 121)

Throughout the process of creating this project I have had a hard time considering myself as an a/r/tographer—an artist, researcher, teacher, and writer of my experiences in those realms (Irwin & deCosson, 2004; Springgay, Irwin, Leggo, & Gouzouasis, 2008). Initially considering myself as a linear, scientific person who values the beauty of logical thinking where thoughts and actions follow a prescribed order, my journey has not been without its twists and turns combined with resistance and fear. Throughout this experience I have found myself going forwards and backwards, inwards and outwards many times over, (re)writing, (re)searching, and (re)learning many of my ideas, values, and lessons that I have (re)created. I am trying to trust in my skills as an educator and as a student to trust the process, as Shaun McNiff (1998) writes, "Trusting the process is based on a belief that something valuable will emerge when we step into the unknown" (p. 27). I try often to visualize what my curriculum project will look like, what the unknown will look like but the many starts and stops that I have made make me wonder if I know what the end looks like, if I know why I am doing this. However, McNiff states, "it has always been the unexpected happenings that have produced the most gratifying results. I prepare by establishing a simple framework of what I want to do, but I always leave room for what is generated by the event" (p. 13). I have begun to understand what is meant by a/r/tography—it is about finding your path amongst the trials and tribulations that allows us to find who we are and who we will become; at the beginning, the end is not known, it is found.

> Creations are like seeds that find their way into tiny chinks in a granite ledge and take rood in the smallest deposits of soil.
>
> McNiff (1998, p. 134)

When I began this journey with Instructional Intelligence, I was frightened that my lack of experience would show immediately. That the other expert teachers that had joined the cohort would immediately pick up on my naïveté and recognize that I was not a "master" teacher, that I needed to put in the years of teaching to reach the point of becoming a "true" teacher researcher. I soon realized that I had joined a group of like-minded educators whose values regarding education complemented mine and that they were the support I needed to become a better teacher. As a cohort, Instructional Intelligence was instilled as a means to create an engaging classroom, but for many of us, the idea of a classroom where the teacher does not transmit information in stand and deliver mode was not in the repertoire of our experiences as graduate student learners. I was pushed many times to take risks, to try tactics and strategies that I was not comfortable with, or familiar with, to use with my students. There was fear of failure, but also a knowingness that mistakes made would help me to become a better, reflexive practitioner. But "in a strange way, the negative performances invariably deepen[s] the process" (McNiff, 1998, p.192), and changing my practice would not be able to occur unless I was willing to let go of my fears and doubts and to trust the art and science of teaching, to trust "becoming pedagogical." I was learning about teaching again, so I had faith in the notion that "planned pedagogic act[s] for which we have certain expectations of the potential of the activity . . . extends students' learning" (Prestage & Perks, 2007, pp. 388–389).

I wanted to break away from the traditional classroom that I had grown up with and to become a teacher who creates "meaningful and powerful learning environments. This implies creative instruction; it implies intelligent instruction; it implies an ever-deepening understanding of subject knowledge" (Bennet & Rolheiser, 2001, p. 4). I was on the right path but my journey was not without its detours. I started out with "small and well-intentioned actions [that will] ultimately contribute to a greater effect" (McNiff, 1998, p. 98), focusing on what it was that I wanted to achieve in a lifetime as a teacher. Curriculum had been my focus as within it there is a creative element that needed to be awakened. I take great joy in spending hours looking into the various ways that a lesson can be taught and the multitude of tactics and strategies that can be used to help students to develop an understanding of concepts.

The mathematics curriculum project became a focus of mine that satisfied my creative spirit yet focused on sound mathematical research that brings about the idea of math as an explorative subject—to use what I was learning in my course of studies to create lessons that illustrates to others the passion that I have for teaching and the joy that can be found in the creative process of lesson design and implementation. I needed to find who I was as a teacher, through who I was becoming as a researcher and artful inquirer. As Patti Pente (2004) states, "it is the entire person who draws from many sources in order to teach" (p. 92). Reflection on what I was teaching and how I was teaching it became the focus of blending theory and practice together.

> Of all the virtues we can learn no trait is more useful, more essential for survival, and more likely to improve the quality of life than the ability to transform adversity into an enjoyable challenge.
>
> Csikszentmihalyi (1990, p. 200)

Praxis. In the world of educational research, I find it awe-inspiring that there are a multitude of new words and terms. However, as an educated person, I sometimes feel lost treading through the litany of terminology. I think this was the first impediment to accepting my role as an artist-teacher-researcher. In quantitative studies, procedures require one to establish a hypothesis, perform a test, use the data to determine a result, and write concrete conclusions. The answers are in the numbers, whereas in qualitative research, the field is left wide open for interpretation and judgment such that results become subjective to the views of the researcher. The path I was to take was to use praxis, turning theory into practice, to create my path of educational understanding and to find myself as a teacher in the process.

The topic was easy to choose, Grade 8 mathematics number sense. The organizer for my lesson plans was the British Columbia's Ministry of Education Guidelines. My inspiration was Barrie Bennett and his ideas surrounding Instructional Intelligence (II). I had been through almost two years of graduate work and readings that focused on changing teachers' instructional repertoire in the classroom. I was ready for the challenge to put my ideas and those of others together in a series of lessons that compliment the directives of the school district that I was employed with. But I was still left staring at a blank page. I had been living "in a state of constant search and exploration," yet I knew that "creative ways of looking at the world offer endless new twists inversions, and challenges to the hegemony of any idea" (McNiff, 1998, p. 69). I needed to put pen to paper and let my ideas flow. However, as the mother of a newborn son and a teacher without a job, I faced a lot of obstacles to my path of teacher-researcher enlightenment.

My goal was to produce a document of lesson plans that would help other teachers but also demonstrate my skills as a forward thinking teacher, essentially an expert teacher in training (see http://www.nvsd44.bc.ca/Math44/math44.html for details on the author's curriculum contribution). But I was juggling a lot of roles. It took time for me to realize that to realize my ideas, I had to accept that "a teacher [is] one who acquires specialized skills and performs in the classroom to a more holistic view of a teacher whose multiple dimensions, background, values, beliefs, and subject knowledge are all important aspects of her/his teaching" (Pente, 2004, p. 92). That the roles that I have taken on in my life—mother, wife, teacher, coach, researcher, and student—would all help me to develop my pedagogical self.

I needed to sit down and write because "[c]reation is a process of emanation. Nothing will happen unless we start working and allow the practice of our particular disciplines to mix with the streams of ideas and experiences that are constantly moving through daily life" (McNiff, 1998, p. 33). Once I began to write and create lessons, I was amazed at the ease and flow that exuded from the endeavor. I was able to find research that complimented and resonated with my values and ideals.

> The way to grow while enjoying life is to create a higher form of order out of the entropy that is an inevitable condition of living. This means taking each

new challenge not as something to be repressed or avoided, but as an opportunity for leaning and for improving skills.

Csikszentmihalyi (1990, p. 172)

As I near the end of my journey, I reflect upon the beginning of this learning process and ask myself what it was that I wanted to achieve through this process of teacher regeneration. I began two and half years ago hoping to develop skills that would help me in the classroom to become a more effective teacher. My goal was to improve my instructional practice and to build a more effective classroom where students are engaged in the learning process. Through connections with other educators, I am engaged in the lifelong process of becoming a more effective teacher, with the hope of becoming a "master" teacher. Through every course, every task, and every doubt, I realized that for me to become a better teacher I needed to be both reflective and reflexive (Etherington, 2004; Steier, 1991). Along the way I have come across the stories of who I am and what I am going to become as a teacher—(re)searcher. I have also realized that the path to becoming a creative, effective teacher in the classroom is an ongoing process that never ends.

Traditionally, all lessons end with some form of assessment, to check into what has been learned and what still needs to be learned. I feel that through these past two and a half years, I have developed a repertoire of teaching tactics and strategies that have made my job as a teacher much easier and much more effective. I set out looking for clarity in how to teach effectively and I think that I found what I was looking for. I am still learning and struggling with the process of becoming pedagogical, of becoming an effective teacher. I think that I will always be a lifelong learner, searching for a better understanding of curriculum and development. I enjoy the process, the creative element of developing lessons that can be enjoyed by myself and as well as my students. Even though there are times that I have come across obstacles that have made me want to quit, I have realized after much reflection that I needed this experience to gain mastery of the art of teaching. I am learning to take the leap, to take risks in the classroom, because if I do not then nothing has been learned nor will it be learned.

"What is an experience unless it is reflected upon and connected to the world?" (Naths, 2004, p. 124). This experience has connected me to the world of education in a way that I would never have imagined. I have made contacts with educators from Kindergarten through Grade 12 in many districts. Most importantly, it has taught me the importance of talking with others about pedagogy—the art and science of teaching. I am creating a community of learners in my classrooms and I too am using this model to develop my community of educators. Through sharing what we are learning and sharing how to improve our learning, we are building sound pedagogy in an out of our classrooms. I am "providing opportunities for students [and myself] to make discoveries through [our] own investigations" (Keeley, 2008, p.11). Where do I go from here? My story as a teacher has not ended as I prepare for the closure of this chapter. My journey is going to take me many places that will help me to develop and create lessons that encourages and promotes learning within my students and within myself.

> The completion of this art piece is the beginning of the next level of inquiry. Thus, this work of art is a pause in process. Pente (2004, p. 101)

Corrine Reid
North Vancouver School District 44
ckinnon@nvsd44.bc.ca

JENNIFER MASSOUD

RECONSIDERING MATHEMATICAL TASK DESIGN

Instructional Intelligence	Intelligences are multiple
Never heard of it?!	New ways to meet diverse needs
Sorting	Thinking in a new way
Tasks	Exploring
Reviewing the chapter	Letting go of the power/center stage
Unknowns exposed	Letting the students lead the way
Classifying	Investigating
Together in pairs and groups	Graphic organizers
Informing our next lesson	Extending our assessment pieces
Outlining activities and strategies	New instructional methods
New meanings and connections made	Construct deeper meaning
All inclusive	Examine how we learn
Learning from your peers	

Introduction

In January of 2008 I walked into Leo Marshall Education Centre without knowing exactly what would be ahead of me for the next two and a half years. I applied to the UBC Masters Program in Curriculum Studies with a focus on instructional intelligence (II). I had no idea what instructional intelligence was and had no idea who Barrie Bennett was. Why would someone want to join a program that they had no idea about? Well, the description of the program was as follows: "This program is designed to respond to the interests and concerns of teachers who wish to become curriculum leaders in school districts. The cohort theme is to *encourage and support teachers who wish to "investigate their practices"* through Barrie Bennett's (2006, 2009) notions of "Instructional Intelligence" ("II") in order to challenge, learn, explore, and renew their understanding of how their engagement with students and curriculum plays a critical role in education." Even without knowing anything about 'II,' the description resonated with me. I had been teaching high school mathematics for five years and had recently taken on a leadership role within my school to coordinate and facilitate the running of the

P. Gouzouasis (ed.), Pedagogy in a New Tonality: Teacher Inquiries on Creative Tactics, Strategies, Graphics Organizers, and Visual Journals in the K-12 Classroom, 285–298.

International Baccalaureate Middle Years Programme. I wanted to become a curriculum leader, I wanted to investigate my practice, and I really wanted to focus on the quality of my engagement with students.

As teachers we ask our students to take risks everyday by trying new things, engaging with material they have never seen before, and finding new ways to become fluent with this new material. As their teacher, how could I ask them to jump into the unknown with me if I wasn't doing that myself? This is how my students and I began our journey into the unknown world of II and mathematics.

In the present inquiry, I intend to look at various ways of teaching and learning mathematics. I will focus on what Barrie Bennett (2006, 2009) refers to as "Instructional Strategies" to create tasks for learning linear and quadratic expressions. I will investigate the design and development process of task creation. I will also take some time to focus on what Bennett (2006, 2009) refers to as "Curriculum Organizers," and more specifically on the notion of "habits of mind" (Cucco, Goldenberg, & Mark, 1996). Since I don't want to simply teach students mathematics concepts, but rather teach skills that help students approach many types of problems in mathematics and in other disciplines, "habits of mind" provided an excellent lens for doing so.

Task Creation Reflection

The first instructional strategy I decided to use was matching and sorting. To begin the process of creating the task I created what Tabach & Freidlander (2010) refer to as the mathematical agenda, deciding what main concepts I'd like to address. I chose slope, y-intercept, parallel lines, perpendicular lines, graphing lines, $y = mx+b$ form, $ax+by+c = 0$ form. Using Swan's (2007, 2008) ideas on the types of tasks that encourage concept development, I worked at creating a task that was mindful of those elements (NB: examples may be obtained form the author).

ELEMENT 1 - CLASSIFYING MATHEMATICAL OBJECTS

I provided three classifying opportunities for the students: (1) *To discriminate between objects* – How is a graph with a slope of 2 different than a graph with a slope of -2?, (2) *To recognize properties* – The relationship between a graph and its slope, and (3) *To use mathematical language and definitions* – How can we recognize parallel and perpendicular lines given equations or graphs?

ELEMENT 2 - INTERPRETING MULTIPLE REPRESENTATIONS

(also recommended by Tabach & Friedlander, through the work of Ainsworth, Bibby, and Wood, 1998)

The interpretation students were required to engage in was the recognition of (1) *Different representations* – two equivalent but different algebraic forms, and a graphical representations and (2) *Distracters or common misconceptions* – the switching of the slope and y-intercept ($y = 3x+2$ versus $y = 2x+3$), having no coefficient in front of x, same slope but positive rather than negative ($y = x$ versus y

$= -x$), equation with the constant term before the variable term ($y = 4 + x$) rather than after.

ELEMENT 3 - CREATING PROBLEMS

When creating the mathematical problem, I considered the sequencing of the task so that the students would work through the matching activities. Once they had completed the activities they were asked to create their own examples (Friedlander, Hershkowitz, & Arcavi, 1989). The way I tried to organize the curriculum through this task provided students the opportunity to develop the following habits of mind (Cuoco, Goldenberg, & Mark, 1996): (1) *Describers* – if working with a partner, students have the opportunity to describe their mental process of matching equations to their graphs, (2) *Tinkerers* – students play with linear equations and working to find algebraic equivalents, (3) *Visualizers* – students visualize relationships between graphs and equations, parallel and perpendicular lines, and (4) *Inventors* – on a simple level students are able to create their own examples of linear relationships.

My Observations and Reflections

I observed that when matching activities offered multiple possible answers, more discussion occurred in the classroom because there was more uncertainty (i.e., deciding whether both representations were correct). That is why I included multiple possible matches for perpendicular equations (i.e., $y = -2x + 3$ matches both $y = 1/2x - 2$ and $2y - x + 10 = 0$). In that way, I hoped to foster a discussion about the definition of perpendicular lines and a recognition that the importance lies in the slope rather than the y-intercept.

Going through the process of creating this task opened my eyes to another tactic of getting students to play and engage with mathematical concepts. I started thinking about all the different mathematical concepts that could suit this type of task (e.g., quadratics, factoring, fractions, trigonometry, number facts, and more). A lack of class time to do exploratory or hands on activities may sometimes prevent me from doing some of these creative tasks, but I have learned that these types of tasks are not overly time consuming. Moreover, they offer deep learning opportunities. It seems to me that students are able to better understand the connections between various representations when they are required to match them. Also, this understanding is further extended when they create their own examples. If the task is created with an awareness to include distracters, so that the opportunity to make common mistakes is available, students have the opportunities to discuss and debate those mistakes. This may provide learners with a fuller understanding, i.e., an understanding that might be difficult to achieve simply by doing questions from a textbook or a teacher telling them to avoid making these common mistakes.

Going through the matching task, the classroom reminded me of the importance of *discussion* in mathematics. Typically, we are so focused on the doing and writing of mathematics that we forget that another level of understanding for other types of learners can be reached by explaining one's mathematical thought processes, debating a mathematical concept, or simply by listening to someone else's approach.

New Ways of Thinking About the Notion of Factoring Trinomials

Throughout this section of my inquiry I will be referring to $x^2+bx+c = (x+p)(x+q)$, where b is the coefficient of the x term and c is the constant in the trinomial with factors $(x+p)(x+q)$, where p and q are constants (NB: examples may be obtained from the author).

The way our textbooks traditionally teach the factoring of trinomials of the form ax^2+bx+c where $a=1$ simply gives students a rule to follow: find the two integers that have a product of c and a sum of b. The students then blindly follow this method. When students are required to factor trinomials with $a \neq 1$, or in the case of difference of squares, students cannot continue to blindly use the rule they were taught. As Schmittau (2003) states "there is no problem of greater importance in the field of task design than that of designing a task that will lay the conceptual groundwork for a new category of mathematical thought" (p. 1). This is why I chose to rethink the way factoring is taught in a traditional classroom. A new instructional strategy may enable students to develop the necessary conceptual groundwork for factoring. Students may work with their prior knowledge of finding the product of two binomials to develop their own technique and understanding of factoring that can extend beyond the simple case of factoring $ax^2 +bx + c$ where $a = 1$.

In using a new instructional strategy, I tried to create a situation that fosters a shift of students' thinking about factoring trinomials from *procedure based* to *encapsulated meaning* (Watson, 2007). Students typically follow a rule (e.g., find the two integers that have a product of c and a sum of b) but a new strategy could offer them an opportunity to develop the relationship between the act of factoring and finding the product of two binomials. As students start to see the relationship between the product and the factorization, I hoped they would be able to move from the act of looking for relationships to seeing properties defined by relationships (Watson, 2007). Students began by multiplying the binomials; when asked to move backwards (factor) they examined how x^2+bx+c is related to $(x + p)(x + q)$, trying to develop a rule that relate b to p and q and/or relate c to p and q. I believe this shift in thinking enabled students to see that $p + q = b$ and $pq = c$, because of the relationship between finding a product and factoring. Thus the relationship they noticed defined the property they used.

I also hoped to foster a shift from example based understanding to making generalizations (Watson, 2007). Students initially worked in situations where the terms of the binomials and trinomials they used were whole numbers. I hoped that the relationships they recognized and the procedures they developed would be strong enough for them to work with the cases where b and/or c are negative and be able to recognize difference of squares as having the same relationship. My rationale was that if they were able to deal with these cases, then the students would have worked toward a generalization about factoring trinomials. Using Prestage & Perks' (2007) tool for adapting and extending a task, I worked to alter the traditional textbook method of teaching factoring.

Step 1: Notice the givens (Prestage & Perks, 2007). The method of teaching factoring the textbook suggests allows students to work with the concept of factoring and mental arithmetic. The question has a single solution where the student is able to find the factor or not.

Step 2: Change, add, or remove a given (Prestage & Perks, 2007). The task was initially changed from "here's the rule now factor the trinomial" to working on finding the product of two binomials. The second change was working to come up with the factorization of the binomial but thinking of it in terms of working backwards from the answer (i.e., the product of the binomials) to the question (i.e., the two binomials that were multiplied) without having been given any rules. The third part of the task had a question where the constant was removed and a question where the coefficient of x was removed to allow the students to find possible values that worked. This third part of the task allowed students to explore the dimensions of possible variation (Watson, 2007) within factoring. Watson proposes that once students are able to work through these explorations then they will come to a fuller understanding of the concept.

Step 3: Analyse the resulting mathematics (Prestage & Perks, 2007) – Students were connected to their prior knowledge about the product of two binomials. This is a concept that they worked with and mastered. Students called upon their knowledge of factors, primes, integer operations/properties, conjecturing, looking for similarities/patterns/ relationships, addition, subtraction, and multiplication of variables, and concept of like terms.

The factoring curriculum has been organized to allow for the development of a variety of habits of mind (Cuoco, Goldenberg & Mark, 1996): (1) *Pattern sniffers* – students discovered the pattern between the product and the factorization, (2) *Guessers and conjecturers* – as students worked to figure out the rule for factoring, and (3) *Experimenters* – students worked to find terms for b or c in Part 3 of the task.

My goal in the alteration of the factoring task was for it to lead to the outcome of micro-modeling (Watson & Mason, 2006). This meant that I had to construct the task "in such a way that desirable regularities might emerge from the learners' engagement with the task" (Watson & Mason, p. 93). In creating my examples in part 1 of the task, I focused on choosing numbers that would lead students to attend to the pattern I wanted ($p + q = b, pq = c$). Using Marton & Tsui's (2004) notion of variation, the first dimension of variation that I was careful to control was the use of whole numbers for p and q, and the second was which whole numbers I would use.

i. p and q are prime resulting with c having only one multiplicative pair
ii. $p = 1$ and q is a nonprime resulting with c having only two multiplicative pairs
iii. p is prime and q is a nonprime resulting with c having three multiplicative pairs
iv. p is prime and q is a nonprime resulting with c having four multiplicative pairs
v. p and q are nonprime resulting with c having five multiplicative pairs

I hoped that by starting with a question where $c = 2$ the connection p and q had to multiply to c would be easier to identify since 2 is prime. Then I systematically varied p and q to increase the number of multiplicative pairs that had a product of c (i.e., increasing the number of multiplicative pairs as they started to develop a conjecture of the relationship and they could test their conjecture on increasingly complicated questions).

In part two of the task where students used the rule they conjectured from part one; I used the same principles of variation as part one. Students started with only positive operators in the examples and with c as prime. I gave the students questions to factor of increasing difficulty as their apparent fluency with the type of questions increased (by increasing the number of factors c had). Once students seemed confident, I introduced what might have been a surprise variation for many students: b as a negative integer (while c is a positive prime). Once they realized that they could use the same rule they had developed, only changing p and q to negative integers, I increased the difficulty of c once again. I continued to give them variations that tested their generalization (i.e., by introducing c as a negative). When students first encountered c as negative, c was prime and b was a whole number. After students were able to deal with c having a greater complexity, I introduced c and b as negative integers where c was prime and again, as understanding permitted, I increased the complexity of c. The final variation where students had to adapt or confirm their conjecture was when $b = 0$. I explicitly offered them the term $0x$ and then removed it hoping they would see that they represent the same thing and are able to use and extend their generalization.

Reflections on the Experience

I was intentional in the order in which I introduced b or c as negatives. This was based on my past experience with students and knowledge of how they are able to make generalizations using negative integers. Depending on the students I am working with and their ability to make the jump to working with negative values of b and/or c, I redo part 1 using p and/or q as negative integers to help them redevelop the generalizations they attempted to make.

In the third part of the task, I removed the c term to help students strengthen their generalizations about the relationship between the values of b and c. Since b

was the only number to work with this focused the students' attention to that relationship. This led to an awareness of the one-to-many relationship that exists between b and c and in turn how that relates to p and q.

Task Development

My final instructional strategy was guided by Tabach & Friedlander's (2010) work on task design considerations. I wanted to look at designing a type of task that is connected to more of a "real world" concept; tasks I don't normally focus on in my classroom. I began creating my task by following Tabach & Friedlander's (2010) design considerations.

1. *Mathematical Content* – work with geometric shapes, geometric language, arithmetic manipulations, pattern identification, multiple representations, ratios, fractions, developing relationships, doing comparisons, making generalizations, and developing habits of mind (Cuoco, Goldenberg, & Mark, 1996).
2. *Context of inquiry* – work with a familiar real world example, the types of tables they have had in their classrooms and have arranged in rows and groups.
3. *Level of openness* – overall, students are not required to follow a predefined algorithm or a certain problem solving method but rather they are to develop their own methods to solve the problems. I put in place some structures to support students in their problem solving by drawing their attention to some of the tools that they have available to them. I specifically asked students in part 1 to create a drawing, table of values, a graph, and gave them manipulatives to help them see different aspects of the problem more clearly (Goldin, 2002). They could then decide if and how they wanted to use these tools to work on the rest of the problem. I also scaffolded the problem by breaking it up into questions that draw the students' attention to what they must consider before they could answer the questions in part 4 and 5. I could have presented students only with the questions from part 4 and 5 without breaking the problem down into smaller problems but I knew for my students this task would have been too open.

   Students would have been overwhelmed and unsure of how/where to start the problem. I am aware that I am taking away part of the problem solving from the students and that there is tremendous value in them setting up their own steps, and not being told any ways to represent or approach the problem. I am also aware that the structure I provide them with is biasing them to approach the problem the way I visualize it. If I was working with more experienced and confident problem solvers I could easily take out part of the structure, but I question whether they would attend to all the 'tricky details.' For instance, students might be developing a generalization for creating a row with hexagonal tables and decide that two people can sit at each table. But, if they only consider the case of an even number of people sitting in a row, they might decide "the number of tables required is equal to the number of people divided by two" but never consider what that means for 5 people (an odd number).

4. *Representations* – students create diagrams, table of values, graphs, develop formulas (algebraic, word, or other).
5. *Sequencing of tasks within an activity* – the problem begins structured (finding how to arrange 5 desks) and moves to less structured (finding a pattern and developing the generalization).

To develop the specific details of the task, I used Marton's concept of variation (Marton & Tsui, 2004). The 'dimensions of variation' that I first considered were the table shapes and how that would affect the problem solving process.

1. Square: Basic familiar table shape and gives an easy one table to one person relationship.
2. Rectangle: Another very familiar table shape and gives an easy one table to two people relationship.
3. Trapezoid: Students are familiar with sitting at these in the classroom but the relationship is more difficult in the row formation because depending on the orientation of the table you're adding either one or two more seats.
4. Hexagon: This offers a relatively visible relationship in the row formation similar to that of the rectangular table. However students are also faced with more practical considerations: Does it make sense to make a row of hexagonal tables? What does it mean to face the board (if the hexagonal tables are joined in a row by an edge the seat will be facing 30° away from the board – see diagram in Key Part 1)?
5. Triangle: A more difficult shape to work with because it is not a normal table shape and students are not as familiar with arranging triangles together. Building a row becomes complicated in the sense that every other table is not usable it is more of a placeholder to keep the edge to edge row formation (see diagram in Key Part 1). Students are again faced with the question of what it means to face the board and will they place a student on the "diagonal" side of the triangle.

Anticipating Student Reactions

The following section is a description of what I anticipated the students would do in developing their understandings of the topic at hand.

PART 1

This was an easy entry point for all students. They were able to easily arrange a row of squares, rectangles, trapezoids, but struggled a little more with the hexagons and triangles because those are a less familiar arrangement for them. I provided a situation where students can be tinkerers (Cuoco, Goldenberg, & Mark, 1996) by giving students the opportunity to play with the shapes (i.e., the manipulatives) and become familiar with the ways of combining them. This also made the task more doable. Students had to revisit what it means to be connected by an edge to be able to work with the unconventional shapes. Students also had to refresh themselves on what a table of values was and had to decide upon the variables. I initially thought that many students would not consider which variable is the dependent and which is the independent. When drawing the graph, I believed they would likely only draw the positive quadrant because that is the way they were most familiar with drawing the coordinate plane (i.e., and not necessarily because they realized they would not have negative number of people or tables). Students at this age are only accustomed to drawing graphs from a table of values thus I hoped what to plot would be clear. I predicted that some students would draw line graphs and some will draw bar graphs because they would not be clear regarding which graph was most useful in any given situation. I also believed some students would develop their generalization for the pattern they were seeing to solve how many tables were needed for 60 or 155 people and use their formula, while others would notice an additive sequence and do repeated addition with their calculator.

I created a "structured variation" (Mason, 2005) in Part 1 where the "dimension of variation" (Marton & Tsui, 2004) is the number of people. The reason I instructed them to calculate for 5 people first is because it is a small diagram-able/visualize-able situation. The case of 60 people started to extend their thinking, got them to 'pattern sniff' (Cuoco, Goldenberg, & Mark, 1996), and recognize that for all shapes except the trapezoids the *even case* is easier to solve. The case of 155 people was included as a type of distracter to bring to light any misconception in the students' development of a generalization – does their generalization work in the case of an odd number (Swan, 2007 & 2008). Finally, I set up a situation where students could be describers (Cuoco, Goldenberg, & Mark, 1996) and conjecturers (Cuoco, Goldenberg & Mark, 1996) as they shifted their thinking from example based (5, 60, 155) to general (Watson, 2007) when developing their method to find the number of tables needed to create a row given any number of people.

PART 2

Students will develop some of Cuoco, Goldenberg, & Mark's (1996) habits of mind—visualizing, tinkering, and experimenting—while they either play with the manipulatives or make drawings to figure out how to create their pods of six (6). The problem is a simple form of a minimization problem (i.e., least number of tables possible to accommodate 6 people). Some students will actually consider multiple formations while others will automatically assume their first formation is the best. Creating the pods should be relatively straightforward for the students because they form either rectangles or hexagons and there are not that many possible formations. I believe that the case of having 60 people is an easy variation for students to figure out because it's divisible by 6. The next variation (250) is more difficult because 250 is not divisible by 6, and they will need to come up with the idea of taking the ceiling of a number—not an idea we discussed.

PART 3

This part of the task was developed with the same framework as Part 2. However, the variation (Marton & Tsui, 2004) of pod size of 10 made figuring out the table formations a little more complex, especially for the trapezoids and the triangles. Considering whether the table formation was created with the least number of tables was more important. At this point in my inquiry, I conjectured that more students would create formations that are not a minimum because they will not take the time to consider all possibilities.

PART 4

Students will need to compare the results for each part of the task for each table type. I think students will get confused while they are doing their comparison because they are being asked "If I wanted to be able to arrange the room in a straight row, pod groups of 6, or pod groups of 10 to accommodate 60 people which type of table should I buy assuming I wanted to buy the least number of tables possible" and they will attend to the word *least* rather than attending to *being able to create all formation types*. I believe that will cause some students to falsely identify the number of tables required to make each formation type (see Table 1 below) because they will look for the least number of tables required to make a formation for each table type. When in actuality, students should be looking for the most number of tables required by each shape and then from that list of data they should pick the shape with the least number of tables required. However, even the students who falsely identify the number of tables required to make all formation types will get the right final answer for Part 4 – hexagon.

Table 1. – Table formations and number of tables required

Shape	*60 people in a row*	*60 people in pods of 6*	*60 people in pods of 10*	*# required to make each formation*	
				Students who attend to create all formation types	*Students who attend to least*
Square	60	60	60	60	60
Rectangle	30	30	30	30	30
Trapezoid	40	30	24	40	24
Hexagon	30	10	12	30	12
Triangle	119	60	84	119	48

PART 5

> This section requires use of the information from Part 4. If the students make the mistake I highlight above (in Table 1 above) then their price calculations will be incorrect. To be able to figure out which table type will be the cheapest, students will have to figure out how to use the price ratios given in the question. I assume that students will arbitrarily pick (e.g., perhaps they will make sure to pick a number they can easily divide by 2 because of the ½ ratios in the question) a cost for one of the table types and figure out the rest based on the given ratios. The idea to pick a number may not come to many students and they may need to be guided a bit more.

My Observations

Jane was quick to start drawing her answers out while Doris started playing with the manipulatives right away (NB: all student names have been changed to protect their anonymity). Both worked on visualizing relationships (Cuoco, Goldenberg, & Mark, 1996). Jane was able to quickly visualize the data of her drawing into table of values, and a graph. However, Jane's visualization of the data was not 100% accurate. She created her graph using all four quadrants and connected her points with a line going through the negative quadrant. This part of the task offers the opportunity to discuss what needs to be considered when creating a graph that describes a "real life" situation.

Doris would not draw anything without first creating it with the manipulatives, giving her the chance to *tinker* (Cuoco, Goldenberg & Mark, 1996) with the various possible formations. She was not feeling confident in her problem solving abilities when she was creating her row of five with rectangles. Doris realized that two tables wasn't enough, but three tables would fit six people, and wasn't sure what to do. She decided to take a look at Jane's work. Jane decided to cut the rectangular table in half so that exactly five (5) people would fit. Doris was then prepared to copy her more confident peer's work. It wasn't until I encouraged them to talk about what the question was asking that they realized that they shouldn't cut the tables. The students were also required to describe (Cuoco, Goldenberg, & Mark, 1996) their interpretation of the question—what does it mean "the minimum number of tables" and "to seat at least five people" and how their solution met these requirements.

When the students were trying to fit the triangular tables together they needed to be reminded of how the tables needed to fit together—what does it mean to be "connected by an edge?" The next discussion was what does it mean to "face the board?" The students took this fuzzy problem of facing the board and developed a new way to describe the situation, i.e., if you were at a 90° angle or greater from the board, you were no longer facing the board (Cuoco, Goldenberg, & Mark, 1996).

The students were worried that the only way they could create a row with triangles would require that some triangles would have no people at them, and they assumed they were making a mistake. They continued to *tinker* and *experiment* (Cuoco, Goldenberg, & Mark, 1996) trying to make various arrangements of the triangles by making pods or putting more than two people at a table. Working to arrange the square, rectangular, and trapezoidal tables was fairly easy because they seemed to be more familiar objects. These formations were done quickly and independently. However, arranging the triangles in a row is a fairly unfamiliar situation because they've never experienced triangular tables in a classroom. The more unfamiliar the situation, the more the students depended on their "habits of mind" (i.e., *describing, tinker, experimenting, conjecturing*, and *guessing*) to try and work out the unfamiliar problem (Cuoco, Goldenberg, & Mark, 1996).

When it came time to make the shift between example (rows of five) to generalization (Watson, 2007), Jane did not consider the case of seating an odd number of people at her row of rectangular tables; she thus created a generalization that would result in half tables. This highlighted the importance of having questions in the task that lead students to re-evaluate the full correctness and applicability of their conjectures. Creating the task so that students work with concrete examples that have the students reflect on the possible variations and then trying to make the shift to a generalization gives students the opportunity to (re)evaluate their ideas/conjectures.

When the students created their row for five (5) using the trapezoidal tables, they had no trouble figuring out how they would do that, but when it came time to develop their generalization there was lots of uncertainty. Jane was resistant to the idea of using table of values or graphs to solve the problem but decided the problem was too hard to solve and wanted to quit, asking "isn't class over yet?" In her struggle, I tried to redirect her attention to only a small aspect of the problem—what were the independent and dependent variables? I realized that even though Jane had marked her independent and dependent variables correctly when making her graph and table of values, she used the dependent variable as if it were the independent value and thus made it very difficult to see the pattern and identify it in the form of $y = mx+b$ as she wanted. I encouraged her to create some more data points and then try to find the number of trapezoidal tables required to fit 60 people. I also tried to encourage her to describe what was happening instead of creating a formula, but she really wanted to create a variable equation. I attempted to foster the visualization of "data, process, and change" (Cuoco, Goldenberg, & Mark, 1996).

This part of the task was a very good opportunity to help develop visualization while focusing on the mathematical concept of independent and dependent variables—what they actually mean, how they relate to forming a generalization, and how to decide which variable is which (i.e., dependent or independent). This also made me realize that I need to find a better way to encourage students, to try different methods of approaching a problem especially when their first approach doesn't work and they are tempted to give up.

Doris was not a very experienced math problem solver, and I think this actually benefitted her because she did not have such a limited view of how to solve the problem. Doris began by creating a list of data below (see Table 2 below).

Table 2. Doris's list

Tables (t)	1	2	3	4	5	6	7	8	9	10
Max # of people (p)	3	4	6	7	9	10	12	13	15	16

First, she noticed the pattern in the maximum number of people as an increase of +1, +2, +1, +2 ... and tried to develop a formula for each ordered pair - (4, 7) would be (t, 2t-1) then (8, 13) would be (t, 2t-3), etc. This offered a good opportunity to explore what it means to make a generalization and explore questions such as, "If each data point has a different formula have you developed a generalization? Is there a pattern in these different formulas that can lead to a better generalization? When should we try a new approach?" When Doris realized her formulas were not helping her make a generalization, I circled groups of her data (as illustrated in Figure 2 above) to see if that could help her sniff a new solution pattern. These circles gave her a new way to attend to the problem, and from that she was able to write the next few groups of data without using the manipulatives and could eventually make a generalization.

It was clear from watching Jane and Doris working on this task that the real value in the task lies in its opportunity to help "students become comfortable with ill-posed and fuzzy problems, to see the benefit of systematizing and abstraction, and to look for and develop new ways of describing situations" (Cuoco, Goldenberg, & Mark, 1996). Within this task students were given various opportunities to pattern sniff, describe, tinker, experiment, make conjectures, visualize data, use multiple points of view, break things into parts, extend things, and represent things (Cuoco, Goldenberg, & Mark, 1996).

Summary

Looking at these instructional strategies and developing these tasks enabled me focus on how I choose and create classroom tasks and learning opportunities for my students. As Swan (2007) says, the purpose is "to develop tasks that foster the generation and re-examination of … concepts through reflection and discussion." I believe that this is exactly what happened in the classroom as students worked on these three tasks. The tactics I selected are by no means the only way to teach these concepts; rather they offer an approach of moving away from content focused lessons. They offered a way to actively engage students collaboratively in the content, encouraging questioning and discussions around their understanding of the concepts.

As I have progressed through the masters program my personal goal has been to loosen my attachment to the textbook lessons that have been firmly ingrained in me as a teacher in a public school system. I have decided to use mathematics as the excuse to develop relationships in the classroom, as an opportunity to both engage in mathematical conversations with my students and foster conversations amongst my students.

If one subscribes to a constructivist learning perspective and believes that one of the criteria of learning is that the learner must take responsibility for their own learning, then one must question how can we teach students unless they are included in the educational conversation. My inquiry illustrates that when students are not working on tasks that foster questioning about what they are doing and learning in school, they are not really engaging in the learning experience. Students need to be given the chance to partake in the conversation of the lesson otherwise they have no ownership in their learning. I have found that when I use a broad variety of instructional strategies and tasks students become more enthusiastic, and actively participate in the lessons. Most of all, more meaningful, applicable learning takes place.

Jennifer Massoud
Vancouver School Board
jmassoud@vsb.bc.ca

Curriculum materials that demonstrate the constructs and task design strategies described in the chapter are available from the author upon request.

PART 5

A STORY FROM THE ADMINISTRATIVE PERSPECTIVE

SANDRA PASCUZZI

STEPPING INTO SYSTEMIC CHANGE

An autobiographical account of a teacher researcher-teacher leader-teacher learner

Teacher as Researcher

Teacher as Leader

Teacher as Learner

It has been three years since stepping into the messy business of change in educational settings. I have seen, heard and done much; yet at other times I feel I have done little. As an educator, this tension often plays an ever-present tug of war inside me. Add to this, a school district's initiative in change, and this tension can be ever consuming. How do I map a course that will enable me to enrich my practice? What will it look like when I get there? How will it affect student achievement? Who will help me to get there? These and many more questions have been swimming through my mind during the past three years. I have been careful, cautiously stepping forward.

I have been an elementary teacher in the North Vancouver School District for more than a dozen years, and became a Vice-Principal at the beginning of this past school year. This appointment has brought me almost full circle to my earliest childhood memory of my public education career. I always wanted so much to be back at school every time I left—be it for summer holidays, or graduating from university. In fact, I was known as "the teacher" from the age of nine, when I used to run regular classroom lessons in our basement for all the neighborhood children who would come over with homework.

I remember my initial visit to Crichton Elementary, an old stone schoolhouse that would become an everlasting sacred sanctuary of many childhood memories. My father's newly shined shoes echoed on the gray stairs as we climbed up to the principal's office. Heavy wooden doors separated the empty spaces in the halls from the interior of his room. School was not yet in session, but we had to register. As new immigrants, we were asked to come and speak directly with the principal. My head peered over the top of the gleaming desk at the high ceilings and tall windows covered with metal grates. With broken English, my father solemnly promised that I would be a good student—that I would listen, behave, and learn well. I kept that oath close to my heart for the rest of my life. I believe it was my right of passage into a life in education.

I began my journey as a teacher-learner, initially curious about improving my practice and with the hopes of fulfilling a life-long dream of obtaining a Master of

P. Gouzouasis (ed.), Pedagogy in a New Tonality: Teacher Inquiries on Creative Tactics, Strategies, Graphics Organizers, and Visual Journals in the K-12 Classroom, 301–319.

Education degree. As I forged a path through this latest phase of change, a metamorphosis has occurred in me. I have embodied three persona—that of learner, that of leader, and that of researcher. The further I traveled along this journey, the less separate and distinct each identity has become. I have been one, and all, at the same time, in varying degrees since the beginning. Now, I can no longer separate those lines—I have become whole, a "learnerleaderresearcher." In this documentation of my personal journey through change, I will weave the stories of other educators and the district's efforts toward the same endeavor.

Stepping into Some Background

More than three years ago, the North Vancouver School District (NVSD44) hired a consultant, Barrie Bennett, to lead our district's initiative in systemic change around the notion of improving instruction in the classroom. Soon thereafter, a partnership was forged with the University of British Columbia to house a Master of Education program in Curriculum Leadership with a focus on Instructional Intelligence. I flipped through the program pamphlet and decided to step forward. I was going on a voyage and the pamphlet was my ticket. Little did I know that through this partnership between the district and the university, I would venture to places and spaces that I would never have thought possible. Little did I know how much this journey was about to change me to the core of my beliefs, values, and understandings about teaching and learning, as well as about our profession, as an educator in our ever-changing world. In my journey, I have taken both baby steps and giant leaps.

Institutionalization

Implementation

Initiation

I will tell the parallel story of the district's initiative by viewing it through the lens of the current literature on change. From my perspective, Michael Fullan's (2001) three phases of initiation, implementation, and institutionalization have provided the structure for the story of the district's change effort. In these categories of change, initiation refers to the process that leads up to and includes a decision to adopt an innovation. Implementation involves putting reform into practice. Institutionalization, or the third phase of change, is characterized by sustainability that is supported by an infrastructure.

> Management of the whole change effort determines its relative success or failure. (Fullan, 2001)

Three years of learning and teaching within the school, the district, and with the university have provided me with numerous opportunities for observations and ruminations upon the whole notion of change. Many dialogues and exchanges with senior leadership, teachers, support staff, and others have led to a new understanding of systemic innovations and their effects on organizations and individuals. Three years of continual growth and learning through the arts have given me a new identity, that of a writer. In this identity, I have had to battle with pen and paper, keyboard and computer, to tell my story. Riding a course through this trajectory of change as a teacher learner, teacher leader and teacher researcher ("learnerleaderresearcher") in the district has sometimes felt like being in a dingy in the middle of the ocean. The only way to survive is to go with the ebb and flow of change, making the most of what you've got, and dealing with the obstacles along the way as best as you can.

Teacher as Researcher

Teacher as Leader

Teacher as Learner

I Am a Teacher and This Is My World

I am a teacher, solid as ice, fluid as liquid, and hot as gas . . . I flow in and out of lands, through places and spaces, with minds, to minds, "inward, outward, backwards, forwards . . ." I touch the world and it touches me. It takes the whole world to tell me who I am, direct my flow, keep my faith, and guide my path.

Yet, I can move mountains and often do by washing ignorance away, cleansing prejudices, bathing wounds, opening new channels and nurturing life. I have a tremendous power. I can be transformative and I can also transform the future. It is up to me whether I baptize in holy waters, rain on a parade, or flow saltily on someone's cheeks. I am a teacher and this is my world.

Figure 1. My beautiful world: The many layers of a teacher's world come together and are split apart in the classroom.

"I want you all to take off your right shoe and throw it in the center of the circle," Peter enthusiastically cajoled us. It wasn't posed as a threat, but I felt threatened. *Oh no, I hope I don't have a hole in my sock. Please, please, don't let me have a hole in my sock. I don't know these people. What have I gotten myself into? What else am I going to be asked to do in this course?* I nervously smiled and looked up and around me. Off to the back of the room, our district senior administrators were looking on and chatting amongst themselves, over the newly formed cohort group. We were sitting shoulder to shoulder in a circle of stackable blue school chairs. All at once, a mountain of shoes, hiking boots, runners, and other footwear fell in a pile on the middle of the brightly lit classroom floor.

"Now, I am going to start sorting into separate piles, and I will point to someone else to continue." Immediately, we were all engaged in the lesson. The circle fell silent as we began to sort piles of shoes in a very active and involved way. *She must be a runner, and he is definitely a hiker. I love those red stilettos.* This was my first experience in what turned out to be a concept formation lesson that sparked my interest, and even diverted it from what could have been an entirely embarrassing episode. I couldn't wait to return to my own class and try it with my students. I couldn't wait to get together again with my new found group of cohort learners and our professors from UBC.

Another Saturday began bright and early. I arrived to the teacher professional center shortly before the usual morning bell at school. The smells of fresh coffee and muffins were a welcome scent as I had little time that morning to get my own java fix. We didn't know who was providing the funding for these refreshments, but all of us were completely grateful at not having to worry about nourishing ourselves through these Saturdays.

We were assigned a project within groups. We were asked to interpret a common school event and then videotape our group's short role-play. The use of video was new to me, and so I asked to be in charge of the videotaping within our group. I wanted to learn as much as possible during this course. Toward the end of the day, we were asked to videotape or make an iMovie of lessons that would incorporate the use of the strategies and tactics in Bennett's book *Beyond Monet* (2001), with our own students. *I can't do this. I've never even videotaped my own children. How am I going to produce a movie while teaching a lesson to my class? I need to figure out the difference between a strategy and a tactic. Honestly! I think I've gotten myself in too deep. What am I doing in this course?*

I decided to keep an open mind about this risk I was facing, as well as the additional risks I would be taking throughout my degree program. I knew the anxiety came from being pushed beyond my comfort zone. This wasn't what I expected. However, at the same time, I was excited about the possibility of doing something new. I knew I could easily change my lesson plan and use a tactic or a strategy. But using a camera, videotaping lessons, now that was pushing me beyond what I expected, but what fun, once again being a student and learning new techniques and ideas! Perhaps I wouldn't become a dinosaur in the classroom after all.

As a generalist teacher at the elementary level, I teach all subject areas and cover a broad curriculum in these subjects. The possibilities of incorporating creative instructional strategies and tactics were endless, but making a movie and using the new software technology of the computers at school was what I became most proud of accomplishing. I was taken to another dimension as a learner. Once again, I experienced the thrill of acquiring a new skill or knowledge. I felt like a kid again! I also felt like I was finally going to have to face the reality of the modern world. Technology was not to be avoided any longer.

After videotaping my lessons, I was able to see myself in action in the classroom, and to reflect upon what I saw afterward. I could dissect each aspect of my lessons—the questioning techniques, the management of the class, and the flow and the pace of the lesson was open to constructive criticism. As a consequence of the deep reflection and subsequent reflexion on these lessons, and allowing the process to flow, a whole unit of study integrating language arts, technology, and community building in the classroom resulted.

I developed a unit on *Heroes* and produced a portfolio with examples of student works in this study. The unit was supported by the *Web In The Classroom* application, a district developed, Internet resource document that enables teachers to easily create a web site for their own students and classroom. Much of what we did in the classroom included the use of technology by the students. The children produced an iMovie and we used the computers to produce books on *Heroes.* This was created with two other teachers, our librarian and our technology teacher in the school. While we worked together, the students also worked in collaborative groups.

The importance of considering learning as a social and collaborative endeavor is well documented in the research literature on change. It is all about relationships (Fullan, 2001; Hargreaves, 2004). When asked about the biggest obstacle that teachers encounter in attempts to change, the major impediment had to do with implementing change alone, i.e., change on one's own (Hargreaves, Earl, Moore & Manning, 2001). Clearly, from the beginning of the whole change effort in the district, I did not feel alone. There have been opportunities for schools to submit action plans and have the district allocate time and resources toward those efforts. The idea of learning together has also been evident. Teachers have been encouraged to share where they are at in their stages of learning. It has been evident that we learn more through the questions we have after initiating change in our practice. Teachers have been encouraged to share these questions and uncertainties. As a result of those experiences, the support network that has emerged has created a powerful community of learners within our district, and most especially within our graduate cohort group of 24 teachers.

The necessity of dialogue and the sharing of ideas are critical to the success of learning that changes teachers to the core of their beliefs. The senior leadership of the district initiated a series of dialogue opportunities for teachers. These opportunities were presented in after school sessions. There was a clear topic statement served up with the idea of promoting a common language. Topics were communicated to the teachers in advance and we were invited to participate in open discussions. I was surprised by the number of participants in attendance, and by the power of these sessions in terms of heightening awareness, creating a common language, and fostering a core group of individuals who were ready to move forward in their thinking. For me, these sessions became like aphrodisiacs to the mind. I never once left the sessions disappointed in either the topic or with the group's level of heightened awareness.

Changes in teachers' skills and beliefs are difficult, because they are embedded at deeper levels. These are the intangibles of change that take time and deliberation in one's own mind after input from other people and through the open exchange of ideas. The "Doers with Big Minds" sessions provided the dialogue and conversations to move me forward. They were effective in promoting a common language in the district. There is no doubt that the language and ideas of *Instructional Intelligence* (Bennett & Rohlheiser, 2001) were now "out there" in the district.

Time is a critical component of learning. Time is needed to process, plan, reflect, revisit, and redo. It means moving from being a mechanical user of a strategy to a higher-level user. Complex change cannot take place without considerable learning, and considerable learning takes time. Time is the scarcest resource for educational innovation, yet it is one of the most important. As a teacher-learner, a mother of young children, and a wife, time has been the one resource that has been the scarcest in my journey to change. What has made the difference is the initial commitment I made to my own professional growth and the vision I had for the future. Time, however, has been limited and I have had to make tough personal and professional choices and prioritize tasks and activities.

Throughout the remainder of this paper, the voices of my colleagues who have shared their professional views on the district's change initiative will be interwoven in this story. I interviewed a teacher-librarian, a vice-principal/district coordinator and a veteran teacher/school associate at the university for their perspectives. Their insights have echoed in my mind throughout my journey, as reminders and indicators of the district's transformation process and how it is interpreted differently or the same depending on certain circumstances and situations.

What has been Most Difficult for You in This Change Effort?

> Time is the biggest problem. Teachers need time to plan, think it through, and make sense of it. Collaboration takes time, and time is what we have little of. The key is release time; we are too exhausted to fit it in at the end of the day.
>
> I found that the summer institutes were a difficult time to attend sessions. It was hard to give up that time. It has to be release time that is provided to work under these master teachers and to watch them in action. It has to be on a regular basis and when teachers are fresh. The pacing of it (the learning) is important. It is not a one-time fix.
>
> School leadership has to be involved, yet the timing of the summer institute was difficult for some administrators to make those sessions. They are needed at the schools at that time in order to get things ready for school start

up. Many were out of the loop for this reason and not able to support their staff or be involved in the change effort.

In *Beyond Monet*, Bennett believes that becoming a conscious practitioner means knowing the underlying reasons why we do, what we do. Learning has to take place in context, specifically in the classroom and with the students that we teach. The most powerful learning that has taken place during the last three years has happened in the classroom and within our schools. Teachers have applied the concepts, strategies, and tactics in *Beyond Monet* in the places and spaces they teach. The space and place of learning is in the classroom, with our students. Within our cohort, we have gone back to our classes, practiced our strategies and tactics, and come together again to discuss our experiences. This has made us more aware of what it is that we are doing in the classroom. To be consciously aware of what you are doing is the difference between what Barrie Bennett calls a painter and a master painter. In course lectures, Gouzouasis referred to it as the difference between an auto mechanic and an automotive design engineer, or a fingerpicker and a well-studied classical guitarist.

The implementation of instructional intelligence in classrooms across the district has provided the opportunity for job-embedded professional development that has fostered far more significant benefits than one-day workshops or seminars. Reflection has been the most useful tool in developing deeper learning and changes in practice. It has forced us to become both reflective and reflexive about our practice and to view it from a variety of perspectives. We have had continual opportunities to go back, try again, review our tactics and applications, revise, and reapply our ideas. It seems that a solid foundation has been laid upon that many of us have built philosophies on teaching and learning that are powerful pillars for our classroom practice. This has been the best form of professional development that I have engaged in since graduating as an undergraduate student from university.

Institutionalization

Implementation

Initiation

In 2003, NVSD44 hired Barrie Bennett to lead our district's initiative in systemic change. An innovative notion entitled Instructional Intelligence was introduced to the district from Bennett & Rolheiser's (2001) book *Beyond Monet: The science and art of teaching*. This approach, called *Instructional Intelligence*, has been the basis of our change effort. It is designed to build teachers' knowledge in eight categories of instructional components.

A two-day conference that brought together elementary and secondary administrators in the Winter of 2003 was followed by an introduction of the concept of the Instructional Institute to the entire district. During the fall term of year one, our superintendent presented *Focus on Instruction* as the topic for Curriculum Implementation Day. Shortly after this introduction, workshops were held with Barrie Bennett and over 140 teachers and administrators for two consecutive months. Summer institutes continued the learning with more in-depth looks at different strategies and tactics such as mind-mapping and framing questions.

A partnership was cemented between the district and the University of British Columbia to implement a Master of Education program in Curriculum Leadership with a focus on Instructional Intelligence, mentored by Peter Gouzouasis, was cemented. A cohort group of teachers from elementary and secondary schools in NVSD44, as well as two teachers from Squamish School District, comprised the group. It was envisioned that a core group of individuals would ensure sustainability in the change effort after the initial introduction phase. The district mapped a five-year plan in which Dr. Bennett would provide repeated introductory sessions in Instructional Intelligence through summer institutes to mobilize every teacher and administrator by open invitation. The university would intensely teach the cohort group, with a focus on research.

What has Led You to Go See Barrie Bennett?

> I was invited initially. I was curious. I wanted to know what was going on.
>
> I saw it as an opportunity—it was district initiated and I decided to be open because it was going to be a five-year focus.
>
> I was very involved at the district level and I saw Barrie in action during an evening session. My reason for continuing was that I was in a leadership position.

Teacher as Researcher

Teacher as Leader

Teacher as Learner

We are always beginning, being, becoming
We are never perfect, and to own up and change
To be resolute in your convictions and values
Is to grow, mature and move forward.

"Moudira, moudira Pascuzzi," crackled the voice on the end of the line. I could tell my father had a lump in his throat as he spoke. It was difficult for him to articulate the feelings that weld up and tried to escape his now skinny frame.

"Yes baba, moudira," I replied, and not for the last time. Relishing the word "moudira" in his mouth, my father wanted to repeat it every time we spoke on the phone. I could tell how proud he was of my accomplishment. I was proud of achieving this goal. I had been appointed Vice-Principal for the upcoming school year. I had suddenly translated all my years of learning into one recognizable word; a word my father could understand in a tangible form.

As the daughter of an immigrant, I knew how important it was to my father for me to become an educated person. My father believed in education as the leveling factor between immigrants and the established community. "Look at Trudeau," my dad would say, "he's still taking courses at the age of seventy." My father believed in life-long learning, and Pierre Elliott Trudeau set a good example. Father encouraged me through two post-graduate degrees, and then my masters degree. In his eyes, citizens needed to become educated, and his daughter was no exception.

Beyond my father's expectations, I also dreamed of an opportunity to lead the educators. This dream came true when I was appointed Vice-Principal for the upcoming 2006–2007 school year. Although I was on maternity leave, my graduate school coursework had ignited a fire within me about the direction that our school district had undertaken in the last four years. In a leadership position, I wanted to effect change positively. I felt I could do so much in this direction. I was continuously energized and inspired in my coursework and through what I saw as results in the classroom. I wanted to share, involve others, visit classrooms, teach teachers about this.

Unfortunately, the summer institute was not a possibility for me during what was going to be my first year as a VP. So much had to be in place before September start-up, and the school was going through a major structural renovation. Both school administrators were needed on location as workers, supplies, equipment were arriving by the hour.

However, shortly after the year began, I was invited as a VP to a session called *Leadership for Learning*. I felt like I had died and gone to heaven. Here I was, a new VP and seeing the best practice on change as described in the research literature actually in action at the district level. The district was using these sessions to carry out its vision, facilitate further learning of the administrative staff, and to provide guidance and direction for its leaders. I felt completely supported and ready to go back to my school with a definite plan in mind. I realized that although I had missed the summer institute, I was not going to be left behind.

I quickly drew up a plan for classroom visitations. I wanted to support my teachers in any way that I could, but I felt that I needed to first touch base and say 'hello' to staff and students, if only for a few minutes, before diving into the professional aspect of the visit. I learned about the make-up of the staff and the student body during those first class visits. I knew where I could potentially succeed in introducing new ideas and where my efforts might not get me very far. Both Hargreaves (2001, 2004) and Fullan (2001, 2005) suggest that with change, you go with the goers, try and shift the neutrals or fence sitters to your side, and leave the others behind. Also, Barrie Bennett repeatedly said that it has to be an open invitation, and teachers have to buy in voluntarily in order for a shift to happen. I knew who the goers were going to be during these class visits.

I wanted to provide the entire staff with opportunities to witness this change effort in action. I knew that some teachers were not interested in this effort, but I made small changes when we got together as a group. One example of my efforts was configuring the desks in a round circle at the beginning of staff meetings. Everyone now faced each other as they do in the Tribes (Gibbs, 2001) community model. I delivered the content of the meeting through visual organizers and graphics, and I involved staff in active participation as much as possible. I looked for ways to pique curiosity in those that were not involved without forcing it upon them. My invitation was to be as open as the district's—the choice was up to each individual to decide if they wanted the opportunity to participate or not.

At the school level, I became the contact person for Instructional Intelligence. I have been able to direct the goers to sharing sessions, after school in-service workshops provided by the district, and to resources that could facilitate their learning. I invited a group of my teachers to an after school sharing session on Instructional Intelligence. Five of our twenty teachers attended. I forwarded information and placed good resources such as books and other curricular support materials in people's boxes.

Although I started the year full of vision and energy for change, I have felt that I am only a small part in making the change effort happen. I realize that change has to come from all levels and people have to be intrinsically motivated themselves to want to learn and change. With my plate full, both on a professional and personal level, I can only do so much. This is where the beauty of the five-year plan comes through and ensures that if you cannot do it now, you will get another opportunity. I have also felt the community support at the district level from senior administrators, other leaders and teachers who are on board. When my energy level is down and I feel like I am not getting far, I once again participate in a workshop, or Leadership Session and get reenergized. The support the district has provided in this way has been invaluable to me as a leader.

Who has Ownership of the Change Effort?

> The administration is instrumental. If administration doesn't care if it happens, then the teachers won't care whether it happens or not.
>
> There has to be leaders at all levels. We have a long way to go. Since it is on a voluntary basis, expectations are not clearly stated, not everyone participates, and it doesn't work. There is always too much on the go, but it is so much easier teaching using these strategies.
>
> There has to be buy-in from both administrators. If one is resistant or indifferent, it makes it hard. The key is to build it into the school culture, at staff meetings. We have to enlighten people and also give them practical stuff to work with.
>
> The (masters) cohort has given rise to a whole new set of leaders who are well versed in Instructional Intelligence. We can't be dismayed by the critics. The integration of the ideas and concepts is what we need to self-sustain. We need leaders at all levels, from the district program people, the unions, and the teachers in the classrooms.

Initiation — ***Implementation*** — Institutionalization

During years three and four of the five-year plan, the district's journey continued with the commencement of Tribes (Gibbs, 2001), as well as continued collegial dialogue and sharing in schools. Two expert Tribes workshop facilitators were brought in to introduce Tribes sessions to more than fifty teachers and administrators.

Bennett describes Tribes as the plate on which Instructional Intelligence is served. Tribes is a process of teaching and learning based on a philosophy of democratic classroom management that uses many cooperative strategies and social inclusion techniques to achieve student success through community building (Gibbs, 2001). The Tribes philosophy has become a focus in the district with top-level personnel now being scheduled for training to become certified Tribes facilitators.

Simultaneously, Barrie Bennett continued to provide introductory workshops to teachers and administrators. He also made presentations to the district's parent association. He taught lessons at various grade levels in NVSD schools, met with both advisory and steering groups to plan for the future, and to some extent mentored the graduate cohort group.

Meanwhile, the Curriculum Implementation Day focus was on Instructional Intelligence and its impact on the NVSD. The district also held workshops on cooperative learning with Johnson's five basic elements, Tribes techniques learning was extended, and action research projects were being implemented by cohort graduate students in over 15 schools at both the elementary and high school levels. The strategies and tactics of Instructional Intelligence could be seen being modeled by workshop presenters and teachers alike. There were workshops held on brain research to provide some background knowledge and to piece it all together. Some of the level of discussion around this has been rather superficial—I have never heard anyone discuss the work of Antonio Damasio and Steven Pinker, yet they are among the leading international researchers in that field.

Further learning through dialogue sessions and sharing occurred through the district's Focus on Instruction website to which every teacher in the district has access. At one point, teachers were given release time to enhance this site with our own ideas on the various components of instruction. Mobilizing a district by providing the necessary resources and support and continuing the vision all happened during this phase of change. As a district, implementation was under full swing. More teachers were getting on board and many were innovating their practice.

To What Extent has Instructional Intelligence Changed Your Practice?

> It has changed my teaching a great deal in the classroom and now in my new role. I use it to teach students and to role model new strategies to student teachers. Children are far more active and social. I have developed new strategies to make learning more authentic and cooperative.

> I haven't been immersed in it. Now, I am using strategies on a regular basis because I see that they work. I fit it into my program whenever I can.

> I definitely use it on a day-to-day basis. I've personally gone through a huge learning curve as I've seen progress in my class. I take bits and pieces of what I've learned and put it all together and integrate to connect with the kids.

> *(Re)searching has blown space into dimensions I never imagined myself capable of examining. It has rendered me aware of the possibility of greater understanding. I will see, not only through my reflexive self as a learner/leader/ researcher. I will see through the eyes of the viewer when I invite dialogue and interpretation in order to extend meaning. The breadth and depth of thought, the borders of the mind, the borderlands have been opened wide. I will explore in, with, through, out, into the (s)p(l)aces of my worlds.*

I am learning a broader understanding of the concept of (s)p(l)ace (deCosson, 2004) and how much the opening up of spaces can affect our practice and me as a teacher learner, leader and researcher. This notion has expanded to include not only my own physical space and environment, but the psychological and social domains of others as well. I was guided to walk with an artist researcher through my journey. I chose Ross Penhall, specifically because of one beautiful painting. In *Juniper Loop*, Penhall (1959) visually represents this broader understanding in an ideal way. The composition projects an air of deep contemplation, thought and a journey through open spaces. The notion of (s)p(l)ace, therefore, not only belongs in a concrete world of pathways, trails, and steps, but also exists in the untouchable aspects that have intangible or non-existent boundaries. This space is embedded in the mind, as well as the inner self.

While Penhall invites us to the open trail with his beautiful use of light, perhaps a metaphor for enlightenment and freedom, I believe that McNiff, in *Trust the process: An artist's guide for letting go,* tells us to be open to new possibilities. He invites us to open up the psychological spaces within ourselves as well as our students. I think he is directly telling us to hold criticism and not to always expect perfect finished products; he warns us to withhold the desire for outcomes (1998). He suggests that the social environment needs to feel safe in order for the teacher artist to create.

A classroom has to be safe, and open in order for students to be able to explore and not feel either threatened or criticized. A school and the district also need these protective factors in place to succeed. Personally, I wonder if my class visitations have a negative impact on my teachers. I have used the "three stars and a wish technique" in which teachers self-assess their own teaching. I ask them to reflect on how the lesson went. I do this only after I have an established a comfortable relationship with the teacher. Yet, I may still unknowingly leave teachers feeling angst through and in the whole process. It is something I have questioned, metaphorically speaking, as perhaps one of the boulders in the pathway in *Juniper Loop* (Penhall, 1959).

Lymburner (2004) states that the process of wandering and wondering in our minds enables connective tissues, new visions, and new meanings to be made. She quotes Clandinin & Connelly's (2000) beautiful idea of perpetual movement in all directions in order to make gains and new insights. This on-going exploration and opening up of the spaces within us that enables us to be reflective and reflexive within our practice is intriguing to me. That is the feeling that *Juniper Loop* gave me when I first saw it. It invited me to open spaces to explore, to wander in, and to wonder about. Not only do we have to have a dialogue within ourselves, but we should include dialogue and learn through interactions with others and with our general surroundings. I have done this within the last few years of change.

This continual (re)search involves the participation of open dialogue from other stakeholders and could very well include groups we have traditionally overlooked. I think that because of the pace of life in our profession, demands on our time often leave us isolated and alone in our decisions making. I will need to reexamine the stakeholders and perhaps invite a few other viewpoints in advance, during the process, or after in order to debrief. Input from various stakeholders has become part of the formative process (McNiff, 1998). If nothing else, the input will open my eyes to other perspectives and give me a wider lens within which to do my planning, teaching and learning.

I also agree whole-heartedly with Lymburner (2004) when she states that the results of self-inquiry leads to a development of inner strength, and an expansion of our repertoire of skills. Self-inquiry builds a foundation upon which we can solidify and justify our practice. It is through this deep examination of our personal and environmental space that we create our own identity and help to shape the identities of our students. We can further examine our beliefs through the perspective of complicity in order to understand our actions and realize the transformative role (Sumara, 1997) we have in the lives of others. Ross Penhall's (1959) message to this end is evident in *Juniper Loop*. He invites us to walk and contemplate through a natural, uncomplicated, and beautiful path leading to a higher ground. This is where we can be open to creating spaces in our otherwise cluttered minds and complicated worlds.

As I stepped into and moved through the district's effort toward change, I have felt as if I have personally walked through *Juniper Loop*. A few questions have surfaced as I traveled along my path. Would we, as a district, be able to maintain this change effort once the five-year implementation phase ended? How many people have actually initiated change in their classrooms? Who would be responsible for continuing the momentum begun by the district? I kept seeking people out who could answer these questions since the beginning of my journey. I kept looking for opportunities to dialogue with teachers, CUPE members, senior level administrators, and anyone else I could find. I have also kept in tune with my surroundings wondering and wandering in various roles at all levels of the organization.

A number of people have traveled the same path. Some were moving in the same direction along with me. These leaders at the district level have hopefully ensured that district developed programs such as Reading 44, Focus on Reading workshops, and Writing 44 had the Instructional Intelligence philosophy embedded within them. Many of the district leaders are facilitators who incorporate Beyond Monet and Tribes tactics in their workshops.

Has the Instructional Intelligence Initiative had an Impact on Student Achievement?

> Very much so, let's take for example, think-pair-share, it gets them to buy in. They are more actively involved and have a higher interest level in their learning. It couldn't but increase their achievement. It is exciting to see the benefits of cooperative work.

> I don't know, I'm not the class teacher, but I think with what I have done it has had an impact. They were motivated and were working till the very last day of school.
>
> I definitely think so, especially with last year's grade seven class. They came away from my class understanding that you need to talk to learn. Learning is social and emotional. You can have skill, but if you don't connect with the kids, you won't get anywhere.

Institutionalization

Implementation

Initiation

During a recent Leadership for Learning Session, our superintendent shared this graphic as a model of our five-year plan, the green portion of the pie signifying the part that we are currently approaching. His message was simultaneously encouraging and realistic. He delivered a clear picture of the initiative continuing with commitment at all levels of senior administration. He also cautioned us about the need to provide for programs of choice, the current climate being one in which public education has to compete to maintain its population base in order to get funding.

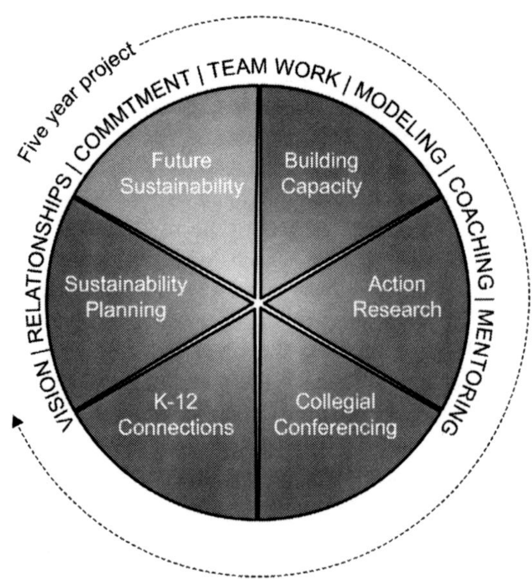

Figure 2. The wheel of change.

As the district moves forward, the question of sustainability arises. Will the district be able to move through the change effort in the future without the top guru, Barrie Bennett, involved? How will a recent change in senior administration affect the outcomes? Will there be enough trust from senior leadership in their administrators in the schools to make site-based decisions? How much accountability from teachers, leaders and students? And what, after all, *does* the research say about student achievement and Instructional Intelligence skills and tactics? Will the University run another cohort group with a focus on Instructional Intelligence methods? Who will be responsible for the planning and continuation of this direction once senior administration moves on?

Table 1. A chart of our district's commitment to systemic change

Systemic change
Instruction as the foundation
Commitment of resources
Structural changes for support
Coherence building
Educational consumerism
Embracing change
Responsiveness and adaptability

We are presently at the stage, as a district, where there are more questions than answers. Much will depend on the willing participation of people at all levels of our organization. I have been invited to participate as a workshop facilitator during this upcoming summer's institute. Along with forty other teachers and administrators, I will present in a series of sharing sessions during three days at the end of the summer. I am eager, and willing, however, this decision to participate has to be weighed against other priorities and needs. Some critical factors need to be addressed. Who owns the expertise now and what will the vision be in the next decade? Will there be adequate tangible resources during these times of budgetary constraints? The district has recently had to make some tough choices due to insufficient provincial funding for public education. Will some of their choices affect the change effort in the future?

At our recent meeting of administrators, I listened to our superintendent give answers to some of these questions. I believe that the direction the district embarked upon almost five years ago will be continued and maintained at the top levels of the organization. I see that the vision illustrated in Figure 2 and Table 1 (see previous page) as evidence that the district has a view for the future. It is clear and forward thinking and there is a plan in place. Yet one may question how effectively this vision will be shared with the entire district as it is ever unfolding, emerging, and becoming.

I also believe that we have worked significantly at all levels of the organization toward this end, and that now, too many people have too much at stake to let the progress diminish. There has been an energy created that will help to sustain the movement. However, it will need to be continually shared, the dialogue will have to happen, and the people and resources have to be deployed to sustain this movement. We will have to work together to make it happen.

Some suggestions regarding ensuring institutionalization have been presented to me along the way. A few people believe the district should develop a curriculum and set out a scope and sequence of learning of Instructional Intelligence for the district. Although this may address a need to make sure we check things off the list, I believe that change has to be flexible and open, especially a systemic change of this magnitude with so many people involved. People are getting on the bandwagon at different stages, at different ages, and with different personal interests. I believe it would be self-defeating to implement change in this manner. There are too many variables involved at the upper levels of administration in making those choices for everyone. There would also be the danger of everyone in the district teaching students the same strategies or tactics at the same time. Also, just as other traditional teaching techniques take on individual interpretations, there is a chance that Instructional Intelligence techniques will become diluted, misinterpreted, and misapplied. Moreover, the techniques may have been perceived by a handful of teachers as a substitute for deep knowledge in content and creative applications of both techniques and curriculum content. In high schools, this could be disastrous. Offering choices and different introduction points seems to be successful. However, based on their own needs and circumstances, these decisions are best left up to an individual teacher to make.

In and of itself, a change effort has to be flexible enough to be adaptable to change. It needs to be open, and serve the needs of the individual as well as the organization. This may be considered at the macro or the micro level. What may work for the district may not work for every school or for every teacher. It will be up to the administration and the teacher to decide. Senior management has to have faith in its top leadership, and administrators have to trust their teachers and allow for distributive decision-making on certain aspects of the change movement. We will need to make this change effort our own by molding it into what serves our own purposes, in our own schools and for our community of learners.

I compiled a list of recommendations for our former superintendent after a few informal conversations about our change effort. Looking back on this list, I still believe my suggestions are as relevant today as they were when I presented them to him.

My professional Recommendations

1. Continued professional development (i.e., use pro-D funds to visit other classes).
2. Create a list of resources, where to get them, who to go to when you need help.
3. Survey teachers on what their needs are, what the stumbling blocks may be.
4. Build trust and mutual understanding and respectful interactions.
5. Give people opportunity to provide feedback and brainstorm ideas.
6. Help foster collaborative learning environment (critical mass for change).
7. Empower teachers by giving them leadership opportunity at many levels.

8. Give teachers some control over the shape and direction we are heading.
9. Create a site-specific teacher leadership role and support with resource base.
10. Review communication network and continue publishing district newsletter.
11. Continue workshops that are both practical and theoretical in nature.

I have also recently prepared a presentation and forwarded it by email to our current superintendent and assistant superintendent with regard to these recommendations.

Where Do You Think We Will Be at After the Five-year Phase is Over?

> I don't know, I haven't informed myself. I don't know what others are doing. We need an overall picture. We need advertisement. We need to know what is out there, a common vision. If there is research that this works, then there should be accountability. Teachers have to see that this is not sucking them dry, but relieving them. They have to see the benefits to students, that they are thinking and learning better, and learning more. It is a way of teaching smarter.
>
> I think we need to become independent, and autonomous in this. The stuff that really works will carry on. I see us moving away from the name of Barrie Bennett. Ideally, every teacher in North Vancouver would be practicing this.
>
> We have a long way to go before sustainability. There are a few teachers embracing this, but there are more that aren't. It is exciting and ideal, but in visiting a number of schools, there are many that are still not on board.

The Next Steps

The implications of who I am now—as a "learnerleaderresearcher"—are many. First and foremost, as a teacher, I will continue to play with the tactics, strategies and graphics organizers in my classroom and with my students. I wish to learn more; I have further questions. I want to fully implement Tribes in my class. I am not an expert on assessment. I need to extend my understanding in the use of rubrics. I want to teach and I want to learn by inquiring into my practice, into student achievement and through research. The new world of technology is changing rapidly, and I will need to keep abreast of these changes in order to serve students and staff alike. I will continue to be a life-long learner at all levels in education.

Equally important is my own influence in the classroom and school community. My personality and character effects, as well as affects, change. When I am in the classroom, setting high expectations for behaviors and learning goals will challenge my students. I need to personally connect with students. Having a grasp on the content of the curriculum will allow me to implement the subject matter with an artful approach. Bennett likens this to an artist's role and the artful integration of all that Instructional Intelligence implies. It is like painting from an artist's palette—a teacher has to use the best shades and colors to provide the best learning situations for her class.

As a leader, I know the paramount importance of building relationships and of maintaining them. It will be critical to build collaborative professional learning teams within my school, so that teachers can support each other in their learning. I will need to keep informed and in tune with what is happening at the district level and look forward to supporting the district in facilitating workshops and mentoring teachers in their practice. The choice for change, I will leave to them. I can affect change positively and directly with my students in my own class. I have the opportunity every year to teach a new set of individuals and perhaps they, in turn, will affect change. Perhaps it will spill out later on.

As a researcher, I have many questions around student achievement using the strategies and tactics of Instructional Intelligence. I am curious on many levels about the implementation of Tribes and how cooperative group work affects the academic, social and emotional development of children. I also have many questions about how my role affects others, the students and the staff that I interact with on a daily basis. How do I transform others? How do they transform me? How much complicity is involved when we interact with each other? Who are the stakeholders and what voices are being heard?

At the district level, the change effort and sustainability will depend on the on-going commitment of people and resources. Every level of the organization has to be involved and interested in maintaining the current wave of change. It will have to be carried on by the internal leaders now. How the district supports those leaders is critical at this point. A commitment of time and money will be required for this. I also believe that a district level position needs to be created in order to ensure success in this effort.

Recently, a British Columbia Ministry Educational Review Team visited NVSD44. Their preliminary observations included comments about our district's strength, high degree of professionalism, dedication to improving student success and outstanding leadership at all levels that our superintendent shared with administrators through an on-line posting (Lewis, 2007). The Team was most impressed with the commitment to the Instructional Institute as a means to focus improving the learning and life chances of students. The ministry team further recognized the breadth and diversity of expressions of student success that are evident throughout our district and encourages us to communicate these successes throughout our community.

North Vancouver School District has an opportunity to affect social change in a positive direction. At the classroom level, teachers need to recognize that this change effort has broader implications for our students and our communities. The district also has a stake in providing the best educational experience for our students. NVSD44 can become progressive and forward thinking in championing the movement to greater achievement and success, for teachers and students alike.

On a more global level, many opportunities abound for sharing our experiences in a technological world. E-learning opportunities and web conferencing are the wave of the future. Those who possess the vision and leadership potential may engage in and create national and international conference opportunities. Already, Instructional Intelligence techniques have spread to many school districts in many countries, and it is an open field for learning in education today. The potential for further research is huge. Change is necessary, change will happen, and whether or not we choose to be involved and stay attuned is up to us as individuals. In education, I do not think we have a choice. We need to continue to learn, to grow, and to change so that we may stay current and create a world worth living in.

My world has been worth living in, the world my father created for me. He made a decision to come to Canada seeking a better life through education. He nurtured my love of learning with continuous support and encouragement all along. He was steadfast in his commitment to my education and never once wavered on this. My father's faith and moral integrity became a beacon of light in my path through change, guiding me to believe in my own purpose and strength to make it through these years. This legacy he left me as a gift. This gift I hope to pass on in my teaching and in my role as a leader. I dedicate this paper to him, for all that he has given me and for all that I have become.

Sandra Pascuzzi
North Vancouver School District 44
spascuzzi@nvsd44.bc.ca

REFERENCES

Abbotsford School District #34. (n.d.). *The developing writer: guided by assessment and instruction.* Curriculum, Instruction, & Assessment Dept. of S.D. No. 34.

Ainsworth, S. E., Bibby, P. A., & Wood, D. J. (1998). Analyzing the costs and benefits of multi-representational learning environment. In M. W. van Someren, P. Reimann, H. P. A. Boshuizen, & T. de Jong. (Eds.). *Learning with multiple representations.* pp. 120-134. Oxford, U.K.: Elsevier Science.

Airasian, P., & Gay, L. R. (2003). *Educational research: competencies for analysis and applications.* Upper Saddle River, OH: Pearson Education, Inc.

Alexander, G. (1995). *District initiatives: Reforming teacher and principal roles.* Idaho: University of Idaho.

Allen, J. (1995). *It's never too late: Leading adolescents to lifelong literacy.* Portsmouth, NH: Heinemann.

Allport, G. W. (1955). Becoming. *Basic considerations for a psychology of personality.* New Haven: Yale University Press.

American Association for the Advancement of Science. (1993). *Benchmarks for science literacy.* New York: Oxford University Press.

Anderman, L. (2003). Academic and social perceptions as predictors of change in middle school students' sense of school belonging. *The Journal of Experimental Education, 72*(1), 5-22.

Anderson, J. (1997). Understanding teacher change: Revisiting the concerns based adoption mode. *Curriculum Inquiry, 27*(3), 331-367.

Anderson, R., & Chance, P. (2003). *The principal's role in standards-based reform: Linking accountability to instructional improvement.* Las Vegas, NV: University of Nevada Las Vegas.

Andrzejczek, N., Trainin, G., & Poldberg, M. (2005). From image to text: Using images in the writing process. *International Journal of Education & the Arts, 6*(12), 1-17.

Apple, M. W. (1992). Educational reform and educational crisis. *Journal of Research in Science Teaching, 29,* 779-789.

Aoki, T. (2005). Inspiriting the curriculum. In W. F. Pinar, & R. L. Irwin (Eds.). *Curriculum in a new key: The collected works of Ted T. Aoki* (pp. 357-366). Mahwah, NJ: Lawrence Erlbaum Associates. Pp. 357-366.

Aoki, T. (2005). Imaginaries of "East and West": Slippery curricular signifiers in education. In W. F. Pinar, & R. L. Irwin (Eds.). *Curriculum in a new key: The collected works of Ted T. Aoki* (pp. 313-320). Mahwah, NJ: Lawrence Erlbaum Associates.

Aoki, T. (2005). Legitimating lived curriculum: Toward a curricular landscape of multiplicity. In W. F. Pinar, & R. Irwin (Eds.), *Curriculum in a new key: The collected works of Ted Aoki* (pp. 199-215). Mahwah, New Jersey: Lawrence Erlbaum Associates.

Aoki, T. T. (2005). Narration and narration in curricular spaces. In W. F. Pinar, & R. L. Irwin (Eds.). *Curriculum in a new key: The collected works of Ted Aoki* (pp. 402-410). Mahwah, NJ: Lawrence Erlbaum Associates.

Annevirta, T., & Vauras, M. (2006). Developmental changes of metacognitive skill in elementary school children. *The Journal of Experimental Education, 74*(3), 197-225.

Arcavi, A. (2003). The role of visual representation in the learning of mathematics. *Educational Studies in Mathematics, 52,* 215-241.

Ashcraft, M. H., & Kirk, E. P. (2001). The relationships among working memory, math anxiety, and performance. *Journal of Experimental Psychology, 130*(2), 224-237.

Avraamidou, L., & Osbourne, J. F. (2009). The role of narrative in communicating science. *International Journal of Science Education, 31,* 1683-1707.

Azzam, A. (2009). Why creativity? A conversation with Sir Ken Robinson. *Educational Leadership. 67(1), 22-26.*

P. Gouzouasis (ed.), Pedagogy in a New Tonality: Teacher Inquiries on Creative Tactics, Strategies, Graphics Organizers, and Visual Journals in the K-12 Classroom, 321–338.

REFERENCES

Baird, J. M. (2006). SHARE and share alike. *Teaching Pre K-8, 36*(5), 54-55.

Baker, L., & Lombardi, B. (1985). Students' lecture notes and their relation to test performance. *Teaching of Psychology, 12* (1), 28-32. New York, NY: Routledge Publishers.

Ballantyne, R., & Packer J. (2006). Promoting learning for sustainability: Principals' perceptions of the role of outdoor and environmental education centers. *Australian Journal of Environmental Education, 22*, 1-15.

Bartsch, K., & Estes, D. (1996). Individual differences in children's developing theory of mind and implications for metacognition. *Learning and Individual Differences, 8*(4), 281-304.

Bartsch, K., Horvath, K., & Estes, D. (2003). Young children's talk about learning events. *Cognitive Development, 18,* 177-193.

Baumeister, R. F., & Leary, M. R. (1995). The need to belong: Desire for interpersonal attachments as a fundamental human motivation. *Psychological Bulletin, 117*(3), 497-529.

Baxter, J., Woodward, J., & Olson. D. (2005). Writing in mathematics: An alternative form of communication for academically low-achieving students. *Learning Disabilities Research & Practice, 20*(2), 119-135.

Bennett, B., & Rolheiser, C. (2001). *Beyond Monet: The artful science of instructional intelligence.* Ajax, ON: Bookation.

Bennett, B. (2009). The artful science of instructional integration. In R. J. Marzano (Ed.). *On Excellence in Teaching,* (pp. 65-91). Alexandria, VA: Solution Tree.

Bennett, B. (n.d.). Instructionally intelligent...socially smart. Retrieved April 21, 2010 from *Orbit Magazine*, OISE/UT's Magazine for Schools: http://www.oise.utoronto.ca/orbit/core5_teach_strat.html

Bennett, B., & Smilanich, P. (2001). *Classroom management: A thinking & caring approach.* Toronto, ON: Bookation.

Bennett, B., Rolheiser, C., & Stevahn, L. (1991). *Cooperative learning: Where heart meets mind.* Toronto, ON: Educational Connections.

Bennett, B., Sangster, S., & Sharratt, L. (2003). *Systemic change: A focus on instructional intelligence... two and one-half years into a five-year journey.* Unpublished manuscript.

Benard, B. (2005). *What is it about Tribes? The research-based components of the developmental process of Tribes learning communities.* Windsor, CA: CenterSource Systems, LLC.

Birks, R., Eng, T., & Walachia, J. (2004). *Landmarks: A process reader.* Toronto, ON: Pearson Canada.

Blakey, E., & Spence, S. (1990). *Thinking for the future.* ERIC Clearinghouse on Information Resources. (ERIC document Reproduction Service No. ED327218).

Blecher, S., & Jaffee, K. (1998). *Weaving in the arts: Widening the learning circle.* Portsmouth, NH: Heinemann.

Borko, H., & Mayfield, V. (1995). The roles of the cooperating teacher and university supervisor in learning to teach. *Teaching and Teacher Education, 11*(5), 501-518.

Bowden, C. (2004). *Psychological assessment report.* North Vancouver, BC: NVSD44.

Bower, B. (2001). Math fears subtract from memory. *Science News, 159*(26), 405.

Brandsford, J., Brown, A., & Cocking, R. (1999). *How people learn: Brain, mind, experience, and school.* Washington, DC: National Academy Press.

Brendtro, L., Brokenleg, M., & Van Bockern, S. (2002). *Reclaiming youth at risk.* Bloomington, IN: Solution Tree.

Brendtro, L., Ness, A., & Mitchell, M. (2005). *No disposable kids.* Bloomington, IN: National Educational Service.

Brighthouse, H. (2008). Education for a flourishing life. *Yearbook of the National Society for the Study of Education, 107* (1), 58-71.

British Columbia Ministry of Education. (2010). *British columbia graduation rates.* Retrieved April 28, 2010, from wwwgov.bc.ca/yourbc/aboriginal_education/

British Columbia Ministry of Education. (n.d.). *Performance standards, writing.* Retrieved April 9, 2010 from http://www.bced.gov.bc.ca/perf_stands/writing.htm

British Columbia Ministry of Education. (2008). *Integrated resource package, IRP 161.* Retrieved April 20, 2010 from http://www.bced.gov.bc.ca/irp/math89.pdf

British Columbia Ministry of Education. (2008). *BC mathematics 8 – 9: Integrated resource package 2008*. Retrieved July 11, 2010 from http://www.bced.gov.bc.ca/irp/math89/2008math8_9.pdf

British Columbia Ministry of Education. (1991). *Thinking in the classroom (resources for teachers), volume one: The context for thoughtful learning.* Victoria, BC: Assessment, Examinations, and Reporting Branch, Ministry of Education and Ministry Responsible for Multiculturalism and Human Rights.

British Columbia Ministry of Education. (2000). *The primary program: A framework for teaching.* Victoria, BC: Ministry of Education, Student Assessment and Program Evaluation Branch.

Browne, D., & Hoover, J. H. (1990). The degree to which student teachers report using instructional strategies valued by university faculty. *Action in Teacher Education, 12*(1), 20-24.

Bruner, J. (1996). *Toward a theory of instruction.* Cambridge MA: Harvard University Press.

Bruner, J. (1977). *The process of education.* Cambridge MA: Harvard University Press.

Buber, M. (1966). *The way of response*. New York: Schocken Books, Inc.

Bullough, R. V. Jr., & Pinnegar, S. (2004). Thinking about the thinking about self-study: An analysis of eight chapters. In Loughran, J. (Author). Hamilton, M. L., & LaBoskey, V. K. (Eds.). *International handbook of self-study of teaching and teacher education practices, Part 1.* Springer Netherlands.

Burns, M. (2010). Snapshots of student misunderstandings. *Educational Leadership, 67(5)*, 18-22.

Buzan, T. (1993). *The mind map book: Radiant thinking.* Woodlands, London: BBC Books.

Buzan, T. (2003). *Mind maps for kids.* Hammersmith, London: Thorsons.

Cameron, J. (2002). *The artist's way: A spiritual path to higher creativity.* New York: Penguin Putnam.

Carter, K. (1993). The place of story in the study of teaching and teacher education. *Educational Researcher, 22* (1), 5-12.

Cazden, C. B. (1983). Peek-a-boo as an instructional model: Discourse development at school and at home. In B.Bain (Ed.). *The sociogenesis of language and human conduct: A multidisciplinary book of readings* (pp. 33-58). New York: Plenum.

Chalmers, F. G. (2004). Painting me into a corner? In R. Irwin, & A. deCosson (Eds.), *a/r/tography: Rendering self through arts based living inquiry* (pp. 173-183). Vancouver, BC: Pacific Educational Press.

Chapin, S. H., & Johnson, A. (2006). *Math matters: Understanding the math you teach (grades K-8).* Sausalito, CA: Math Solutions Publications.

Chapman, R. (1998). Improving student performance through the arts. *Principal, 77*(4), 20-22, 24.

Chessin, D., & Zander, M. (2006). The nature of science and art. *Sciencescope, 29*(8), 42-46.

Clarke, A., & Erickson, G. (Eds.). (2003). *Teacher inquiry: Living the research in everyday practice*. London: RoutledgeFalmer.

Clarke, A., & Erickson, G. (2004). The nature of teaching and learning in self-study. In J. Loughran et al. (Eds.). *International handbook of self-study of teaching and teacher education practices, part 1.* Springer Netherlands.

Cobb, J. B. (1998). The social contexts of tutoring: Mentoring the older at-risk student. *Reading Horizons, 39*(1), 49-75.

Cohen, J. (2006). Social, emotional, ethical, and academic education: Creating a climate for learning, participation in democracy, and well-being. *Harvard Education Review, 76*(2), 201-237.

Cohen, J. (1986). Theoretical considerations of peer tutoring. *Psychology in the Schools, 23,* 175-186.

Cohen, P., Kulik, J.A., & Kulik, C. (1982). Educational outcomes of tutoring: A metaanalysis of findings. *American Educational Research Journal, 19,* 237-248.

Colvin, J., Ainge, D., & Nelson, R. (1997). How to defuse defiance, threats, challenges, confrontations. *Teaching Exceptional Children, 29*(6), 47-51.

Colwell, R. (2006). *MENC handbook of research methodologies*. Oxford University Press USA. Retrieved April 24, 2010 from http://lib.myilibrary.com/Browse/open.asp?ID=65558&loc=333

Common Curriculum Framework for Grades 10 – 12 Mathematics: Western and Northern Canadian Protocol. (2008). Ministry of Education. Retrieved July 11, 2010, from http://www.wncp.ca/media/38771/math10to12.pdf

REFERENCES

Connolly, M., & Clandinin, J. (1990). Stories of experience and narrative inquiry. *Educational Researcher, 19*(5), *2-14.*

Constantino, T. (2007). Articulating aesthetic understandings through art making. *International Journal of Education and the Arts, 8*(1), 1-25.

Corkill, A. J. (1996). Individual differences in metacognition. *Learning and Individual Differences, 8*(4), 275-279.

Costa, A. L. (1985). *Developing minds: A resource book for teaching thinking.* Alexandria, VA: ASCD.

Costa, A. L. (1998). Teaching for intelligence: Recognizing and encouraging skillful thinking and behavior. In *Context, 18,* 22-30.

Costa, A. L. (2008). The thought-filled curriculum. *Educational Leadership, 65* (5), 20-24.

Covey, S. (2008). *The 7 habits of happy kids.* Toronto, ON: Simon & Schuster Books for Young Readers.

Cramer, J. (2008). Reviving the connection between children and nature. *Nativeplants, 9*(3), 279-286.

Csikszentmihalyi, M. (1990). *Flow: The psychology of optimal experience, steps toward enhancing the quality of life.* New York: Harper & Row.

Cuoco, A., Goldenberg, E. P., & Mark, J. (1996). Habits of mind: An organizing principle for mathematics curriculum. *Journal of Mathematical Behavior, 15* (4), 375-402.

Curran, L. (1998). *Lessons for little ones: Mathematics.* San Clemente, CA: Kagan Publishing.

Curran, L. (2000). *Lessons for little ones: Language arts.* San Clemente, CA: Kagan Publishing.

Daane, C., & Latham, D. (1998). Helping supervising teachers stay abreast of effective instructional strategies. *Contemporary Education, 69*(3), 141.

Day, C. (2000). Beyond transformational leadership. *Educational Leadership, 57*(7), 56-59.

Davenport, S. V., Arnold, M., & Lassmann, M. (2004). The impact of cross-age tutoring on reading attributes and reading achievement. *Reading Improvement, 41*(1), 3-13.

Davis, B., & Sumara, D. (1997). *Enlarging the space of the possible: Complexity, complicity, and action-research practices.* In Terrance Carson, & Dennis Sumara (Eds.), *Action research as a living practice* (pp. 299-312). New York: Peter Lang.

de Bono, E. (1991). *Six thinking hats for schools: K-2 resource book.* Logan, IA: Perfection Learning.

de Cosson, A. F., Irwin, R. L., Kind, S., & Springgay, S. (2007). Walking in wonder: Encountering the visual through living inquiry. In G. Knowles, T. Luciani, A. Cole, & L. Neilsen (Eds.), *The art of visual inquiry* (pp. 135-152). Halifax, Nova Scotia: Backalong Books.

de Cosson, A. F. (2004). The hermeneutic dialogic: Finding patterns midst the aporia of the artist/researcher/teacher. In R. L. Irwin, & A. de Cosson (Eds.), *a/r/tography: Rendering self through arts-based living Inquiry* (pp. 127-152). Vancouver, BC: Pacific Educational Press.

Desoete, A., & Roeyers, H. (2002). Off-line metacognition: A domain specific retardation in young children with learning disabilities? *Learning Disability Quarterly, 25,* 123-139.

Dewey, J. (1934). *Art as experience.* New York: Perigee Books.

Dignath, C., & Büttner, G. (2008). Components of fostering self-regulated learning among students: A meta-analysis on intervention studies at primary and secondary school level. *Metacognition Learning, 3,* 231-264.

Doonan, J. (2005). *Looking at pictures in picture books.* Stroud, UK: Thimble Press.

Douglas, O., Smith Burton, K., & Reese-Durham, N. (2008). The effects of multiple intelligence teaching strategy on the academic achievement of eighth grade math students. *Journal of Instructional Psychology, 35*(2), 182-187.

Douville, P. (2004). Use mental imagery across the curriculum. *Preventing School Failure, 49*(1), 36-39.

Duke, D. L. (1988). Why principals consider quitting. *Phi Delta Kappan,* 70(4), 308-313.

Dyson, H. (1994). *Confronting the split between the child and children: Toward new curricular visions of the child writer.* Occasional paper #35 presented at the National Center for the Study of Writing and Literacy, Berkeley, CA.

Eisner, E. W. (1982). *Curriculum and instruction.* New York, NY: Longman.

Eisner, E. W. (2005). *Reimagining schools: The selected works of Elliot W. Eisner*. New York, NY: Routledge.

Elias, M. (2003). *Academic and social-emotional learning. Educational Practices Series Booklet #11*. Geneva, Switzerland: UNESCO, International Academy of Education and the International Bureau of Education.

Elliot, D. J. (1995). *Music matters: A new philosophy of music education*. New York: Oxford University Press.

Ellis, C., & Bochner, A. (2000). Autoethnography personal narrative, reflexity: Researcher as subject. In N.K. Denzin, & Y.S. Lincoln (Eds.). *Handbook of qualitative research,* second edition (pp. 733-767). Thousand Oaks, CA: Sage.

Ellis, K., Keeling-Walter, W., Evans, M., & Reissner, C. (2006). *Instructional strategies for K-12: Strategies for teaching*. Otterville, ON: Otterville Public School Teachers.

Ellsworth, J. (2001). A survey of educational change models. *Teacher Librarian, 29*(2), 22-24.

Empson, S.B., & Junk, D.L. (2004). Teachers' knowledge of children's mathematics after implementing a student-centered curriculum. *Journal of Mathematics Teacher Education 7,* 121-144.

Englert, C. S., & Hiebert, E. H. (1984). Children's sensitivity to expository text structure. *Journal of Educational Psychology, 76,* 65-74.

Epstein, A. S. (2003). How planning and reflection develop young children's thinking skills. *Young Children, 58* (5), 28-36.

Epstein, A. S. (2008). An early start on thinking. *Educational Leadership, 65* (5), 38-42.

Ernst, K. (1997). Student sketch journals: Art in your curriculum. *Teaching PreK – 8, 27*(6), 26-27.

Ernst, K. (2001). The artist's workshop: Widening the reading, writing, and art connections. *Reading and Writing Quarterly, 13*(4), 355-367.

Etherington, K. (2004). *Becoming a reflexive researcher: Using our selves in research*. London & Philadelphia: Jessica Kingsley Publishers.

Farris, R. (1991). Changing mathematics teaching. Clearing House, *65*(1), 48-50.

Feiler, R., Heritage, M., & Gallimore, R. (2000). Teachers leading teachers. *Educational Leadership, 57* (7), 66-69.

Finley, S. (2008). Arts-based research. In G. Knowles, & A. Cole (Eds.). *Handbook of the arts in qualitative research: Perspectives, methodologies, examples and issues* (pp. 70-80). Thousand Oak, CA: Sage.

Flavell, J. H. (1979). Metacognition and cognitive monitoring: A new area of cognitive-developmental inquiry. *American Psychologist, 34* (10), 906-911.

Flavell, J. H. (1999). Cognitive development: Children's knowledge about the mind. *Annual Review Psychology, 50,* 21-45.

Flavell, J. H. (2004). Theory-of-mind development: Retrospect and prospect. *Merrill-Palmer Quarterly, 50*(3), 274-290.

Flavell, J. H., Green, F. L., Flavell, E. R., & Grossman, J. B. (1997). The development of children's knowledge about inner speech. *Child Development, 68*(1), 39-47.

Fraser, S. (2006). *Authentic childhood: Experiencing Reggio Emilia in the classroom* (2nd ed.). Toronto, ON: Thomson & Nelson.

Freedman, J. (2000). *Wall of fame*. San Diego, CA: AVID Academic Press.

Freire, P. (1970). *Pedagogy of the oppressed*. New York, NY: Continuum International Publishing Group, Inc.

Friedlander, A., Hershkowitz, R., & Arcavi, A. (1989). Incipient "algebraic" thinking in pre-algebra students. *Proceedings of the 13th Conference of the International Group for the Psychology of Mathematics Education, Vol. 1* (pp. 283-290). Paris, France.

Fuchs, D., & Fuchs, L. (2001). Peer-assisted learning strategies in reading. *Remedial and Special Education, 22* (1), 1-11.

Fulford, R. (2001). *The triumph of narrative: Storytelling in the age of mass culture*. New York, NY: Broadway.

Fullan, M. (2002). The change leader. *Educational Leadership, 59*(8), 16-20.

REFERENCES

Fullan, M. (2005). *Leadership and sustainability: system thinkers in action.* Thousand Oaks, CA: Corwin Press.

Fullan, M. (2001). *Leading in a culture of change.* San Francisco, CA: John Wiley & Sons, Inc.

Fullan, M. (1999). *Change forces: The sequel.* Philadelphia, PA: Falmer Press, Taylor & Francis, Inc.

Fullan, M. (2000). *The role of the principal in school reform: Principal's institute at Bank Street College.* Retrieved February 1, 2011 from http://www.michaelfullan.ca/Articles_00/11_00.pdf

Fullan, M. (2001). *The new meaning of educational change.* Toronto, ON: Irwin.

Fullan, M., & Hargreaves, A. (1996). *What's worth fighting for in your school.* New York, NY: Teacher's College Press.

Gagne, R. (1965). *The conditions of learning.* New York: Holt, Rinehart & Winston.

Gardner, H. (1983). *Frames of mind: The theory of multiple intelligences.* New York: Basic Books.

Gardner, H. (2006). *Multiple intelligences: New horizons.* New York: Basic Books.

Gardner, H. (1993). *Multiple Intelligences: The theory in practice.* New York: Basic Books.

Gawain, S. (1978). *Creative visualization.* San Rafael, CA: New World Library, 1978.

Gay, L.R., Mills, G.E., & Airasian, P. W. (2003). *Educational research: Competencies for analysis and applications* (7th ed.). Columbus, Ohio: Merrill Prentice-Hall.

Gibbs, J. (1999). *Guiding your school community to live a culture of caring and learning: The process is called tribes.* Windsor, CA: Centersource Systems, LLC.

Gibbs, J. (2001). *Discovering gifts in middle school: Learning in a caring culture called Tribes.* Windsor, CA: CenterSource Systems, LLC.

Gibbs, J. (2001). *Tribes: A new way of learning and being together.* Oakland, CA: Centersource Systems, LLC.

Glickman, C. D. (2003). *Holding sacred ground: Essays on leadership, courage and endurance in our schools.* San Francisco, CA: John Wiley & Sons, Inc.

Goleman, D. (1998). *Working with emotional intelligence.* Toronto, Ontario: Bantam Books.

Goleman, D., Byatzis, R., & McKee, A. (2002). *Primal leadership: Realizing the power of emotional intelligence.* Boston, MA: Harvard Business School Press.

Goldin, G. A. (2002). Representation in mathematical learning and problem solving. In English, L. (Ed.). *Handbook of international research in mathematics education* (pp. 197-218). Mahwah, NJ: Lawrence Erlbaum Associates.

Goldsworthy, A. (2004). *Passage.* London: Thames & Hudson.

Gordon, C., Sheridan, M., & Paul, W. (1998). Strategic learning for life: Learning to learn. In *content literacy for secondary teachers.* Toronto, ON: Harcourt Brace.

Gough, N. (1993). Environmental education, narrative complexity and postmodern science fiction. *International Journal of Science Education, 15*(5), 607-625.

Gouzouasis, P. (2008). Toccata on assessment, validity, and interpretation. *Being with a/r/t/ography.* Springgay, S., Irwin, R. L., Gouzouasis, P., & Leggo, C. (Eds.). (pp. 219-230). Rotterdam: SensePublishers.

Grauer, K. (1984). Art and writing: Enhancing expression in images and words. *Art Education, 37*(5), 32-34.

Grauer, K. (2006). Starting with art: Relating children's visuals and written expression. In K. Grauer, & R. Irwin (Eds.). *StarTing With* (pp. 110-117). Toronto, ON: Canadian Society for Education through Art.

Gripman, S. (2009). Macworld. *Canadian Reference Centre, 26* (3), 26-32.

Grout, N., Ratzburg, E., & Todd, T. (2005). *Examining the factors that are contributing to or detracting from the implementation of the five-year instructional strategies institute in North Vancouver School District.* Unpublished M.Ed. thesis. The University of British Columbia.

Gouzouasis, P. (2008). Toccata on assessment, validity, and interpretation. *Being with a/r/t/ography.* Springgay, S., Irwin, R. L., Gouzouasis, P., & Leggo, C. (Eds.). (pp. 219-230). Rotterdam: SensePublishers.

Gouzouasis, P. (in press). An ethos of music education in the 21st century: An (im)possibility? *Action, Criticism and Theory for Music Education,* 20 page ms.

Grossman, R. (2008). Structures for facilitating student reflection. *College Teaching, 57*(1), 15-22.

Hall, G. E., & Hord, S. (2001, 2006). *Implementing change: patterns, principles, and potholes*. Needham Heights, MA: Allyn and Bacon.

Halstead, M. (1995). How metaphors structure our spiritual understanding. In C. Ota, & C. Erricker (Eds.). *Spiritual education: Literary, empirical and pedagogical approaches* (pp. 149-172). London: Cassell.

Hanson, J. (2002). *Improving student learning in mathematics and science through the integration of visual art.* Master of Art Action Research Project, Saint Xavier University and IRI/Skylight Professional Development Field Based Masters Program. (ERIC Document Reproduction Service No. ED465534)

Hargreaves, A. (2004). Inclusive and exclusive educational change: Emotional responses of teachers and implications for leadership. *School Leadership and Management, 24,* 287-309.

Hargreaves, A., Earl, L., Moore, S., & Manning, S. (2001). *Learning to change: Teaching beyond subjects and standards.* San Francisco, CA: Jossey-Bass Inc.

Hargreaves, A. (2000). Four ages of professionalism and professional learning. *Teachers and Teaching: History and Practice, 6*(2), 151-182.

Harris, A., & Muijs, D. (2003). Teacher leadership: A review of the research. Retrieved May 23, 2005 from http://www.ncsl.org.uk/researchpublications

Hartley, J., & Marshall, S. (1974). On notes and note-taking. *Universities Quarterly*, 28(2), 225-235.

Hattie, J. (2006). Cross age tutoring and the reading together program. *Studies in Educational Evaluation, 32(2),*100-124.

Hekimoglu, S., & Kittrell, E. (2010). Challenging students' beliefs about mathematics: The use of documentary to alter perceptions of efficacy. *Primus: problems, resources and issues in mathematics undergraduate studies, 20*(4), 299-331.

Hertberg-Davis, H., & Callahan, C. M. (2008). A narrow escape: Gifted students' perceptions of advanced placement and international baccalaureate programs. *Gifted Child Quarterly, 52*(3), 199-216.

Hershkowitz, R., Arcavi, A., & Bruckheimer, M. (2001). Reflections on the status and nature of visual reasoning-the case of the matches. *Journal of Mathematics, Science and Technology, 32*(2), 255-265.

Hodgins, J. (1993). *A passion for narrative: A guide for writing fiction.* Toronto, ON: McClelland & Stewart.

Hopkins, M. (2008). A vision for the future: Collective effort for systemic change. *Phi Delta Kappan , 89*(10), 737-740.

Hord, S. (1997). Issues about change. Professional learning communities: What are they and why are they important? Retrieved May 23, 2005 from http://www.sedl.org/change/issues/issues61.html

Horsley, D. L., & Loucks-Horsley, S. (1998). CBAM brings order to the tornado of change. *Journal of Staff Development, 19*(4). Retrieved April 25, 2005 from http://www.nsdc.org/library/publications/jsd/horsley194.cfm

Howitt, C. (2009). Teaching science. *The Journal of the Australian Science Teachers Association, 55*(2), 42-46.

Hoyt, L. (1992). Many ways of knowing: Using drama, oral interactions, and the visual arts to enhance reading comprehension. *The Reading Teacher, 45*(8), 580-584.

Hungerford, H., & Volk, T. (1990). Changing learner behavior through environmental education. *Journal of Environmental Education, 21*(3), 8-12.

Hunter, M. (1994). *Enhancing teaching.* New York: Macmillan College.

Hyde, K. L., Lerch, J., Norton, A., Forgeard, M., Winner, E., Evans. A. C., & Schlaug, G. (2009). Musical training shapes structural brain development. *The Journal of Neuroscience, 29*(10), 3019-3025.

International Baccalaureate Organization. (2006a). *Diploma programme mathematics SL.* Chippenham, UK: Antony Rowe Ltd.

REFERENCES

International Baccalaureate Organization. (2006b). *IB learner profile booklet.* Chippenham, UK: Antony Rowe Ltd.

Irwin, R. (2004). a/r/tography: A metonymic metissage. In R. Irwin, & A. deCosson (Eds.). *a/r/tography: Rendering self through arts based living inquiry* (pp. 27-40). Vancouver, BC: Pacific Educational Press.

Jackson, S. (2003). Weeding the garden. In M. Shamsher, E. Decker, & C. Leggo., (Eds.). *Teacher research in the backyard* (pp. 187-218). Vancouver, BC: BCTF Program for Quality Teaching.

Jacobson, J., Thrope, L., fisher, D., Lapp, D., Frey, N., & Flood, J. (2001). Cross-age tutoring: A literacy improvement approach for struggling adolescent readers. *Journal of Adolescent & Adult Literacy, 44,* 528-536.

James, W. (1899). *Talks to teachers on psychology; and to students on some of life's ideals.* Complete text retrieved on February 4, 2011 from http://www.bookrags.com/ebooks/16287/. Also available at http://www.gutenberg.org/files/16287/16287-h/16287-h.htm

Janeczko, P., & Raschka, C. (2005). *Poke in the I: A collection of concrete poems.* Somerville, MA: Candlewick Press.

Jardine, D. (1997). Their bodies swelling with messy secrets. In T.R. Carson, & D. J. Sumara (Eds.). *Action research as a living practice* (161-166). New York: Peter Lang.

Jensen, E. (1998). *Teaching with the brain in mind.* Alexandria, VA: Association for Supervision and Curriculum Development.

Jobe, R., & Dayton-Sakari, M. (1999). *Reluctant readers: Connecting students and books for successful reading experiences.* Markham, ON: Pembroke Publishers.

Johnson, D., & Johnson, R. (2004). The three Cs of promoting social and emotional learning. In J. Zins, R. Weissberg, M.C. Wang, & H. Whalberg (Eds.). *Building school successes on social emotional learning: What does the research say?* New York, NY: Teachers College Press.

Johnson, S. (2008). *Brainy quotes.* Retrieved January 12, 2010 from http://www.brainyquote.com/quotes/authors/s/samuel_johnson.html

Johnson, J., Carlson, S., Kastl, J., & Kastl, R. (1992). Developing conceptual thinking: The concept attainment model. *The Clearing House, 66*(2), 117-121.

Johnston, S. (2010). *Environmental sustainability and ecological systems: A curriculum project for grade 10 students at the North Vancouver outdoor school.* Unpublished document, 22 page manuscript (available from the author upon request).

Juel, C. (1991). What makes literacy tutoring effective? *Reading Research Quarterly, 31,* 268-289.

Kagan, L. (2000). *Multiiple intelligencs: Structure and activities.* San Clemente, CA: Kagan Publishings.

Kalin, N., Grauer, K., Baird, J., & Meszaro, C. (2007). Provoking points of convergence: Museum and university collaborating and co-evolving. *Jade, 26*(2), 199-205.

Kalin, N. (2007). Art teachers learning from the personal through autobiographical inquiry. *Arts and Learning Research Journal, 24,* 77-89.

Keeley, P. (2008). *Science formative assessment.* Thousand Oaks, CA: Corwin Press & NSTA Press.

Keeley, P. (2005). *75 practical strategies for linking assessment, instruction, and learning* (Paperback). Thousand Oaks: Corwin Press.

Kelchtermans, G., & Hamilton, M. L. (2004). The dialectics of passion and Theory: Exploring the relation between self-study and emotion. In Loughran, J. (Author) Hamilton, M. L., & LaBoskey, V. K. (Eds.). *International handbook of self-study of teaching and teacher education practices, Part 1.* Springer Netherlands.

Kewra, K., & Robinson, D. (1995). Visual argument: Graphic organizers are superior to outlines in improving learning from text, *Journal of Educational Psychology, 87*(5), 455-467, Washington, DC: American Psychological Association.

Koirala, H. P. (2002). Facilitating student learning through math journals. In *Proceedings of the Annual Meeting of the International Group for the Psychology of Mathematics Education* (*3*, pp. 217-223). Norwich, England. (ERIC Document Reproduction Service No. ED476099)

Kottler, J. (2002). *Students who drive you crazy: Succeeding with resistant, unmotivated, and otherwise difficult young people*. Thousand Oaks, California: Corwin Press, Inc.

Krasiejko, I. (2010). The role of metacognition in education. *The New Educational Review, 20*(1), 120-128.

Kruse, K. (n.d.). Retrieved May 30, 2010, from *Gagne's nine events of instruction: An introduction*, at http://www.e-learningguru.com/articles/art3_3.htm

Labbo, L., & Teale, W. (1990). Cross-age reading: A strategy for helping poor readers. *The Reading Teacher, 43,* 362-369.

Lai, K. (1999). Freedom to Learn: A study of the experiences of secondary school teachers and students in a geography field trip. *International Research in Geographical and Environmental Education, 8*(3), 239-255.

Lamarche-Bisson, D. (2004). Learning styles – What are they? Hey can they help? *World and I, 17*(9), 268, Washington, DC.

Lane, A. (2009). Communication World. *Business Source Premier, 26*(1), 24-25.

Lazear, D. (1991). *Seven Ways of Knowing.* Palatine, Illinois: Skylight Publishing, Inc.

Leggo, C. (2004). Living poetry: Five ruminations. *Language and Literacy, 6*(2), 27-42.

Leinhardt, G. (1986). Expertise in mathematics teaching. *Educational Leadership, 43*(7), 28-33.

Leithwood, K., & Aitken, R. (1995). *Making schools smarter.* Thousand Oaks, CA: Corwin Press, Inc.

Lemke, J. L. (1990). *Talking science: language, learning and values.* Norwood, NJ: Ablex Publishing Corporation.

Lewis, J. (2007, May 4). District review team—preliminary observations. Message posted to ManagerCentral, archived at http://www.nvsd44.bc.ca.

Lewison, M., Seely Flint, A., & Van Sluys, K. (2002). Taking on critical literacy: The journey of newcomers and novices. *Language Arts, 79*(5), 382-392.

Likona, T. (1988). Four strategies for fostering character development in children. *Phi Delta Kappan, 69*(6), 421.

Lim, L., & Pugalee, D. K. (2004). Using journal writing to explore "They communicate to learn mathematics and they learn to communicate mathematically." *Ontario Action Researcher, 7*(2), 1-15.

Lim, L., & Pugalee, D. K. (2006). The effects of writing in a secondary applied mathematics class: Collaborative action research project. Retrieved July 10, 2010 from http://math.coe.uga.edu/tme/issues/v13n2/v13n2.lshii.pdf

Livingston, J. A. (1997). Metacognition: An overview. Retrieved October 31, 2009 from http://www.gse.buffalo.edu/fas/shuell/cep564/Metacog.htm

Lockl, K., & Schneider, W. (2006). Precursors of metamemory in young children: The role of theory of mind and metacognitive vocabulary. *Metacognition Learning, 1*, 15-31.

Long, N. (1996). The conflict cycle paradigm on how troubled students get teachers out of control. In J.L. Long & W.C. Morris (Eds.). *Conflict in the classroom: The education of at-risk and troubled students* (pp. 244-265). (5th ed.). Austin, Texas: Pro-Ed, Inc.

Long, N. (2000). Personal struggles in reclaiming troubled students. *Reclaiming Children and Youth, 9*(2), 95-8.

Longworth, N. (2003). Lifelong learning in action: transforming education in the 21st century. London, UK: Kogan Page Limited.

Loewenstein, G. (1994). The psychology of curiosity: A review and reinterpretation. *Psychological Bulletin, 116,* 75-98.

Lougheed, T. (2008). Wild child: Giving the child back to nature. *Environmental Health Perspectives, 116*(10), 346-349.

Loughran, J. (Author), Hamilton, M. L., LaBoskey, V. K. (Eds.). (2004). What's the title of the paper? *International handbook of self-study of teaching and teacher education practices, Part 1.* Springer Netherlands.

Loughran, J. (2005). Researching teaching about teaching: self-study of teacher education practices. *Studying Teacher Education, 1*(1), 5-16.

REFERENCES

Louv, R. (2006). *Last child in the woods: Saving our children from the nature-deficit disorder.* Chapel Hill, North Carolina: Algonquin Books of Chapel Hill.

Lymburner, J. (2004). Interwoven threads: Theory, practice and research coming together. In R. Irwin, & A. deCosson (Eds.). *a/r/tography: Rendering self through arts based living inquiry* (pp. 75-90). Vancouver, BC: Pacific Educational Press.

MacDonald, B. (2005). *Boy smarts: Mentoring boys for success at school.* New York, NY: Mentoring Boys Press.

Mallonee, R. L. (1998). Applying multiple intelligence theory in the music classroom. *Choral Journal, 38*(8), 37-41.

Marchisan, M., & Alber, S. (2001). The write way: Tips for teaching the writing process to resistant writers. *Intervention in School and Clinic, 36*(3), 154-162.

Martin, J. (1991). *Flowers for mom.* Toronto, ON: Annick Press.

Marton F., & Tsui, A. (2004). *Classroom discourse and the space of the learning.* Mahwah, NJ: Lawrence Erlbaum.

Marzano, R. J., Pickering, D. J., & Pollock, J. E. (2005). *Classroom instruction that works: Research-based strategies for increasing student achievement.* Upper Saddle River, NJ: Merrill Prentice Hall.

Marzano, R. J. (2007). *The art and science of teaching.* Alexandria, VA: Association for Supervision and Curriculum Development.

Marzano, R. J. (2009). *Designing & teaching learning goals & objectives.* Alexandria, VA: Solution Tree.

Marzano, R. J. (2009b). *Formative assessment & standards-based grading.* Alexandria: Solution Tree.

Mason, J. (2005). Frameworks for learning, teaching and research: Theory and practice. Retrieved July 10, 2010 from http://mcs.open.ac.uk/jhm3/SVGrids/SVGRids_Files/PMENAPlenary Oct05.pdf

McGinnis, S. (2010, May 16). Mathematics is the most 'catastrophic' subject for students, and even induces panic in many adults. *Calgary Herald.* Retrieved July 12, 2010, from http://www.calgaryherald.com/technology/methods+take+anxiety+math/3034118/story.html#ixzz0tVyeVFp1

McNeely, C., & Falci, C. (2004). School connectedness and the transition into and out of health-risk behavior among adolescents: A comparison of social belonging and teacher support. *Journal of School Health, 74*(7), 284-292.

McNiff, S. (1998). *Trust the process: An artist's guide to letting go.* Boston: Shambhala.

Miller, L. J., Kohler, F.W., Ezell, H., Hoel, K., & Strain, P. S. (1993, Spring). Winning with peer tutoring: A teacher's guide. *Preventing School Failure,* 14–18. North Vancouver School District. 2005. *Catchment Areas.* Retrieved May, 11, 2007 from http://www.nvsd44.bc.ca/Schools/CatchmentAreas.aspx.

Monroe, M., Andrews, E., & Biedenweg, K. (2007). A framework for environmental education strategies. *Applied Environmental Education and Communication, 6,* 205-216.

Moore, P. (1994). Authoring. *English in Education, 28*(3), 11-14.

Moriarty, M. W. (2009). Evaluating children's use of symbol in some recent research. *International Journal of Children's Spirituality, 14*(1), 47-61.

Morton, B. (2007, April 28). Interpersonal skills put focus on a 'we' not 'me' attitude. In *The Vancouver Sun,* p. E1.

Nada, N., Kholief, M., Tawfik, S., & Metwally, N. (2009). Mobile knowledge tool-kit to create a paradigm shift in higher education. *Electronic Journal of Knowledge Management, 7(2),* 255-260.

Nardi, E., & Steward, S. (2003). Is mathematics T.I.R.E.D.? A profile of quiet disaffection in the secondary mathematics classroom. *British Educational Research Journal, 29*(3), 345-367.

Naths A. J. (2004). Of mango trees and woven tales. In R. L. Irwin, & A. de Cosson (Eds.). *a/r/tography: Rendering self through arts-based living Inquiry* (pp. 116-126). Vancouver, BC: Pacific Educational Press.

National Research Council. (2000). *Inquiry and the national science education standards.* Washington, DC: National Academy Press.

Negrete, A. (2003). *Fact via fiction. The Pantaneto Forum, 12.* Retrieved on April 24, 2010 from http://www.pantaneto.co.uk/issue12/front12.htm.

North Vancouver School District. (2007). *Writing 44 Intermediate: A core writing framework.* Victoria, BC: Queen's Printer.

North Vancouver School District 44. (2007). *Math 44: Teaching for proficiency.* Retrieved August 25, 2010 from http://www.nvsd44.bc.ca/Math44/math44.html

North Vancouver School District. (2008). Math 44: Teaching for proficiency (2nd Ed.). North Vancouver, BC.

North Vancouver School District. (2006). *School district performance plan: Accountability contract.*

North Vancouver School District. (2006). *School district performance plan: School district context.*

North Vancouver School District. (1999). *Reading 44 Intermediate: A core reading framework.* Victoria, BC. Queen's Printer.

Olson, J. (2006). Perspectives: The myth of catering to learning styles. *Science & Children, 44*(2), 56-57, Arlington, VA: National Science Teachers Association.

Olson, J. (1992). *Envisioning writing.* Portsmouth, NH: Heinemann.

Onika, D., Smith Burton, K., & Reese-Curham, N. (2008). The effects of multiple intelligence teaching strategy on the academic achievement of eighth grade math students. *Journal of Instructional Psychology, 35*(2), 182-187.

Op't Eynde, P., De Corte, E., & Verschaffel, L. (2002). Framing students' mathematics-related beliefs: A quest for conceptual clarity and a comprehensive categorization. In G. C. Leder, E. Pehkonen, & G. Törner (Eds.), *Beliefs: A Hidden Variable in Mathematics Education?* (pp. 13-37). Netherlands: Kluwer Academic Publishers.

Osbourne, J. F., & Collins, S. (2001). Pupils' views of the role and value of the science curriculum: a focus group study. *International Journal of Science Education, 23*(5), 441-468.

Osterman, K. F. (2000). Students' need for belonging in the school community. *Review of Educational Research, 70*(3), 323-367.

Palmberg I., & Kuru J. (2000). Outdoor activities as a basis for environmental responsibility. *The Journal of Environmental Education, 31*(4), 32-36.

Parry, T., & Gregory, G. (2003). *Designing brain-compatible learning* (2nd ed.). Glenview, IL: Pearson Education, Inc.

Pearse, H. (2004). Praxis in perspective. In A. de Cosson & R. L. Irwin (Eds.). *a/r/tography: Rendering self through arts-based living inquiry* (pp. 184-197). Vancouver, BC: Pacific Educational Press.

Penhall, R. (1959). Juniper loop [Painting in oil on canvas]. *Artist for Kids Gallery.* Leo Marshall Curriculum Centre, North Vancouver, BC.

Pente, P. (2004). Reflections on artist/researcher/teacher identities: A game of cards. In R. L. Irwin, & A. de Cosson (Eds.). a/r/tography: Rendering Self Through Arts-Based Living Inquiry (pp. 91-102). Vancouver: Pacific Educational Press.

Pepper, S. C. (1942/1970). *World hypotheses: A study in evidence.* Berkley, CA: University of California Press.

Phillips, L. (2000, July). *Image to word-word to image: Literally a vision.* Preliminary Policy Brief Presented for Pacific Resources for Education and Learning, Honolulu, HI.

Pirie, S., & Kieren. (1994). Growth in mathematical understanding: how can we characterise it and how can we represent it? *Educational Studies in Mathematics, 26*(2-3), 165-190.

Pillow, B. H. (2008). Development of children's understanding of cognitive activities. *The Journal of Genetic Psychology, 169*(4), 297-321.

Pinar, W. (1999). Not burdens – Breakthroughs. *Curriculum Inquiry, 29*(3), 365-367.

Pinar, W. (2004). Foreword. In A. de Cosson, & R. L. Irwin (Eds.). *a/r/tography: Rendering self through arts-based living inquiry* (pp. 9-25). Vancouver, BC: Pacific Educational Press.

Pintrich, P. R. (2002). The role of metacognitive knowledge in learning, teaching, and assessing. *Theory Into Practice, 41*(4), 219-225.

Pinzker, V. (2001). *Increasing the engagement and understanding of concepts in mathematics.* Master of Arts Action Research Project, Saint Xavier University and Skylight Professional Development. (ERIC Document Reproduction Service No. ED455117)

REFERENCES

Porter, N. (2004). Exploring the making of wonder. In R. Irwin, & A. deCosson (Eds.). *a/r/tography: Rendering self through arts based living inquiry* (pp.103-115). Vancouver, BC: Pacific Educational Press.

Powell, A. B., & Lopez, J. A. (1989). Writing as a vehicle to learn mathematics: A case study. In: P. Connolly, & T. Vilardi (Eds.). *Writing to learn mathematics and science* (pp.157-177). New York: Teachers College Press. Retrieved August 23, 2010 from http://andromeda.rutgers.edu/~powellab/docs/chapters/PowellLopez%281989%29.pdf

Prestage, S., & Perks, P. (2007). Developing teacher knowledge using a tool for creating tasks for the classroom. *Journal of Mathematics Teacher Education, 10*(4–6), 381-390.

Pryer, A. (2004). Living within marginal spaces: intellectual nomadism and artists/researcher/teacher praxis. R. L. Irwin & A. deCossen (Eds.). *a/r/tography: Rendering self through arts based living inquiry* (pp. 116-126). Vancouver, BC: Pacific Educational Press.

Pugalee, D. K. (1998). Promoting mathematical learning through writing. *Mathematics in School, 27*(1), 20-22.

Reder, L. M. (1996). Different research programs on metacognition: Are the boundaries imaginary? *Learning and Individual Differences, 8*(4), 383-390.

Ritchart, R., & Perkins, D. (2008). Making thinking visible. *Educational Leadership, 65*(5), 57-61.

Rivkin, M. (2000). Outdoor experiences for young children. *ERIC® Clearinghouse on Rural Education and Small Schools.* 1-5.

Roller, C. M. (1996). *Variability not disability: Struggling readers in a workshop classroom.* Newark, DE: International Reading Association.

Rosell, S.A. (2000). *Changing frames: Leadership and governance in the information age—report of the roundtable on renewing governance.* Retrieved October 21, 2008 from http://www.viewpointlearning.ca/publications/books/changing_frames.pdf

Rosenblatt, L. (1994). The transactional theory of reading and writing. In R.B. Ruddell, M.R. Ruddell, & H. Singer (Eds.). *Theoretical models and processes of reading* (4th ed., pp. 1057-1092). Newark, DE: International Reading Association.

Sagor, R. (1996). Building resiliency in students. *Educational Leadership, 54,* 38-43.

Salomon, G. (1984). Television is "easy" and print is "tough:" The differential investment of mental effort in learning as a function of perceptions and attributions. *Journal of Educational Psychology, 76*(4), 833-846, Washington, DC: American Psychological Association.

Sanders-Bustle, L. (2008). Visual artifacts journals as creative and critical springboards for meaning making. *Art Education, 5*, 8014.

Santrock, J. (2004). *Cognitive development approaches.* New York, NY: McGraw-Hill.

Sarason, S. B. (1999). *Teaching as a performing art.* New York, NY: Teachers College Press.

Sax, L. (2005). *Why gender matters.* New York, NY: Broadway Books.

Schank, R. C., & Berman, T. R. (2002). The pervasive role of stories in knowledge and action. In Solomon, J. (Ed.). Science stories and science texts: What can they do for our students? *Studies in Science Education, 37*(1), 85-105.

Schlaug, G., Janke, L., Huang, Y., Staiger, J. F., & Steinmetz, H. (1995). Increased corpus callosum size in musicians. *Neuropsychologia, 33*(8), 1047-1055.

Schmittau, J. (2003). Task framework/principles. *International Congress for Mathematics Education, 11.* Retrieved June 26, 2010 from http://tsg.icme11.org/document/get/292

Schoenfeld, A. H. (1988). When good teaching leads to bad results: The disasters of 'well-taught' mathematics courses. *Educational Psychologist, 23*(2), 145-166.

Schraw, G., & Moshman, D. (1995). Metacognitive theories. *Educational Psychology Review, 7*(4), 351-371.

Schunk, D. H. (1986). Verbalization and young children's self-regulated learning. *Contemporary Educational Psychology, 11,* 347-369.

Schwarz, L. (2006). About wishes and invitations: Four meditations on life writing with Carl Leggo. *Vitae Scholasticae Annual,* 65-72.

Scruggs, T. E., Mastropieri, M. A., Monson, J., & Jorgensen, C. (1985). Maximizing what gifted students can learn: Recent findings of learning strategy research. *Gifted Child Quarterly, 29,* 181-185.

Senge, P. (1990). *The fifth discipline: The art and practice of the learning organization.* New York, NY: Doubleday.

Senge, P., Kleiner, A., Roberts, C., Ross, R., & Smith, B. (1994). *The fifth disciple fieldbook.* Toronto, ON: Doubleday.

Sewell, S., & Hazzard, B. (Hosts). (2006). Inclusion is the salad dressing (Podcast episode 7).in Tribes tips: The active learning and inclusion podcast. Retrieved October 25, 2006 from pdtogo.com/tribes

Sewell, S., & Hazzard, B. (Hosts). (2006). Why use Tribes? (Podcast episode 2).in Tribes tips: The active learning and inclusion podcast. Retrieved October 25, 2006 from pdtogo.com/tribes

Shanahan, T. (1998). On the effectiveness and limitations of tutoring in reading. *Review of Research in Education, 23,* 217-234.

Siegler, R. S., & Ellis, S. (1996). Piaget on childhood. *Psychological Science, 7*(4), 211-215.

Silver, H., Strong, R., & Perini, M. (1997). Integrating learning styles and multiple intelligences, *Educational Leadership* (September), 22-27. Alexandria, VA: Association for Supervision and Curriculum Development.

Sinatra, R., & Stahl-Gemake, J. (1983, March). *How curriculum leaders can involve the right brain in active reading and writing development.* Presented at the 38th Annual Meeting of the Association for Supervision and Curriculum Development, Houston, Texas.

Singer, D. G., & Singer, J. L. (1999). *The house of make-believe: Children's play and the developing imagination.* Boston, MA: Harvard University Press.

Skirrow, I. H., & Barrett, Y. (2008). What is the role of the library in IB world schools? *ECIS Librarians Conference 2008.* Retrieved June 20, 2010 from http://my-i-experience.com/experiences/ecis/skirrow%20barrett%20RoleofLibrary%20ECISBerlin08.pdf

Smith, G. (2002). Place-based education: Learning to be where we are. *The Phi Delta Kappan, 83*(8), 584-594.

Smith-Sebasto, N., & Cavern, L. (2006). Effects of pre- and post –trip activities associated with a residential education experience on student's attitudes toward the environment. *The Journal of Environmental Education, 37*(4), 4-17.

Smits, H. (1997). Living within the space of practice: Action research inspired by hermeneutics. In T. Carson, & D. Sumara (Eds.). *Action Research as a Living Practice* (pp. 229-312). New York, NY: Peter Lang.

Southworth, G. (2003). National College for School Leadership: Instructional Leadership in Schools: Reflections and empirical evidence. Retrieved May 23, 2005 from http://www.ncsl.org.uk/researchpublications

Sparkes, A. C. (2005). *Telling tales in sport and physical activity: A qualitative journey.* Champaign, IL: Human Kinetics.

Spitalli, S. (2005). The don't's of student discipline. *Education Digest: Essential Readings Condensed for Quick Review, 70*(5), 28-31.

Springgay, S., Irwin, R. L., Leggo, C., & Gouzouasis, P. (Eds.). (2008). *Being with a/r/t/ography.* Rotterdam: SensePublishers.

Squamish Nation, Tsleil-Waututh Nation, North Vancouver School District, BC Ministry of Education (2006). *Aboriginal education enhancement agreement.* North Vancouver, BC: North Vancouver School District 44.

Steier, F. (Ed.).(1991). *Research and reflexivity.* London: Sage.

Stix, A. (1994). Pic-jour math: Pictorial journal writing in mathematics. *Arithmetic Teacher, 41*(5), 264-269.

Stix, A. (1995). *The link between art and mathematics.* Cincinatti, OH: Annual Conference of the National Middle School Association. (ERIC Document Reproduction Service No. ED398170).

Stix, A. (1996). *The need for pictorial journal writing.* Hartdale, NY: Westchester Teachers' Center Conference, "Math Enrichment For All." (ERIC Document Reproduction Service No. ED410555).

Strahm, M. (2007). Cooperative learning: Group processing and students needs for self worth and belonging. *Alberta Journal of Educational Research, 53*(1), 63-77.

Strand, J. A., & Peacock, T. (2002). *Nurturing resilience and school success in American Indian and Alaskan native students.* Charleston, WV: ERIC Clearinghouse on Rural Education and Small Schools. (ERIC Document Reproduction Service No. ED471488)

Sudzina, M., Giebelhaus, C., & Coolican, M. (1997). Mentor or tormentor: The role of the cooperating teacher in student teacher success or failure. *Action in Teacher Education, 18*(4), 23-25.

Sumara, D., & Davis, B. (1997). Enlarging the space of the possible: Complexity, complicity, and action-research practices. In Terrance Carson & Dennis Sumara (Eds.). *Action research as a living practice* (pp. 299-312). New York: Peter Lang.

Suominen, A. (2006). Writing with photographs writing self: Using artistic methods in the investigation of identity. *International Journal of Education through Art, 2*(2), 139-156.

Swan, M. (2007). The impact of task-based professional development on teachers' practices and beliefs: A design research study. *Journal of Mathematics Teacher Education, 10*(4-6), 217-237.

Sutton, C. (1992). *Words, science and learning.* Buckingham: Open University Press.

Swan M. (2008). The design of multiple representation tasks to foster conceptual development. *International Congress for Mathematics Education, 11.* Retrieved July 6, 2008 from http://tsg.icme11.org/tsg/show/35

Swan, M. (2007). *The design of multiple representation tasks to foster conceptual development.* Nottingham: University of Nottingham.

Swanson, M. C., Marcus, M., & Elliott, J. (2000). Rigor with support: Lessons from AVID. *Leadership, 30*(2), 26-27, 37-38.

Swartz, R. J. (n.d.).Thinking-based learning: Making the most of what we have learned about teaching in the regular classroom to bring out the best in our students. Retrieved from. http://www.nctt.net/lessonsarticles.php#ARTICLES.

Stigler, J. W., & Hiebert, J. (1999). *The teaching gap: Best ideas from the world's teachers for improving education in the classroom.* New York, NY: The Free Press.

Taylor, A., & Kuo, F.E. (2006). Is contact with nature important for healthy child development? State of the evidence. In Spencer, C., & Blades, M. (Eds.). *Children and their environments: Learning, using and designing spaces.* Cambridge University Press, Cambridge, U.K. Available online at http://www.lhhl.uiuc.edu/

Tabach, M., & Friedlander, A. (2010). Designer concerns versus student work: The case of improving grades. Retrieved June 24, 2010 from http://tsg.icme11.org/document/get/293

Thorsen, K. (2010, June 6). *Art therapy with Kat 2009 – 2010.* Retrieved July 14, 2010 from Sock Monkey Monthly Web site, http://klasssockmonkey.wordpress.com/

Tishman, S., & Palmer, P. (2005). Visible thinking. *Leadership Compass, 2*(4), 1-3.

Tomlinson. C. (1999). *The differentiated classroom: Responding to the needs of all learners.* Alexandria, VA: Association for Supervision and Curriculum Development.

Topping, K. (1987). Peer tutored paired reading: Outcome data from ten projects. *Educational Psychology, 7*(2), 133-145.

UNESCO. (1980). *Environmental education in the light of the Tbilisi Conference.* Paris: Unesco.

Urzua, C. (1995). Cross-age tutoring in the literacy club. *ERIC digest, ED386949, 1-7.*

Van De Walle, J. A., & Folk, S. (2005). Elementary and middle school mathematics: Teaching developmentally. Toronto, ON: Pearson.

Veenman, M. V. J., & Spaans, M. A. (2005). Relation between intellectual and metacognitive skills: Age and task differences. *Learning and Individual Differences, 15,* 159-176.

Veenman, M. V. J., Van Hout-Wolters, B. H. A. M., & Afflerbach, P. (2006). Metacognition and learning: Conceptual and methodological considerations. *Metacognition Learning, 1,* 3-14.

Von Glasersfeld, E. (1989). Cognition, construction of knowledge, and teaching. *Synthese, 80*(1), 121-140.

Vygotsky, L. S. (1978). *Mind and society: The development of higher psychological processes.* Cambridge, MA: Harvard University Press.

Waldman, C., & Crippen, K. (2009). Integrating interactive notebooks. *The Science Teacher* (January), 51-55, Arlington, VA: National Science Teachers Association.

Walker, I., & Crogan, M. (1998). Academic performance, prejudice, and the jigsaw classroom: New pieces to the puzzle. *Journal of Community & Applied Social Psychology, 8*(6), 381-393.

Wallace, G. (1996). Engaging with learning. In J. Rudduck (Ed.). *School improvement: What can pupils tell us?* London: David Fulton.

Wan, C. Y., & Schlaug, G. (2010). Music making as a tool for promoting brain plasticity across the lifespan. *The Neuroscientist, 16*(5), 566-577.

Wasik, B. A. (1998). Volunteer tutoring programs in reading: A review. *Reading Research Quarterly, 33,* 266-291.

Watson, A. (Nov 2007). Mathematical thinking in adolescence: possible shifts of perspective. University of Nottingham, Mathematical Thinking conference. Retrieved June 26, 2010 from http://www.education.ox.ac.uk/uploaded/Mathematical%20thinking%20in%20adolescence.pp

Watson, A., & Mason, J. (2006). Seeing an exercise as a single mathematical object: Using variation to structure sense-making. *Mathematical Thinking and Learning, 8*(2), 91-111.

Watts, M., & McGrath, C. (1998). SATIS factions: Approaches to relevance in science education. *School Science Review, 79,* 61-65.

Weber, S. J. (2008). Visual images in research. In G. Knowles & A. Cole (Eds.). *Handbook of the arts in qualitative research: Perspectives, methodologies, example and issues* (pp. 41-53). Thousand Oak, CA: Sage.

Wellington, J., & Osbourne, J. (2001). *Language and literacy in science education.* Buckingham, UK: Open University Press.

Wells, N., & Lekies, K. (2006). Nature and the life course: Pathways from childhood nature experiences to adult environmentalism. *Children, Youth and Environments, 16*(1), 1-24.

Western and Northern Canadian Protocol. (2006). *The common curriculum framework for K-9 Mathematics.* Retrieved September 22, 2010 from http://www.wncp.ca/media/38765/ccfkto9.pdf

Whitebread, D., Coltman, P., Pasternak, D., Sangster, C., Grau, V., Bingham, S., Almeqdad, Q., & Demetriou, D. (2009). The development of two observational tools for assessing metacognition and self-regulated learning in young children. *Metacognition Learning, 4,* 63-85.

Wiggins, G., & McTighe, J. (2005). *Understanding by design.* Alexandria, VA: Association for Supervision and Curriculum Design.

Wilhelm, J. D. (2009). The power of teacher inquiry: Developing a critical literacy for teachers. *Voices from the Middle, 17*(2), 36-39.

Wilson, S. (2004). Fragments: Life writings in image and in text. In R.L. Irwin, & A. de Cosson (Eds.). *a/r/tography: Rendering self through arts-based living inquiry* (pp. 41-74). Vancouver, BC: Pacific Educational Press.

Wolfe, P. (2001). *Brain matters.* Alexandria, VA: Association for Supervision and Curriculum Development.

Wray, D., & Lewis, M. (1997). *Extending literacy: Children reading and writing no fiction.* London: Routledge.

Yankelovich, D. (1999). *The magic of dialogue: Transforming conflict into cooperation.* New York, NY: Simon & Schuster.

Yilmaz, O., Boone, W., & Andersen, H. (2004). Views of elementary and middle school Turkish students towards environmental issues. *International Journal of Science Education, 26*(12), 1527-1546.

Yost, D., & Mosca, F. (2002). Beyond behavior strategies: Using reflection to manage youth in crisis. *Clearing House, 75*(5), 264-67.

Young, J. (2003). Science interactive notebooks in the classroom. *Science Scope* (January), 44-47. Arlington, VA: National Science Teachers Association.

Zasalavsky, O. (2008). *Attention to similarities and differences: A fundamental principle for task design and implementation in mathematics education.* Haifa: Department of Education.

Zimmerman, B. J. (2002). Becoming a self-regulated learner: An overview. *Theory Into Practice, 41*(2), 64-70.

Additional references

Artzt, A. F., & Armour-Thomas, E. (1999). A cognitive model for examining teachers' instructional practice in mathematics: A guide for facilitating teacher reflection. *Educations Studies in Mathematics, 40*(3), 211-235.

*British Columbia Ministry of Education. (1991). Thinking in the classroom (resources for teachers), volume two: Experiences that enhance thoughtful learning. V*ictoria, BC: Assessment, Examinations, and Reporting Branch, Ministry of Education and Ministry Responsible for Multiculturalism and Human Rights.

Bromme, R., Pieschl, S., & Stahl, E. (2010). Epistemological beliefs are standards for adaptive learning: A functional theory about epistemological beliefs and metacognition. *Metacognition Learning, 5, 7-26.*

Brown, R. (2002). Mathematical modeling in the international baccalaureate, teacher beliefs and technology usage. *Teaching Mathematics and Its Applications, 21*(2), 67-74.

Brown, R., & Davies, E. W. (2002). The introduction of graphic calculators into assessment in mathematics in the international baccalaureate organization; opportunities and challenges. *Teaching Mathematics and Its Applications, 21*(4), 173-187.

City of North Vancouver. (2008). *Community profile.* Retrieved October 23, 2008, from http://www.cnv.org/printer_friendly.aspx?c=3&i=254

Cobb, P., McClain, K., de Silva Lamberg, T., & Dean, C. (2003). Situating teachers' instructional practices in the institutional setting of the school and district. *Educational Researcher, 32*(6), 13-24.

Costa, A. L. (2008). *The school as a home for the mind: Creating mindful curriculum, instruction, and dialogue.* Thousand Oaks, CA: Corwin Press.

Coutinho, S., Wiemer-Hastings, K., Skowronski, J. J., & Britt, M. A. (2005). Metacognition, need for cognition and use of explanations during ongoing learning and problem solving. *Learning and Individual Differences, 15,* 321-337.

District of North Vancouver. (2008). *Economic Development: Demographics.* Retrieved October 23, 2008, from http://www.dnv.org/article.asp?c=77

Eisenhart, M., Borko, H., Underhill, R., Brown, C., Jones, D., & Agard, P. (1993). Conceptual knowledge falls through the cracks: Complexities of learning to teach mathematics for understanding. *Journal for Research in Mathematics Education, 24*(3), 8-40.

Even, R., & Tirosh, D. (2002). Teacher knowledge and understanding of students' mathematical learning. *Handbooks of International Research in Mathematics Education.* Mahwah, NJ: Erlbaum.

Flavell. J. H., Miller, P. H., & Miller, S. A. (1993). *Cognitive development: Third edition.* Englewood Cliffs, NJ. Prentice Hall.

Fogarty, R., & Opeka, K. (1988). *Start them thinking: A handbook of classroom strategies for the early years.* Palatine, IL: IRI Group.

Goldhaber, D. D., & Brewer, D. J. (2000). Does teacher certification matter? High school teacher certification status and student achievement. *Educational Evaluation and Policy Analysis, 22*(2), 129-145.

Gopnik, A., & Astington, J. W. (1998). Children's understanding of representational change and its relation to the understanding of false belief and the appearance-reality distinction. *Child Development, 59*(1), 26-37.

Graeber, A. O. (1999). Forms of knowing mathematics: What preservice teachers should learn, *Educational Studies in Mathematics, 38,* 189-208.

Hinrichs, J. (2004). A comparision of levels of international understanding among the students of the international baccalaureate diploma and advancement placement programs in the USA. *Journal of Research in International Education, 2*(3), 331-348.

Krathwohl, D. R. (2002). A revision of Bloom's taxonomy: An overview. *Theory Into Practice, 41*(4), 212-218.

Matthews, D., & Kitchen, J. (2007). School-within-a-school gifted programs: Perceptions of students and teachers in public secondary schools. *Gifted Child Quarterly, 51*(3), 256-271.

Mayer, R. E. (2002). Rote versus meaningful learning. *Theory Into Practice, 41*(4), 226-232.

McGuinness, C. (1999). From thinking skills to thinking classrooms–Department for Education and Employment Research Brief No. 115. Retrieved from http://www.dcsf.gov.uk/research/data/uploadfiles/RB115.doc

North Vancouver School District. (2008). *North Vancouver snapshot.* Retrieved October 23, 2008 from http://nvsd44.bc.ca/AboutUs/NorthVancouverSnapshot.aspx

Novak, J. D. (1990). Concept maps and Vee diagrams: Two metacognitive tools to facilitate meaningful learning. *Instructional Science, 19,* 29-52.

Opeka, K. (1991). *Keep them thinking: Level one* (2nd ed.). Pallatine, IL: Skylight Publishing.

Peskin, J., & Astington, J. W. (2004). The effects of adding metacognitive language to story texts. *Cognitive Development, 19,* 253-273.

Rice, J. K. (1999). The impact of class size on instructional strategies and the use of time in high school mathematics and science courses. *Educational Evaluation and Policy Analysis, 21*(2), 215-229.

Ritchart, R., Palmer, P., Church, M., & Tishman, S. (April, 2006). Thinking routines: Establishing patterns of thinking in the classroom. Paper prepared for AERA Conference.

Robson, S. (2006). *Developing thinking and understanding in young children: An introduction for students.* New York, NY: Routledge.

Schoenfeld, A. (2006). Learning to think mathematically: Problem solving, metacognition, and sense making in mathematics. *Handbook on research in mathematics.* Mahwah, NJ: Erlbaum.

Siegler, R. S. (2000). The rebirth of children's learning. *Child Development, 71*(1), 26-35.

Siegler, R. S. (2004). Learning about learning. *Merrill-Palmer Quarterly, 50*(3), 353-368.

Springer, L., Stanne, L. E., & Donovan, S. S. (1999). Effects of small-group learning on undergraduates in science, mathematics, engineering, and technology: A meta-analysis. *Review of Educational Research, 69*(1), 21-51.

The University of British Columbia: Faculty of Education. (2008). *Teacher education programs.* Retrieved October 24, 2008, from http://teach.educ.ubc.ca/bachelor/cohorts/elementary.html#FAME

Van der Stel, M., & Veenman, M.V. J. (2010). Development of metacognitive skillfulness: A longitudinal study. *Learning and Individual Differences, 20,* 220-224.

Wasserman, S. (1978). *Put some thinking in your classroom.* Chicago, IL: Benefic Press.

Whitehead, D. (2006). Justifying what we do: Criteria for the selection of literacy and thinking tools. *English in Aotearoa, 60,* 27-40

Winne, P. H. (1995). Inherent details in self-regulated learning. *Educational Psychologist, 30*(4), 173-187.

Winne, P. H. (1996). A metacognitive view of individual differences in self-regulated learning. *Learning and Individual Differences, 8*(4), 327-354.

Student Readings

Albom, M. (1997). *Tuesday's with Morrie.* New York, NY: Doubleday.

Bauby, J. (1997). *The Diving bell and the butterfly.* London, England: Harper Perennial.

Bolte-Taylor, J. (2006). *My stroke of insight.* New York, NY: Plume.

Bunting, E. (1991). *Fly away home.* New York: Clarion Books.

Christopher, M. (2002). Michael Jordan. In K.T. Froloff (Ed.). *Basketball* (p.33). Westminster, CA: Teacher Created Materials, Inc.

DuPrau, J. (2003). *City of ember.* New York: Yearling.

Farmer, N. (2002). *House of the scorpion.* New York: Simon Pulse.

Francis, D. (2000). Catching and Canning. In *Connections Canada 5* (pp. 158-161). Toronto: Oxford University Press.

REFERENCES

Friedman, L. (2008). Angel Girl. Minneapolis, MN.: Carolrhoda Books.

Gawande, A. (2002). *Complications.* New York, NY: Picador.

Genova, L. (2009). *Still Alice.* New York, NY: Simon and Schuster.

O'Kelly, E. (2008). *Chasing Daylight.* New York, NY: McGraw Hill.

Pausch, R. (2008). *The last lecture.* New York, NY: Hyperion.

Powrie, S., & Sterling, S. (2001). Thinking about culture. *Connections Canada, 6*, 48-49. Toronto: Oxford University Press.

Raskin, E. (1978). *The westing game*. New York: Scholastic Inc.

Sapolsky, R. (1997). *The trouble with testosterone.* New York, NY: Simon and Schuster.

Schiller, B. (1999). Mandela. In A. Barlow-Kedves, T. O'Grady, J. Onody, W. Mathieu, & S. Tywonink (Eds.). *Sightlines 8* (pp. 161-164). Scarborough, ON.: Prentice Hall.

Turner, M.W. (1996). *The thief.* New York: Harper Collins.

Movies

Demme, J., Saxon, E., & Demme, J. (1993). *Philadelphia.* USA: Tristar.

Iron, D., Urdl, S., Weiss, J., & Polley, S. (2007). *Away from me.* UK: Film Farm

Kennedy, K., Kilik, J., & Schnabel, J. (2007). *The diving bell and the Butterfly.* France: Pathe Renn.

Pillsbury, S., & Spottiswoode, R. (1993). *And the band played on.* USA: HBO.

CPSIA information can be obtained at www.ICGtesting.com
Printed in the USA
LVOW071816101111

254429LV00002B/1/P

9 789460 916670